A
MARVEL COMICS
PRESENTATION

CIVIL WAR
THE AMAZING SPIDER-MAN

WRITER J. MICHAEL STRACZYNSKI	**ASSISTANT EDITOR** MICHAEL O'CONNOR	**SVP PRINT, SALES & MARKETING** DAVID GABRIEL
PENCILER RON GARNEY	**EDITOR** AXEL ALONSO	**BOOK DESIGNER** DAYLE CHESLER
	COLLECTION EDITOR JENNIFER GRÜNWALD	**EDITOR IN CHIEF** AXEL ALONSO
INKER BILL REINHOLD	**ASSISTANT EDITOR** SARAH BRUNSTAD	**CHIEF CREATIVE OFFICER** JOE QUESADA
COLORIST MATT MILLA	**ASSOCIATE MANAGING EDITOR** ALEX STARBUCK	**PUBLISHER** DAN BUCKLEY
LETTERER VC'S CORY PETIT	**EDITOR, SPECIAL PROJECTS** MARK D. BEAZLEY	**EXECUTIVE PRODUCER** ALAN FINE
	SENIOR EDITOR, SPECIAL PROJECTS JEFF YOUNGQUIST	**SPIDER-MAN CREATED BY** STAN LEE & STEVE DITKO

VIL WAR: AMAZING SPIDER-MAN. Contains material originally published in magazine form as AMAZING SPIDER-MAN #532-538. Fourth printing 2015. ISBN# 978-0-7851-2237-1. Published by MARVEL WORLDWIDE, C., a subsidiary of MARVEL ENTERTAINMENT, LLC. OFFICE OF PUBLICATION: 135 West 50th Street, New York, NY 10020. Copyright © 2007 MARVEL No similarity between any of the names, characters, persons, d/or institutions in this magazine with those of any living or dead person or institution is intended, and any such similarity which may exist is purely coincidental. **Printed in the U.S.A.** ALAN FINE, President, Marvel tertainment; DAN BUCKLEY, President, TV, Publishing and Brand Management; JOE QUESADA, Chief Creative Officer; TOM BREVOORT, SVP of Publishing; DAVID BOGART, SVP of Operations & Procurement, Publishing; B. CEBULSKI, VP of International Development & Brand Management; DAVID GABRIEL, SVP Print, Sales & Marketing; JIM O'KEEFE, VP of Operations & Logistics; DAN CARR, Executive Director of Publishing Technology; SAN CRESPI, Editorial Operations Manager; ALEX MORALES, Publishing Operations Manager; STAN LEE, Chairman Emeritus. For information regarding advertising in Marvel Comics or on Marvel.com, please contact nathan Rheingold, VP of Custom Solutions & Ad Sales, at jrheingold@marvel.com. For Marvel subscription inquiries, please call 800-217-9158. **Manufactured between 3/4/2015 and 4/6/2015 by R.R. DONNELLEY,** C., SALEM, VA, USA.

9 8 7 6 5 4

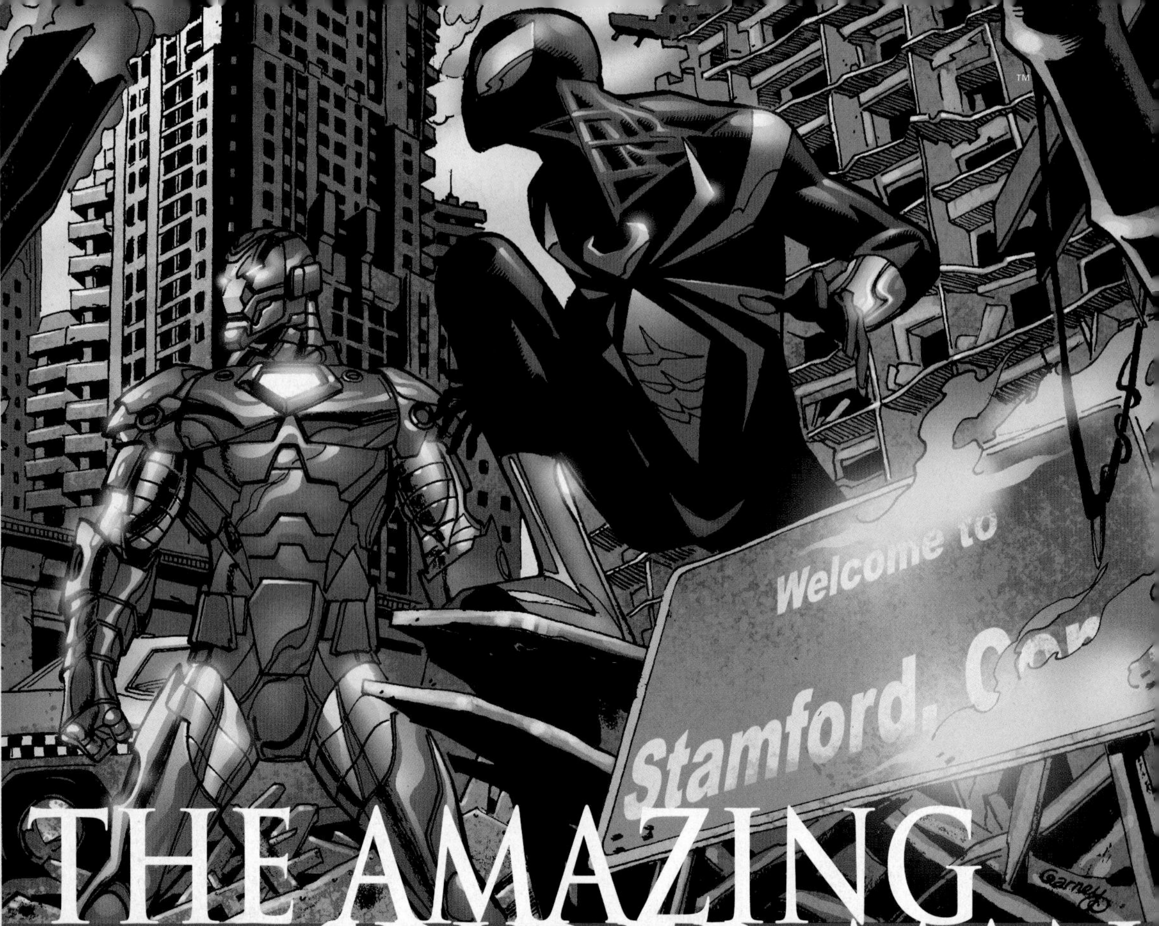

Welcome to
Stamford,

THE AMAZING SPIDER-MAN

A MARVEL COMICS EVENT

CIVIL WAR

AMAZING SPIDER-MAN #532

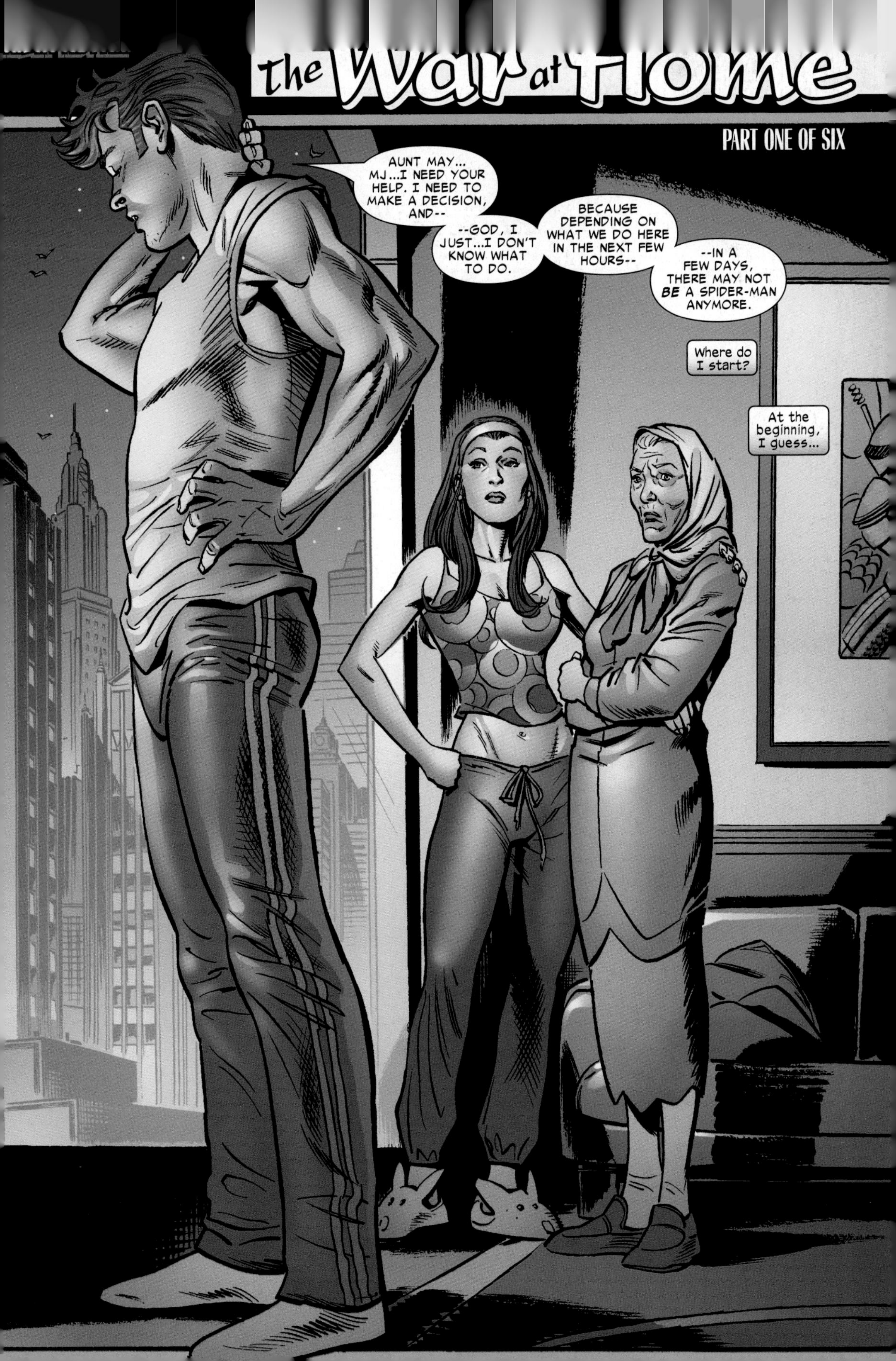
The War at Home
PART ONE OF SIX
AUNT MAY... MJ...I NEED YOUR HELP. I NEED TO MAKE A DECISION, AND--
--GOD, I JUST...I DON'T KNOW WHAT TO DO.
BECAUSE DEPENDING ON WHAT WE DO HERE IN THE NEXT FEW HOURS--
--IN A FEW DAYS, THERE MAY NOT BE A SPIDER-MAN ANYMORE.
Where do I start?
At the beginning, I guess...

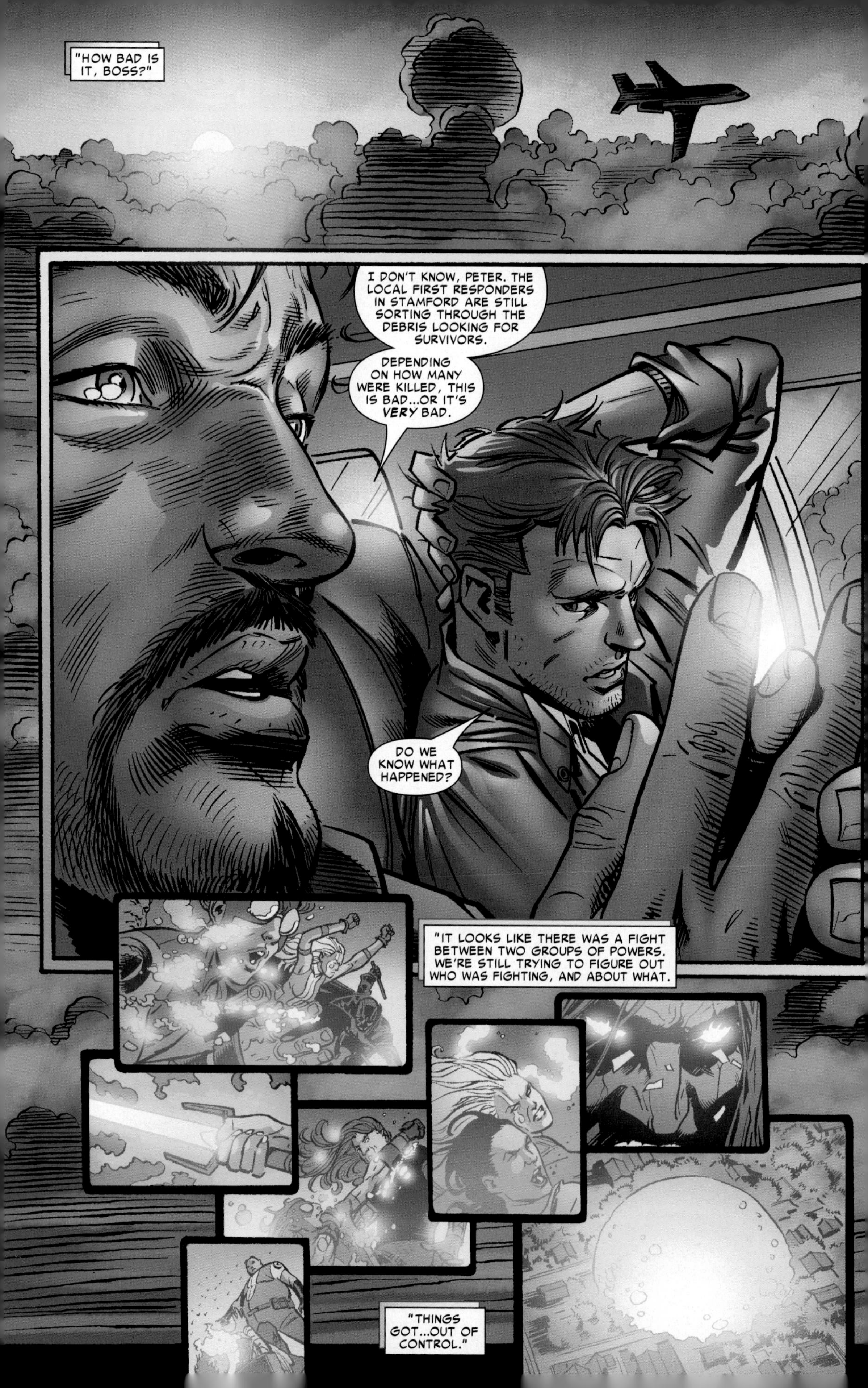
"HOW BAD IS IT, BOSS?"
I DON'T KNOW, PETER. THE LOCAL FIRST RESPONDERS IN STAMFORD ARE STILL SORTING THROUGH THE DEBRIS LOOKING FOR SURVIVORS.
DEPENDING ON HOW MANY WERE KILLED, THIS IS BAD...OR IT'S VERY BAD.
DO WE KNOW WHAT HAPPENED?
"IT LOOKS LIKE THERE WAS A FIGHT BETWEEN TWO GROUPS OF POWERS. WE'RE STILL TRYING TO FIGURE OUT WHO WAS FIGHTING, AND ABOUT WHAT.
"THINGS GOT...OUT OF CONTROL."

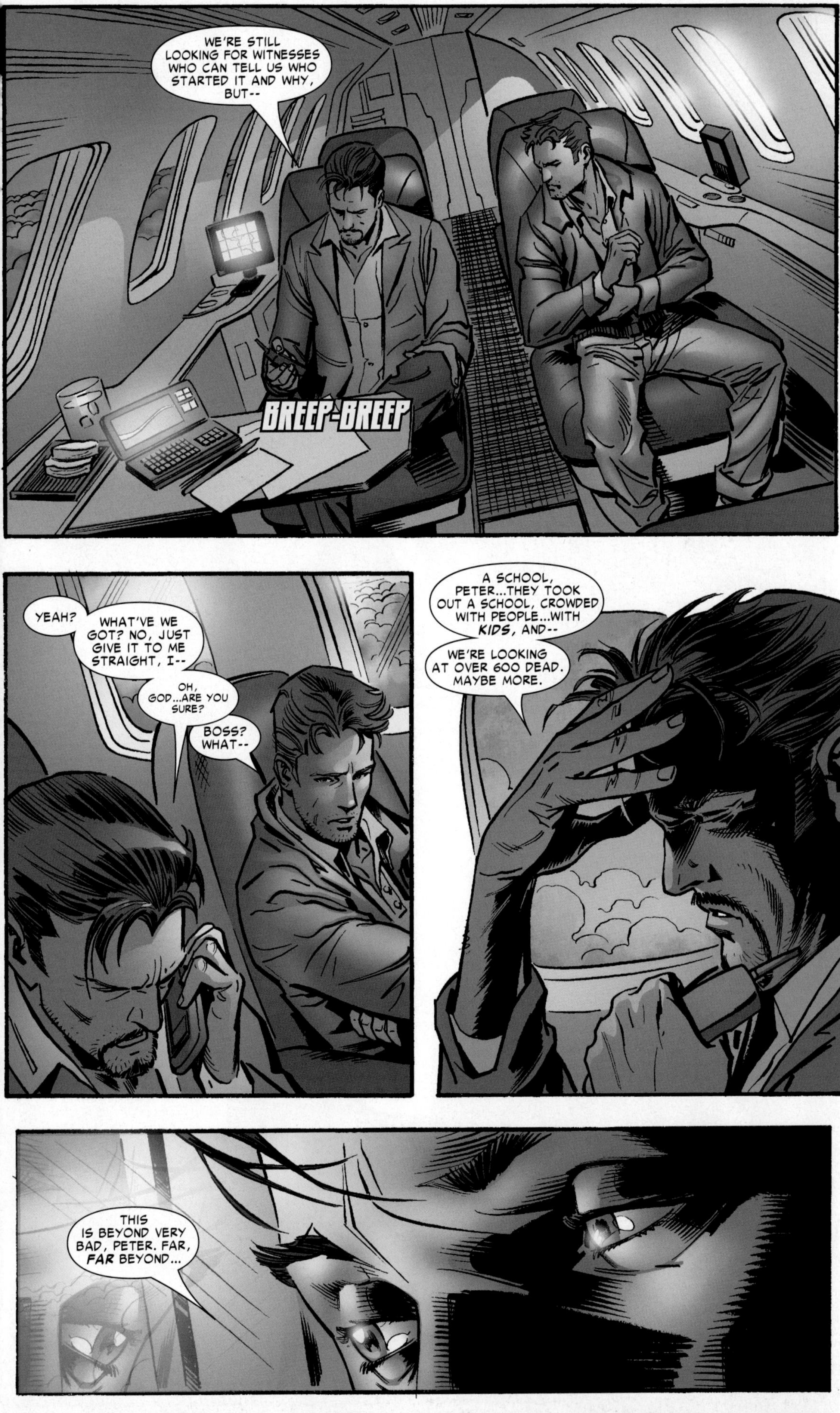
WE'RE STILL LOOKING FOR WITNESSES WHO CAN TELL US WHO STARTED IT AND WHY, BUT--
BREEP-BREEP
YEAH?
WHAT'VE WE GOT? NO, JUST GIVE IT TO ME STRAIGHT, I--
OH, GOD...ARE YOU SURE?
BOSS? WHAT--
A SCHOOL, PETER...THEY TOOK OUT A SCHOOL, CROWDED WITH PEOPLE...WITH KIDS, AND--
WE'RE LOOKING AT OVER 600 DEAD. MAYBE MORE.
THIS IS BEYOND VERY BAD, PETER. FAR, FAR BEYOND...

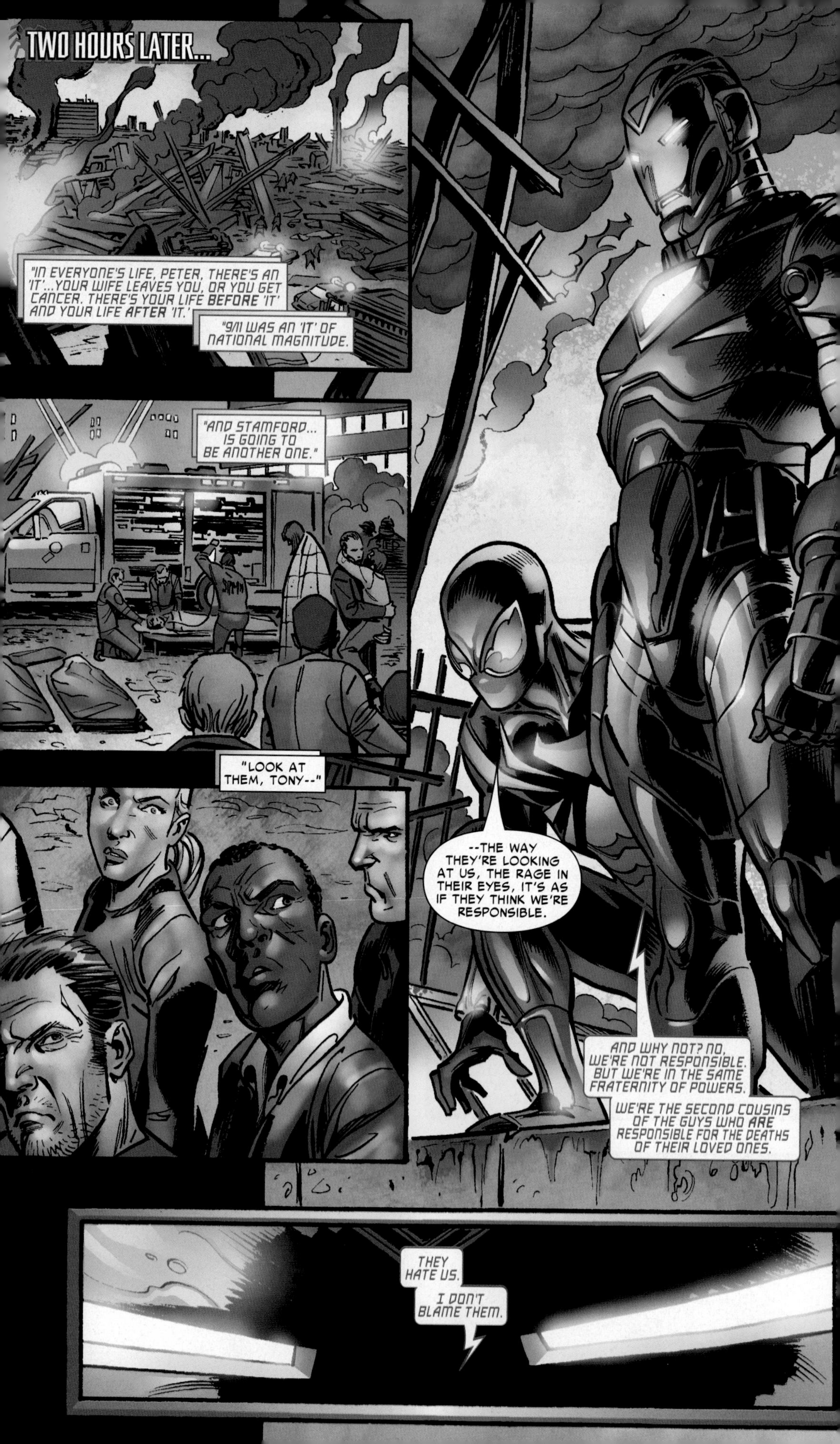
TWO HOURS LATER...
"IN EVERYONE'S LIFE, PETER, THERE'S AN 'IT'...YOUR WIFE LEAVES YOU, OR YOU GET CANCER. THERE'S YOUR LIFE BEFORE 'IT' AND YOUR LIFE AFTER 'IT.'
"9/11 WAS AN 'IT' OF NATIONAL MAGNITUDE.
"AND STAMFORD... IS GOING TO BE ANOTHER ONE."
"LOOK AT THEM, TONY--"
--THE WAY THEY'RE LOOKING AT US, THE RAGE IN THEIR EYES, IT'S AS IF THEY THINK WE'RE RESPONSIBLE.
AND WHY NOT? NO, WE'RE NOT RESPONSIBLE. BUT WE'RE IN THE SAME FRATERNITY OF POWERS.
WE'RE THE SECOND COUSINS OF THE GUYS WHO ARE RESPONSIBLE FOR THE DEATHS OF THEIR LOVED ONES.
THEY HATE US.
I DON'T BLAME THEM.

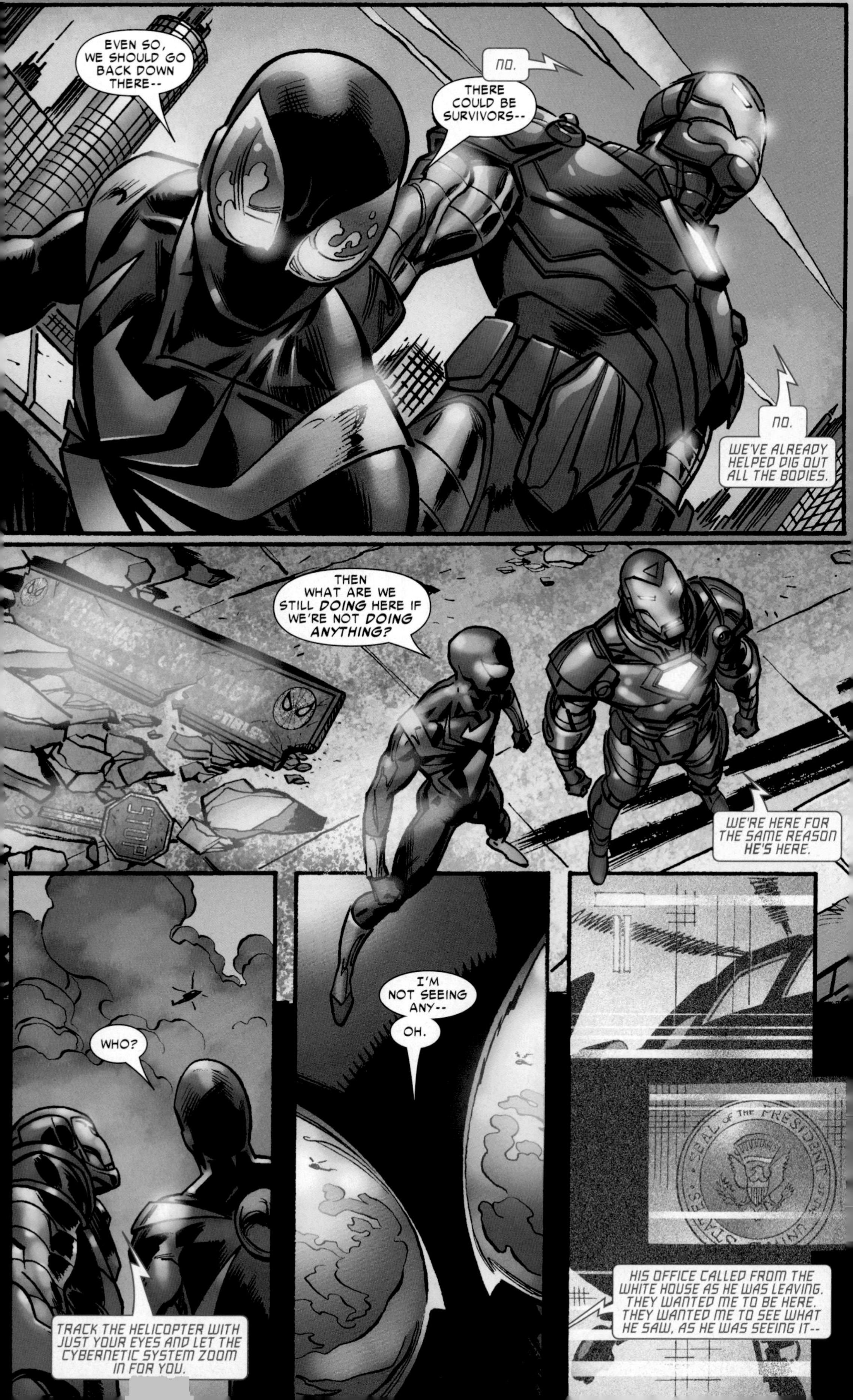
EVEN SO, WE SHOULD GO BACK DOWN THERE--
NO.
THERE COULD BE SURVIVORS--
NO.
WE'VE ALREADY HELPED DIG OUT ALL THE BODIES.
THEN WHAT ARE WE STILL DOING HERE IF WE'RE NOT DOING ANYTHING?
WE'RE HERE FOR THE SAME REASON HE'S HERE.
STOP
WHO?
TRACK THE HELICOPTER WITH JUST YOUR EYES AND LET THE CYBERNETIC SYSTEM ZOOM IN FOR YOU.
I'M NOT SEEING ANY--
OH.
SEAL OF THE PRESIDENT
HIS OFFICE CALLED FROM THE WHITE HOUSE AS HE WAS LEAVING. THEY WANTED ME TO BE HERE. THEY WANTED ME TO SEE WHAT HE SAW, AS HE WAS SEEING IT--

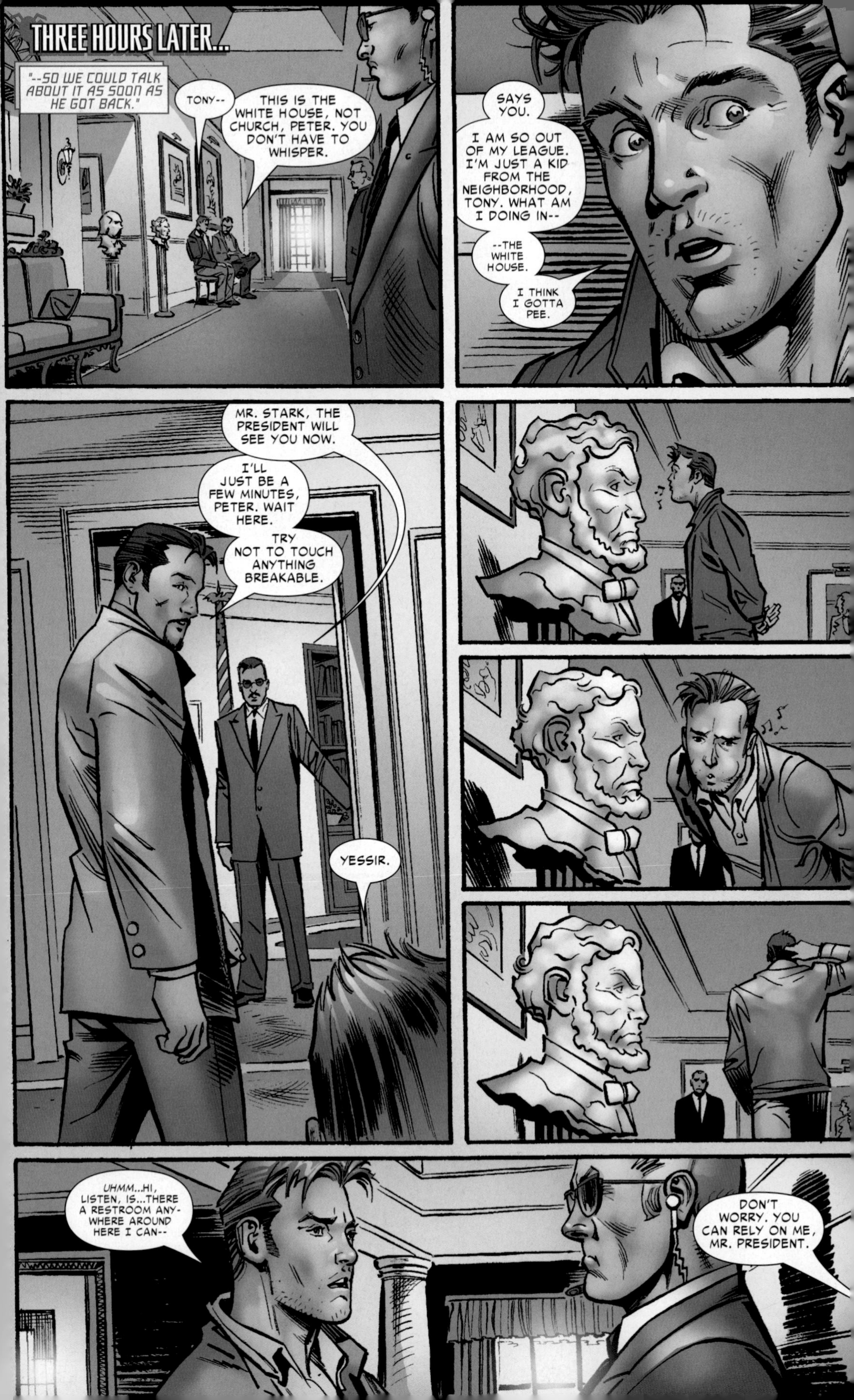
THREE HOURS LATER...
"--SO WE COULD TALK ABOUT IT AS SOON AS HE GOT BACK."
TONY--
THIS IS THE WHITE HOUSE, NOT CHURCH, PETER. YOU DON'T HAVE TO WHISPER.
SAYS YOU.
I AM SO OUT OF MY LEAGUE. I'M JUST A KID FROM THE NEIGHBORHOOD, TONY. WHAT AM I DOING IN--
--THE WHITE HOUSE.
I THINK I GOTTA PEE.
MR. STARK, THE PRESIDENT WILL SEE YOU NOW.
I'LL JUST BE A FEW MINUTES, PETER. WAIT HERE.
TRY NOT TO TOUCH ANYTHING BREAKABLE.
YESSIR.
UHMM...HI, LISTEN, IS...THERE A RESTROOM ANYWHERE AROUND HERE I CAN--
DON'T WORRY. YOU CAN RELY ON ME, MR. PRESIDENT.

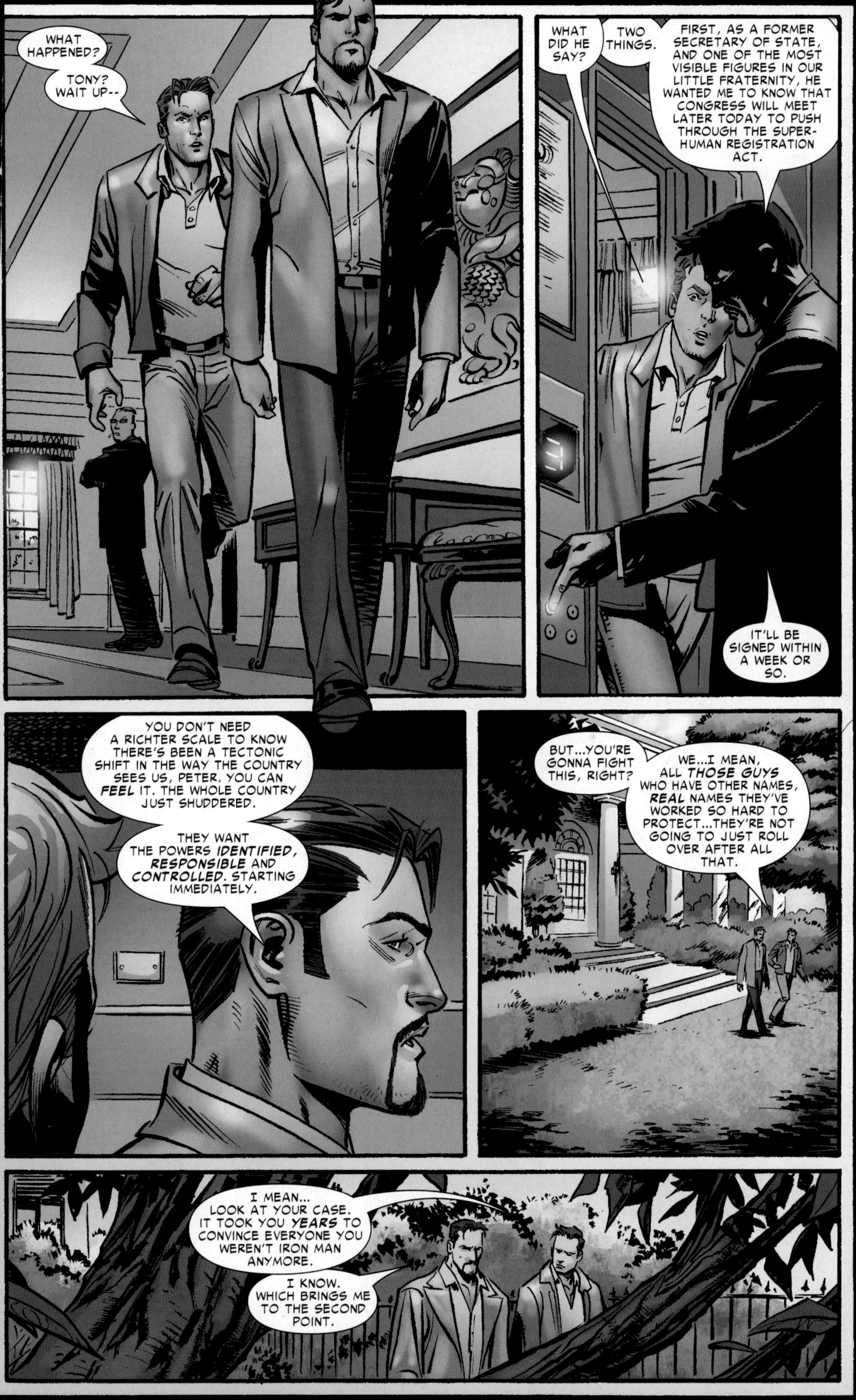
WHAT HAPPENED?
TONY? WAIT UP--
WHAT DID HE SAY?
TWO THINGS.
FIRST, AS A FORMER SECRETARY OF STATE, AND ONE OF THE MOST VISIBLE FIGURES IN OUR LITTLE FRATERNITY, HE WANTED ME TO KNOW THAT CONGRESS WILL MEET LATER TODAY TO PUSH THROUGH THE SUPER-HUMAN REGISTRATION ACT.
IT'LL BE SIGNED WITHIN A WEEK OR SO.
YOU DON'T NEED A RICHTER SCALE TO KNOW THERE'S BEEN A TECTONIC SHIFT IN THE WAY THE COUNTRY SEES US, PETER. YOU CAN *FEEL* IT. THE WHOLE COUNTRY JUST SHUDDERED.
THEY WANT THE POWERS *IDENTIFIED, RESPONSIBLE* AND *CONTROLLED*. STARTING IMMEDIATELY.
BUT...YOU'RE GONNA FIGHT THIS, RIGHT?
WE...I MEAN, ALL *THOSE GUYS* WHO HAVE OTHER NAMES, *REAL* NAMES THEY'VE WORKED SO HARD TO PROTECT...THEY'RE NOT GOING TO JUST ROLL OVER AFTER ALL THAT.
I MEAN... LOOK AT YOUR CASE. IT TOOK YOU *YEARS* TO CONVINCE EVERYONE YOU WEREN'T IRON MAN ANYMORE.
I KNOW. WHICH BRINGS ME TO THE SECOND POINT.

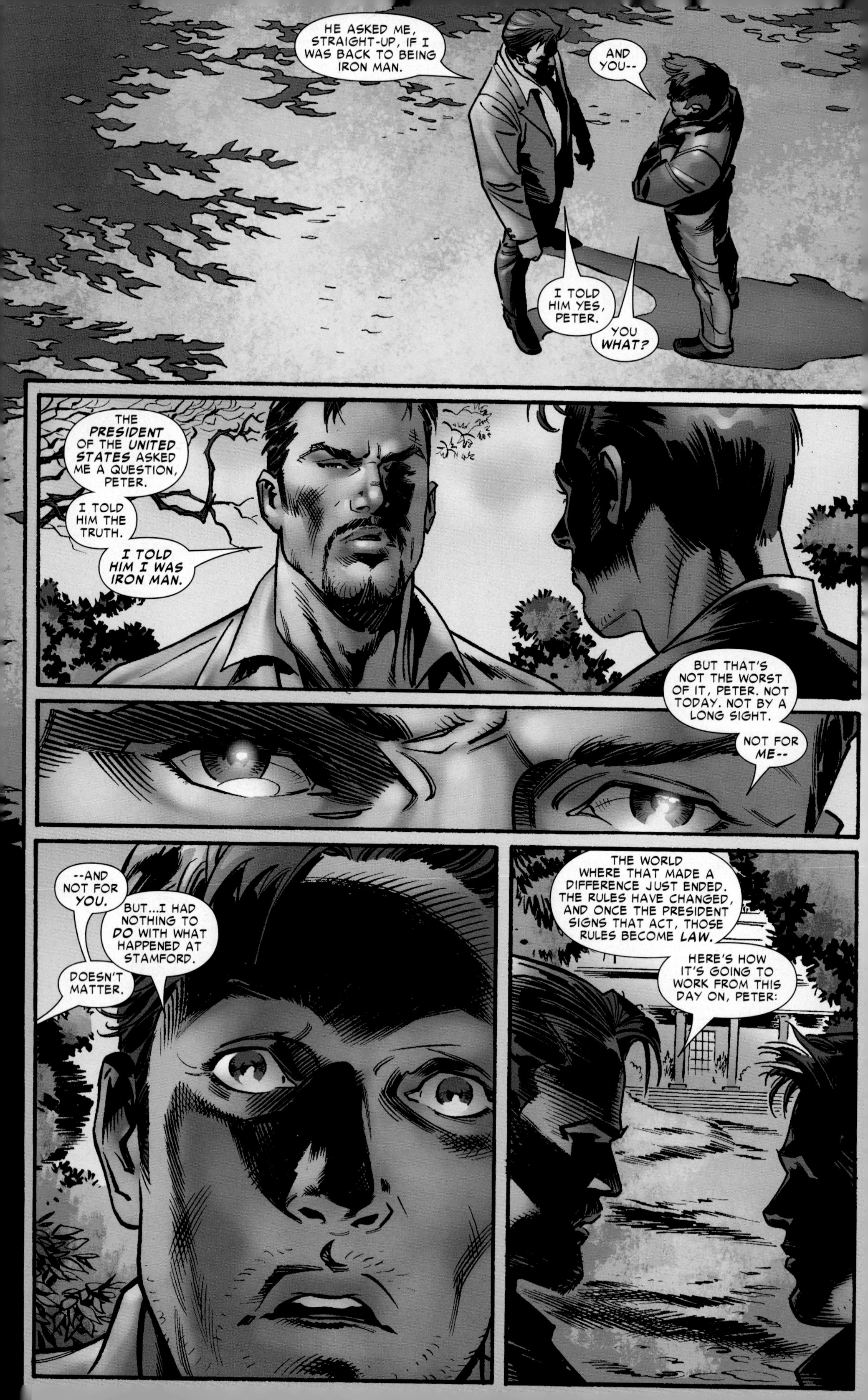
HE ASKED ME, STRAIGHT-UP, IF I WAS BACK TO BEING IRON MAN.
AND YOU--
I TOLD HIM YES, PETER.
YOU WHAT?
THE PRESIDENT OF THE UNITED STATES ASKED ME A QUESTION, PETER.
I TOLD HIM THE TRUTH.
I TOLD HIM I WAS IRON MAN.
BUT THAT'S NOT THE WORST OF IT, PETER. NOT TODAY. NOT BY A LONG SIGHT.
NOT FOR ME--
--AND NOT FOR YOU.
BUT...I HAD NOTHING TO DO WITH WHAT HAPPENED AT STAMFORD.
DOESN'T MATTER.
THE WORLD WHERE THAT MADE A DIFFERENCE JUST ENDED. THE RULES HAVE CHANGED, AND ONCE THE PRESIDENT SIGNS THAT ACT, THOSE RULES BECOME LAW.
HERE'S HOW IT'S GOING TO WORK FROM THIS DAY ON, PETER:

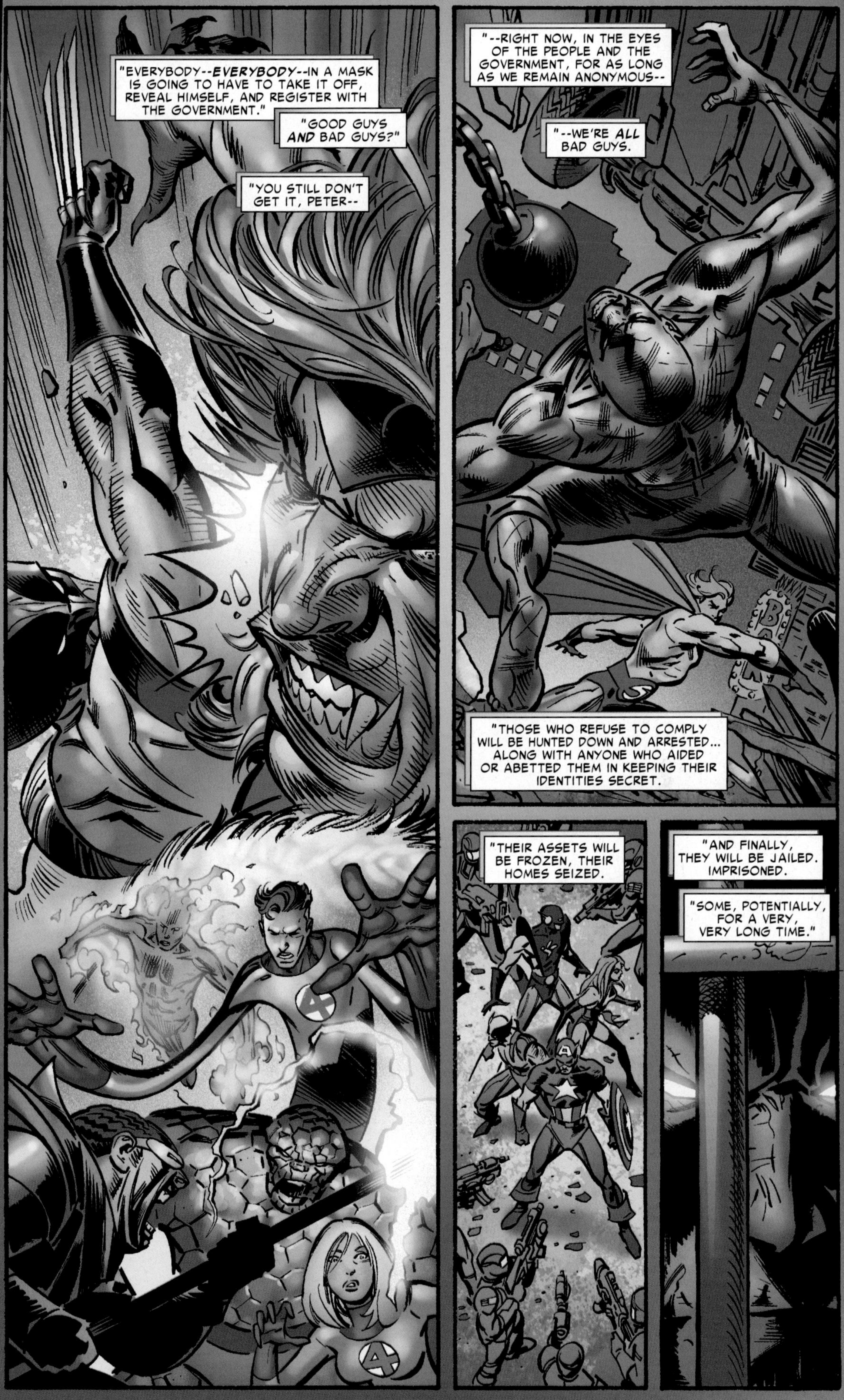
"EVERYBODY--EVERYBODY--IN A MASK IS GOING TO HAVE TO TAKE IT OFF, REVEAL HIMSELF, AND REGISTER WITH THE GOVERNMENT."
"GOOD GUYS AND BAD GUYS?"
"YOU STILL DON'T GET IT, PETER--
"--RIGHT NOW, IN THE EYES OF THE PEOPLE AND THE GOVERNMENT, FOR AS LONG AS WE REMAIN ANONYMOUS--
"--WE'RE ALL BAD GUYS.
"THOSE WHO REFUSE TO COMPLY WILL BE HUNTED DOWN AND ARRESTED... ALONG WITH ANYONE WHO AIDED OR ABETTED THEM IN KEEPING THEIR IDENTITIES SECRET.
"THEIR ASSETS WILL BE FROZEN, THEIR HOMES SEIZED.
"AND FINALLY, THEY WILL BE JAILED. IMPRISONED.
"SOME, POTENTIALLY, FOR A VERY, VERY LONG TIME."

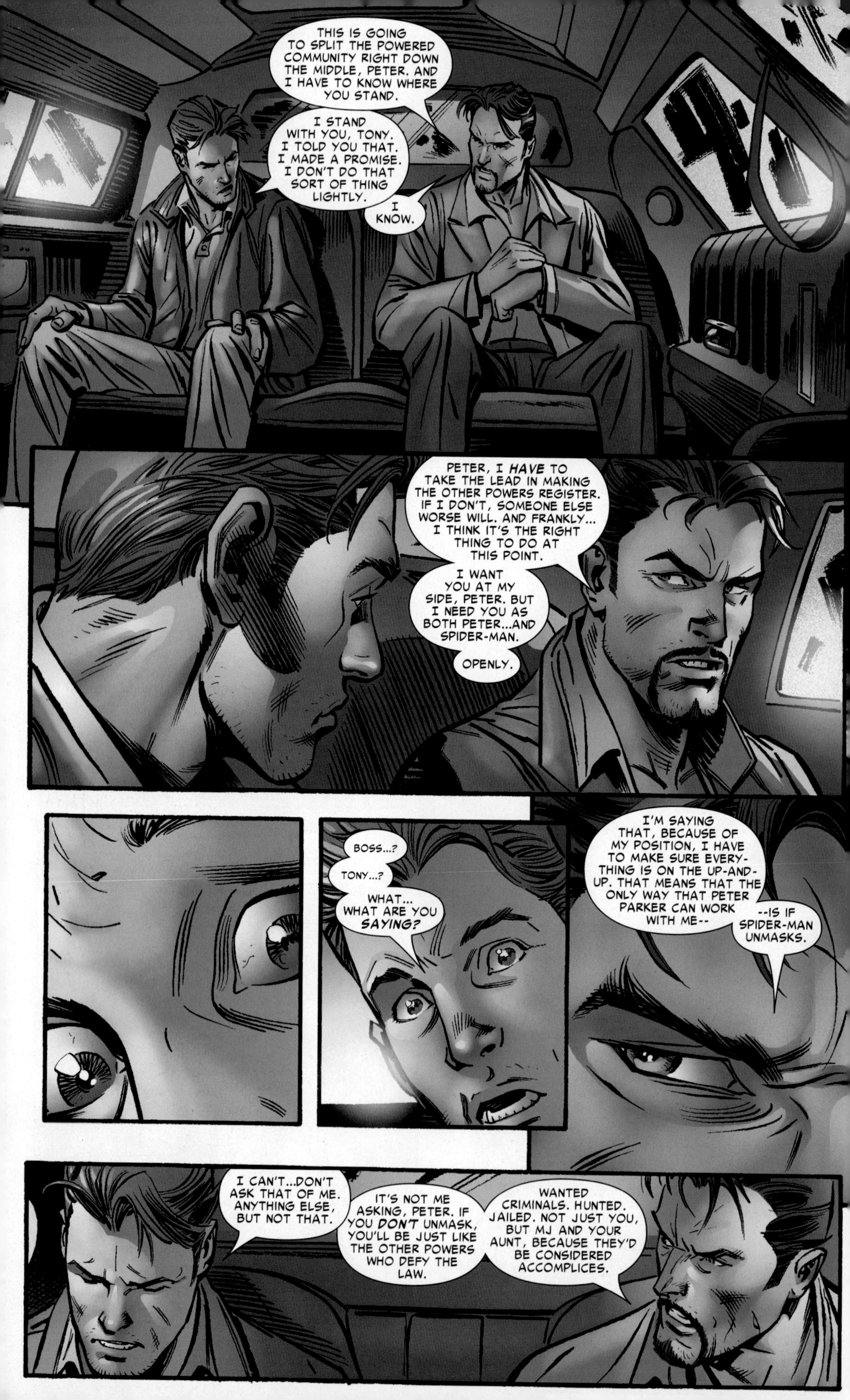
THIS IS GOING TO SPLIT THE POWERED COMMUNITY RIGHT DOWN THE MIDDLE, PETER. AND I HAVE TO KNOW WHERE YOU STAND.
I STAND WITH YOU, TONY. I TOLD YOU THAT. I MADE A PROMISE. I DON'T DO THAT SORT OF THING LIGHTLY.
I KNOW.
PETER, I *HAVE* TO TAKE THE LEAD IN MAKING THE OTHER POWERS REGISTER. IF I DON'T, SOMEONE ELSE WORSE WILL. AND FRANKLY... I THINK IT'S THE RIGHT THING TO DO AT THIS POINT.
I WANT YOU AT MY SIDE, PETER. BUT I NEED YOU AS BOTH PETER...AND SPIDER-MAN.
OPENLY.
BOSS...?
TONY...?
WHAT... WHAT ARE YOU *SAYING?*
I'M SAYING THAT, BECAUSE OF MY POSITION, I HAVE TO MAKE SURE EVERY-THING IS ON THE UP-AND-UP. THAT MEANS THAT THE ONLY WAY THAT PETER PARKER CAN WORK WITH ME--
--IS IF SPIDER-MAN UNMASKS.
I CAN'T...DON'T ASK THAT OF ME. ANYTHING ELSE, BUT NOT THAT.
IT'S NOT ME ASKING, PETER. IF YOU *DON'T* UNMASK, YOU'LL BE JUST LIKE THE OTHER POWERS WHO DEFY THE LAW.
WANTED CRIMINALS. HUNTED. JAILED. NOT JUST YOU, BUT MJ AND YOUR AUNT, BECAUSE THEY'D BE CONSIDERED ACCOMPLICES.

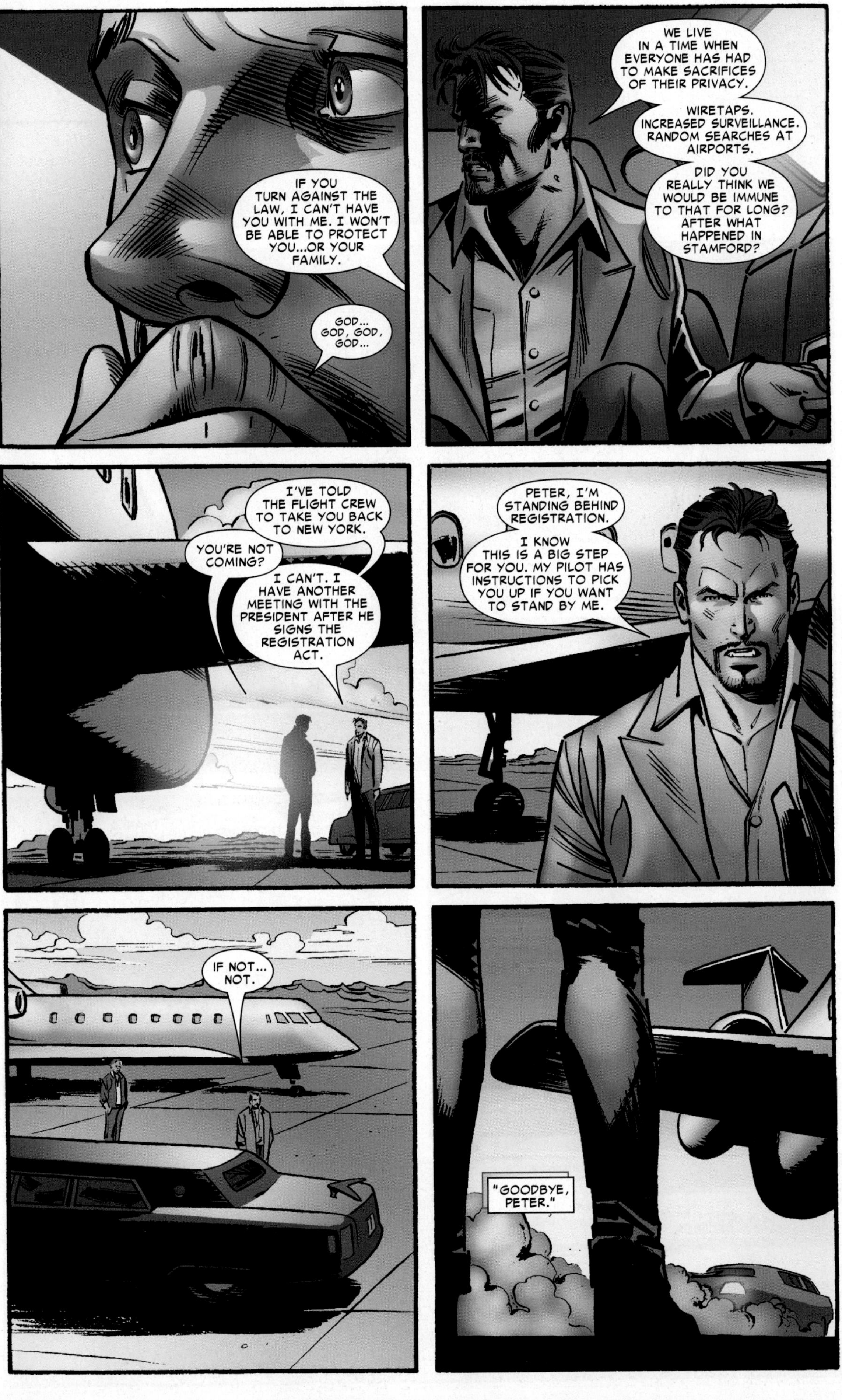
IF YOU TURN AGAINST THE LAW, I CAN'T HAVE YOU WITH ME. I WON'T BE ABLE TO PROTECT YOU...OR YOUR FAMILY.
GOD... GOD, GOD, GOD...
WE LIVE IN A TIME WHEN EVERYONE HAS HAD TO MAKE SACRIFICES OF THEIR PRIVACY.
WIRETAPS. INCREASED SURVEILLANCE. RANDOM SEARCHES AT AIRPORTS.
DID YOU REALLY THINK WE WOULD BE IMMUNE TO THAT FOR LONG? AFTER WHAT HAPPENED IN STAMFORD?
I'VE TOLD THE FLIGHT CREW TO TAKE YOU BACK TO NEW YORK.
YOU'RE NOT COMING?
I CAN'T. I HAVE ANOTHER MEETING WITH THE PRESIDENT AFTER HE SIGNS THE REGISTRATION ACT.
PETER, I'M STANDING BEHIND REGISTRATION.
I KNOW THIS IS A BIG STEP FOR YOU. MY PILOT HAS INSTRUCTIONS TO PICK YOU UP IF YOU WANT TO STAND BY ME.
IF NOT... NOT.
"GOODBYE, PETER."

RIGHT, YES, I...YES, I KNOW IT'S LATE AND YOU'RE ABOUT TO CLOSE, BUT COULD YOU GIVE ME THE TOTAL AMOUNT IN MY ACCOUNTS?

NO, NOT THE SHARED ACCOUNTS WITH MY WIFE, JUST MINE. RIGHT, SAVINGS, CHECKING, EVERYTHING.

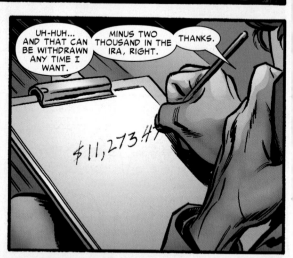

UH-HUH... AND THAT CAN BE WITHDRAWN ANY TIME I WANT.

MINUS TWO THOUSAND IN THE IRA, RIGHT.

THANKS.

$11,273.47

"AUNT MAY...MJ...I NEED YOUR HELP. I NEED TO MAKE A DECISION, AND--

"--GOD, I JUST... I DON'T KNOW WHAT TO DO."

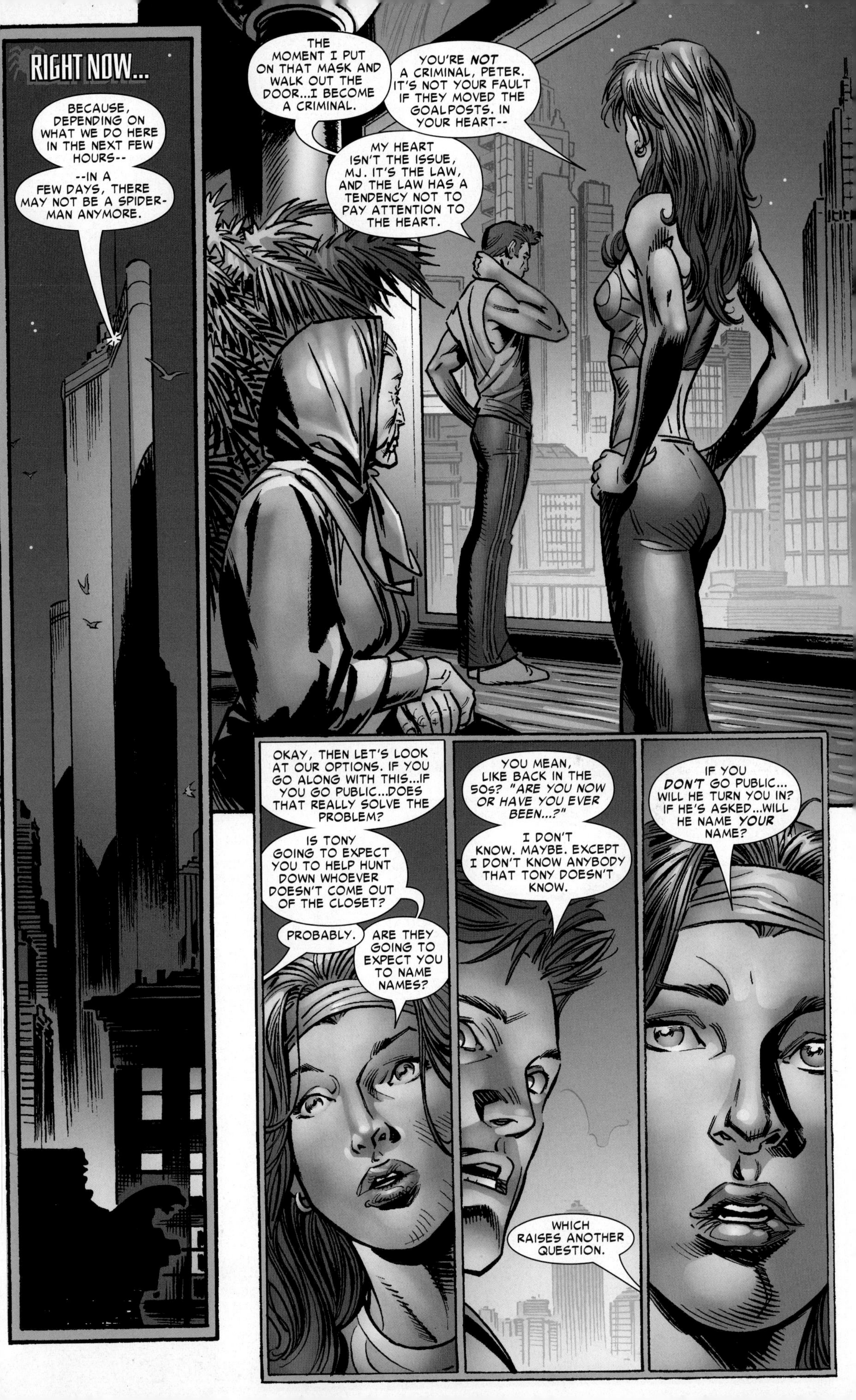
RIGHT NOW...
BECAUSE, DEPENDING ON WHAT WE DO HERE IN THE NEXT FEW HOURS--
--IN A FEW DAYS, THERE MAY NOT BE A SPIDER-MAN ANYMORE.
THE MOMENT I PUT ON THAT MASK AND WALK OUT THE DOOR...I BECOME A CRIMINAL.
YOU'RE NOT A CRIMINAL, PETER. IT'S NOT YOUR FAULT IF THEY MOVED THE GOALPOSTS. IN YOUR HEART--
MY HEART ISN'T THE ISSUE, MJ. IT'S THE LAW, AND THE LAW HAS A TENDENCY NOT TO PAY ATTENTION TO THE HEART.
OKAY, THEN LET'S LOOK AT OUR OPTIONS. IF YOU GO ALONG WITH THIS...IF YOU GO PUBLIC...DOES THAT REALLY SOLVE THE PROBLEM?
IS TONY GOING TO EXPECT YOU TO HELP HUNT DOWN WHOEVER DOESN'T COME OUT OF THE CLOSET?
PROBABLY.
ARE THEY GOING TO EXPECT YOU TO NAME NAMES?
YOU MEAN, LIKE BACK IN THE 50s? "ARE YOU NOW OR HAVE YOU EVER BEEN...?"
I DON'T KNOW. MAYBE. EXCEPT I DON'T KNOW ANYBODY THAT TONY DOESN'T KNOW.
WHICH RAISES ANOTHER QUESTION.
IF YOU DON'T GO PUBLIC... WILL HE TURN YOU IN? IF HE'S ASKED...WILL HE NAME YOUR NAME?

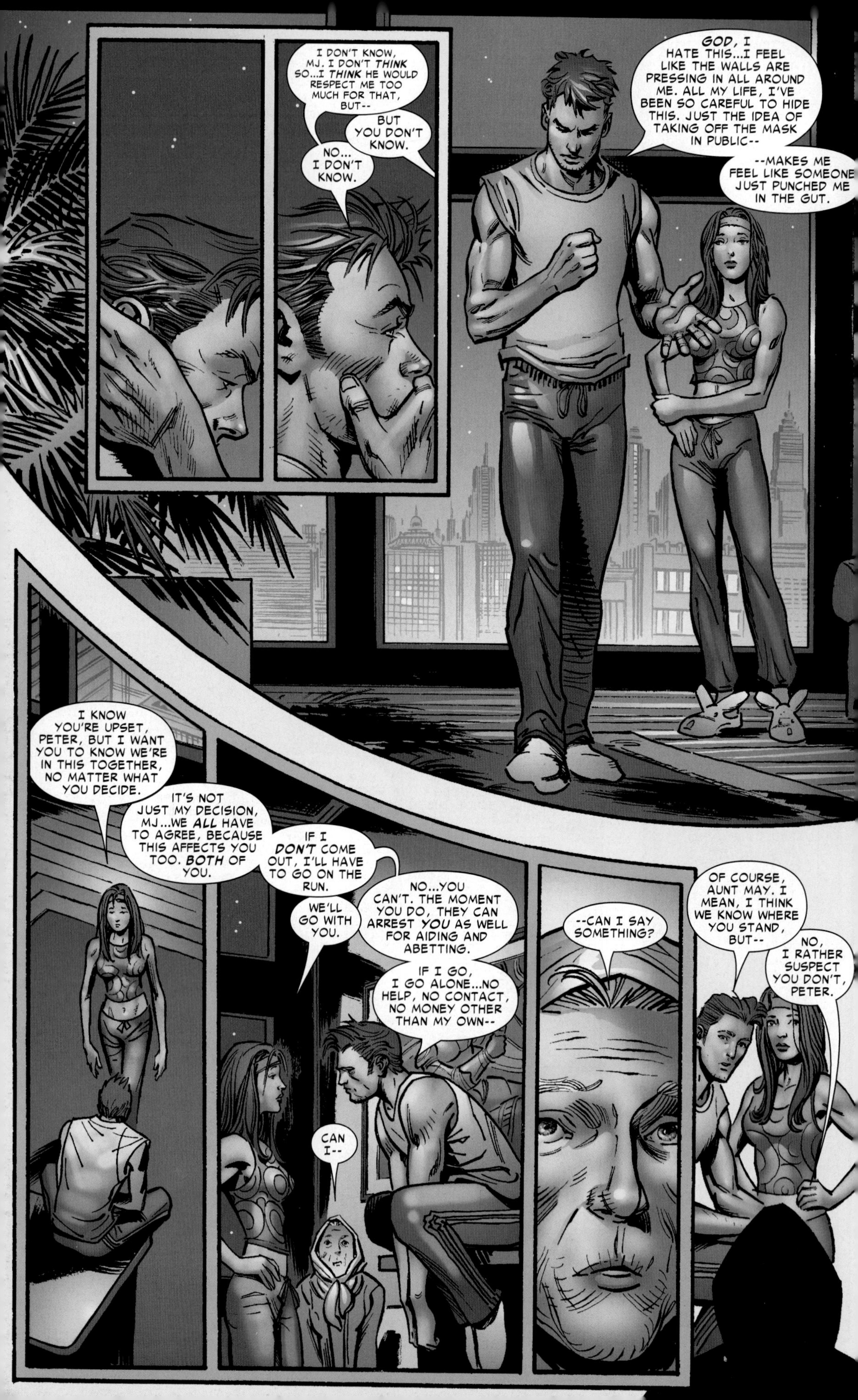
I DON'T KNOW, MJ. I DON'T THINK SO...I THINK HE WOULD RESPECT ME TOO MUCH FOR THAT, BUT--
BUT YOU DON'T KNOW.
NO... I DON'T KNOW.
GOD, I HATE THIS...I FEEL LIKE THE WALLS ARE PRESSING IN ALL AROUND ME. ALL MY LIFE, I'VE BEEN SO CAREFUL TO HIDE THIS. JUST THE IDEA OF TAKING OFF THE MASK IN PUBLIC--
--MAKES ME FEEL LIKE SOMEONE JUST PUNCHED ME IN THE GUT.
I KNOW YOU'RE UPSET, PETER, BUT I WANT YOU TO KNOW WE'RE IN THIS TOGETHER, NO MATTER WHAT YOU DECIDE.
IT'S NOT JUST MY DECISION, MJ...WE ALL HAVE TO AGREE, BECAUSE THIS AFFECTS YOU TOO. BOTH OF YOU.
IF I DON'T COME OUT, I'LL HAVE TO GO ON THE RUN.
WE'LL GO WITH YOU.
NO...YOU CAN'T. THE MOMENT YOU DO, THEY CAN ARREST YOU AS WELL FOR AIDING AND ABETTING.
IF I GO, I GO ALONE...NO HELP, NO CONTACT, NO MONEY OTHER THAN MY OWN--
CAN I--
--CAN I SAY SOMETHING?
OF COURSE, AUNT MAY. I MEAN, I THINK WE KNOW WHERE YOU STAND, BUT--
NO, I RATHER SUSPECT YOU DON'T, PETER.

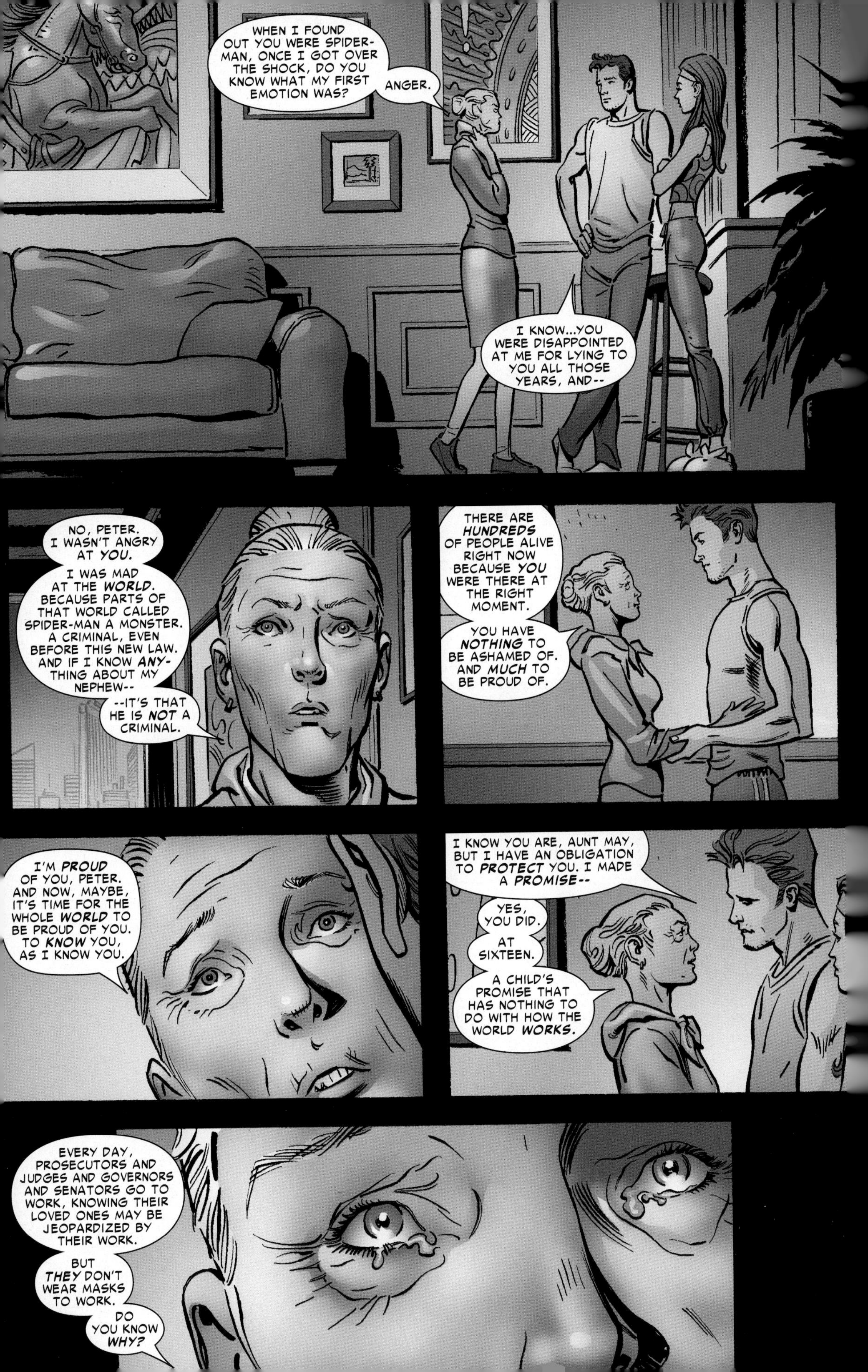
WHEN I FOUND OUT YOU WERE SPIDER-MAN, ONCE I GOT OVER THE SHOCK, DO YOU KNOW WHAT MY FIRST EMOTION WAS?
ANGER.
I KNOW...YOU WERE DISAPPOINTED AT ME FOR LYING TO YOU ALL THOSE YEARS, AND--
NO, PETER. I WASN'T ANGRY AT *YOU.*
I WAS MAD AT THE *WORLD*. BECAUSE PARTS OF THAT WORLD CALLED SPIDER-MAN A MONSTER. A CRIMINAL, EVEN BEFORE THIS NEW LAW. AND IF I KNOW *ANY*-THING ABOUT MY NEPHEW--
--IT'S THAT HE IS *NOT* A CRIMINAL.
THERE ARE *HUNDREDS* OF PEOPLE ALIVE RIGHT NOW BECAUSE *YOU* WERE THERE AT THE RIGHT MOMENT.
YOU HAVE *NOTHING* TO BE ASHAMED OF. AND *MUCH* TO BE PROUD OF.
I'M *PROUD* OF YOU, PETER. AND NOW, MAYBE, IT'S TIME FOR THE WHOLE *WORLD* TO BE PROUD OF YOU. TO *KNOW* YOU, AS I KNOW YOU.
I KNOW YOU ARE, AUNT MAY, BUT I HAVE AN OBLIGATION TO *PROTECT* YOU. I MADE A *PROMISE*--
YES, YOU DID.
AT SIXTEEN.
A CHILD'S PROMISE THAT HAS NOTHING TO DO WITH HOW THE WORLD *WORKS*.
EVERY DAY, PROSECUTORS AND JUDGES AND GOVERNORS AND SENATORS GO TO WORK, KNOWING THEIR LOVED ONES MAY BE JEOPARDIZED BY THEIR WORK.
BUT *THEY* DON'T WEAR MASKS TO WORK.
DO YOU KNOW *WHY?*

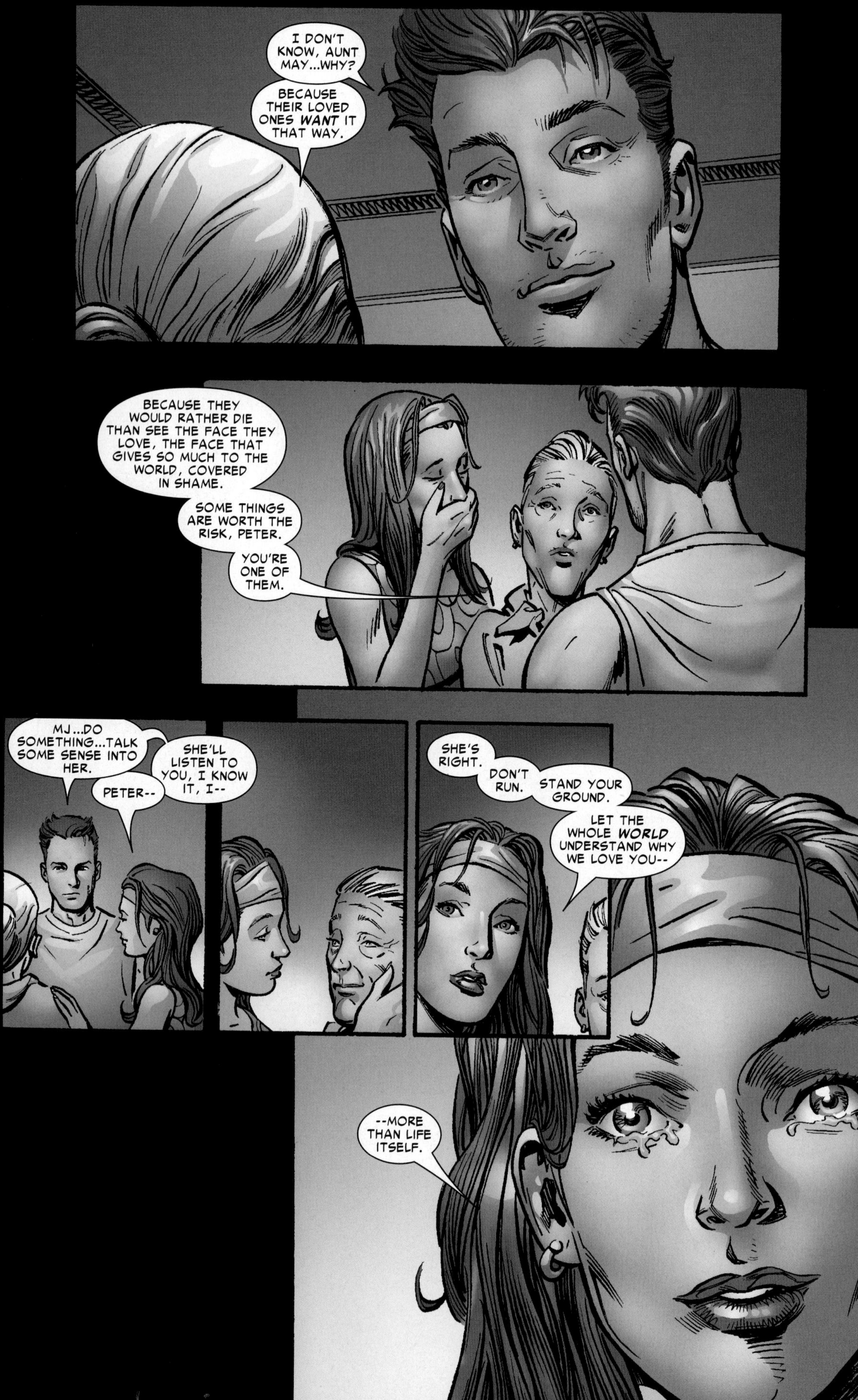
I DON'T KNOW, AUNT MAY...WHY?
BECAUSE THEIR LOVED ONES *WANT* IT THAT WAY.
BECAUSE THEY WOULD RATHER DIE THAN SEE THE FACE THEY LOVE, THE FACE THAT GIVES SO MUCH TO THE WORLD, COVERED IN SHAME.
SOME THINGS ARE WORTH THE RISK, PETER.
YOU'RE ONE OF THEM.
MJ...DO SOMETHING...TALK SOME SENSE INTO HER.
SHE'LL LISTEN TO YOU, I KNOW IT, I--
PETER--
SHE'S RIGHT.
DON'T RUN.
STAND YOUR GROUND.
LET THE WHOLE *WORLD* UNDERSTAND WHY WE LOVE YOU--
--MORE THAN LIFE ITSELF.

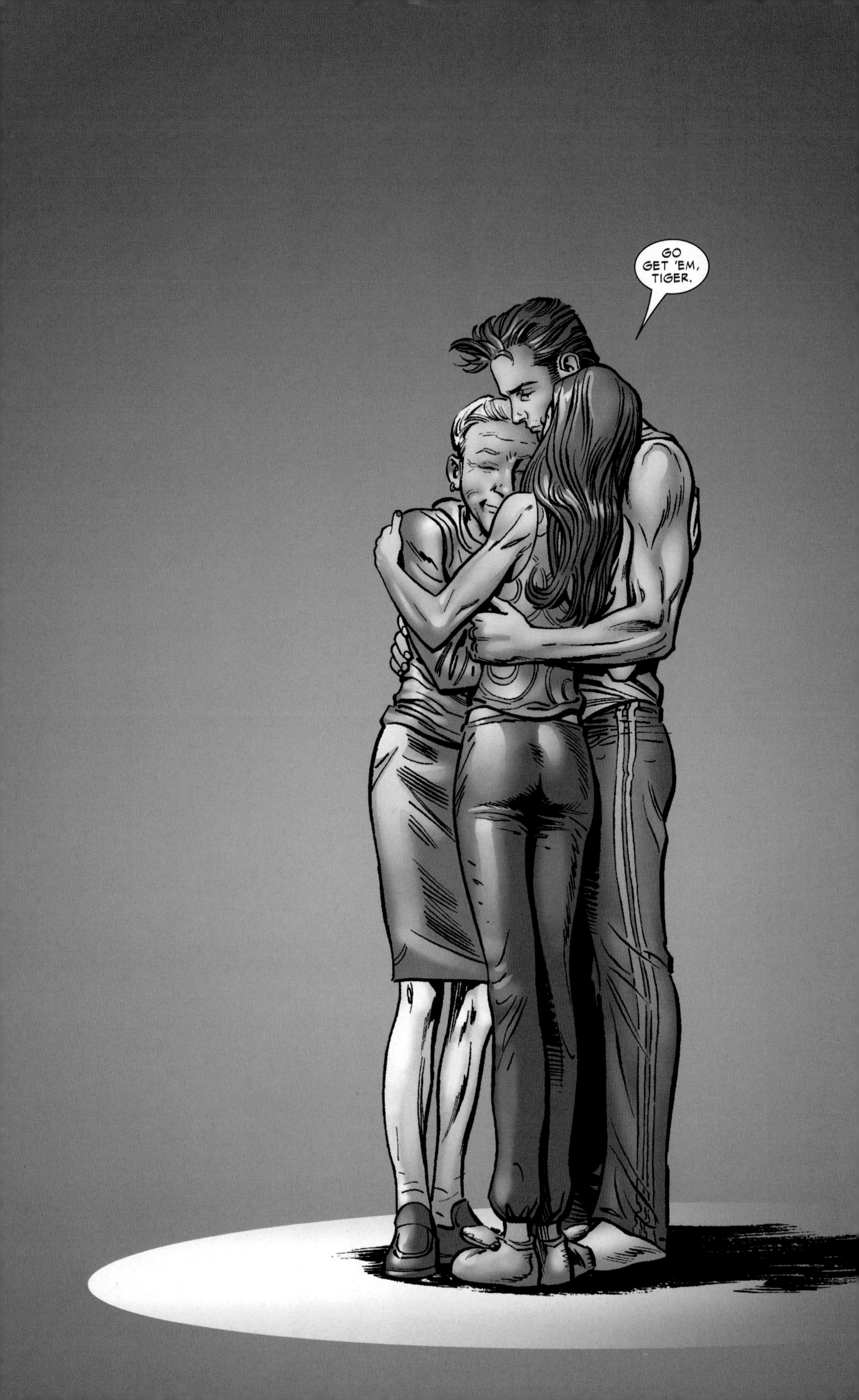
GO GET 'EM, TIGER.

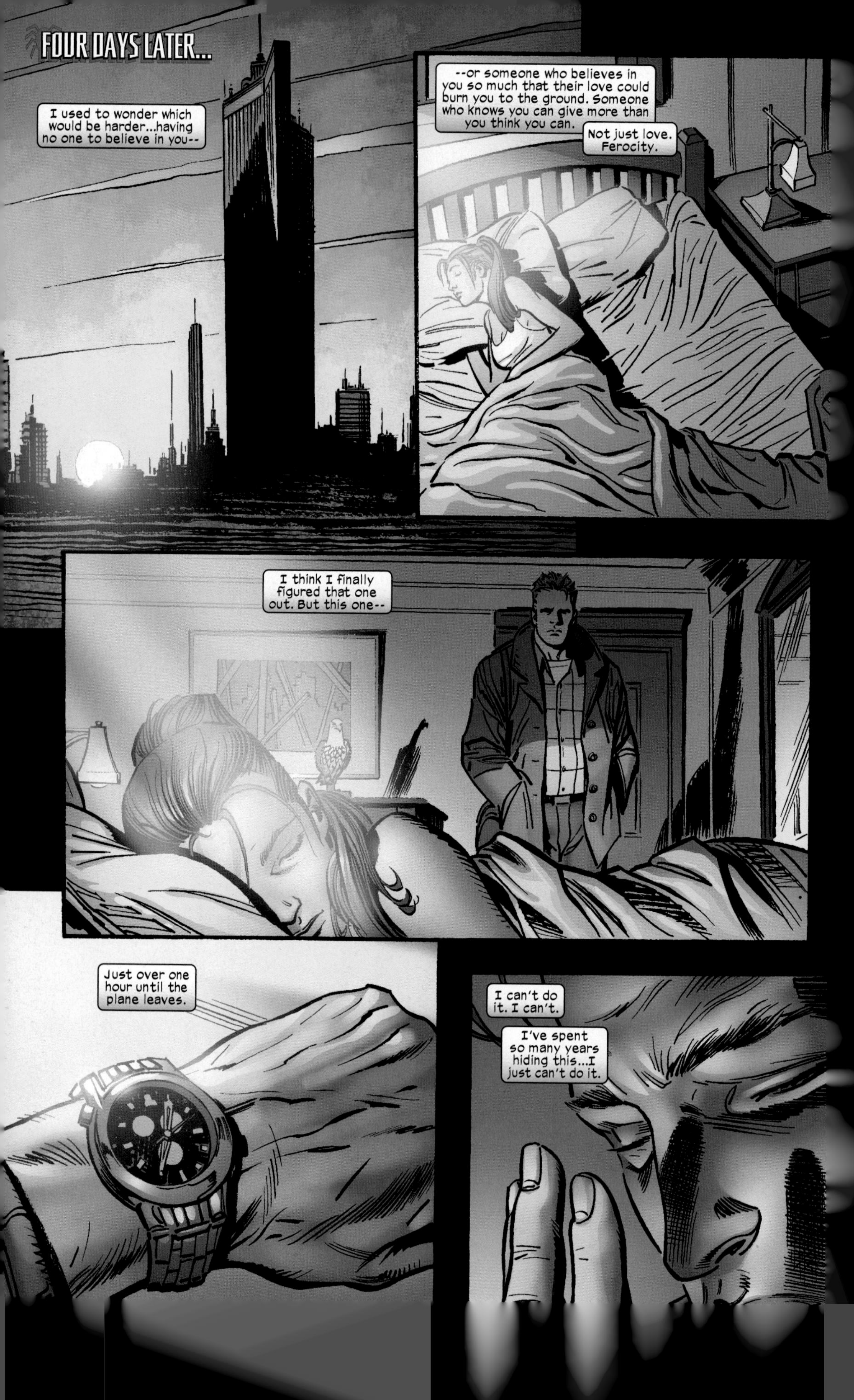
FOUR DAYS LATER...
I used to wonder which would be harder...having no one to believe in you--
--or someone who believes in you so much that their love could burn you to the ground. Someone who knows you can give more than you think you can.
Not just love. Ferocity.
I think I finally figured that one out. But this one--
Just over one hour until the plane leaves.
I can't do it. I can't.
I've spent so many years hiding this...I just can't do it.

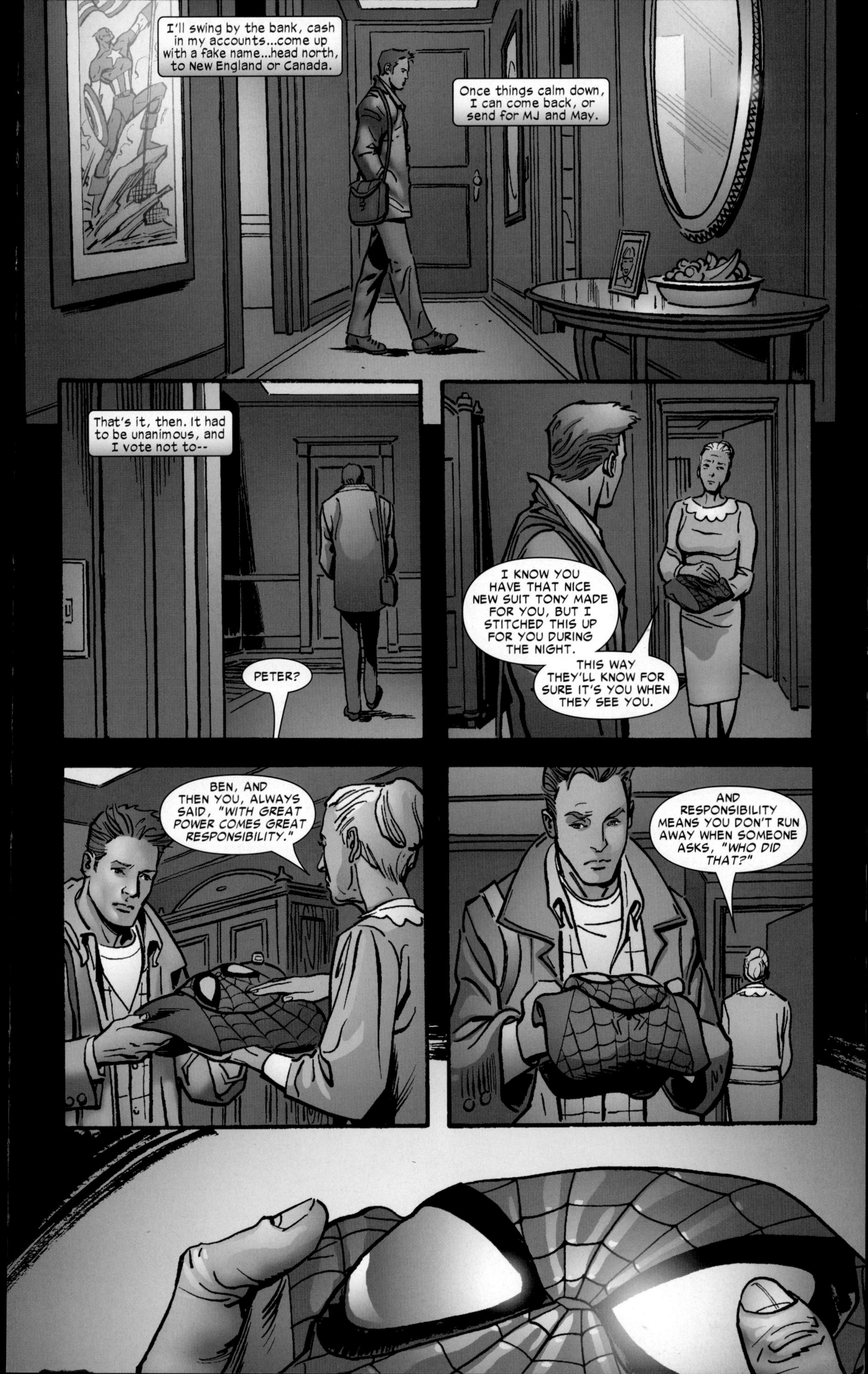
I'll swing by the bank, cash in my accounts...come up with a fake name...head north, to New England or Canada.
Once things calm down, I can come back, or send for MJ and May.
That's it, then. It had to be unanimous, and I vote not to--
PETER?
I KNOW YOU HAVE THAT NICE NEW SUIT TONY MADE FOR YOU, BUT I STITCHED THIS UP FOR YOU DURING THE NIGHT.
THIS WAY THEY'LL KNOW FOR SURE IT'S YOU WHEN THEY SEE YOU.
BEN, AND THEN YOU, ALWAYS SAID, "WITH GREAT POWER COMES GREAT RESPONSIBILITY."
AND RESPONSIBILITY MEANS YOU DON'T RUN AWAY WHEN SOMEONE ASKS, "WHO DID THAT?"

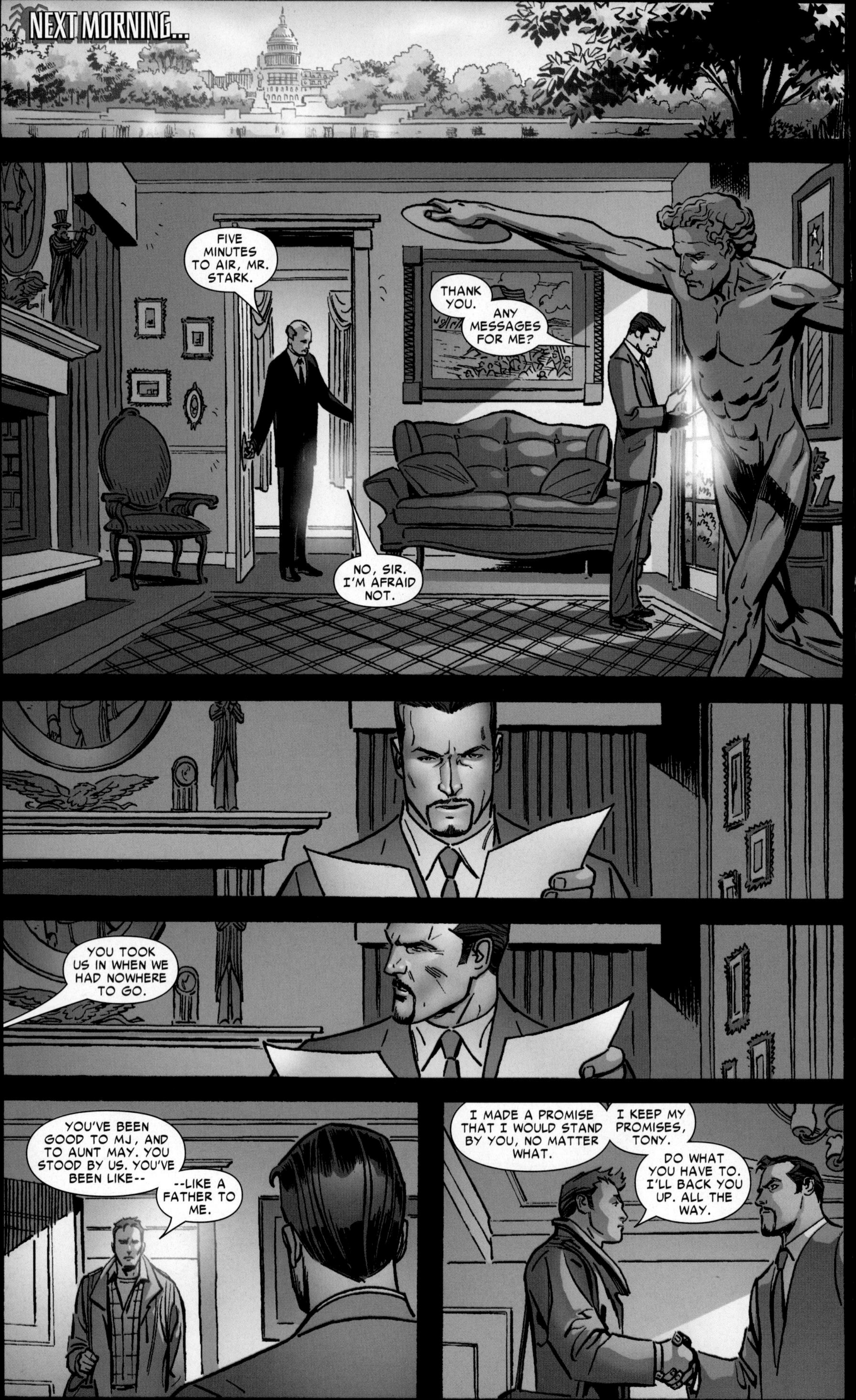
NEXT MORNING...
FIVE MINUTES TO AIR, MR. STARK.
THANK YOU.
ANY MESSAGES FOR ME?
NO, SIR. I'M AFRAID NOT.
YOU TOOK US IN WHEN WE HAD NOWHERE TO GO.
YOU'VE BEEN GOOD TO MJ, AND TO AUNT MAY. YOU STOOD BY US. YOU'VE BEEN LIKE--
--LIKE A FATHER TO ME.
I MADE A PROMISE THAT I WOULD STAND BY YOU, NO MATTER WHAT.
I KEEP MY PROMISES, TONY.
DO WHAT YOU HAVE TO. I'LL BACK YOU UP. ALL THE WAY.

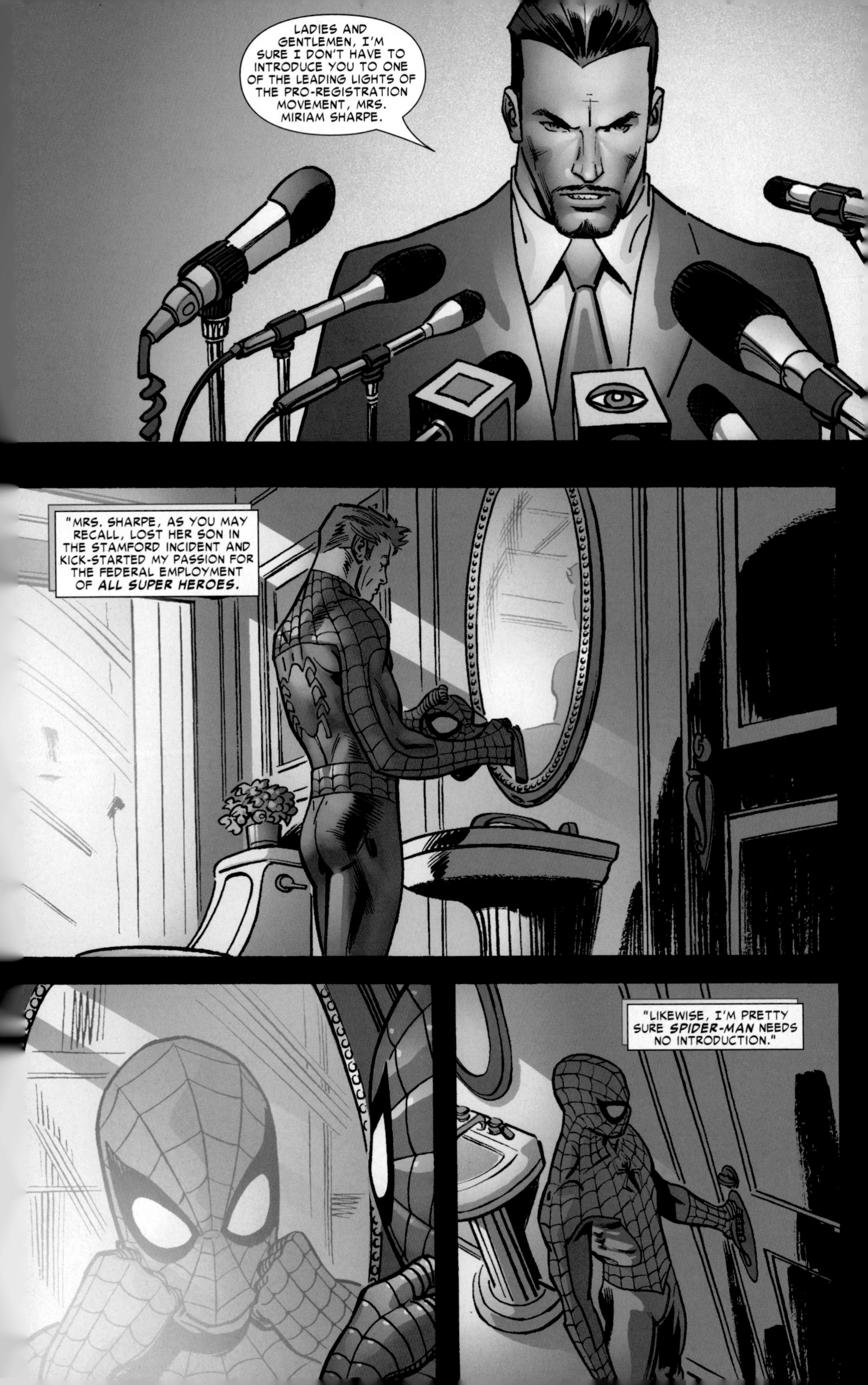
LADIES AND GENTLEMEN, I'M SURE I DON'T HAVE TO INTRODUCE YOU TO ONE OF THE LEADING LIGHTS OF THE PRO-REGISTRATION MOVEMENT, MRS. MIRIAM SHARPE.
"MRS. SHARPE, AS YOU MAY RECALL, LOST HER SON IN THE STAMFORD INCIDENT AND KICK-STARTED MY PASSION FOR THE FEDERAL EMPLOYMENT OF ALL SUPER HEROES.
"LIKEWISE, I'M PRETTY SURE SPIDER-MAN NEEDS NO INTRODUCTION."

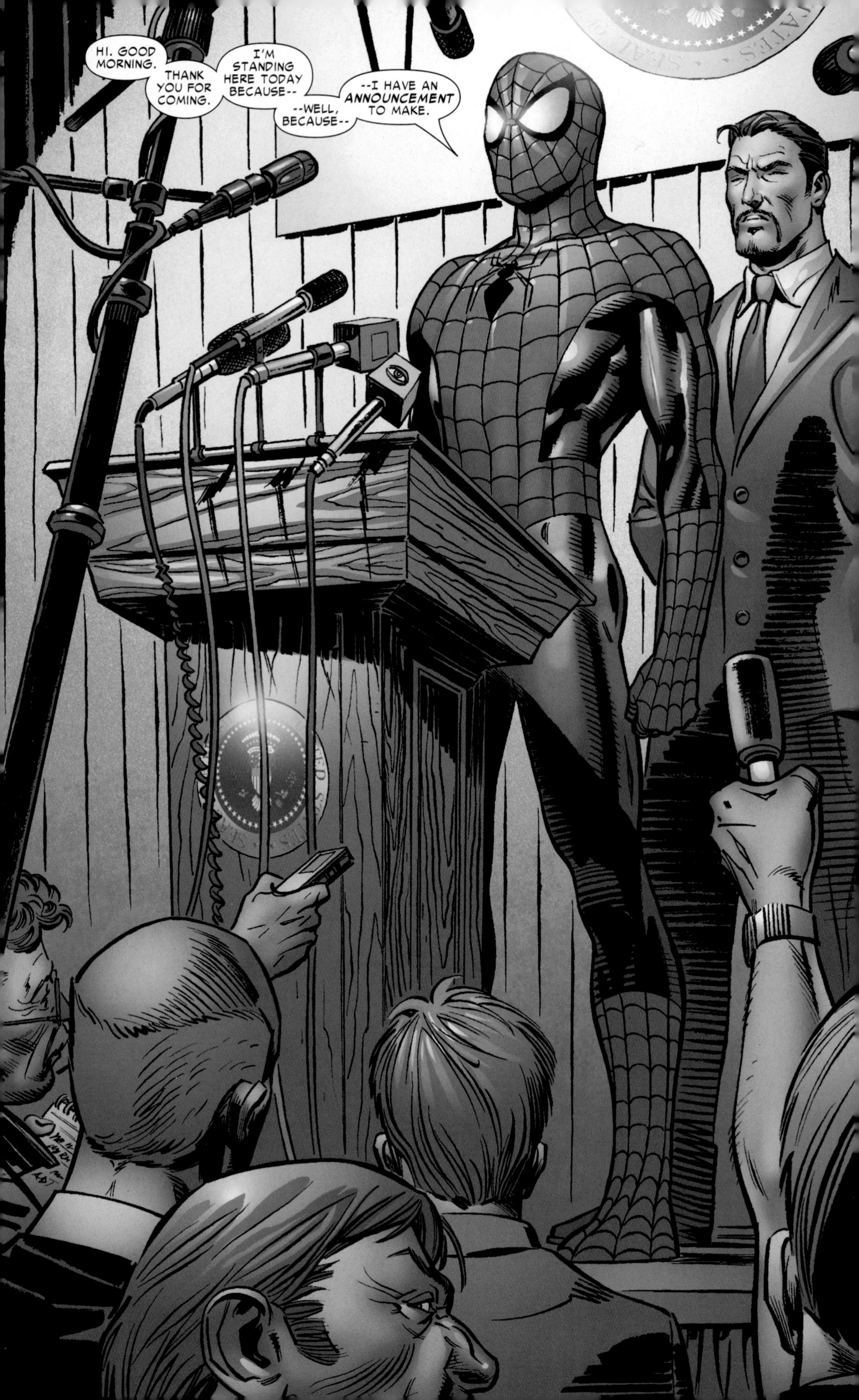
HI. GOOD MORNING.
THANK YOU FOR COMING.
I'M STANDING HERE TODAY BECAUSE--
--WELL, BECAUSE--
--I HAVE AN ANNOUNCEMENT TO MAKE.

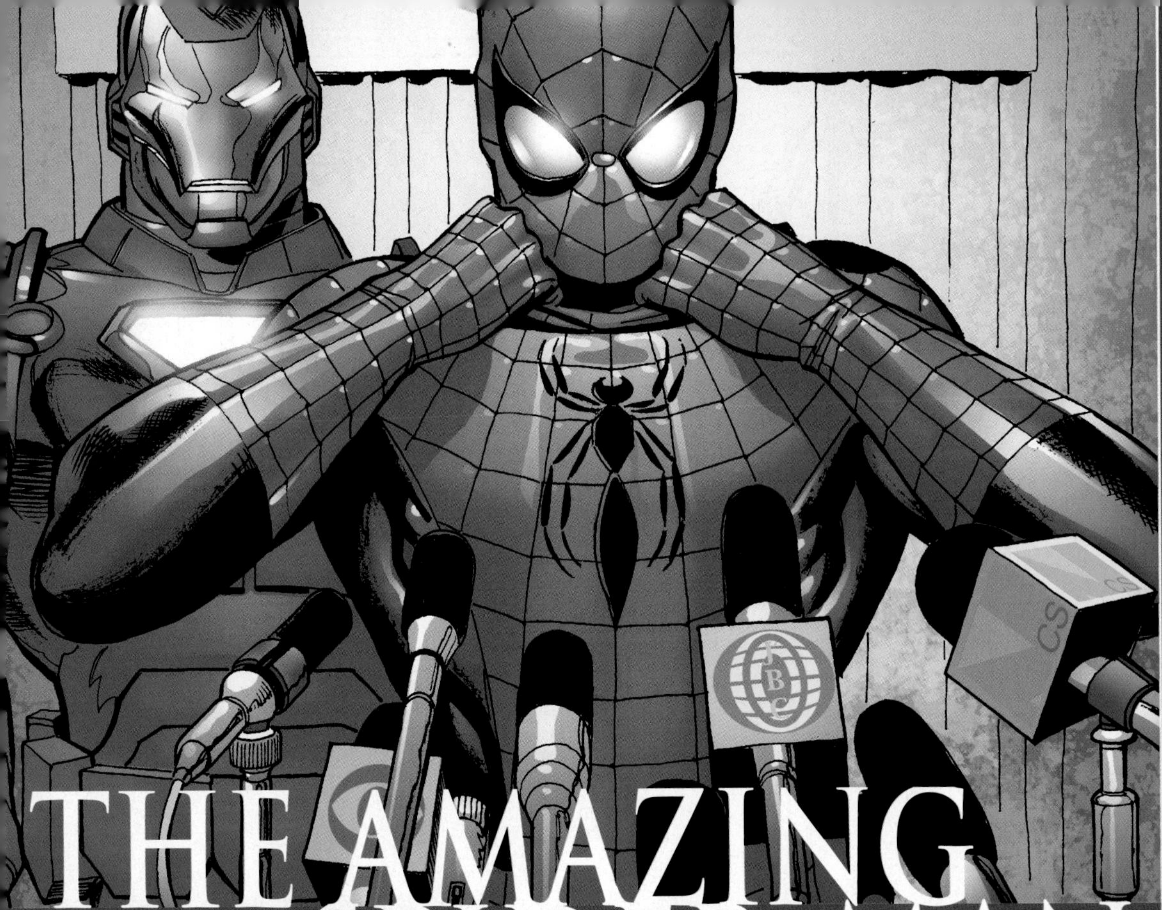
JBC
CS

THE AMAZING SPIDER-MAN

A MARVEL® COMICS EVENT

CIVIL WAR

AMAZING SPIDER-MAN #533

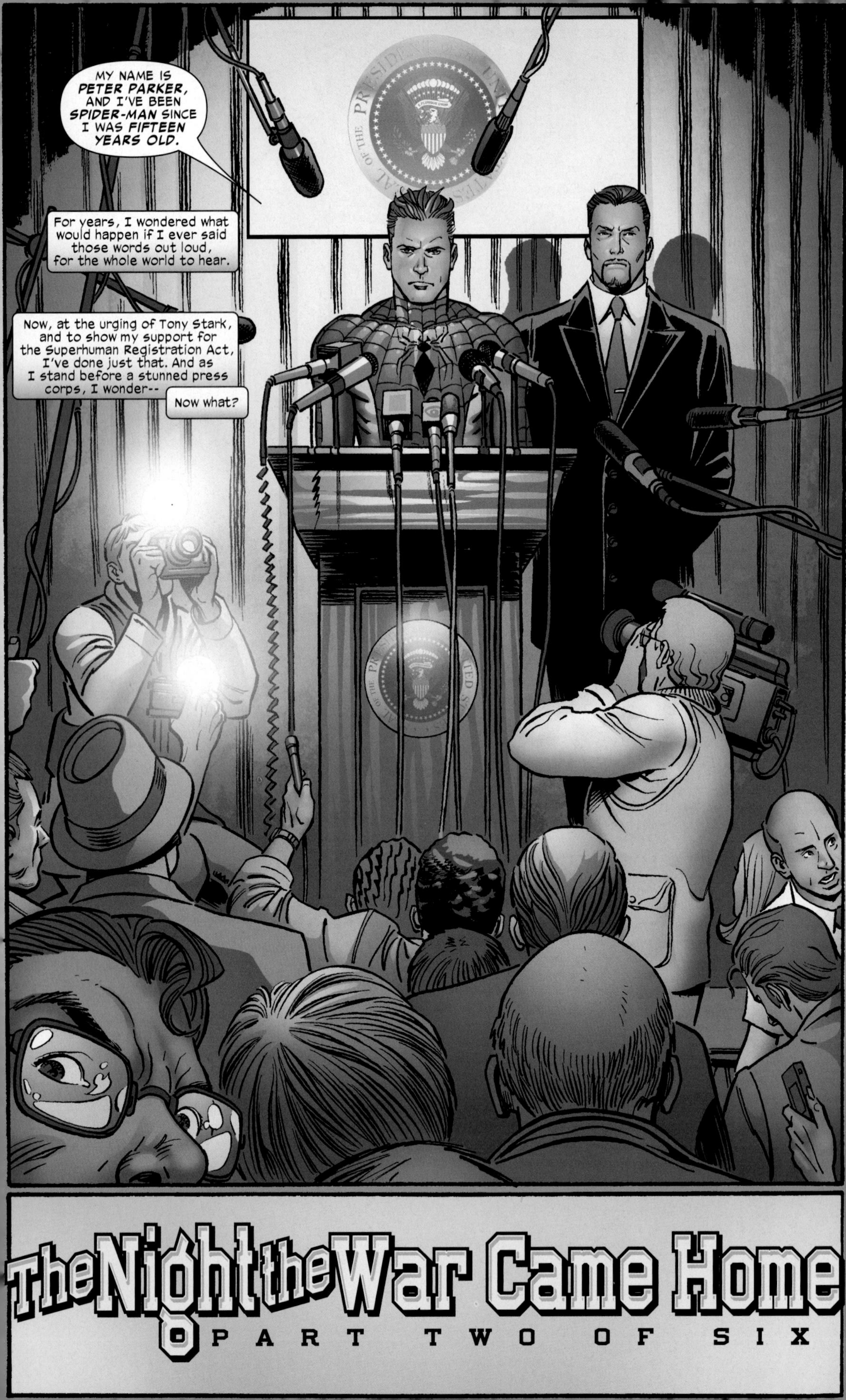
MY NAME IS PETER PARKER, AND I'VE BEEN SPIDER-MAN SINCE I WAS FIFTEEN YEARS OLD.
For years, I wondered what would happen if I ever said those words out loud, for the whole world to hear.
Now, at the urging of Tony Stark, and to show my support for the Superhuman Registration Act, I've done just that. And as I stand before a stunned press corps, I wonder--
Now what?
The Night the War Came Home
PART TWO OF SIX

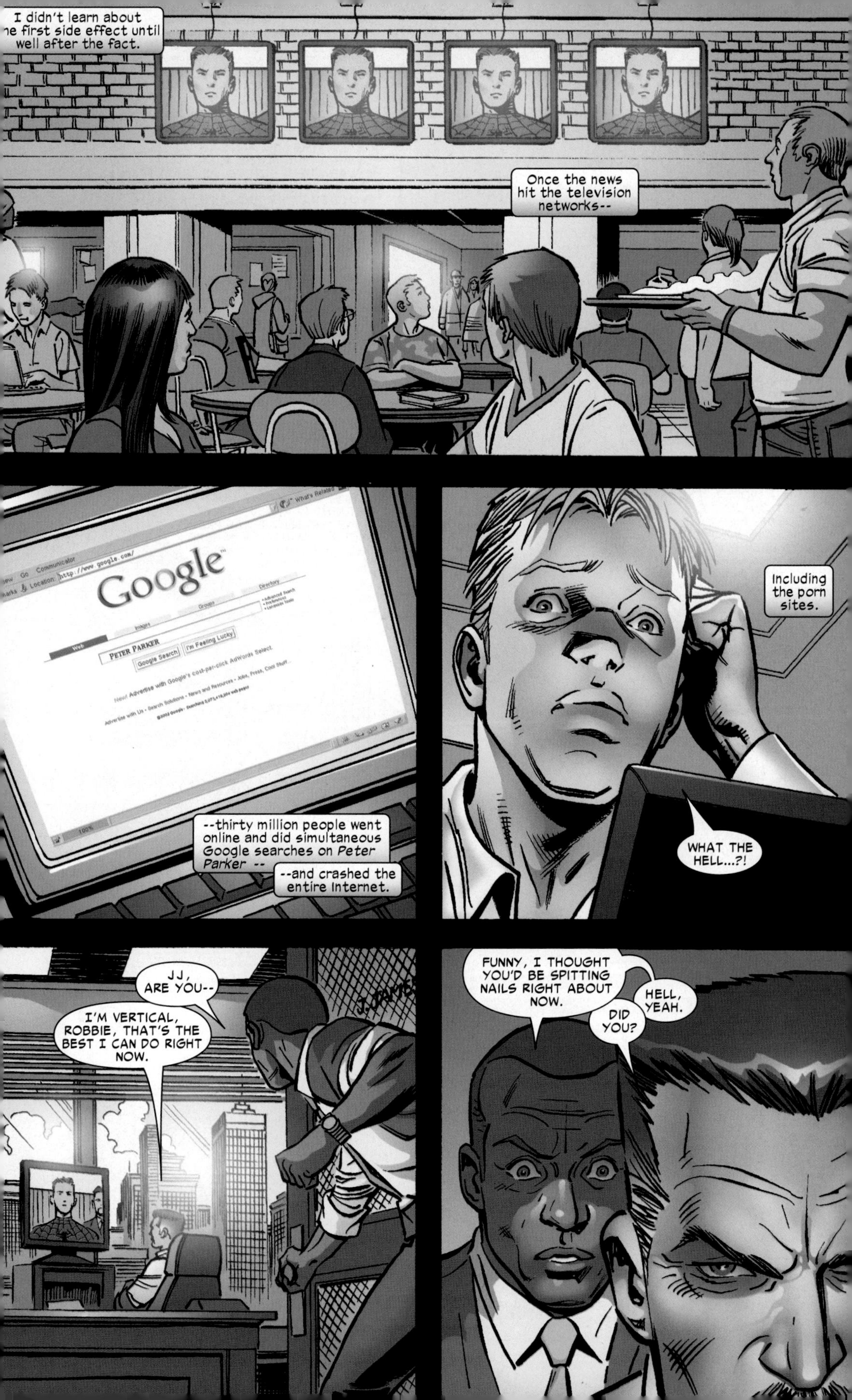

I didn't learn about
he first side effect until
well after the fact.
Once the news hit the television networks--
Google
PETER PARKER
--thirty million people went online and did simultaneous Google searches on *Peter Parker* --
--and crashed the entire Internet.
Including the porn sites.
WHAT THE HELL...?!
JJ, ARE YOU--
I'M VERTICAL, ROBBIE, THAT'S THE BEST I CAN DO RIGHT NOW.
FUNNY, I THOUGHT YOU'D BE SPITTING NAILS RIGHT ABOUT NOW.
HELL, YEAH.
DID YOU?

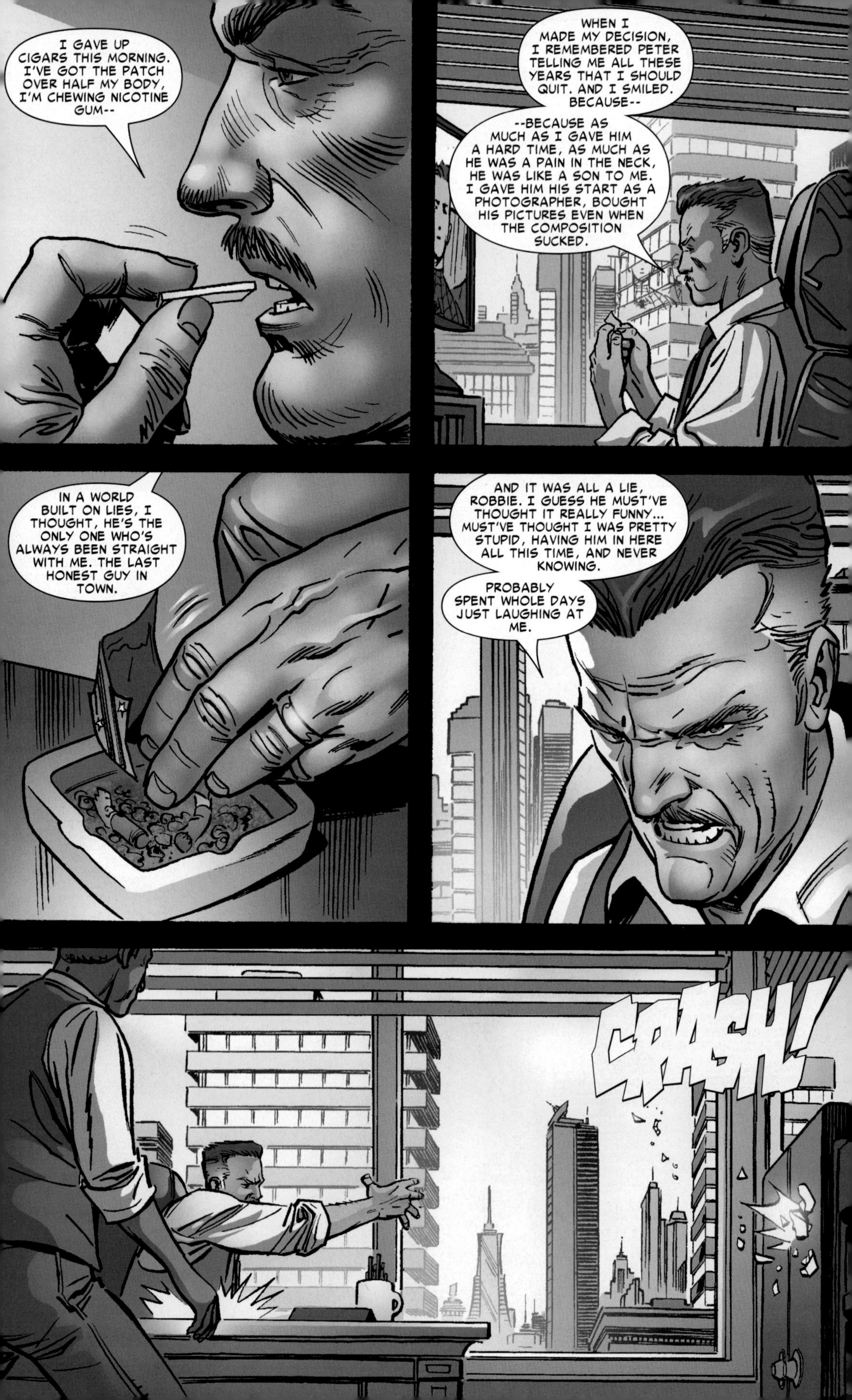
I GAVE UP CIGARS THIS MORNING. I'VE GOT THE PATCH OVER HALF MY BODY, I'M CHEWING NICOTINE GUM--
WHEN I MADE MY DECISION, I REMEMBERED PETER TELLING ME ALL THESE YEARS THAT I SHOULD QUIT. AND I SMILED. BECAUSE--
--BECAUSE AS MUCH AS I GAVE HIM A HARD TIME, AS MUCH AS HE WAS A PAIN IN THE NECK, HE WAS LIKE A SON TO ME. I GAVE HIM HIS START AS A PHOTOGRAPHER, BOUGHT HIS PICTURES EVEN WHEN THE COMPOSITION SUCKED.
IN A WORLD BUILT ON LIES, I THOUGHT, HE'S THE ONLY ONE WHO'S ALWAYS BEEN STRAIGHT WITH ME. THE LAST HONEST GUY IN TOWN.
AND IT WAS ALL A LIE, ROBBIE. I GUESS HE MUST'VE THOUGHT IT REALLY FUNNY... MUST'VE THOUGHT I WAS PRETTY STUPID, HAVING HIM IN HERE ALL THIS TIME, AND NEVER KNOWING.
PROBABLY SPENT WHOLE DAYS JUST LAUGHING AT ME.
CRASH!

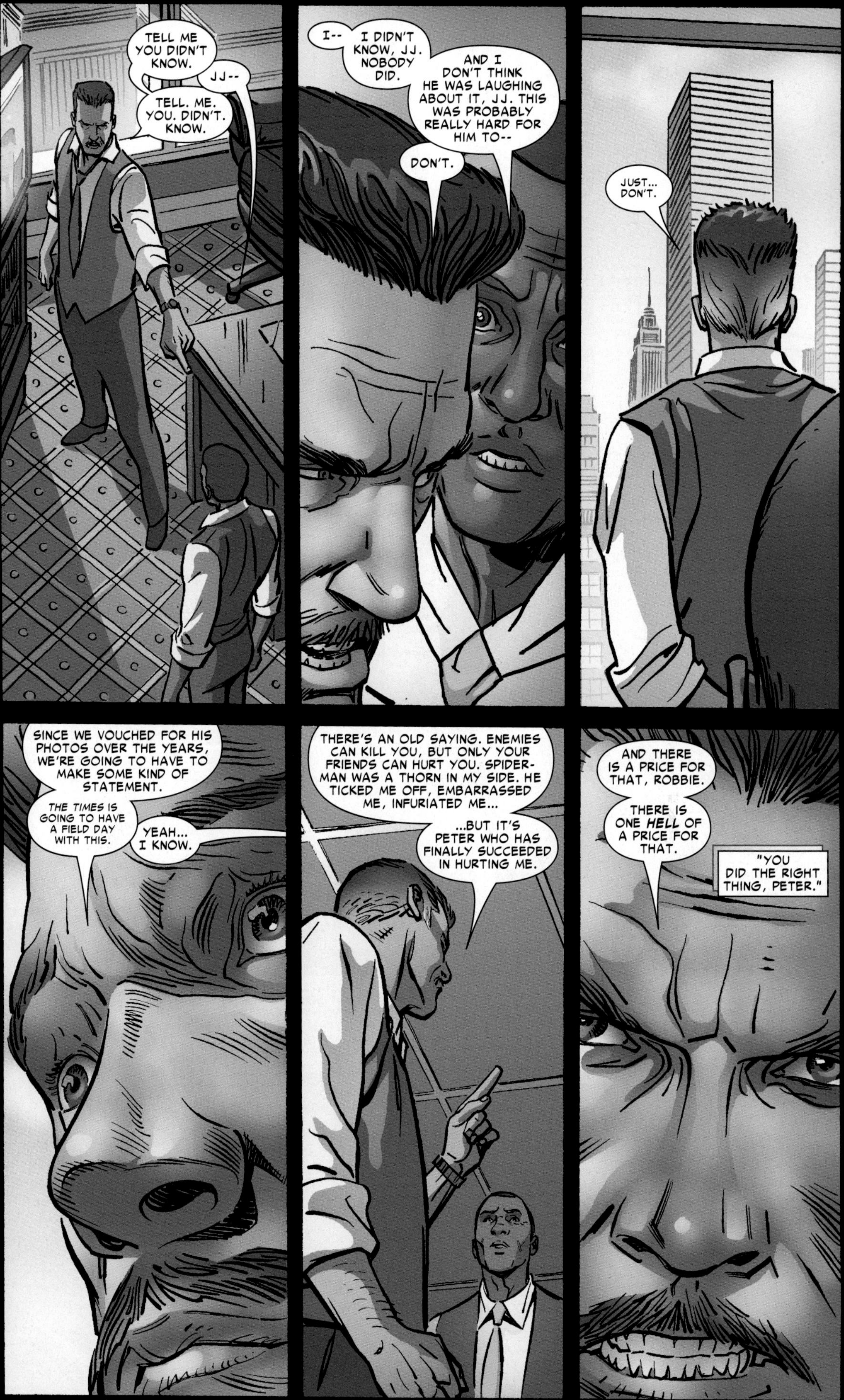
TELL ME YOU DIDN'T KNOW.
JJ--
TELL. ME. YOU. DIDN'T. KNOW.
I--
I DIDN'T KNOW, JJ. NOBODY DID.
AND I DON'T THINK HE WAS LAUGHING ABOUT IT, JJ. THIS WAS PROBABLY REALLY HARD FOR HIM TO--
DON'T.
JUST... DON'T.
SINCE WE VOUCHED FOR HIS PHOTOS OVER THE YEARS, WE'RE GOING TO HAVE TO MAKE SOME KIND OF STATEMENT.
THE TIMES IS GOING TO HAVE A FIELD DAY WITH THIS.
YEAH... I KNOW.
THERE'S AN OLD SAYING. ENEMIES CAN KILL YOU, BUT ONLY YOUR FRIENDS CAN HURT YOU. SPIDER-MAN WAS A THORN IN MY SIDE. HE TICKED ME OFF, EMBARRASSED ME, INFURIATED ME...
...BUT IT'S PETER WHO HAS FINALLY SUCCEEDED IN HURTING ME.
AND THERE IS A PRICE FOR THAT, ROBBIE.
THERE IS ONE HELL OF A PRICE FOR THAT.
"YOU DID THE RIGHT THING, PETER."

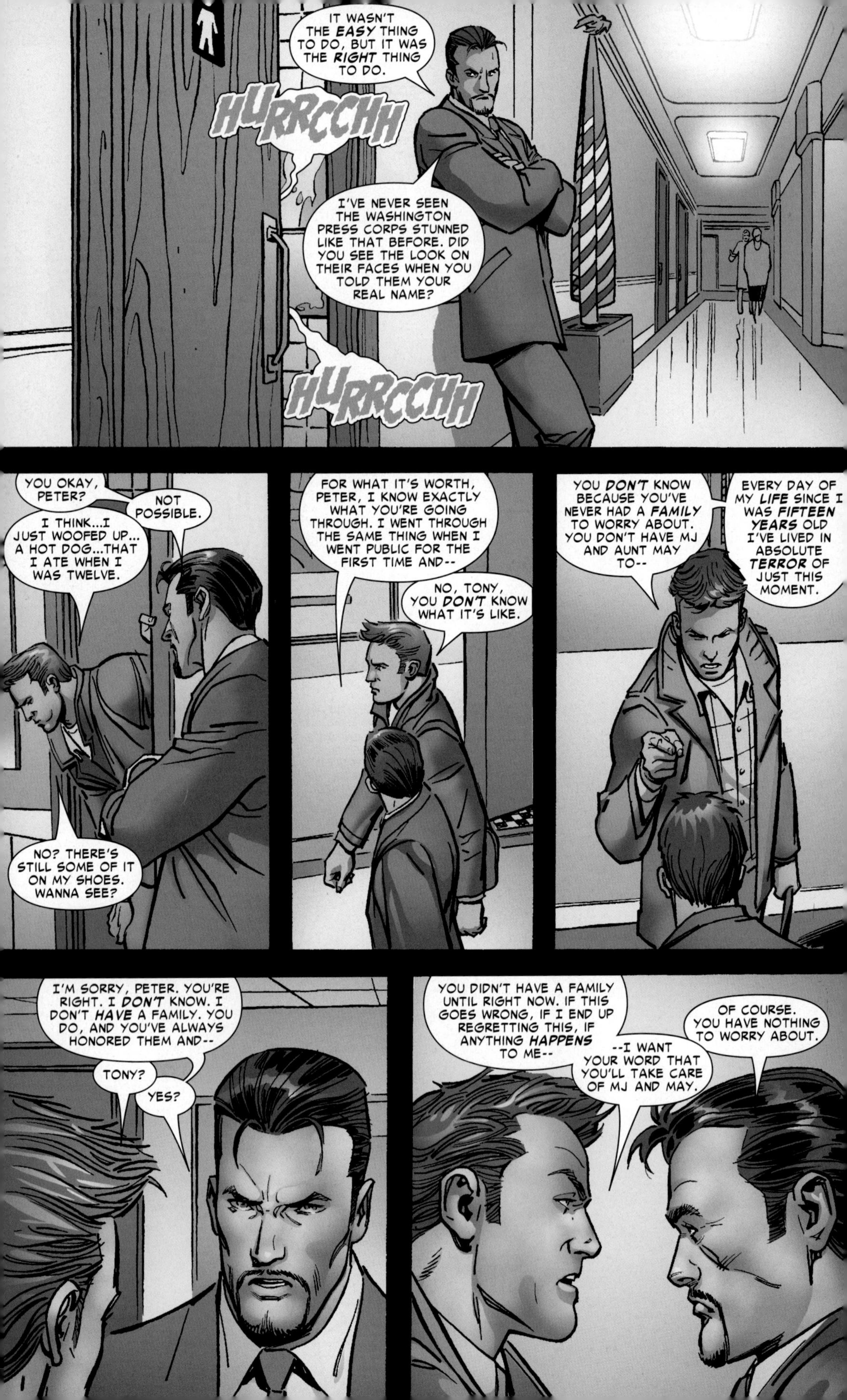
IT WASN'T THE EASY THING TO DO, BUT IT WAS THE RIGHT THING TO DO.
HURRCCHH
I'VE NEVER SEEN THE WASHINGTON PRESS CORPS STUNNED LIKE THAT BEFORE. DID YOU SEE THE LOOK ON THEIR FACES WHEN YOU TOLD THEM YOUR REAL NAME?
HURRCCHH
YOU OKAY, PETER?
NOT POSSIBLE.
I THINK...I JUST WOOFED UP... A HOT DOG...THAT I ATE WHEN I WAS TWELVE.
NO? THERE'S STILL SOME OF IT ON MY SHOES. WANNA SEE?
FOR WHAT IT'S WORTH, PETER, I KNOW EXACTLY WHAT YOU'RE GOING THROUGH. I WENT THROUGH THE SAME THING WHEN I WENT PUBLIC FOR THE FIRST TIME AND--
NO, TONY, YOU DON'T KNOW WHAT IT'S LIKE.
YOU DON'T KNOW BECAUSE YOU'VE NEVER HAD A FAMILY TO WORRY ABOUT. YOU DON'T HAVE MJ AND AUNT MAY TO--
EVERY DAY OF MY LIFE SINCE I WAS FIFTEEN YEARS OLD I'VE LIVED IN ABSOLUTE TERROR OF JUST THIS MOMENT.
I'M SORRY, PETER. YOU'RE RIGHT. I DON'T KNOW. I DON'T HAVE A FAMILY. YOU DO, AND YOU'VE ALWAYS HONORED THEM AND--
TONY?
YES?
YOU DIDN'T HAVE A FAMILY UNTIL RIGHT NOW. IF THIS GOES WRONG, IF I END UP REGRETTING THIS, IF ANYTHING HAPPENS TO ME--
--I WANT YOUR WORD THAT YOU'LL TAKE CARE OF MJ AND MAY.
OF COURSE. YOU HAVE NOTHING TO WORRY ABOUT.

GOOD.

BECAUSE IF ANYTHING HAPPENS TO *THEM* BECAUSE OF THIS AND I'M STILL ALIVE, *YOU'RE* THE ONE WHO'S GOING TO HAVE SOMETHING TO WORRY ABOUT.

IT WON'T, PETER.

I'M JUST SAYING.

I KNOW.

I HAD THEM BRING THE CAR AROUND BACK. THE PLANE IS WAITING TO TAKE YOU BACK TO NEW YORK.

BUT--

I'LL NEED YOU SOON, BUT RIGHT NOW, YOUR PLACE IS WITH YOUR FAMILY.

THIS IS WHERE YOU'RE SUPPOSED TO SAY, "I GUESS MAYBE YOU DO UNDERSTAND WHAT IT'S LIKE TO HAVE A FAMILY."

NOT TODAY, TONY...

...MAYBE TOMORROW, OR THE DAY AFTER, BUT NOT TODAY.

SPIDER-MAN!

Love You, Peter!

...OES HIDE BEHIND MASKS!

SPIDER-FREAK REVEALED!

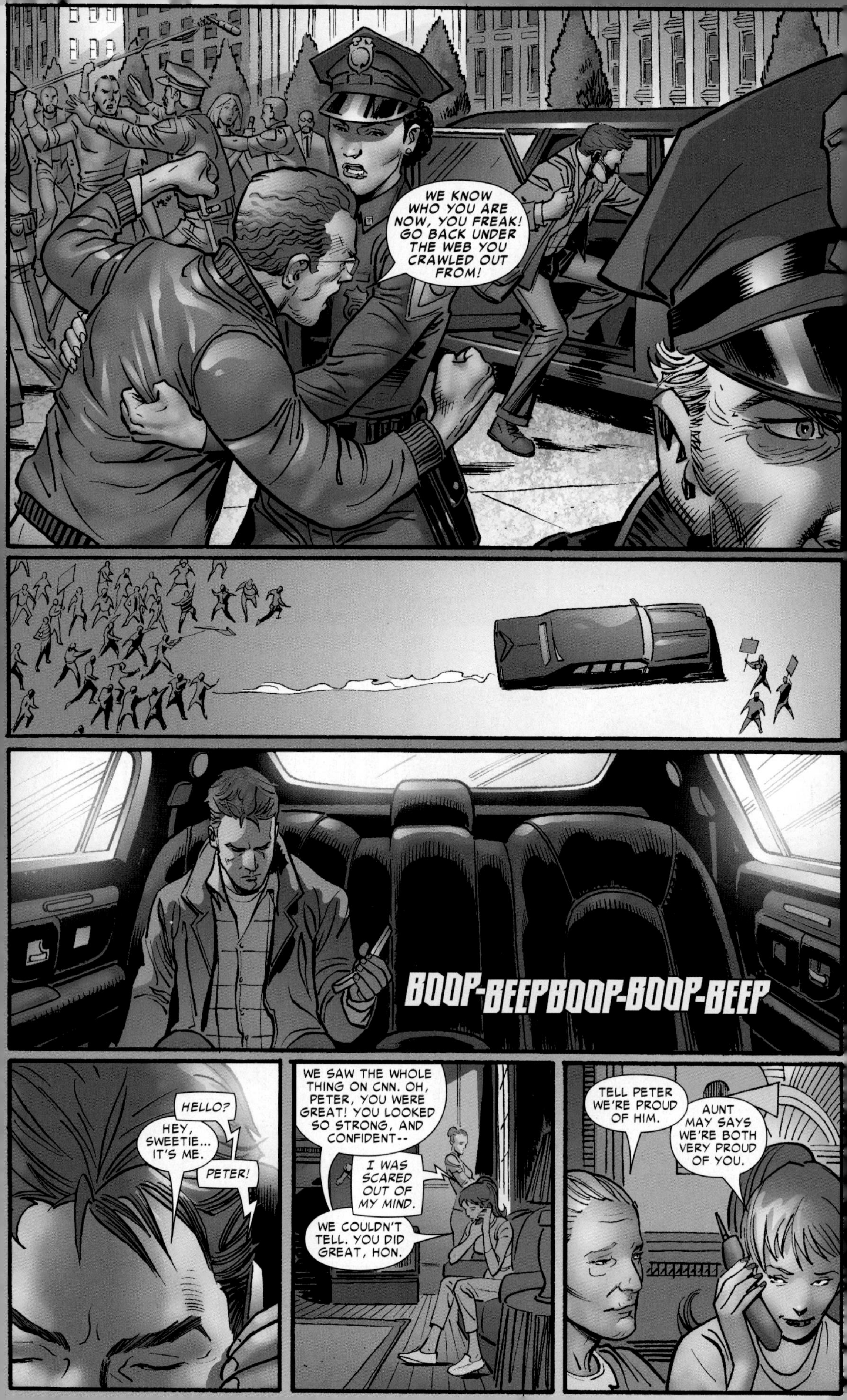
WE KNOW WHO YOU ARE NOW, YOU FREAK! GO BACK UNDER THE WEB YOU CRAWLED OUT FROM!
BOOP-BEEPBOOP-BOOP-BEEP
HELLO?
HEY, SWEETIE... IT'S ME.
PETER!
WE SAW THE WHOLE THING ON CNN. OH, PETER, YOU WERE GREAT! YOU LOOKED SO STRONG, AND CONFIDENT--
I WAS SCARED OUT OF MY MIND.
WE COULDN'T TELL. YOU DID GREAT, HON.
TELL PETER WE'RE PROUD OF HIM.
AUNT MAY SAYS WE'RE BOTH VERY PROUD OF YOU.

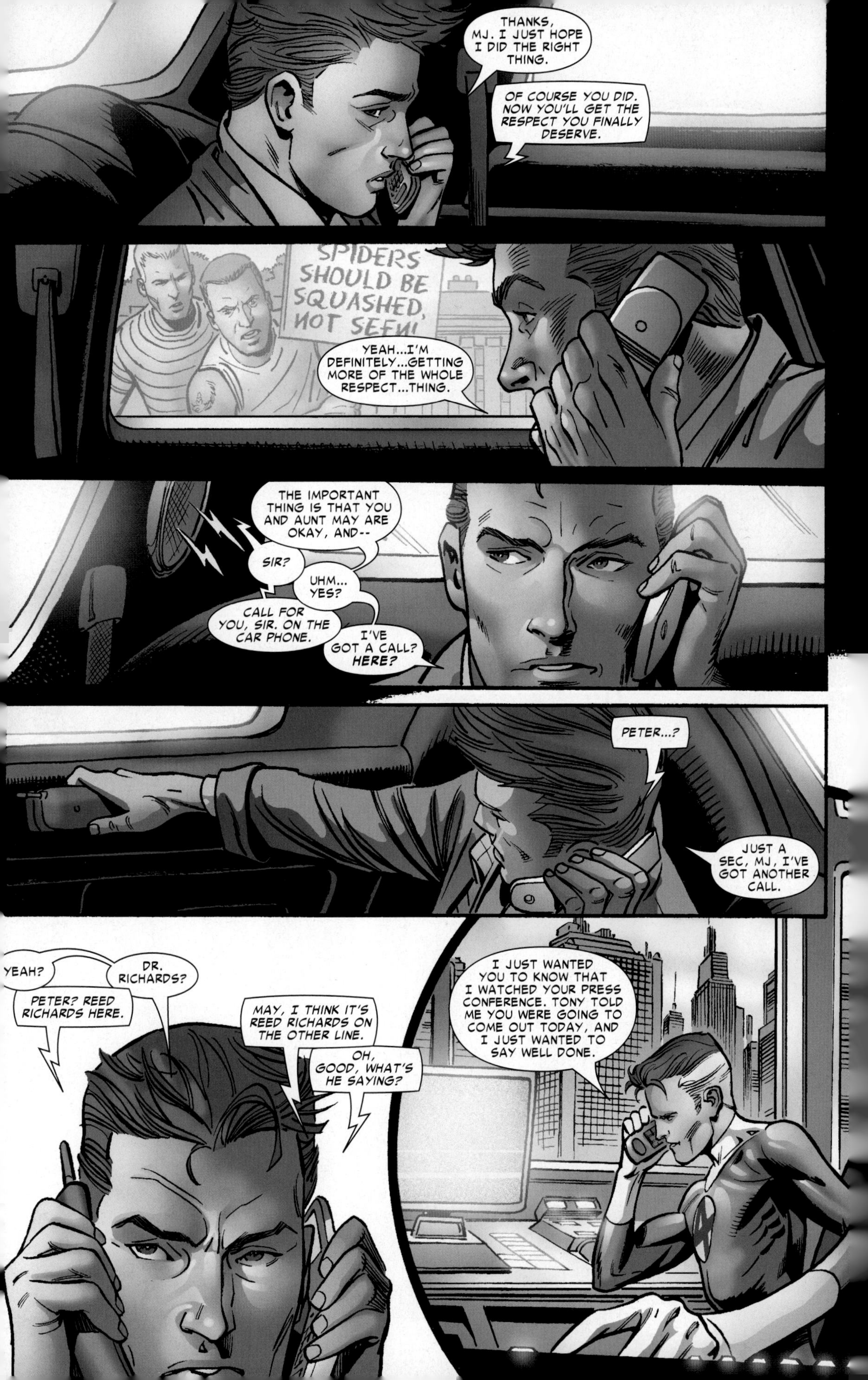
THANKS, MJ. I JUST HOPE I DID THE RIGHT THING.
OF COURSE YOU DID. NOW YOU'LL GET THE RESPECT YOU FINALLY DESERVE.
SPIDERS SHOULD BE SQUASHED, NOT SEEN!
YEAH...I'M DEFINITELY...GETTING MORE OF THE WHOLE RESPECT...THING.
THE IMPORTANT THING IS THAT YOU AND AUNT MAY ARE OKAY, AND--
SIR?
UHM... YES?
CALL FOR YOU, SIR. ON THE CAR PHONE.
I'VE GOT A CALL? HERE?
PETER...?
JUST A SEC, MJ, I'VE GOT ANOTHER CALL.
YEAH?
DR. RICHARDS?
PETER? REED RICHARDS HERE.
MAY, I THINK IT'S REED RICHARDS ON THE OTHER LINE.
OH, GOOD, WHAT'S HE SAYING?
I JUST WANTED YOU TO KNOW THAT I WATCHED YOUR PRESS CONFERENCE. TONY TOLD ME YOU WERE GOING TO COME OUT TODAY, AND I JUST WANTED TO SAY WELL DONE.

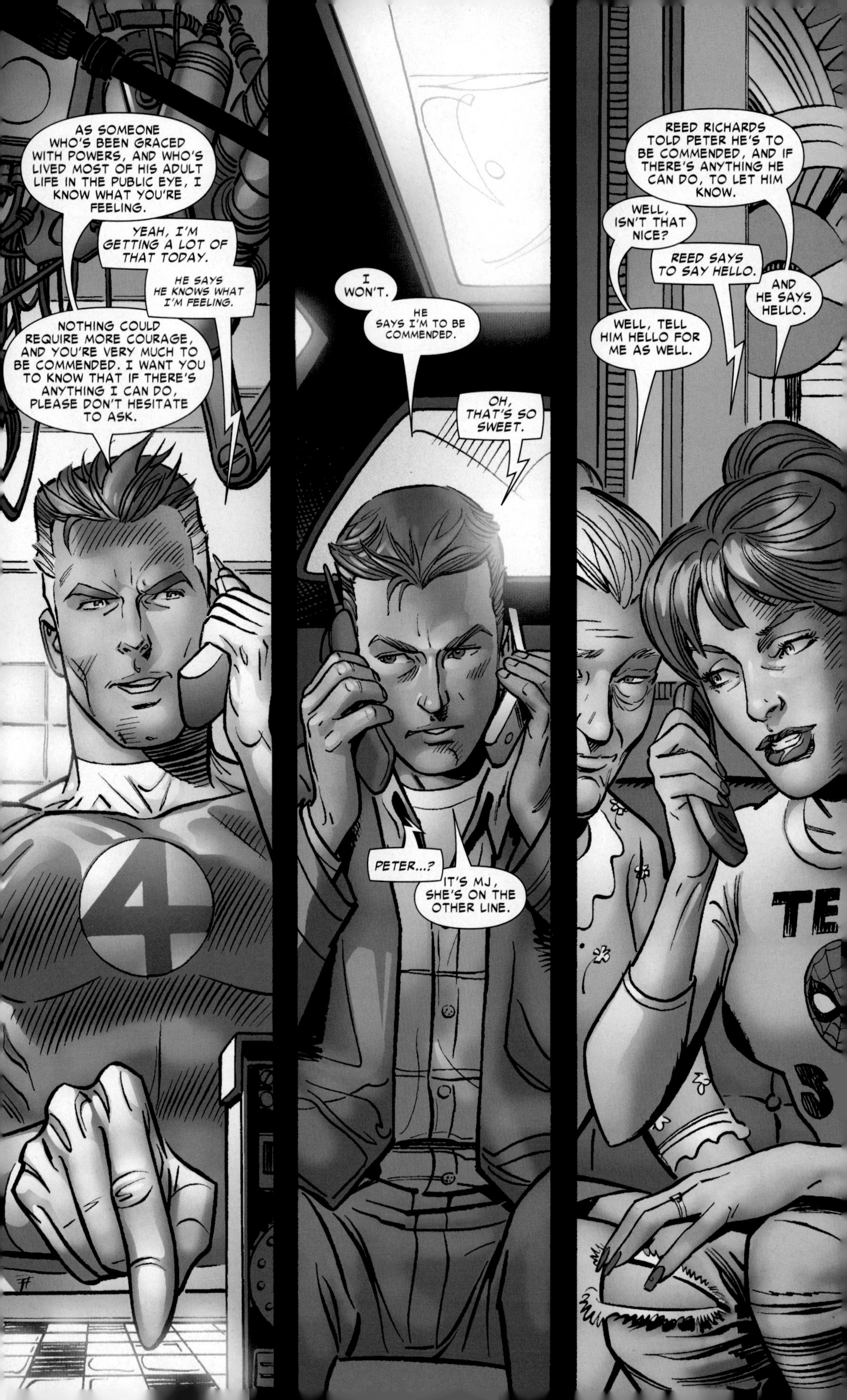
AS SOMEONE WHO'S BEEN GRACED WITH POWERS, AND WHO'S LIVED MOST OF HIS ADULT LIFE IN THE PUBLIC EYE, I KNOW WHAT YOU'RE FEELING.
YEAH, I'M GETTING A LOT OF THAT TODAY.
HE SAYS HE KNOWS WHAT I'M FEELING.
NOTHING COULD REQUIRE MORE COURAGE, AND YOU'RE VERY MUCH TO BE COMMENDED. I WANT YOU TO KNOW THAT IF THERE'S ANYTHING I CAN DO, PLEASE DON'T HESITATE TO ASK.
I WON'T.
HE SAYS I'M TO BE COMMENDED.
OH, THAT'S SO SWEET.
PETER...?
IT'S MJ, SHE'S ON THE OTHER LINE.
REED RICHARDS TOLD PETER HE'S TO BE COMMENDED, AND IF THERE'S ANYTHING HE CAN DO, TO LET HIM KNOW.
WELL, ISN'T THAT NICE?
REED SAYS TO SAY HELLO.
AND HE SAYS HELLO.
WELL, TELL HIM HELLO FOR ME AS WELL.

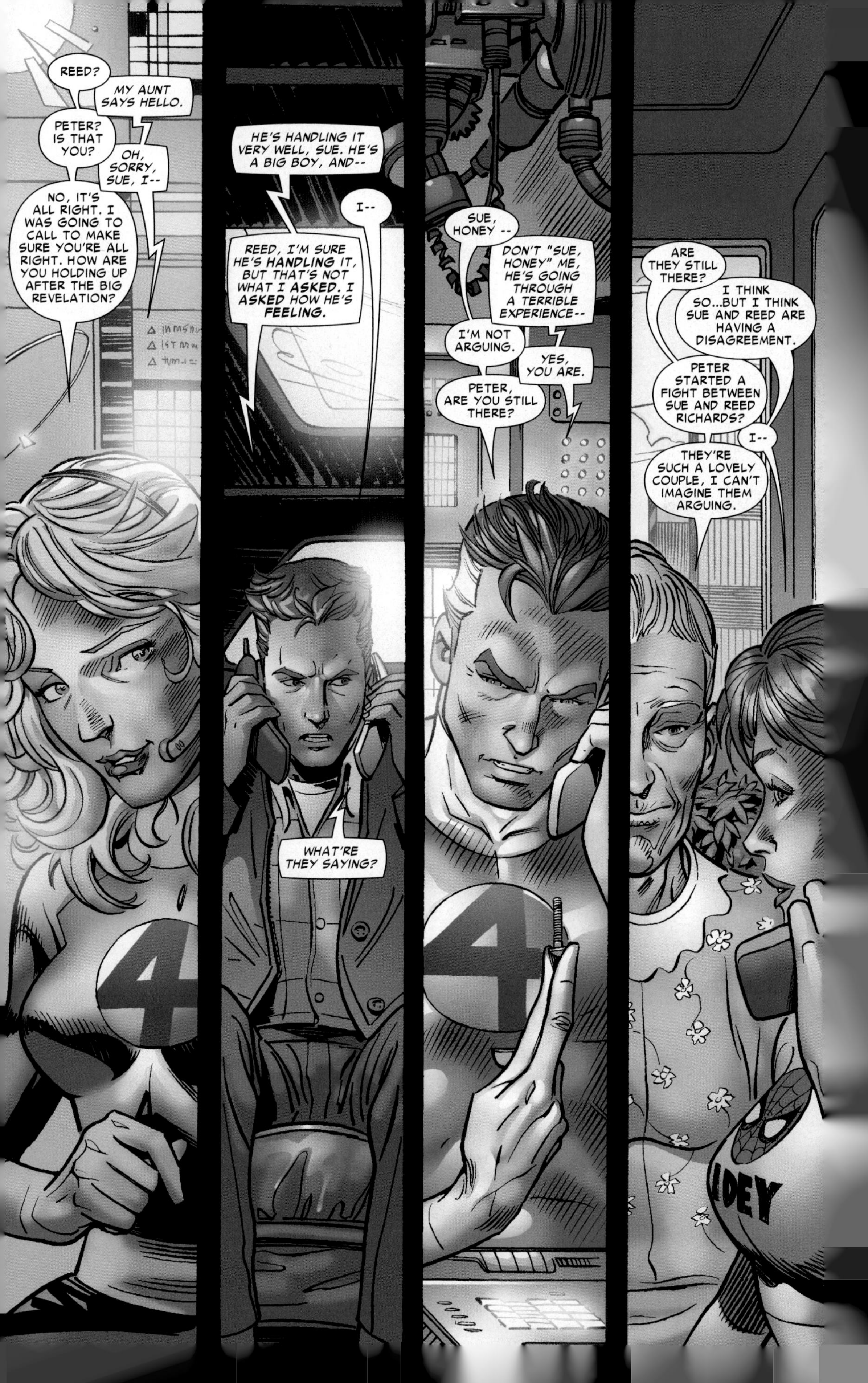
REED?
MY AUNT SAYS HELLO.
PETER? IS THAT YOU?
OH, SORRY, SUE, I--
NO, IT'S ALL RIGHT. I WAS GOING TO CALL TO MAKE SURE YOU'RE ALL RIGHT. HOW ARE YOU HOLDING UP AFTER THE BIG REVELATION?
HE'S HANDLING IT VERY WELL, SUE. HE'S A BIG BOY, AND--
I--
REED, I'M SURE HE'S HANDLING IT, BUT THAT'S NOT WHAT I ASKED. I ASKED HOW HE'S FEELING.
WHAT'RE THEY SAYING?
SUE, HONEY --
DON'T "SUE, HONEY" ME, HE'S GOING THROUGH A TERRIBLE EXPERIENCE--
I'M NOT ARGUING.
YES, YOU ARE.
PETER, ARE YOU STILL THERE?
ARE THEY STILL THERE?
I THINK SO...BUT I THINK SUE AND REED ARE HAVING A DISAGREEMENT.
PETER STARTED A FIGHT BETWEEN SUE AND REED RICHARDS?
I--
THEY'RE SUCH A LOVELY COUPLE, I CAN'T IMAGINE THEM ARGUING.

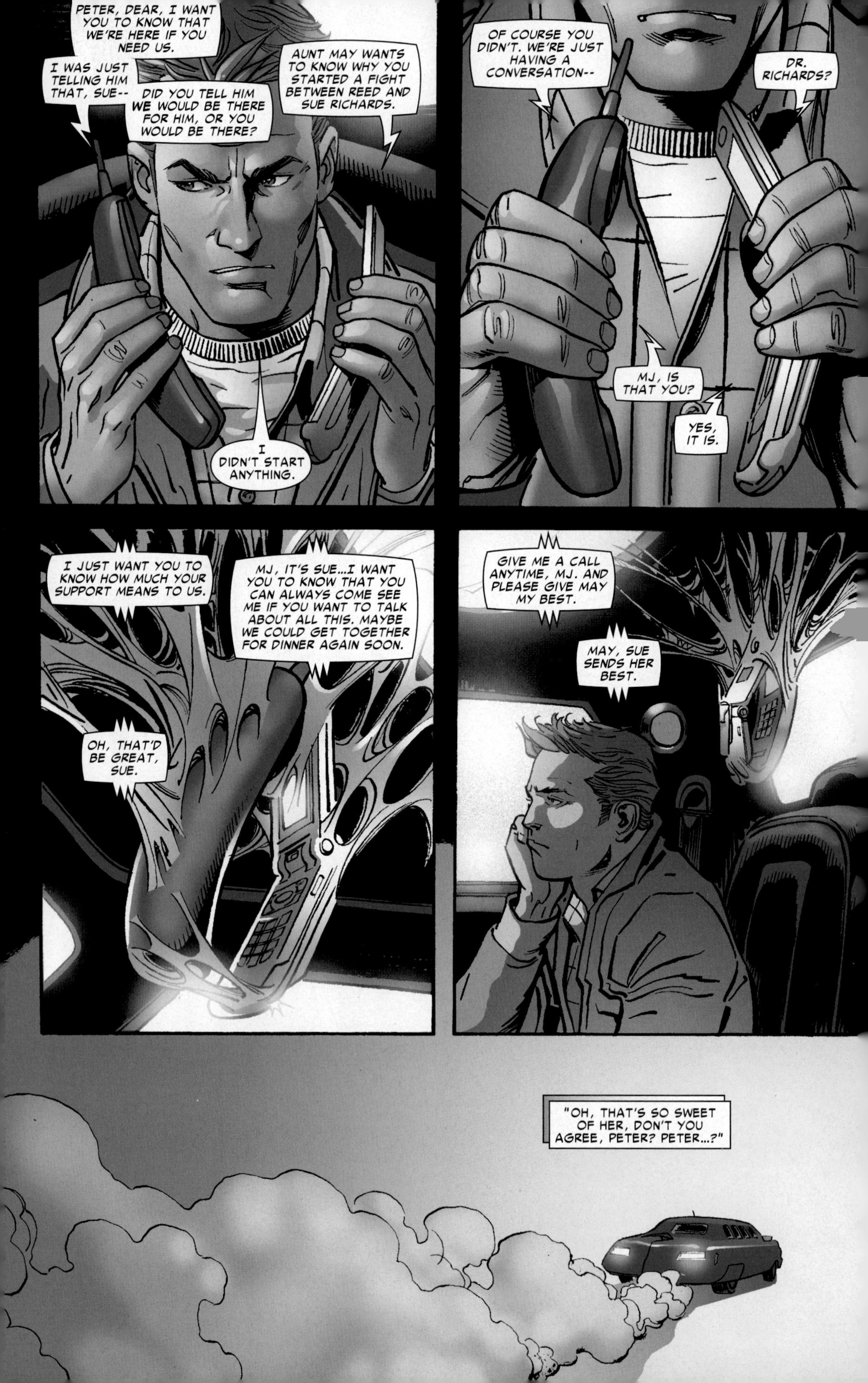
PETER, DEAR, I WANT YOU TO KNOW THAT WE'RE HERE IF YOU NEED US.
I WAS JUST TELLING HIM THAT, SUE--
DID YOU TELL HIM WE WOULD BE THERE FOR HIM, OR YOU WOULD BE THERE?
AUNT MAY WANTS TO KNOW WHY YOU STARTED A FIGHT BETWEEN REED AND SUE RICHARDS.
I DIDN'T START ANYTHING.
OF COURSE YOU DIDN'T. WE'RE JUST HAVING A CONVERSATION--
DR. RICHARDS?
MJ, IS THAT YOU?
YES, IT IS.
I JUST WANT YOU TO KNOW HOW MUCH YOUR SUPPORT MEANS TO US.
MJ, IT'S SUE...I WANT YOU TO KNOW THAT YOU CAN ALWAYS COME SEE ME IF YOU WANT TO TALK ABOUT ALL THIS. MAYBE WE COULD GET TOGETHER FOR DINNER AGAIN SOON.
OH, THAT'D BE GREAT, SUE.
GIVE ME A CALL ANYTIME, MJ. AND PLEASE GIVE MAY MY BEST.
MAY, SUE SENDS HER BEST.
"OH, THAT'S SO SWEET OF HER, DON'T YOU AGREE, PETER? PETER...?"

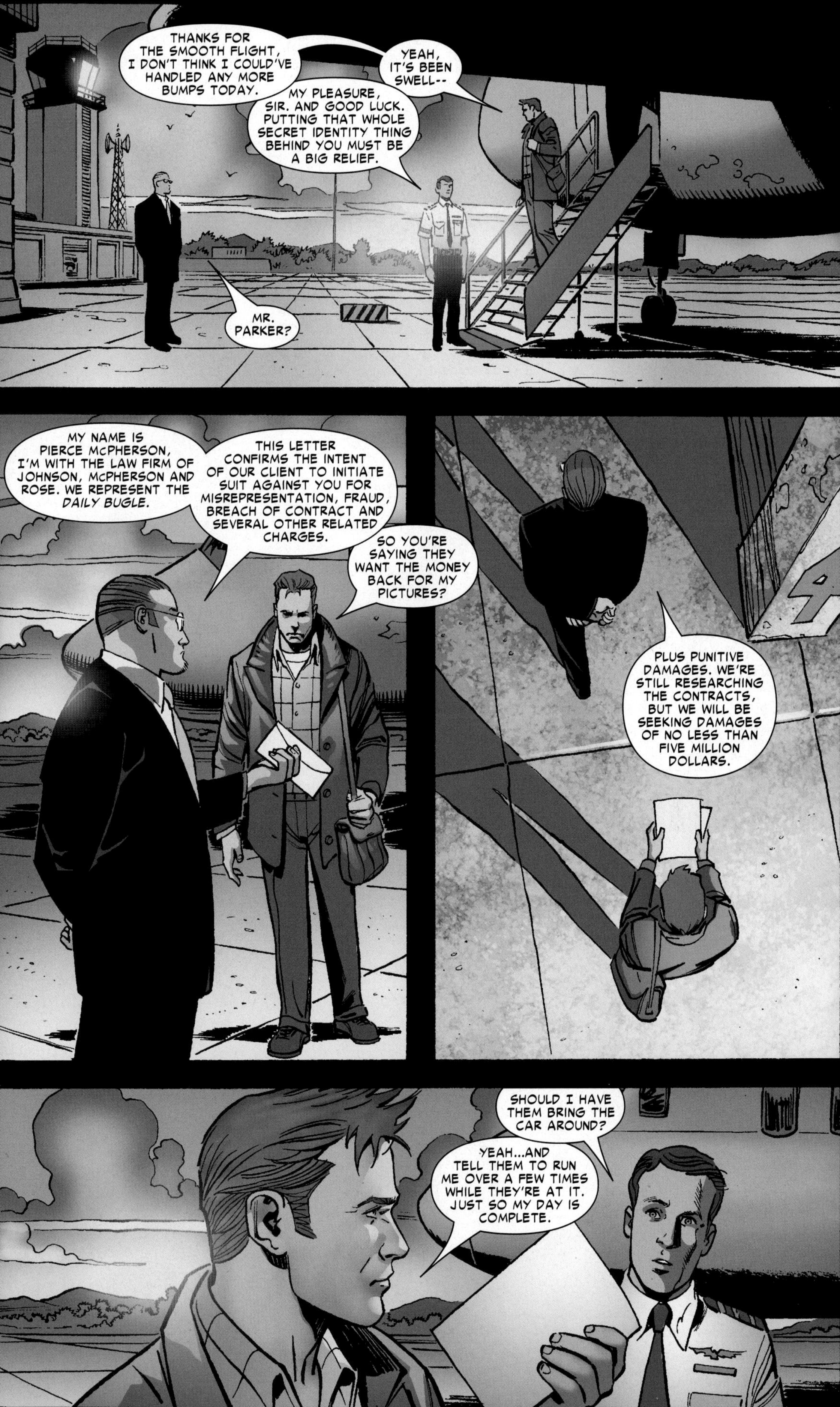
THANKS FOR THE SMOOTH FLIGHT, I DON'T THINK I COULD'VE HANDLED ANY MORE BUMPS TODAY.
YEAH, IT'S BEEN SWELL--
MY PLEASURE, SIR. AND GOOD LUCK. PUTTING THAT WHOLE SECRET IDENTITY THING BEHIND YOU MUST BE A BIG RELIEF.
MR. PARKER?
MY NAME IS PIERCE McPHERSON, I'M WITH THE LAW FIRM OF JOHNSON, McPHERSON AND ROSE. WE REPRESENT THE *DAILY BUGLE*.
THIS LETTER CONFIRMS THE INTENT OF OUR CLIENT TO INITIATE SUIT AGAINST YOU FOR MISREPRESENTATION, FRAUD, BREACH OF CONTRACT AND SEVERAL OTHER RELATED CHARGES.
SO YOU'RE SAYING THEY WANT THE MONEY BACK FOR MY PICTURES?
PLUS PUNITIVE DAMAGES. WE'RE STILL RESEARCHING THE CONTRACTS, BUT WE WILL BE SEEKING DAMAGES OF NO LESS THAN FIVE MILLION DOLLARS.
SHOULD I HAVE THEM BRING THE CAR AROUND?
YEAH...AND TELL THEM TO RUN ME OVER A FEW TIMES WHILE THEY'RE AT IT. JUST SO MY DAY IS COMPLETE.

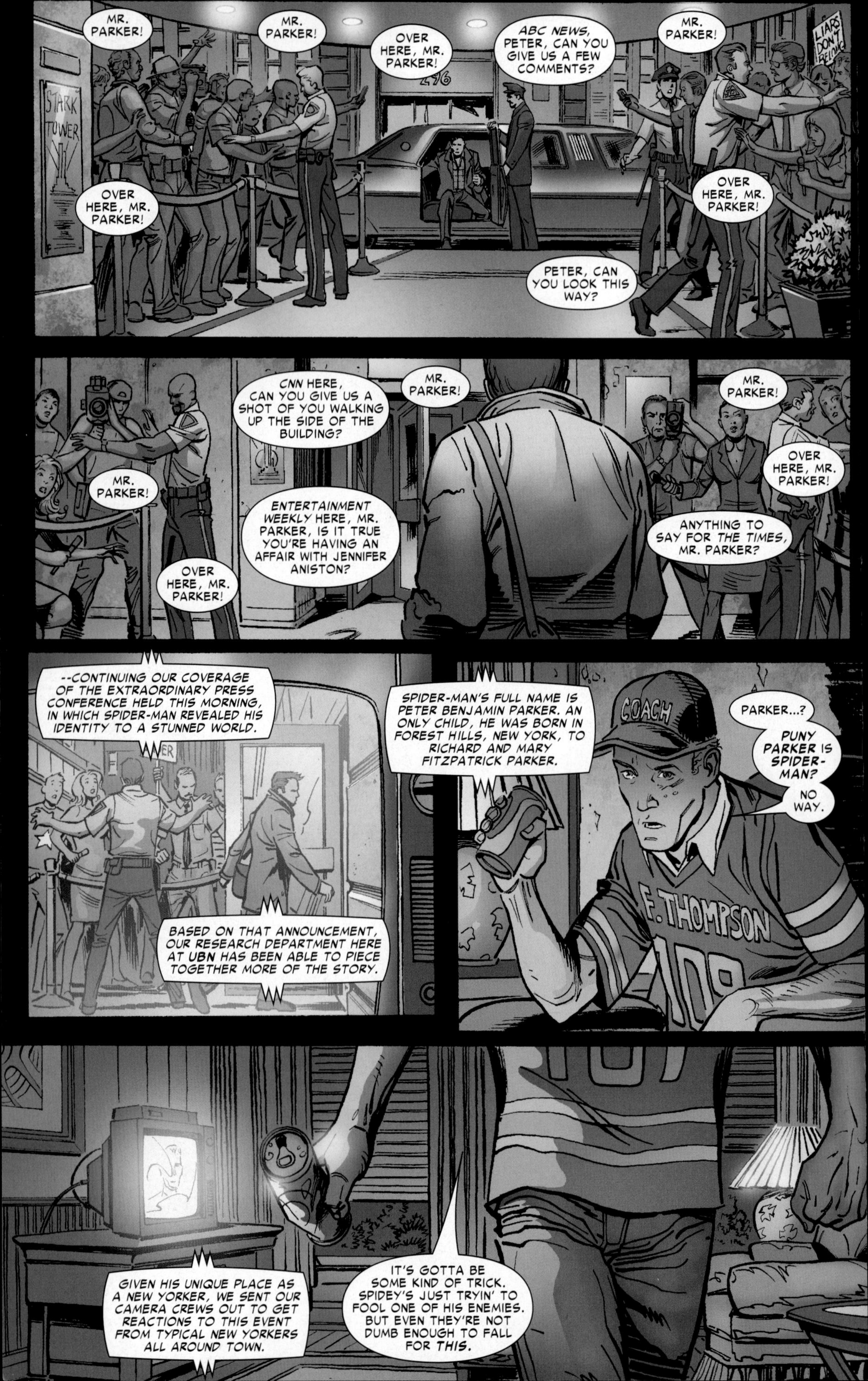
MR. PARKER!
MR. PARKER!
OVER HERE, MR. PARKER!
ABC NEWS, PETER, CAN YOU GIVE US A FEW COMMENTS?
MR. PARKER!
STARK TOWER
LIARS DON'T BELONG
OVER HERE, MR. PARKER!
OVER HERE, MR. PARKER!
PETER, CAN YOU LOOK THIS WAY?
CNN HERE, CAN YOU GIVE US A SHOT OF YOU WALKING UP THE SIDE OF THE BUILDING?
MR. PARKER!
MR. PARKER!
MR. PARKER!
OVER HERE, MR. PARKER!
ENTERTAINMENT WEEKLY HERE, MR. PARKER, IS IT TRUE YOU'RE HAVING AN AFFAIR WITH JENNIFER ANISTON?
OVER HERE, MR. PARKER!
ANYTHING TO SAY FOR THE TIMES, MR. PARKER?
--CONTINUING OUR COVERAGE OF THE EXTRAORDINARY PRESS CONFERENCE HELD THIS MORNING, IN WHICH SPIDER-MAN REVEALED HIS IDENTITY TO A STUNNED WORLD.
BASED ON THAT ANNOUNCEMENT, OUR RESEARCH DEPARTMENT HERE AT UBN HAS BEEN ABLE TO PIECE TOGETHER MORE OF THE STORY.
SPIDER-MAN'S FULL NAME IS PETER BENJAMIN PARKER. AN ONLY CHILD, HE WAS BORN IN FOREST HILLS, NEW YORK, TO RICHARD AND MARY FITZPATRICK PARKER.
COACH
E. THOMPSON
PARKER...?
PUNY PARKER IS SPIDER-MAN?
NO WAY.
GIVEN HIS UNIQUE PLACE AS A NEW YORKER, WE SENT OUR CAMERA CREWS OUT TO GET REACTIONS TO THIS EVENT FROM TYPICAL NEW YORKERS ALL AROUND TOWN.
IT'S GOTTA BE SOME KIND OF TRICK. SPIDEY'S JUST TRYIN' TO FOOL ONE OF HIS ENEMIES. BUT EVEN THEY'RE NOT DUMB ENOUGH TO FALL FOR THIS.

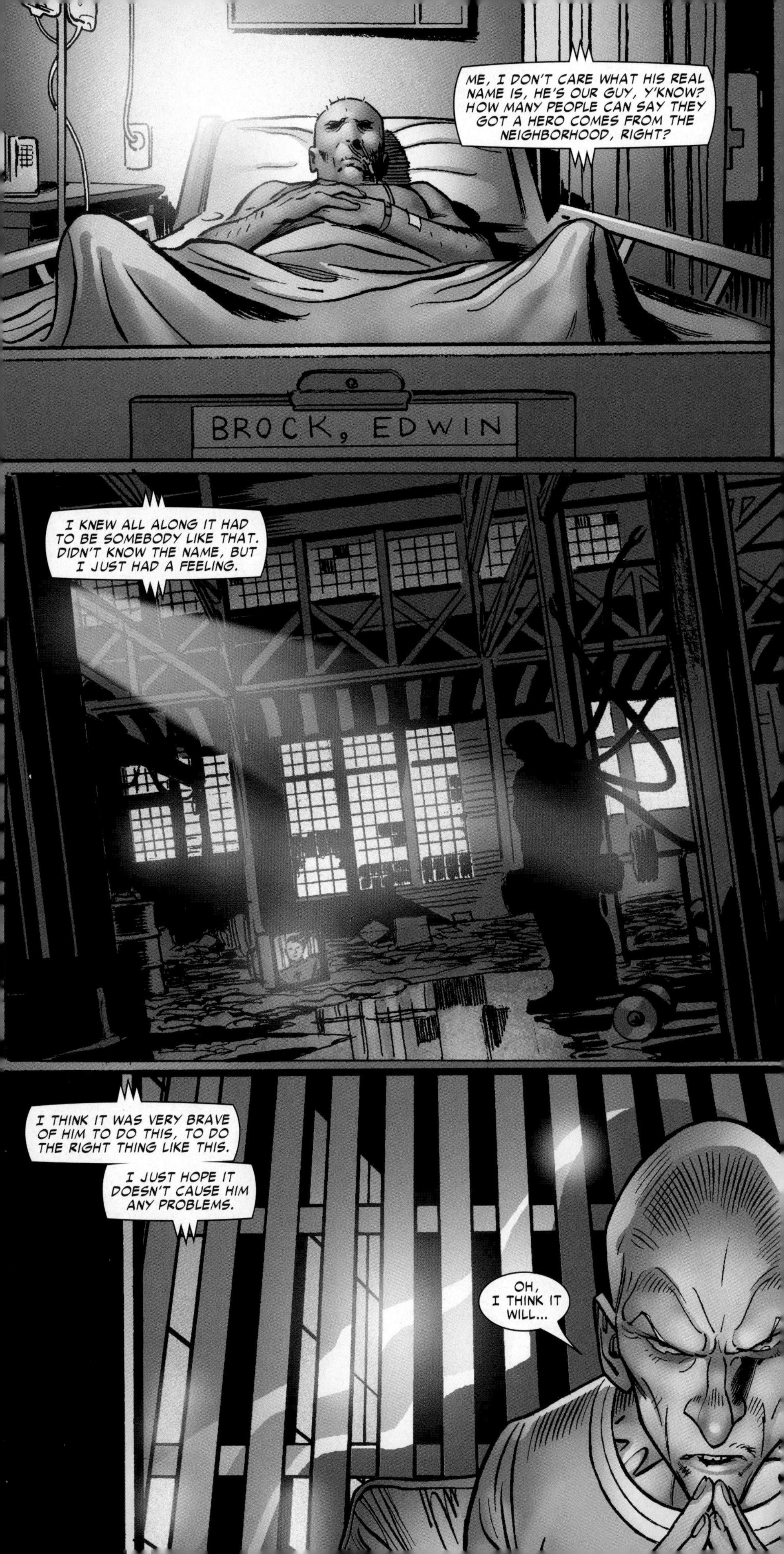
ME, I DON'T CARE WHAT HIS REAL NAME IS, HE'S OUR GUY, Y'KNOW? HOW MANY PEOPLE CAN SAY THEY GOT A HERO COMES FROM THE NEIGHBORHOOD, RIGHT?
BROCK, EDWIN
I KNEW ALL ALONG IT HAD TO BE SOMEBODY LIKE THAT. DIDN'T KNOW THE NAME, BUT I JUST HAD A FEELING.
I THINK IT WAS VERY BRAVE OF HIM TO DO THIS, TO DO THE RIGHT THING LIKE THIS.
I JUST HOPE IT DOESN'T CAUSE HIM ANY PROBLEMS.
OH, I THINK IT WILL...

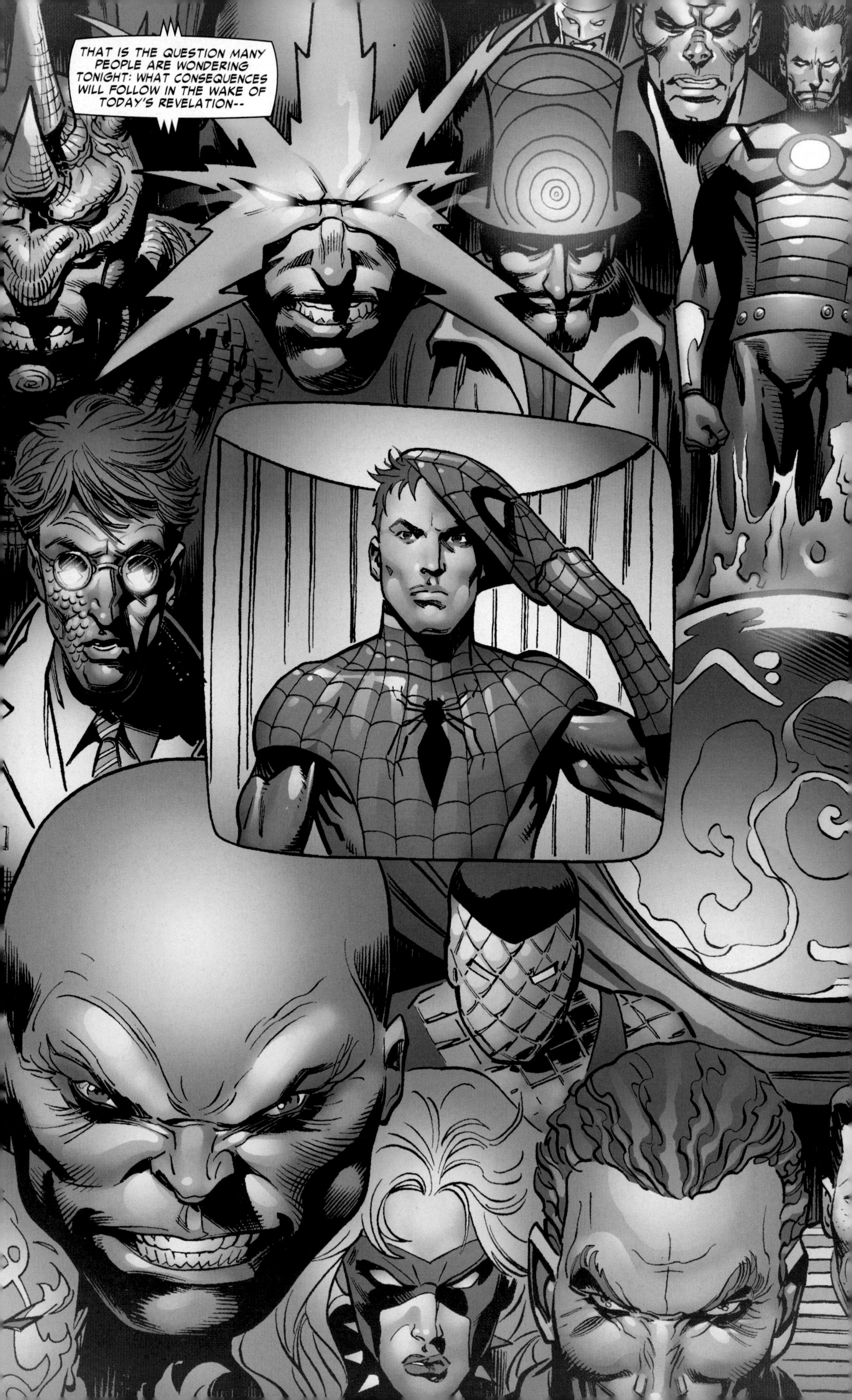
THAT IS THE QUESTION MANY PEOPLE ARE WONDERING TONIGHT: WHAT CONSEQUENCES WILL FOLLOW IN THE WAKE OF TODAY'S REVELATION--

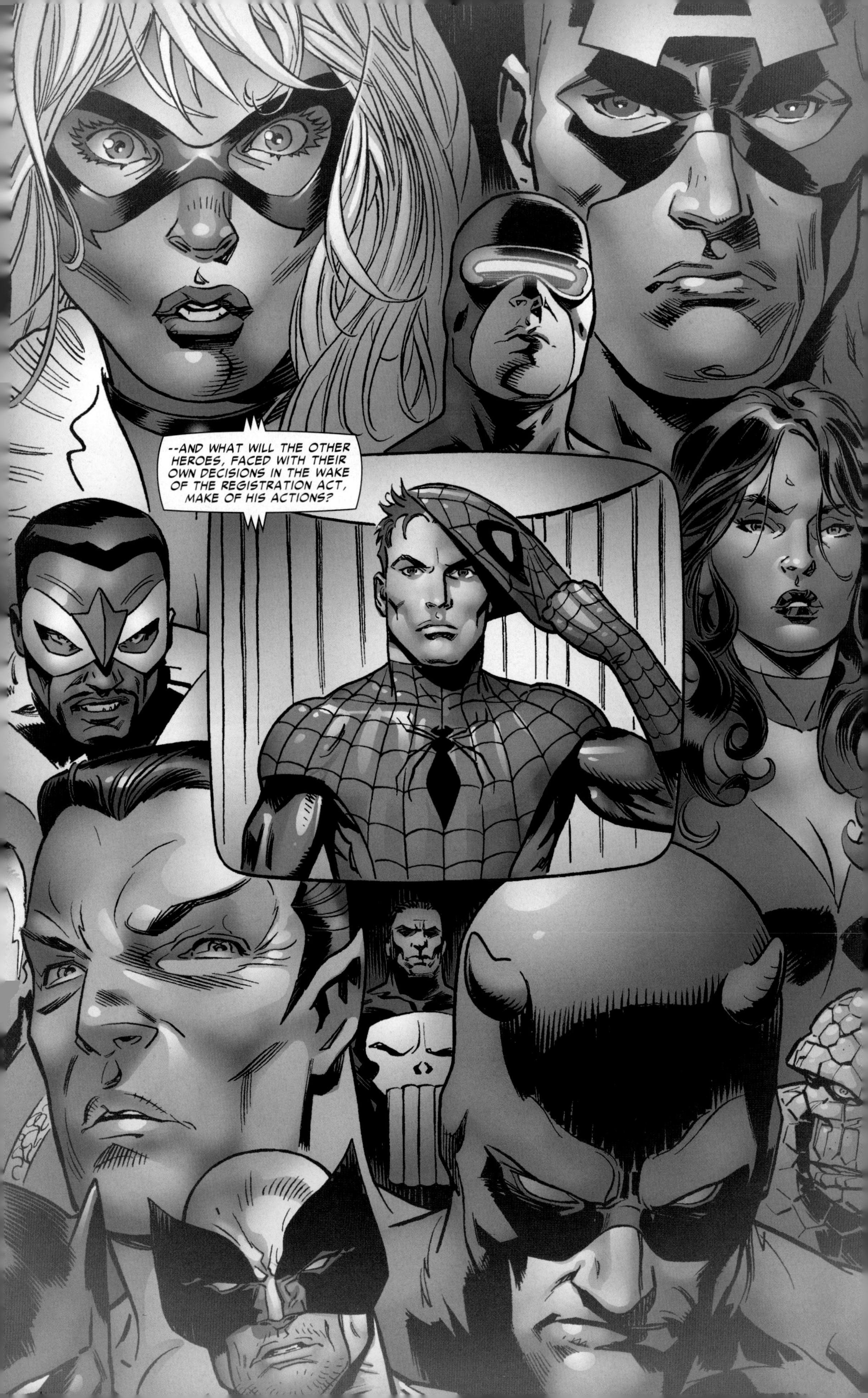
--AND WHAT WILL THE OTHER HEROES, FACED WITH THEIR OWN DECISIONS IN THE WAKE OF THE REGISTRATION ACT, MAKE OF HIS ACTIONS?

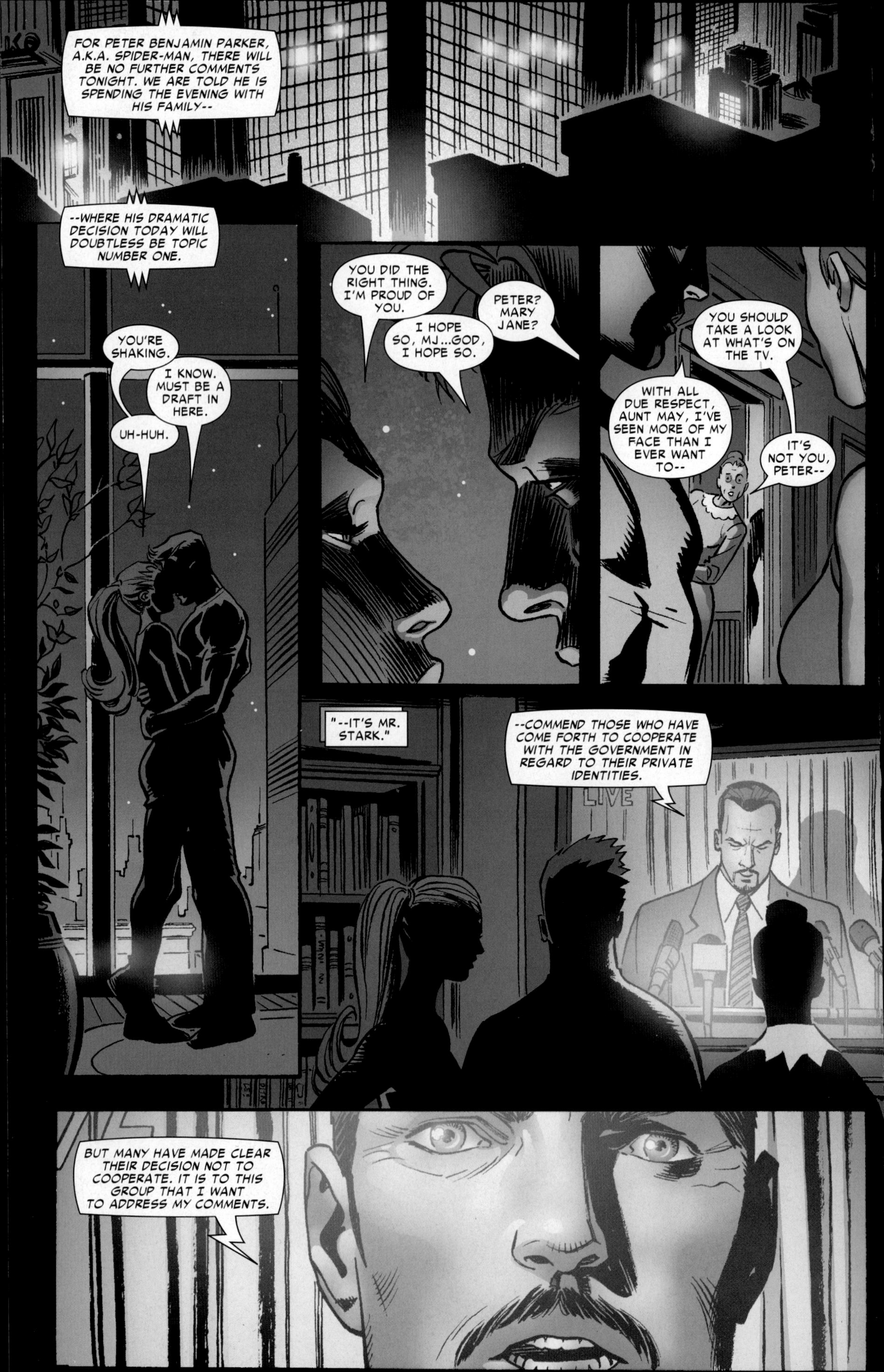
FOR PETER BENJAMIN PARKER, A.K.A. SPIDER-MAN, THERE WILL BE NO FURTHER COMMENTS TONIGHT. WE ARE TOLD HE IS SPENDING THE EVENING WITH HIS FAMILY--
--WHERE HIS DRAMATIC DECISION TODAY WILL DOUBTLESS BE TOPIC NUMBER ONE.
YOU'RE SHAKING.
I KNOW. MUST BE A DRAFT IN HERE.
UH-HUH.
YOU DID THE RIGHT THING. I'M PROUD OF YOU.
I HOPE SO, MJ...GOD, I HOPE SO.
PETER? MARY JANE?
YOU SHOULD TAKE A LOOK AT WHAT'S ON THE TV.
WITH ALL DUE RESPECT, AUNT MAY, I'VE SEEN MORE OF MY FACE THAN I EVER WANT TO--
IT'S NOT YOU, PETER--
"--IT'S MR. STARK."
--COMMEND THOSE WHO HAVE COME FORTH TO COOPERATE WITH THE GOVERNMENT IN REGARD TO THEIR PRIVATE IDENTITIES.
LIVE
BUT MANY HAVE MADE CLEAR THEIR DECISION NOT TO COOPERATE. IT IS TO THIS GROUP THAT I WANT TO ADDRESS MY COMMENTS.

OVER THE LAST TEN YEARS, CASUALLY AND THROUGH MY OWN INVESTIGATIONS, I HAVE DETERMINED THE IDENTITIES OF 137 OTHER HEROES. THOSE NAMES ARE ON THE LIST I HAVE IN MY HAND HERE TONIGHT.

THE DEADLINE FOR REGISTRATION HAS COME AND GONE. STARTING THIS TIME TOMORROW, ANYONE ON THIS LIST WHO HAS NOT COME FORWARD TO REGISTER, OR WHO GIVES AID AND COMFORT TO THOSE WHO REFUSE--

--WILL BE HUNTED DOWN, ARRESTED AND IMPRISONED. WITHOUT EXCEPTION.

WHAT ABOUT CAPTAIN AMERICA? HIS IDENTITY IS KNOWN, BUT WORD IS HE'S HELPING HEROES WHO WON'T REGISTER.

WITHOUT EXCEPTION MEANS WITHOUT EXCEPTION.

HOW DO YOU INTEND TO APPREHEND THESE INDIVIDUALS?

WE WILL USE WHATEVER MEANS ARE NECESSARY.

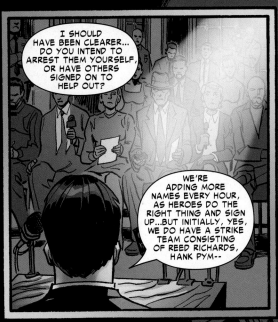

I SHOULD HAVE BEEN CLEARER... DO YOU INTEND TO ARREST THEM YOURSELF, OR HAVE OTHERS SIGNED ON TO HELP OUT?

WE'RE ADDING MORE NAMES EVERY HOUR, AS HEROES DO THE RIGHT THING AND SIGN UP...BUT INITIALLY, YES, WE DO HAVE A STRIKE TEAM CONSISTING OF REED RICHARDS, HANK PYM--

--AND SPIDER-MAN.

WHAT THE--?

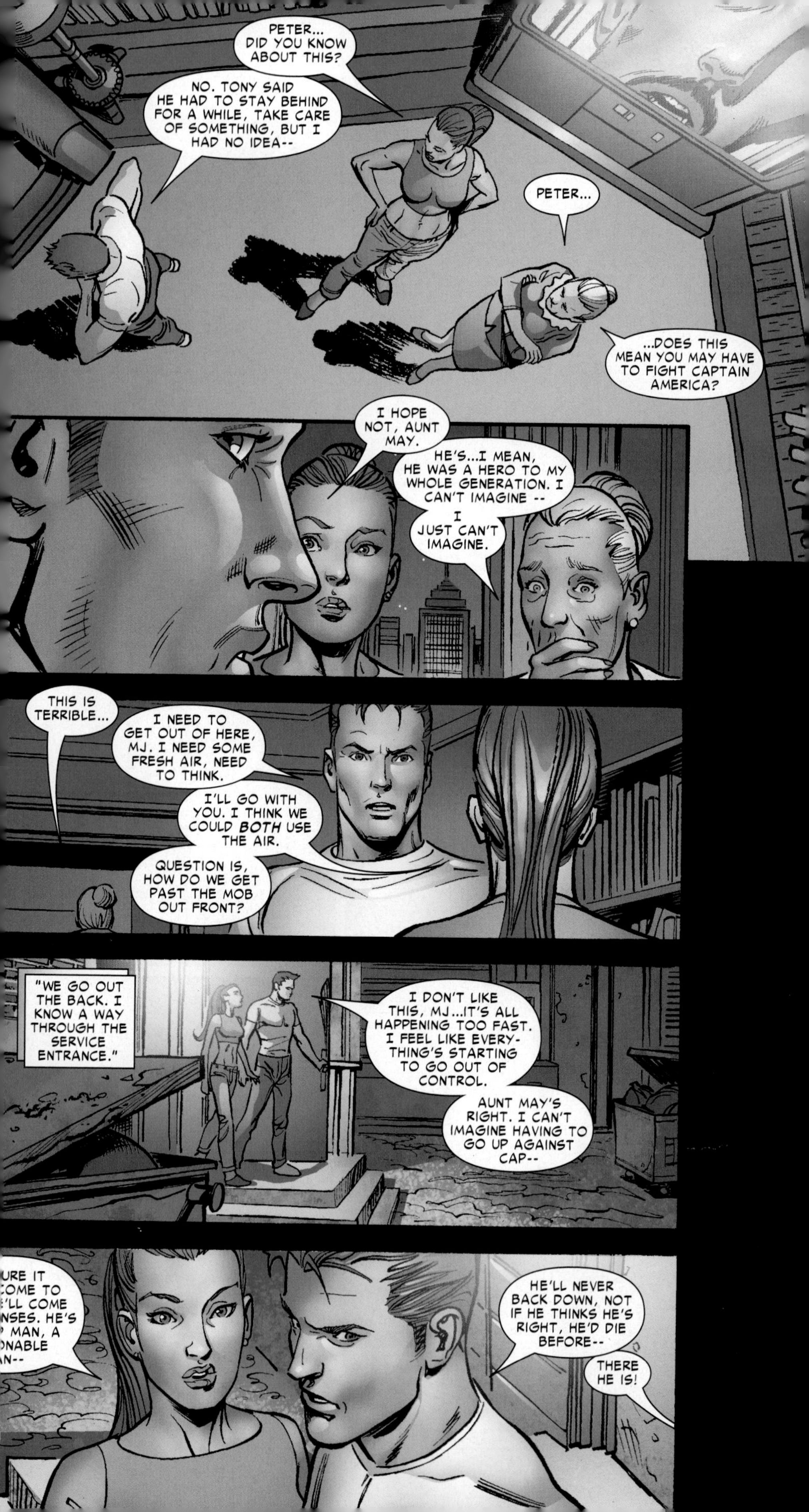

PETER... DID YOU KNOW ABOUT THIS?
NO. TONY SAID HE HAD TO STAY BEHIND FOR A WHILE, TAKE CARE OF SOMETHING, BUT I HAD NO IDEA--
PETER...
...DOES THIS MEAN YOU MAY HAVE TO FIGHT CAPTAIN AMERICA?
I HOPE NOT, AUNT MAY.
HE'S...I MEAN, HE WAS A HERO TO MY WHOLE GENERATION. I CAN'T IMAGINE --
I JUST CAN'T IMAGINE.
THIS IS TERRIBLE...
I NEED TO GET OUT OF HERE, MJ. I NEED SOME FRESH AIR, NEED TO THINK.
I'LL GO WITH YOU. I THINK WE COULD BOTH USE THE AIR.
QUESTION IS, HOW DO WE GET PAST THE MOB OUT FRONT?
"WE GO OUT THE BACK. I KNOW A WAY THROUGH THE SERVICE ENTRANCE."
I DON'T LIKE THIS, MJ...IT'S ALL HAPPENING TOO FAST. I FEEL LIKE EVERYTHING'S STARTING TO GO OUT OF CONTROL.
AUNT MAY'S RIGHT. I CAN'T IMAGINE HAVING TO GO UP AGAINST CAP--
HE'LL NEVER BACK DOWN, NOT IF HE THINKS HE'S RIGHT, HE'D DIE BEFORE--
THERE HE IS!

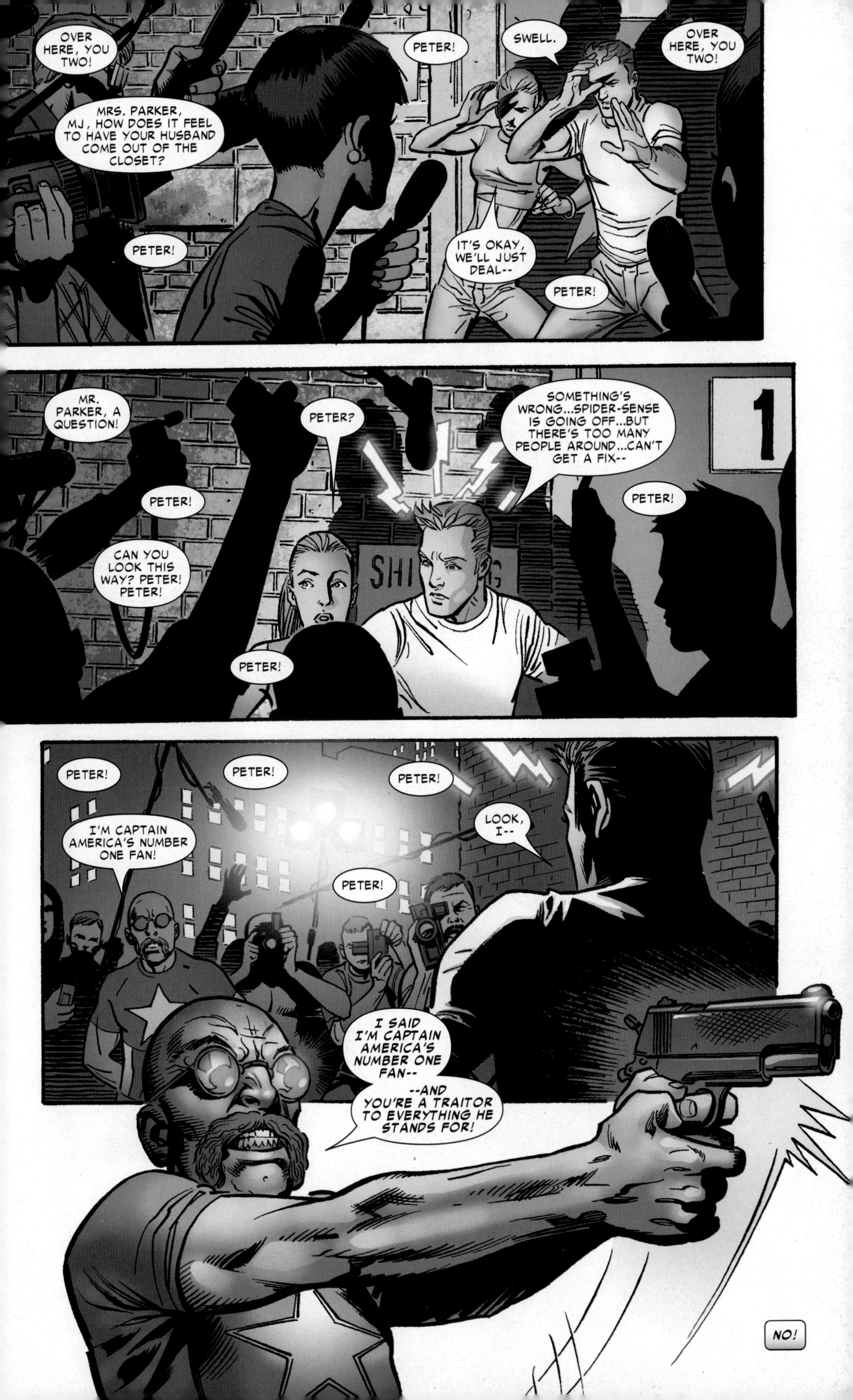
OVER HERE, YOU TWO!
MRS. PARKER, MJ, HOW DOES IT FEEL TO HAVE YOUR HUSBAND COME OUT OF THE CLOSET?
PETER!
PETER!
SWELL.
OVER HERE, YOU TWO!
IT'S OKAY, WE'LL JUST DEAL--
PETER!
MR. PARKER, A QUESTION!
PETER?
SOMETHING'S WRONG...SPIDER-SENSE IS GOING OFF...BUT THERE'S TOO MANY PEOPLE AROUND...CAN'T GET A FIX--
1
PETER!
PETER!
CAN YOU LOOK THIS WAY? PETER! PETER!
SHI G
PETER!
PETER!
PETER!
PETER!
I'M CAPTAIN AMERICA'S NUMBER ONE FAN!
LOOK, I--
PETER!
I SAID I'M CAPTAIN AMERICA'S NUMBER ONE FAN--
--AND YOU'RE A TRAITOR TO EVERYTHING HE STANDS FOR!
NO!

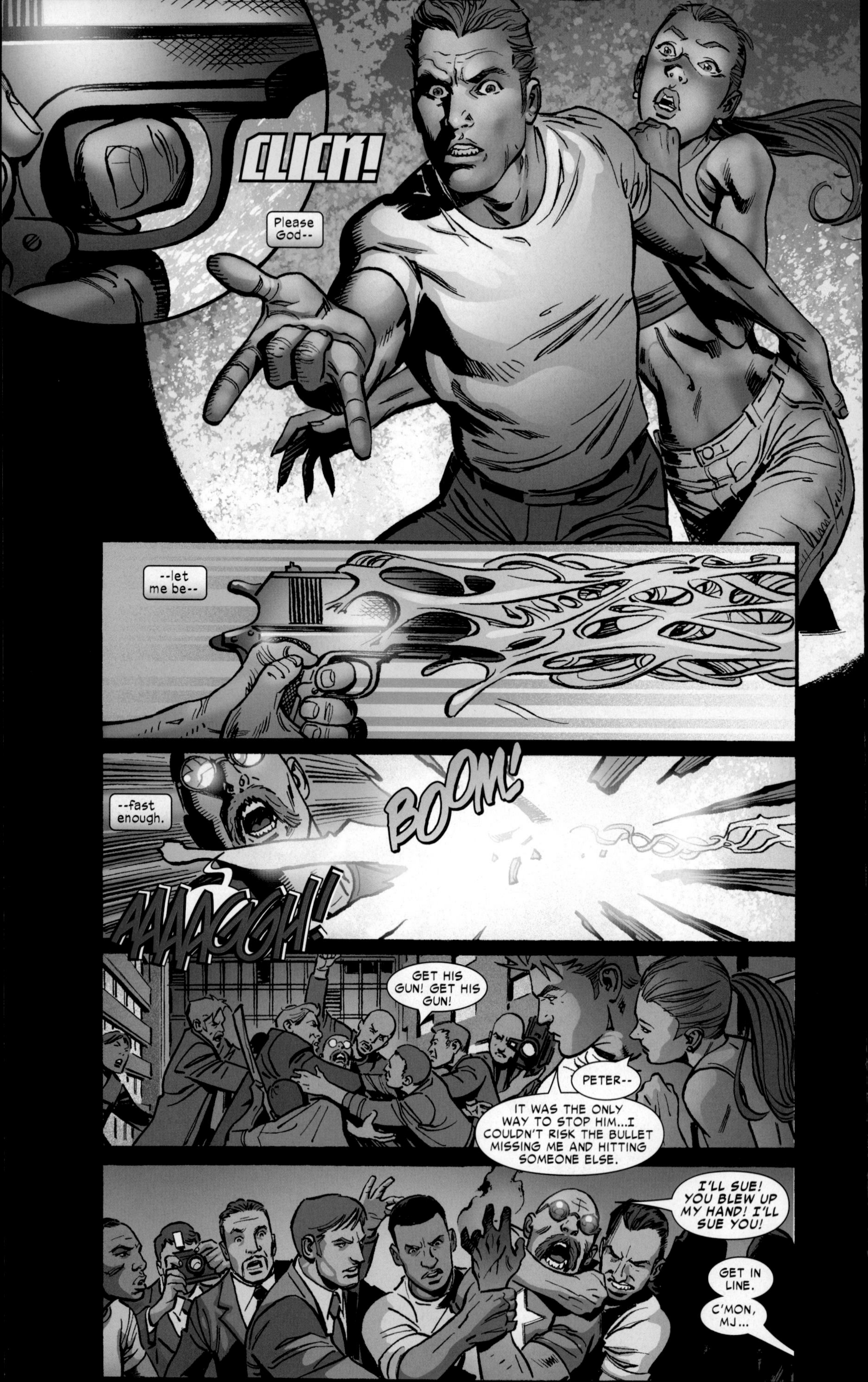
CLICK!
Please God--
--let me be--
--fast enough.
BOOM!
AAAAGGGH!
GET HIS GUN! GET HIS GUN!
PETER--
IT WAS THE ONLY WAY TO STOP HIM...I COULDN'T RISK THE BULLET MISSING ME AND HITTING SOMEONE ELSE.
I'LL SUE! YOU BLEW UP MY HAND! I'LL SUE YOU!
GET IN LINE.
C'MON, MJ...

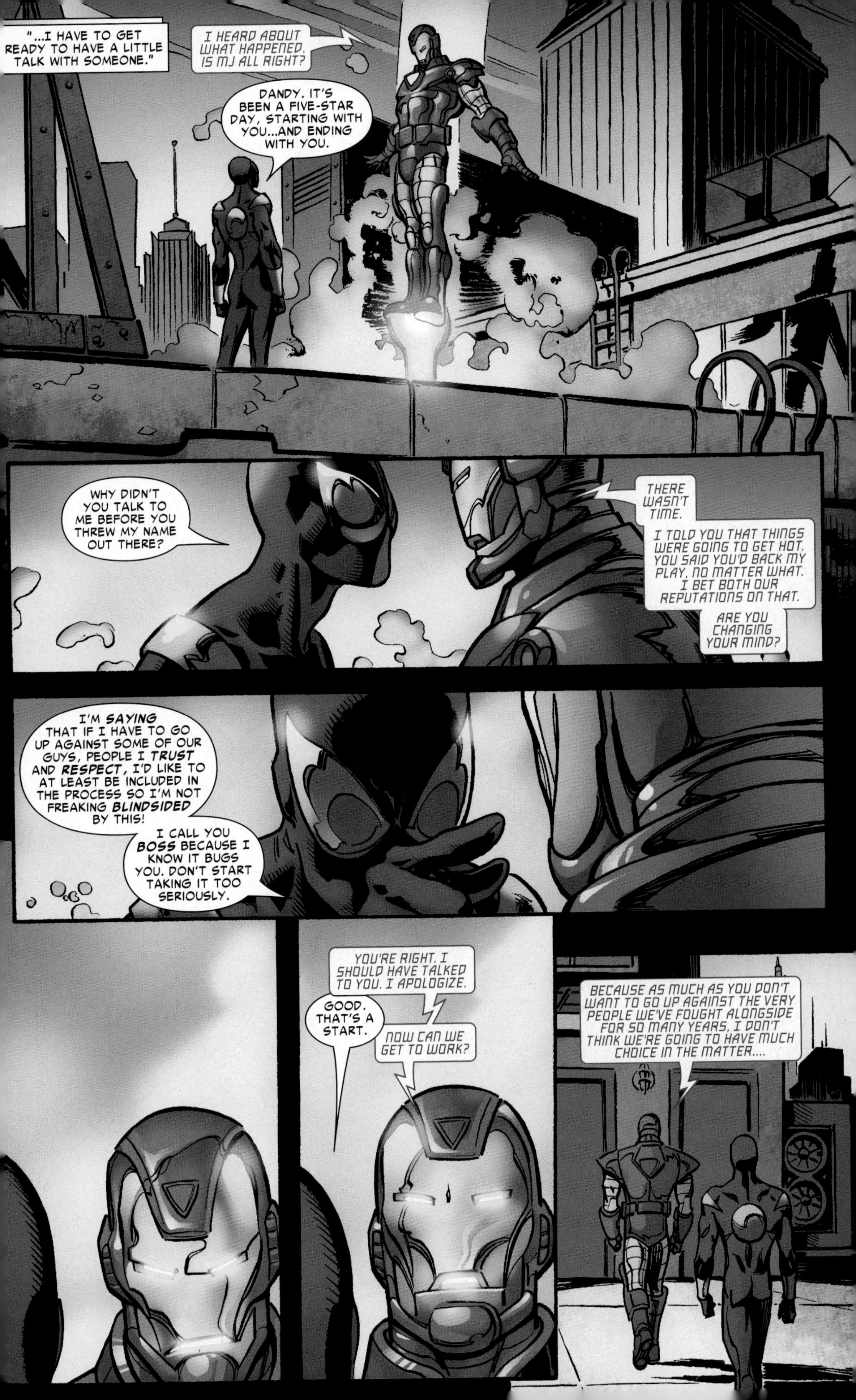
"...I HAVE TO GET READY TO HAVE A LITTLE TALK WITH SOMEONE."
I HEARD ABOUT WHAT HAPPENED. IS MJ ALL RIGHT?
DANDY. IT'S BEEN A FIVE-STAR DAY, STARTING WITH YOU...AND ENDING WITH YOU.
WHY DIDN'T YOU TALK TO ME BEFORE YOU THREW MY NAME OUT THERE?
THERE WASN'T TIME.
I TOLD YOU THAT THINGS WERE GOING TO GET HOT. YOU SAID YOU'D BACK MY PLAY, NO MATTER WHAT. I BET BOTH OUR REPUTATIONS ON THAT.
ARE YOU CHANGING YOUR MIND?
I'M SAYING THAT IF I HAVE TO GO UP AGAINST SOME OF OUR GUYS, PEOPLE I TRUST AND RESPECT, I'D LIKE TO AT LEAST BE INCLUDED IN THE PROCESS SO I'M NOT FREAKING BLINDSIDED BY THIS!
I CALL YOU BOSS BECAUSE I KNOW IT BUGS YOU. DON'T START TAKING IT TOO SERIOUSLY.
YOU'RE RIGHT. I SHOULD HAVE TALKED TO YOU. I APOLOGIZE.
GOOD. THAT'S A START.
NOW CAN WE GET TO WORK?
BECAUSE AS MUCH AS YOU DON'T WANT TO GO UP AGAINST THE VERY PEOPLE WE'VE FOUGHT ALONGSIDE FOR SO MANY YEARS, I DON'T THINK WE'RE GOING TO HAVE MUCH CHOICE IN THE MATTER....

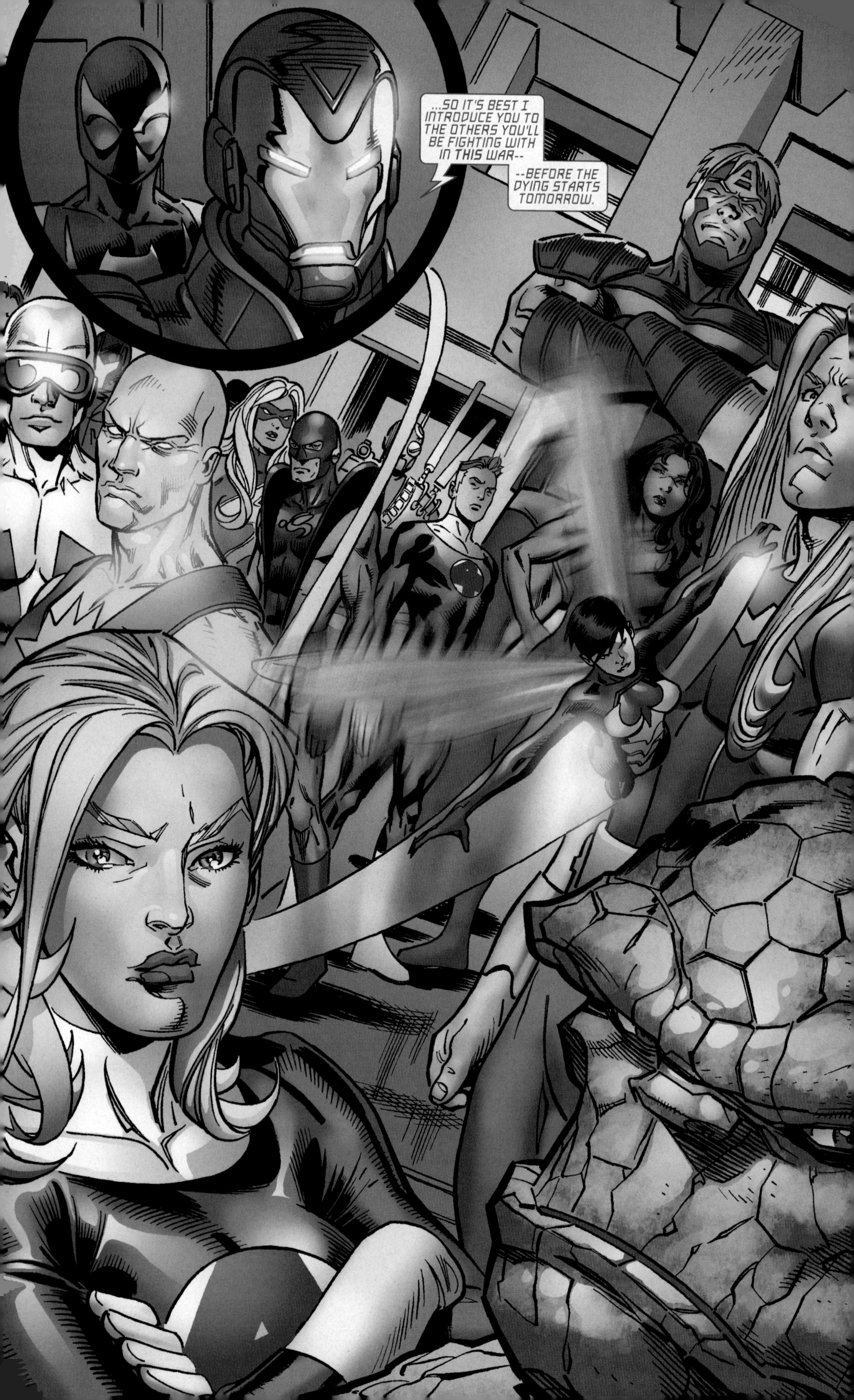
...SO IT'S BEST I INTRODUCE YOU TO THE OTHERS YOU'LL BE FIGHTING WITH IN THIS WAR--
--BEFORE THE DYING STARTS TOMORROW.

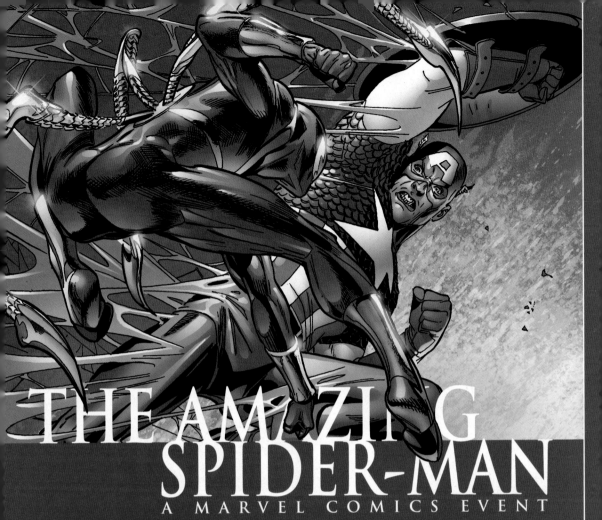

THE AMAZING SPIDER-MAN

A MARVEL COMICS EVENT

CIVIL WAR

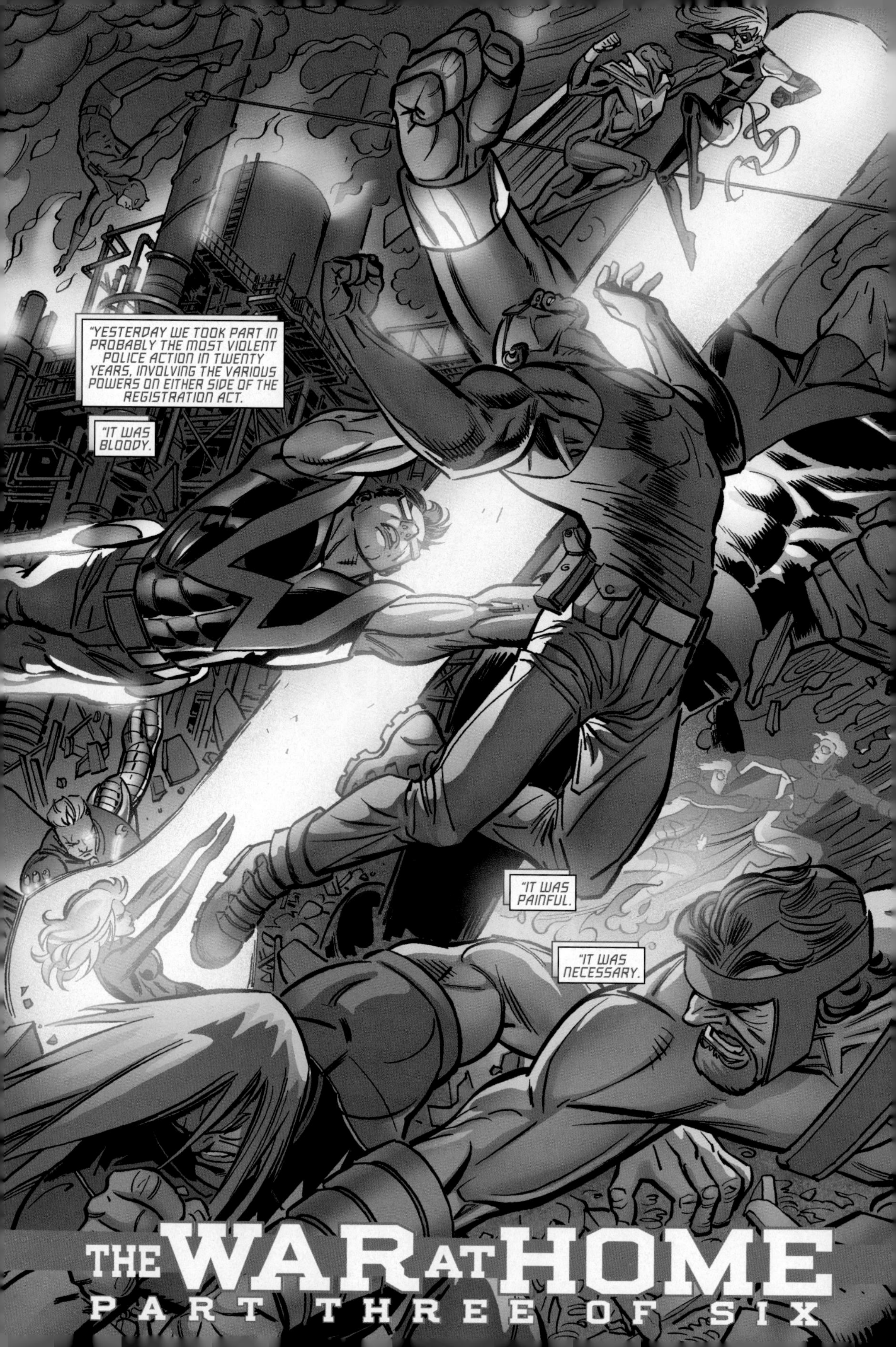
"YESTERDAY WE TOOK PART IN PROBABLY THE MOST VIOLENT POLICE ACTION IN TWENTY YEARS, INVOLVING THE VARIOUS POWERS ON EITHER SIDE OF THE REGISTRATION ACT.
"IT WAS BLOODY.
"IT WAS PAINFUL.
"IT WAS NECESSARY.
THE WAR AT HOME
PART THREE OF SIX

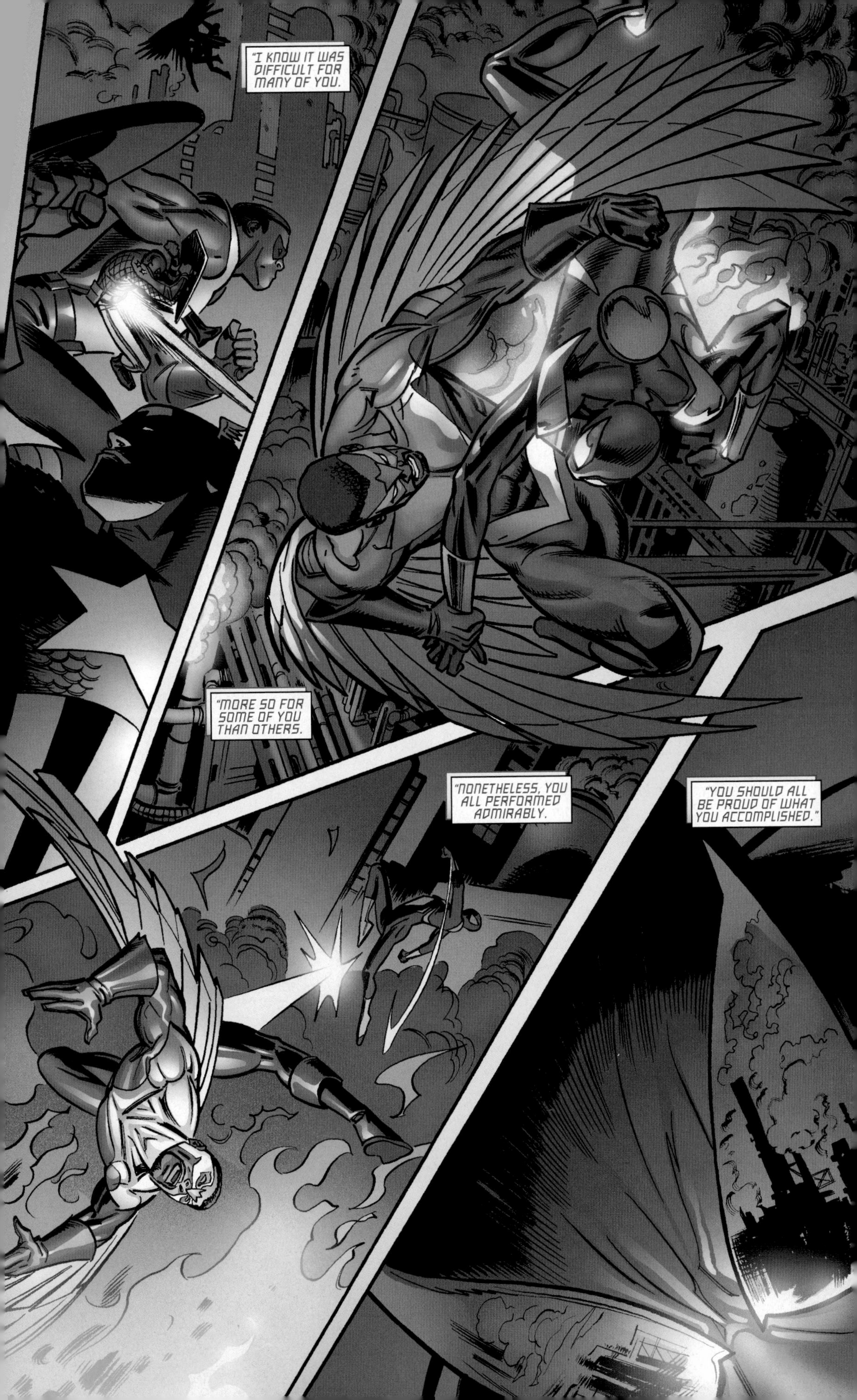
"I KNOW IT WAS DIFFICULT FOR MANY OF YOU.
"MORE SO FOR SOME OF YOU THAN OTHERS.
"NONETHELESS, YOU ALL PERFORMED ADMIRABLY.
"YOU SHOULD ALL BE PROUD OF WHAT YOU ACCOMPLISHED."

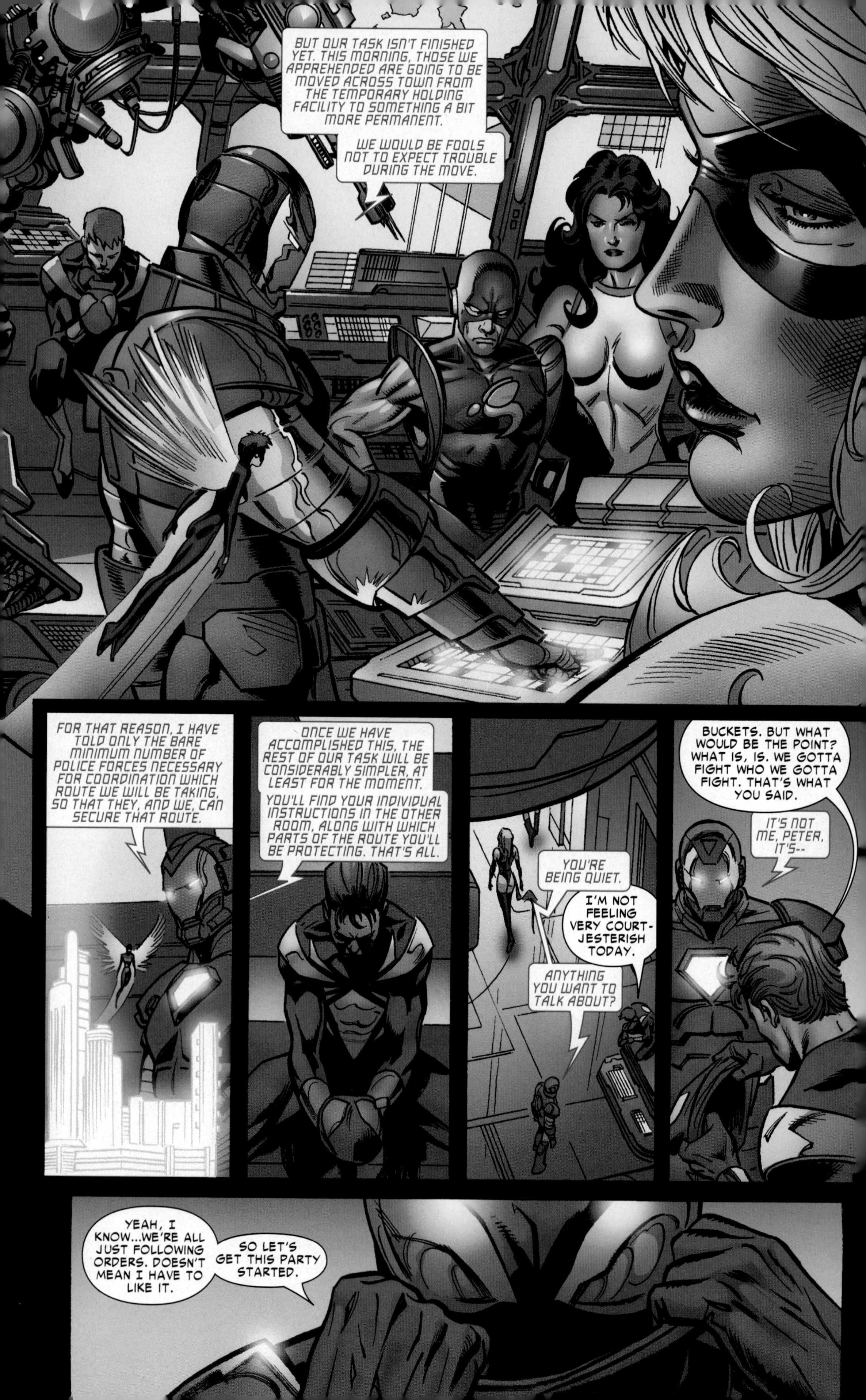
BUT OUR TASK ISN'T FINISHED YET. THIS MORNING, THOSE WE APPREHENDED ARE GOING TO BE MOVED ACROSS TOWN FROM THE TEMPORARY HOLDING FACILITY TO SOMETHING A BIT MORE PERMANENT.
WE WOULD BE FOOLS NOT TO EXPECT TROUBLE DURING THE MOVE.
FOR THAT REASON, I HAVE TOLD ONLY THE BARE MINIMUM NUMBER OF POLICE FORCES NECESSARY FOR COORDINATION WHICH ROUTE WE WILL BE TAKING, SO THAT THEY, AND WE, CAN SECURE THAT ROUTE.
ONCE WE HAVE ACCOMPLISHED THIS, THE REST OF OUR TASK WILL BE CONSIDERABLY SIMPLER, AT LEAST FOR THE MOMENT.
YOU'LL FIND YOUR INDIVIDUAL INSTRUCTIONS IN THE OTHER ROOM, ALONG WITH WHICH PARTS OF THE ROUTE YOU'LL BE PROTECTING. THAT'S ALL.
YOU'RE BEING QUIET.
I'M NOT FEELING VERY COURT-JESTERISH TODAY.
ANYTHING YOU WANT TO TALK ABOUT?
BUCKETS. BUT WHAT WOULD BE THE POINT? WHAT IS, IS. WE GOTTA FIGHT WHO WE GOTTA FIGHT. THAT'S WHAT YOU SAID.
IT'S NOT ME, PETER, IT'S--
YEAH, I KNOW...WE'RE ALL JUST FOLLOWING ORDERS. DOESN'T MEAN I HAVE TO LIKE IT.
SO LET'S GET THIS PARTY STARTED.

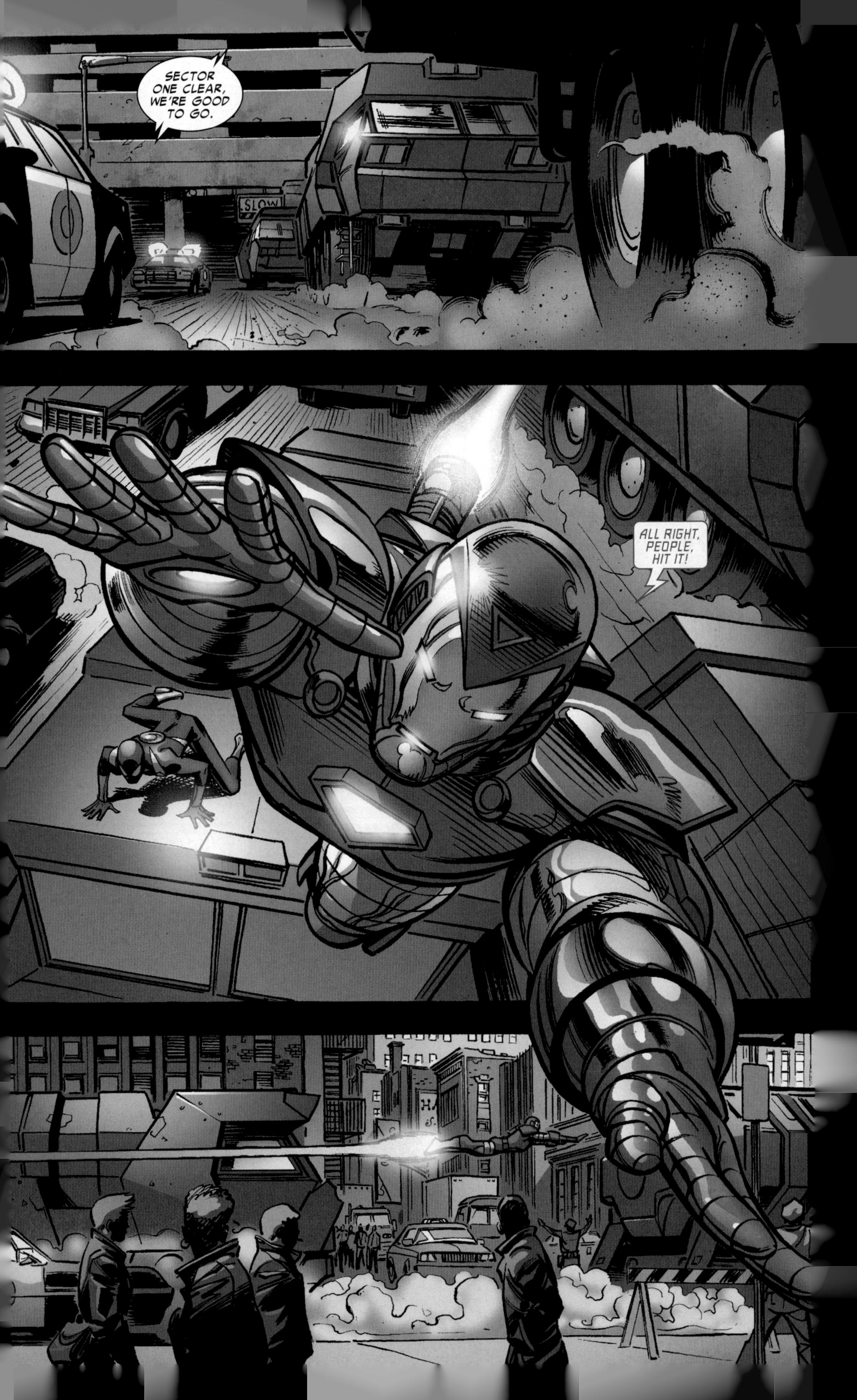
SECTOR ONE CLEAR, WE'RE GOOD TO GO.
SLOW
ALL RIGHT, PEOPLE, HIT IT!

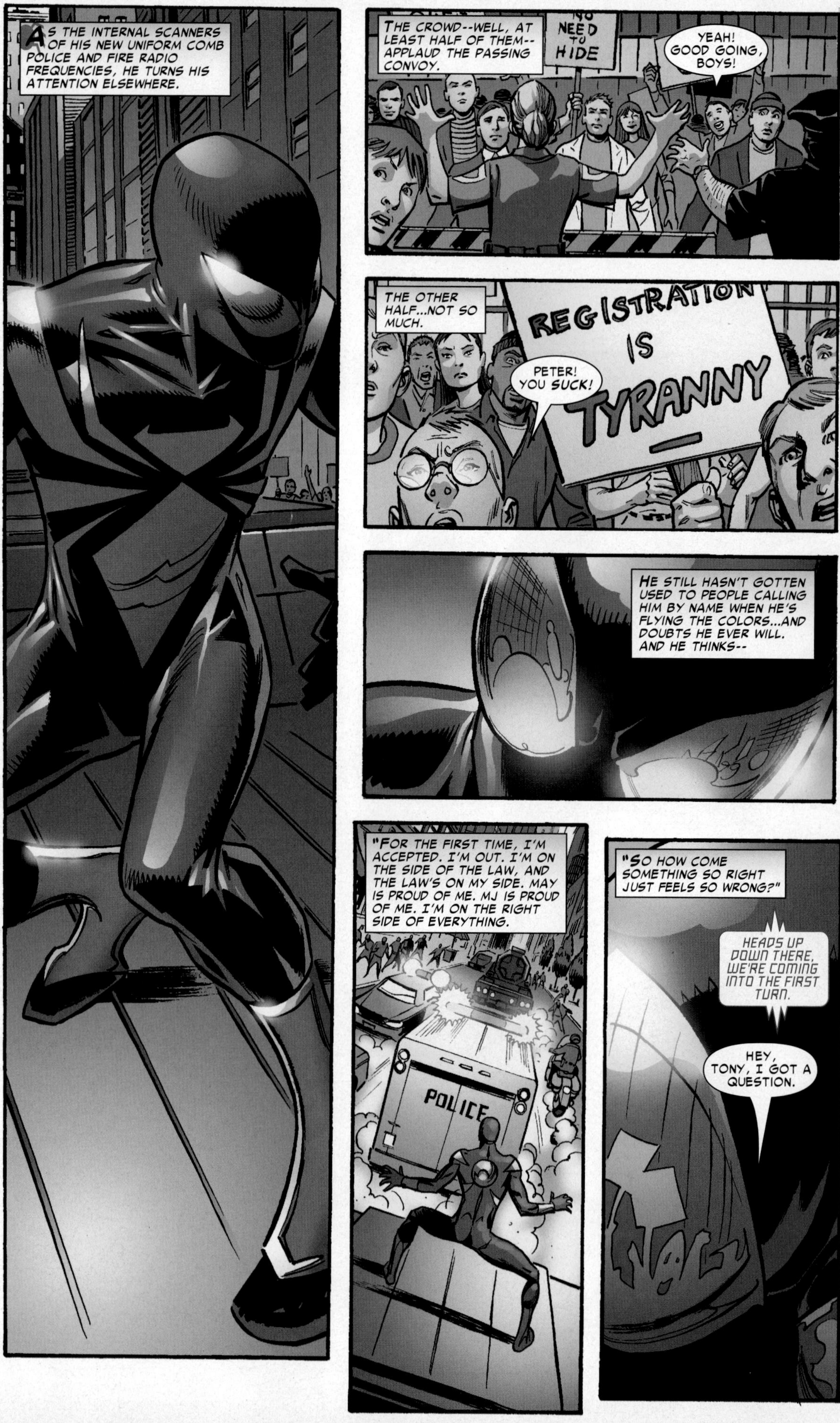
AS THE INTERNAL SCANNERS OF HIS NEW UNIFORM COMB POLICE AND FIRE RADIO FREQUENCIES, HE TURNS HIS ATTENTION ELSEWHERE.
THE CROWD--WELL, AT LEAST HALF OF THEM--APPLAUD THE PASSING CONVOY.
NO NEED TO HIDE
YEAH! GOOD GOING, BOYS!
THE OTHER HALF...NOT SO MUCH.
REGISTRATION IS TYRANNY
PETER! YOU SUCK!
HE STILL HASN'T GOTTEN USED TO PEOPLE CALLING HIM BY NAME WHEN HE'S FLYING THE COLORS...AND DOUBTS HE EVER WILL. AND HE THINKS--
"FOR THE FIRST TIME, I'M ACCEPTED. I'M OUT. I'M ON THE SIDE OF THE LAW, AND THE LAW'S ON MY SIDE. MAY IS PROUD OF ME. MJ IS PROUD OF ME. I'M ON THE RIGHT SIDE OF EVERYTHING.
POLICE
"SO HOW COME SOMETHING SO RIGHT JUST FEELS SO WRONG?"
HEADS UP DOWN THERE, WE'RE COMING INTO THE FIRST TURN.
HEY, TONY, I GOT A QUESTION.

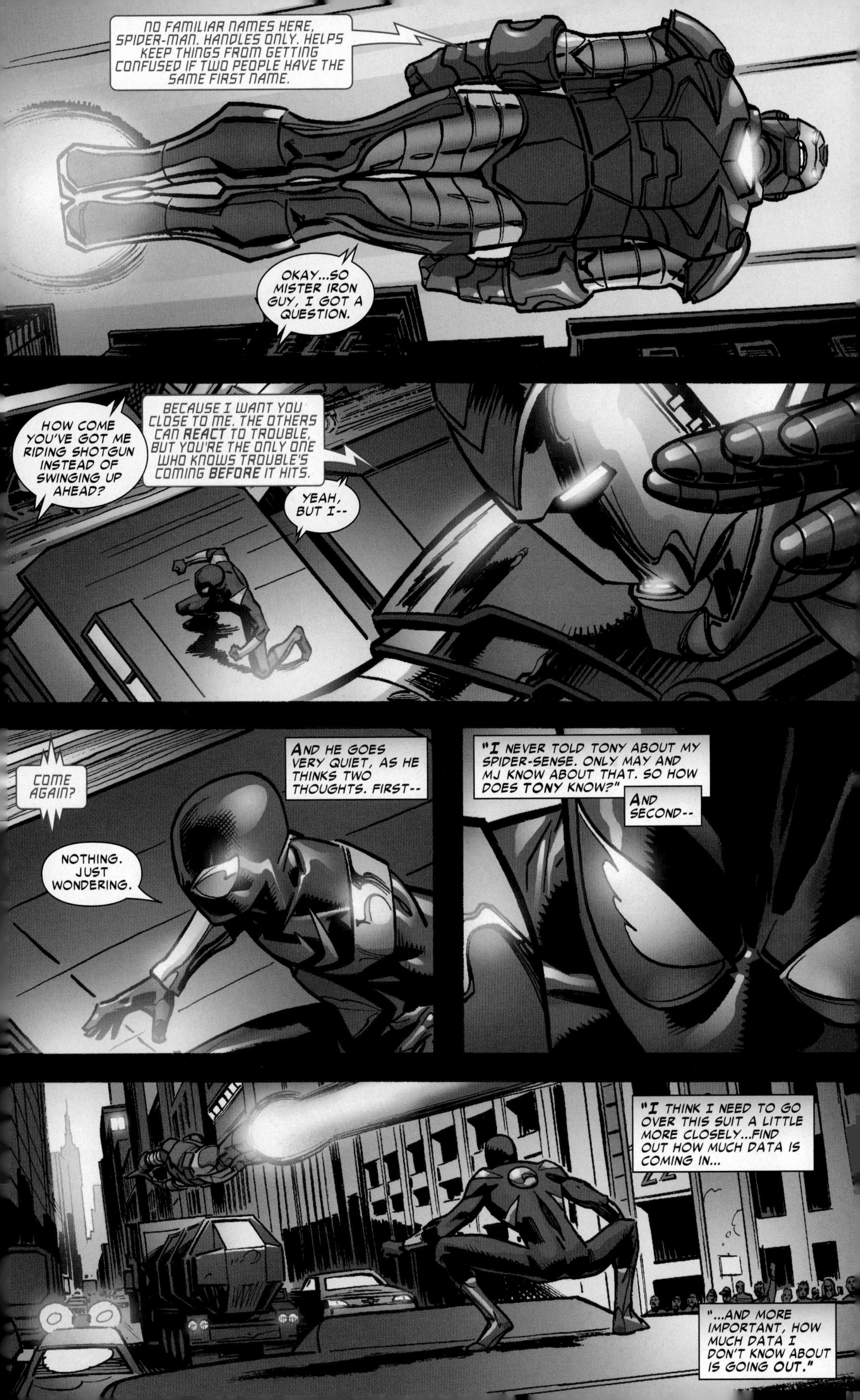

NO FAMILIAR NAMES HERE, SPIDER-MAN. HANDLES ONLY. HELPS KEEP THINGS FROM GETTING CONFUSED IF TWO PEOPLE HAVE THE SAME FIRST NAME.
OKAY...SO MISTER IRON GUY, I GOT A QUESTION.
HOW COME YOU'VE GOT ME RIDING SHOTGUN INSTEAD OF SWINGING UP AHEAD?
BECAUSE I WANT YOU CLOSE TO ME. THE OTHERS CAN REACT TO TROUBLE, BUT YOU'RE THE ONLY ONE WHO KNOWS TROUBLE'S COMING BEFORE IT HITS.
YEAH, BUT I--
COME AGAIN?
NOTHING. JUST WONDERING.
AND HE GOES VERY QUIET, AS HE THINKS TWO THOUGHTS. FIRST--
"I NEVER TOLD TONY ABOUT MY SPIDER-SENSE. ONLY MAY AND MJ KNOW ABOUT THAT. SO HOW DOES TONY KNOW?"
AND SECOND--
"I THINK I NEED TO GO OVER THIS SUIT A LITTLE MORE CLOSELY...FIND OUT HOW MUCH DATA IS COMING IN...
"...AND MORE IMPORTANT, HOW MUCH DATA I DON'T KNOW ABOUT IS GOING OUT."

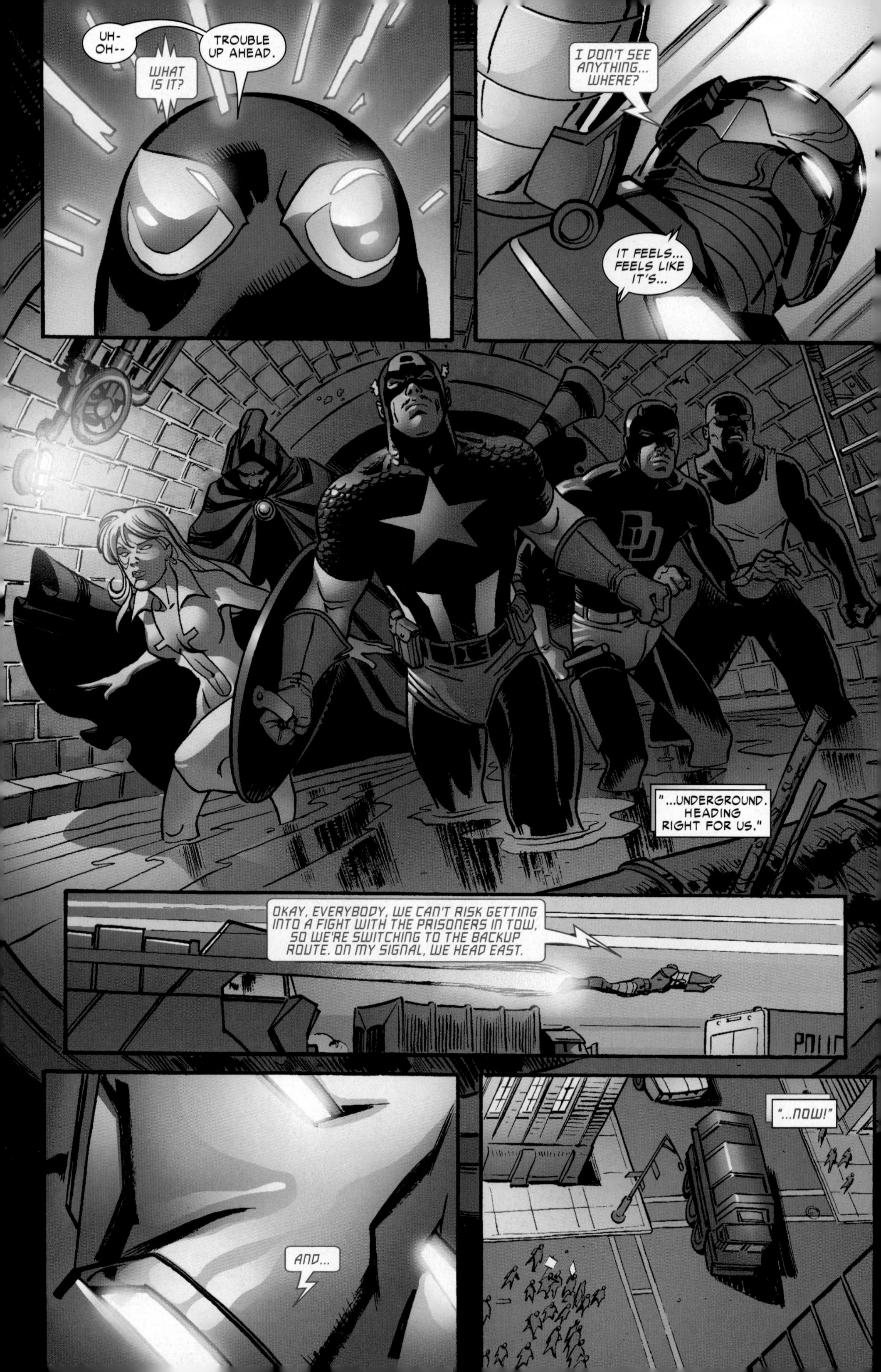
UH-OH--
WHAT IS IT?
TROUBLE UP AHEAD.
I DON'T SEE ANYTHING... WHERE?
IT FEELS... FEELS LIKE IT'S...
"...UNDERGROUND. HEADING RIGHT FOR US."
OKAY, EVERYBODY, WE CAN'T RISK GETTING INTO A FIGHT WITH THE PRISONERS IN TOW, SO WE'RE SWITCHING TO THE BACKUP ROUTE. ON MY SIGNAL, WE HEAD EAST.
AND...
"...NOW!"

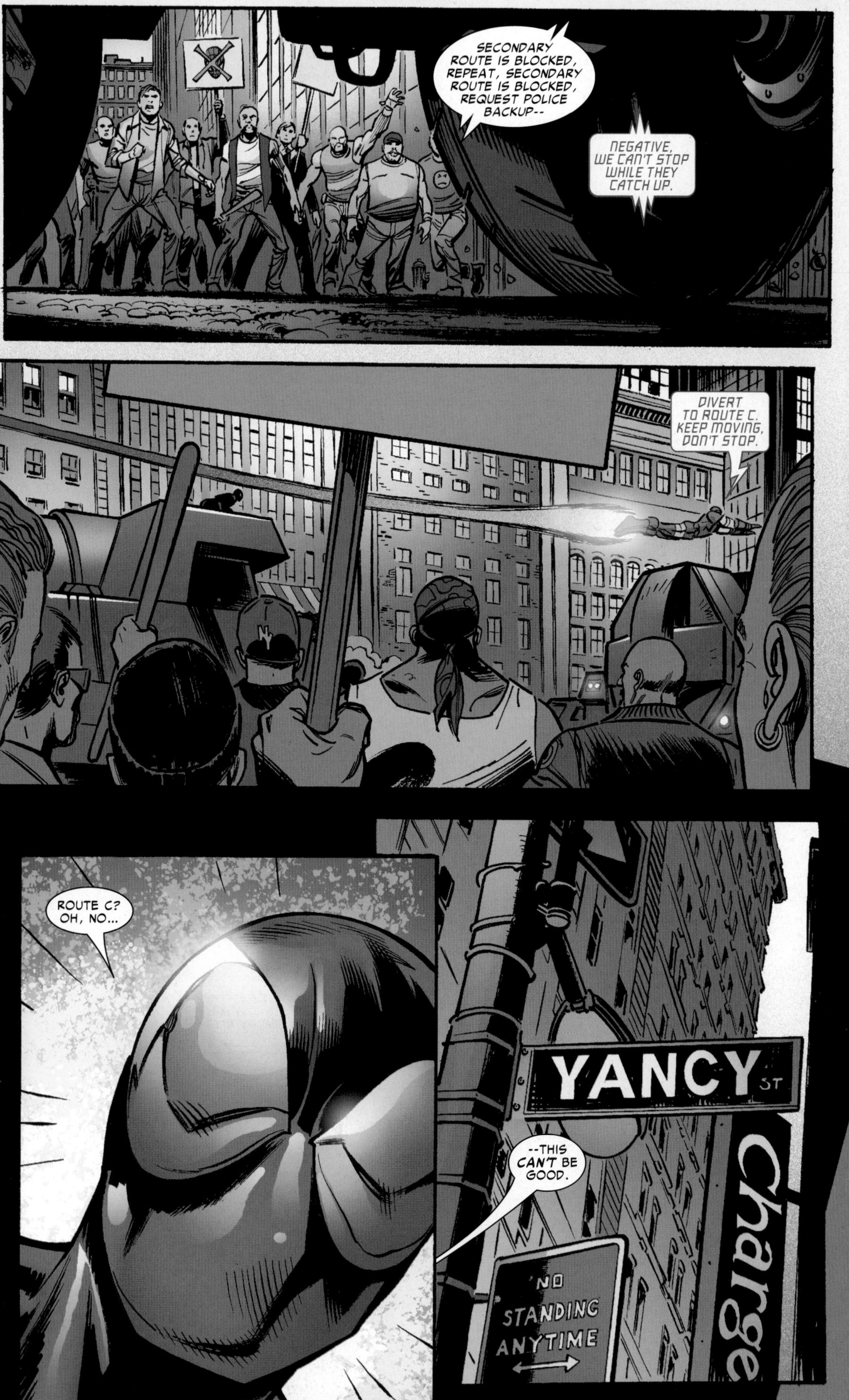
SECONDARY ROUTE IS BLOCKED, REPEAT, SECONDARY ROUTE IS BLOCKED, REQUEST POLICE BACKUP--
NEGATIVE, WE CAN'T STOP WHILE THEY CATCH UP.
DIVERT TO ROUTE C. KEEP MOVING, DON'T STOP.
ROUTE C? OH, NO...
YANCY ST
--THIS CAN'T BE GOOD.
NO STANDING ANYTIME
Charge

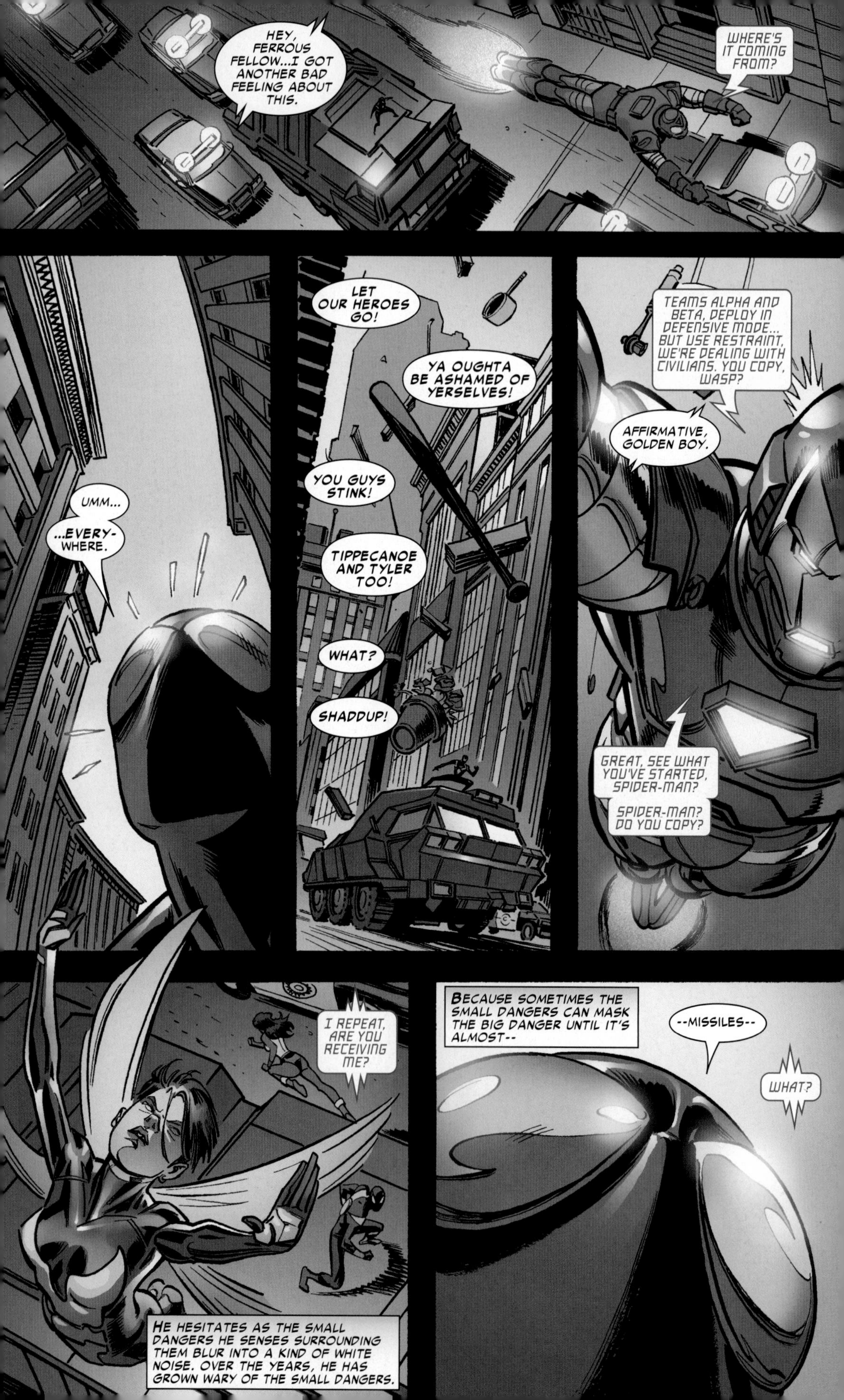
HEY, FERROUS FELLOW...I GOT ANOTHER BAD FEELING ABOUT THIS.
WHERE'S IT COMING FROM?
UMM...
...EVERY-WHERE.
LET OUR HEROES GO!
YA OUGHTA BE ASHAMED OF YERSELVES!
YOU GUYS STINK!
TIPPECANOE AND TYLER TOO!
WHAT?
SHADDUP!
TEAMS ALPHA AND BETA, DEPLOY IN DEFENSIVE MODE... BUT USE RESTRAINT, WE'RE DEALING WITH CIVILIANS. YOU COPY, WASP?
AFFIRMATIVE, GOLDEN BOY.
GREAT, SEE WHAT YOU'VE STARTED, SPIDER-MAN?
SPIDER-MAN? DO YOU COPY?
I REPEAT, ARE YOU RECEIVING ME?
HE HESITATES AS THE SMALL DANGERS HE SENSES SURROUNDING THEM BLUR INTO A KIND OF WHITE NOISE. OVER THE YEARS, HE HAS GROWN WARY OF THE SMALL DANGERS.
BECAUSE SOMETIMES THE SMALL DANGERS CAN MASK THE BIG DANGER UNTIL IT'S ALMOST--
--MISSILES--
WHAT?

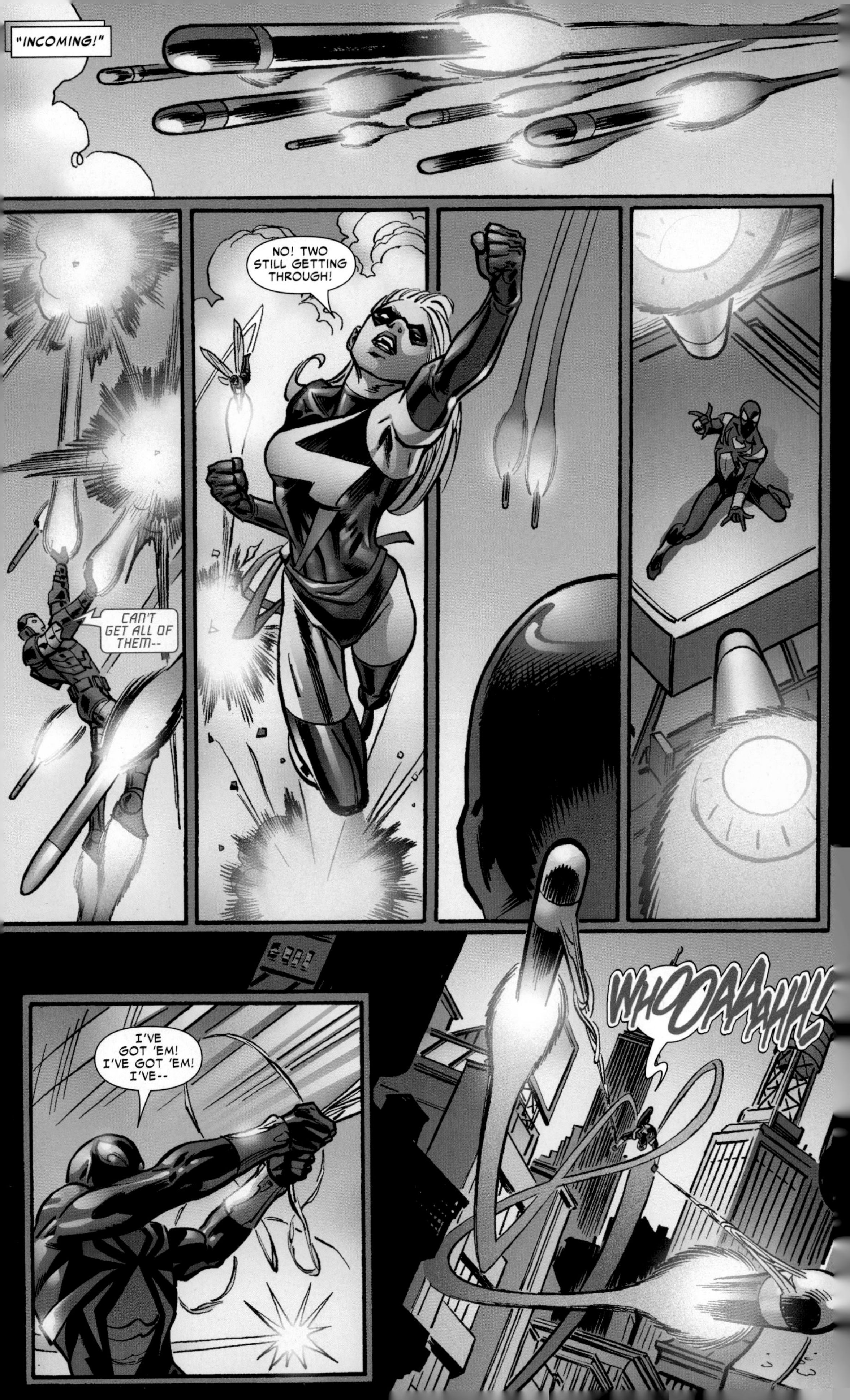
"INCOMING!"
NO! TWO STILL GETTING THROUGH!
CAN'T GET ALL OF THEM--
I'VE GOT 'EM! I'VE GOT 'EM! I'VE--
WHOOAAAHH!

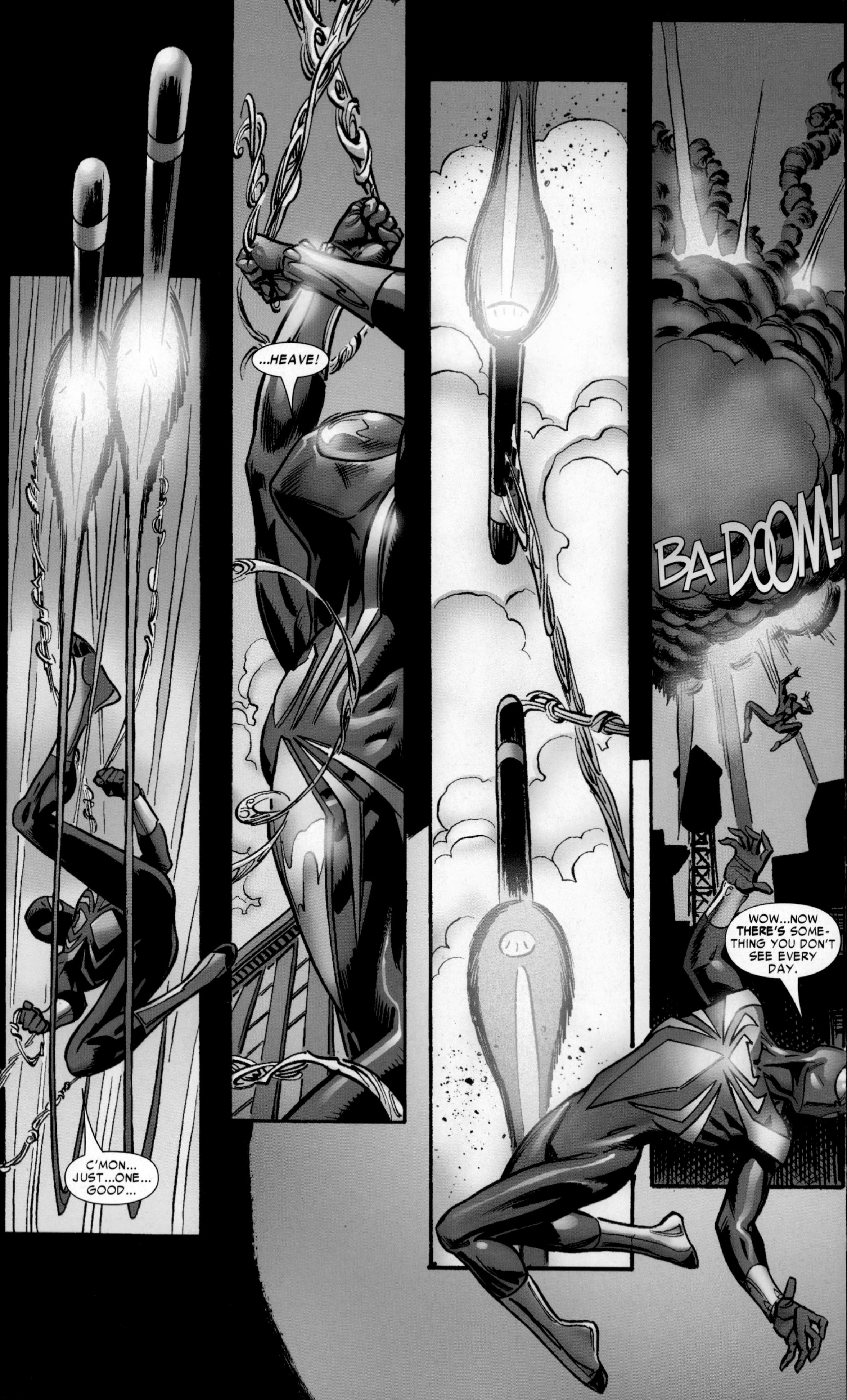
C'MON... JUST...ONE... GOOD...
...HEAVE!
BA-DOOM!
WOW...NOW THERE'S SOME-THING YOU DON'T SEE EVERY DAY.

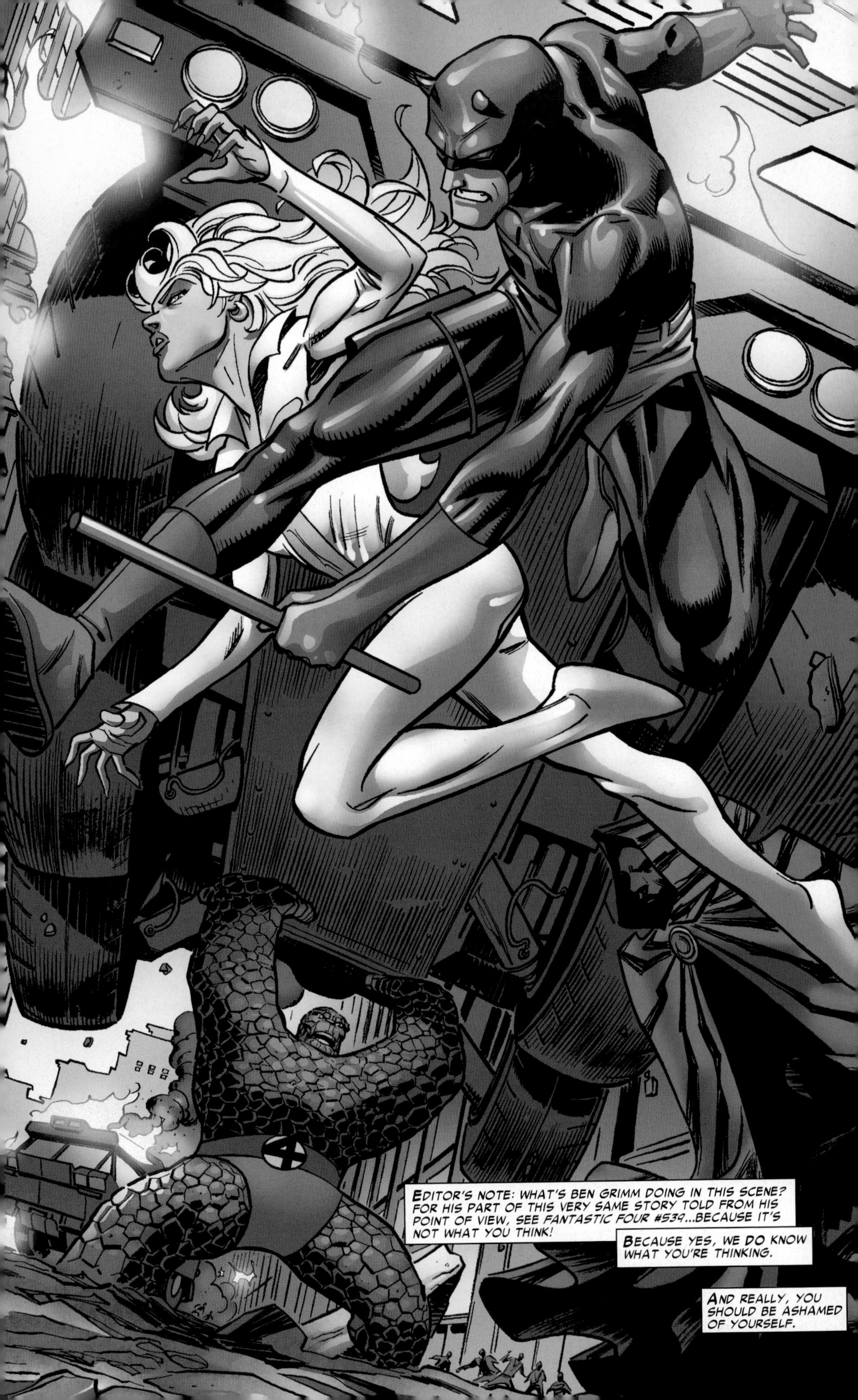
EDITOR'S NOTE: WHAT'S BEN GRIMM DOING IN THIS SCENE? FOR HIS PART OF THIS VERY SAME STORY TOLD FROM HIS POINT OF VIEW, SEE FANTASTIC FOUR #539...BECAUSE IT'S NOT WHAT YOU THINK!
BECAUSE YES, WE DO KNOW WHAT YOU'RE THINKING.
AND REALLY, YOU SHOULD BE ASHAMED OF YOURSELF.

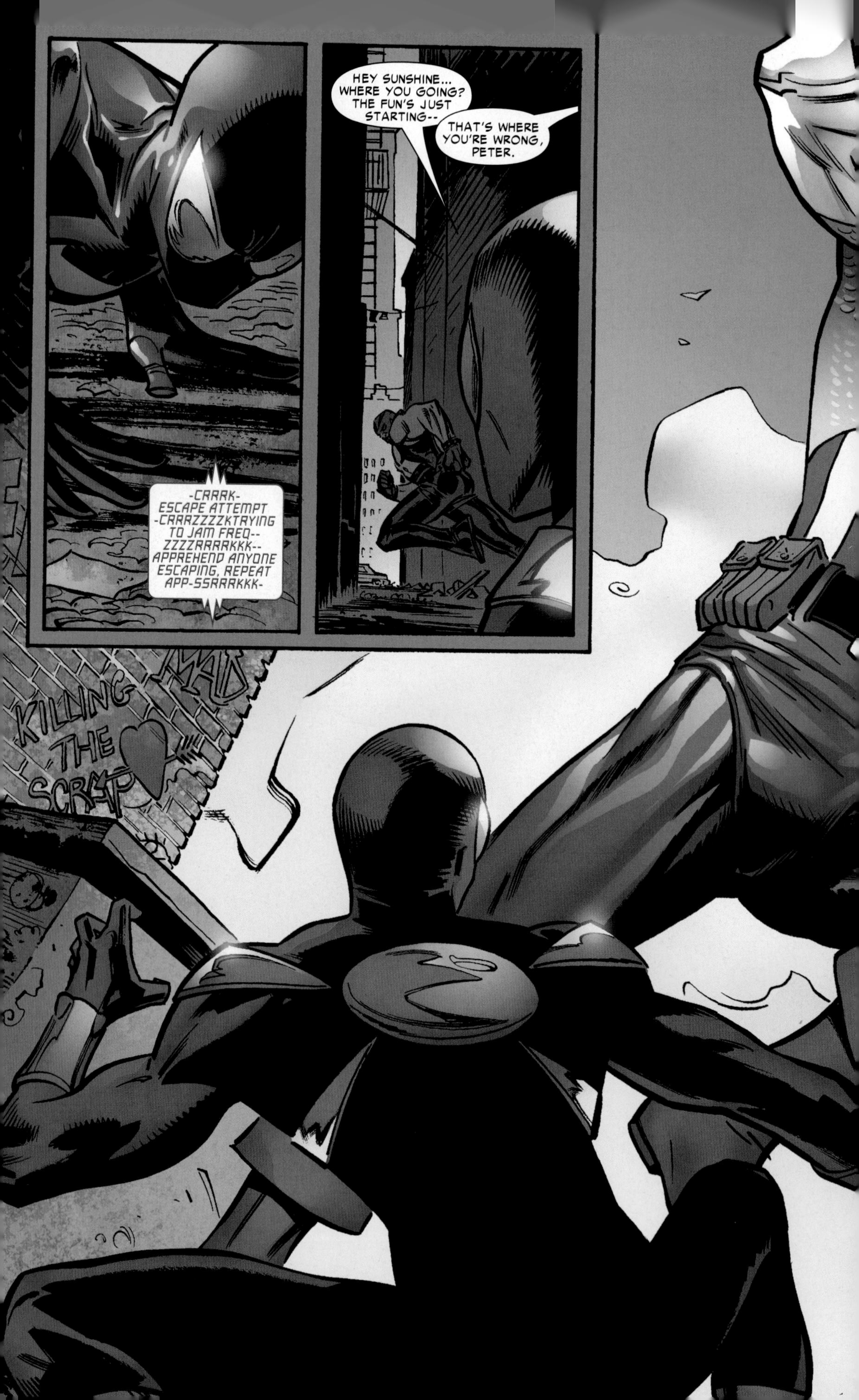
-CRRRK-
ESCAPE ATTEMPT
-CRRRZZZZKTRYING
TO JAM FREQ--
ZZZZRRRRKKK--
APPREHEND ANYONE
ESCAPING, REPEAT
APP-SSRRRKKK-
HEY SUNSHINE... WHERE YOU GOING? THE FUN'S JUST STARTING--
THAT'S WHERE YOU'RE WRONG, PETER.
KILLING THE SCRAP
MAD

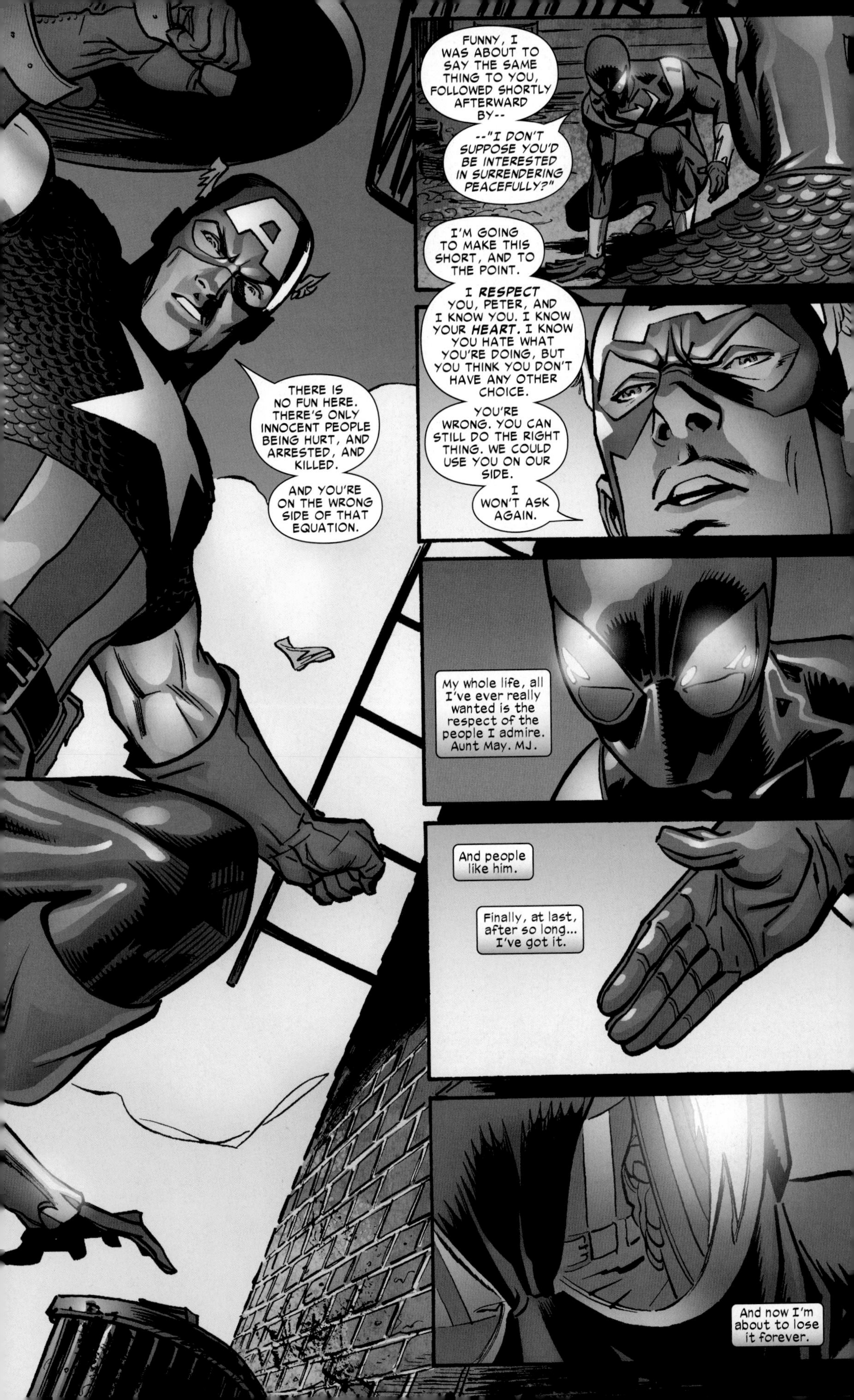
FUNNY, I WAS ABOUT TO SAY THE SAME THING TO YOU, FOLLOWED SHORTLY AFTERWARD BY--
--"I DON'T SUPPOSE YOU'D BE INTERESTED IN SURRENDERING PEACEFULLY?"
THERE IS NO FUN HERE. THERE'S ONLY INNOCENT PEOPLE BEING HURT, AND ARRESTED, AND KILLED.
AND YOU'RE ON THE WRONG SIDE OF THAT EQUATION.
I'M GOING TO MAKE THIS SHORT, AND TO THE POINT.
I RESPECT YOU, PETER, AND I KNOW YOU. I KNOW YOUR HEART. I KNOW YOU HATE WHAT YOU'RE DOING, BUT YOU THINK YOU DON'T HAVE ANY OTHER CHOICE.
YOU'RE WRONG. YOU CAN STILL DO THE RIGHT THING. WE COULD USE YOU ON OUR SIDE.
I WON'T ASK AGAIN.
My whole life, all I've ever really wanted is the respect of the people I admire. Aunt May. MJ.
And people like him.
Finally, at last, after so long... I've got it.
And now I'm about to lose it forever.

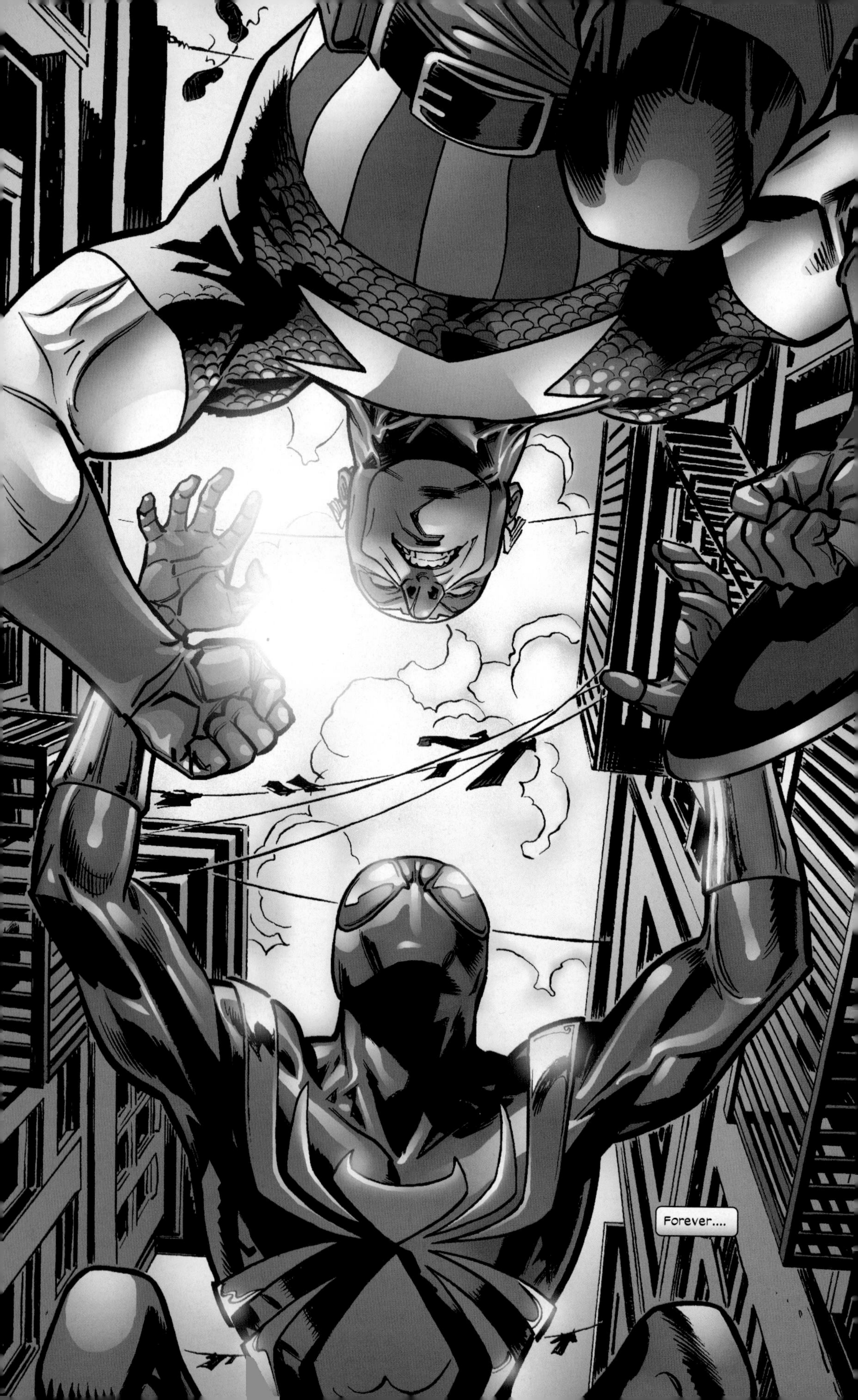
Forever....

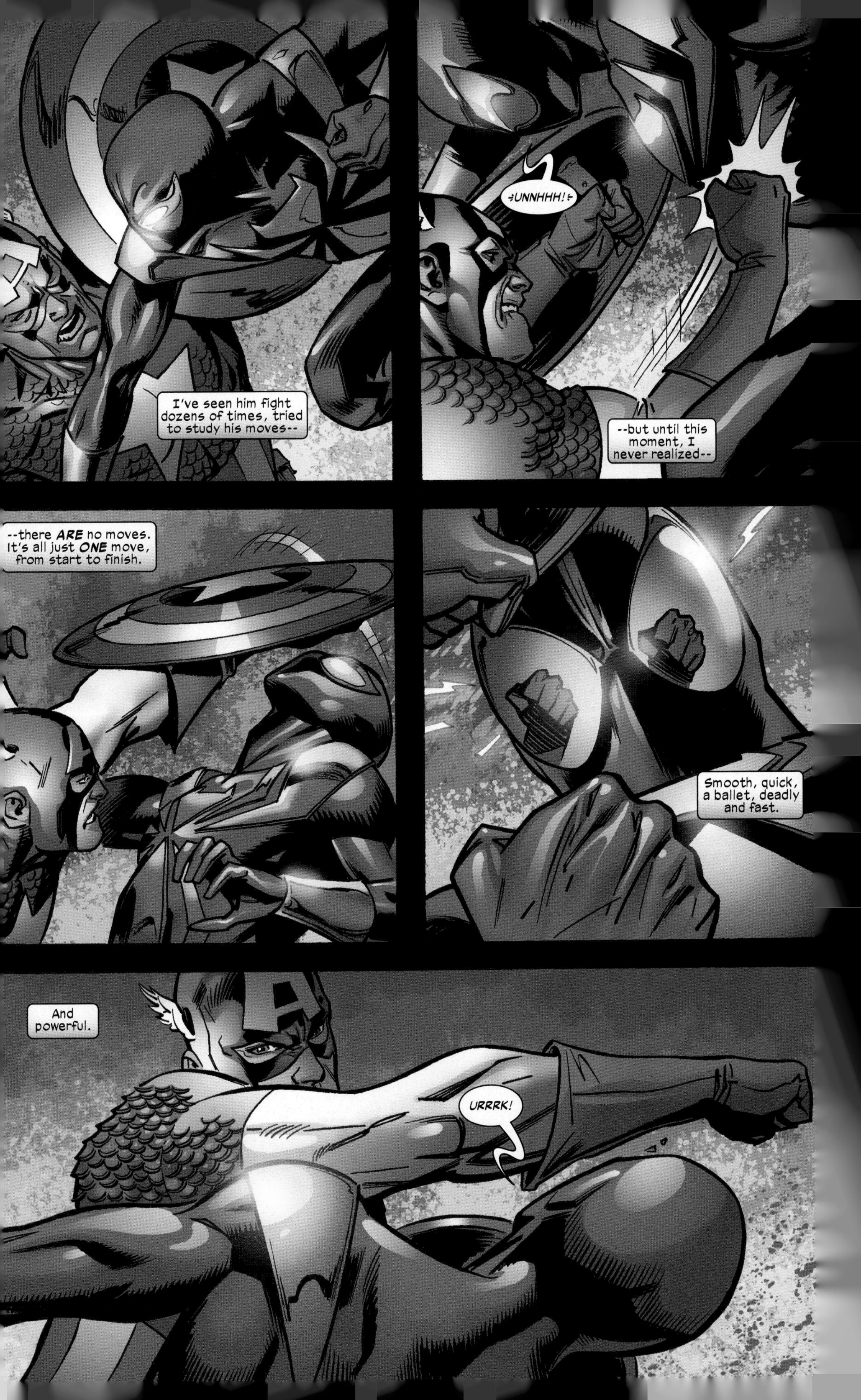
I've seen him fight dozens of times, tried to study his moves--
UNNHHH!
--but until this moment, I never realized--
--there ARE no moves. It's all just ONE move, from start to finish.
Smooth, quick, a ballet, deadly and fast.
And powerful.
URRRK!

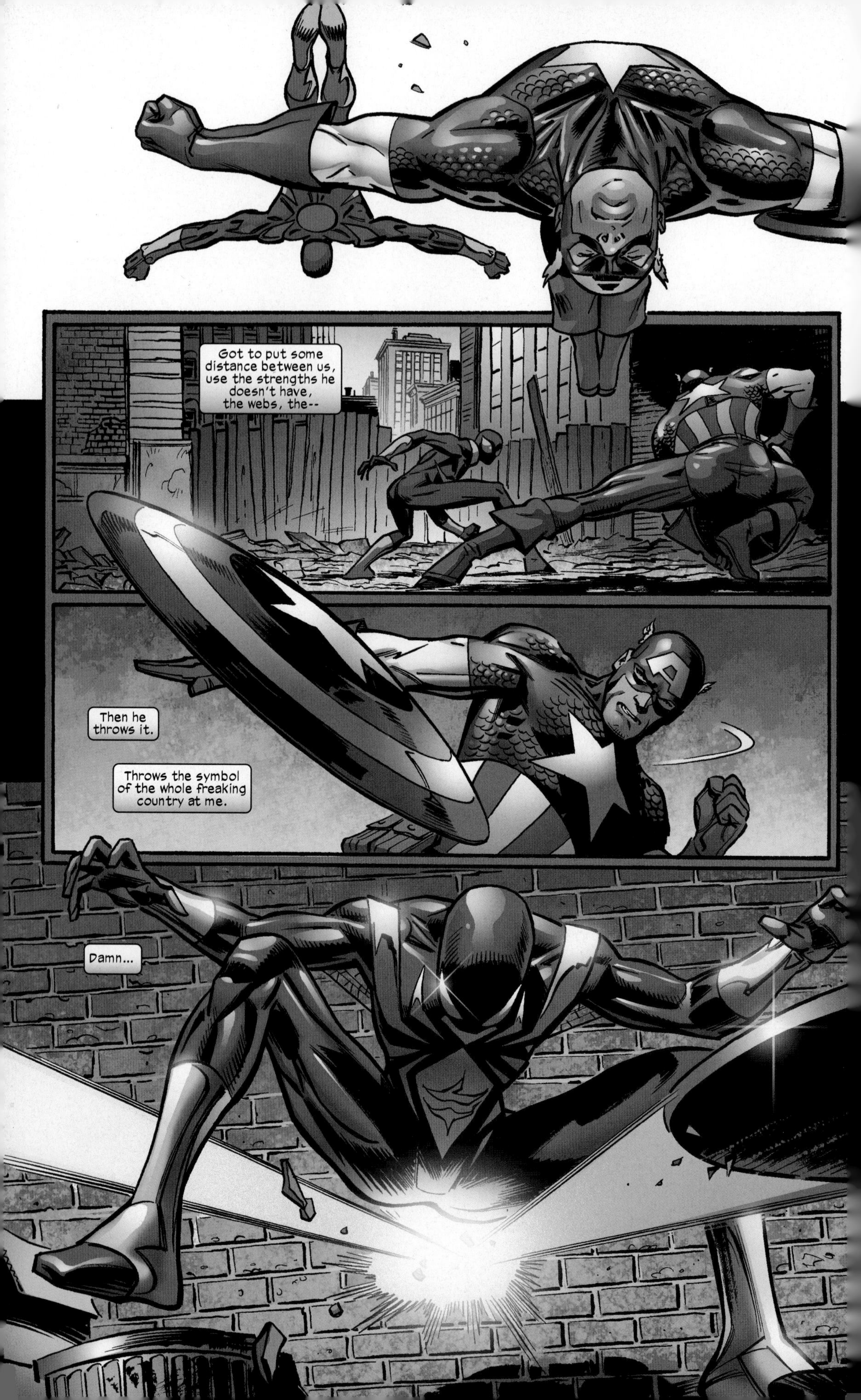
Got to put some distance between us, use the strengths he doesn't have, the webs, the--
Then he throws it.
Throws the symbol of the whole freaking country at me.
Damn...

The shield is perfect geometry in flight...but I have one advantage... I can SENSE where it's going to end up.

I use it--

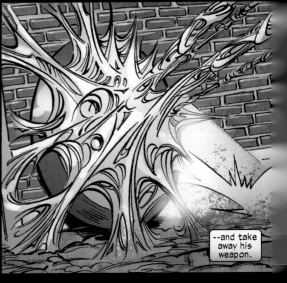

--and take away his weapon.

And as I turn, still in midair, I realize I've exposed my back--

--and did exactly what he wanted me to do.

AGGGGH!

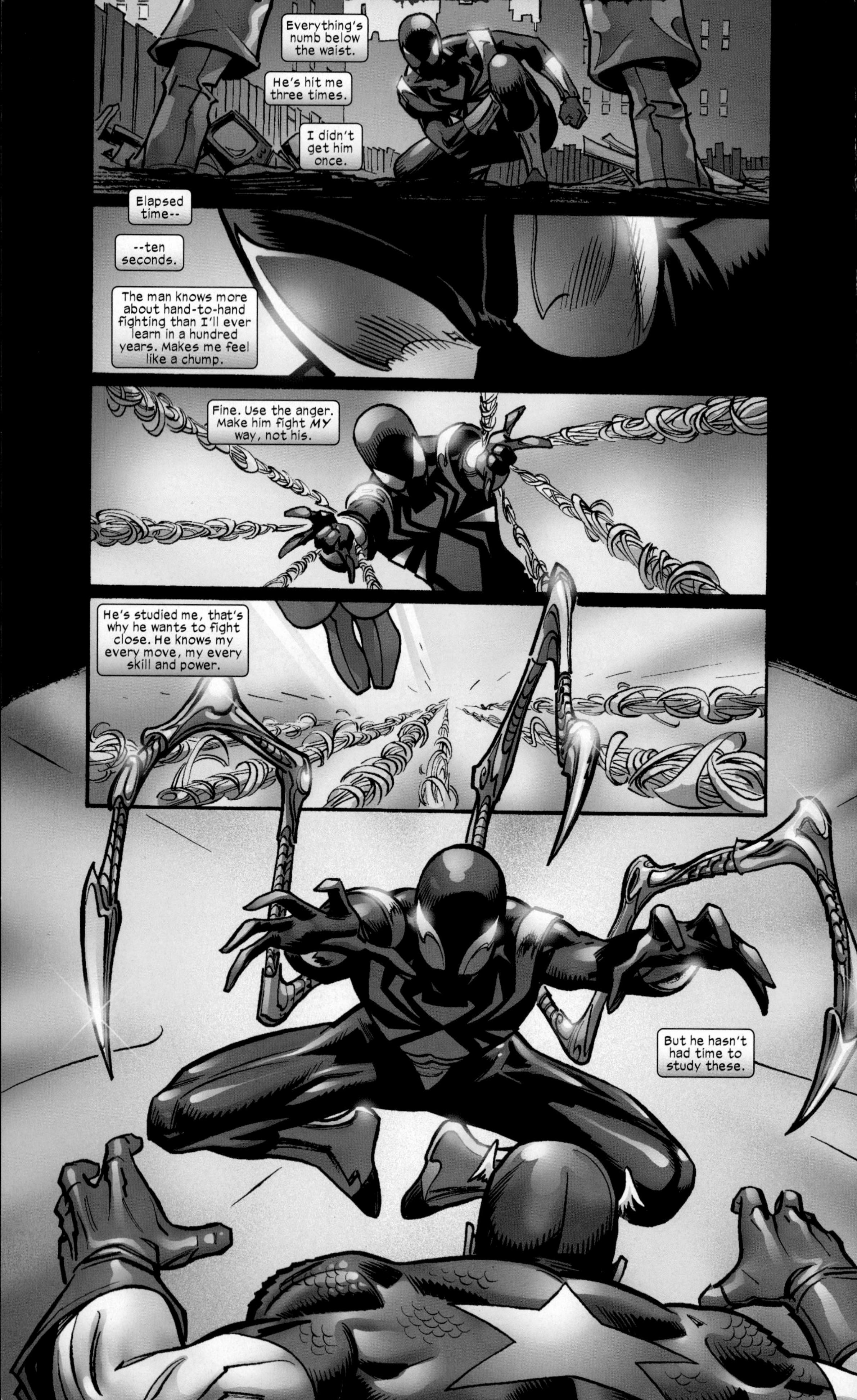
Everything's numb below the waist.
He's hit me three times.
I didn't get him once.
Elapsed time--
--ten seconds.
The man knows more about hand-to-hand fighting than I'll ever learn in a hundred years. Makes me feel like a chump.
Fine. Use the anger. Make him fight *MY* way, not his.
He's studied me, that's why he wants to fight close. He knows my every move, my every skill and power.
But he hasn't had time to study these.

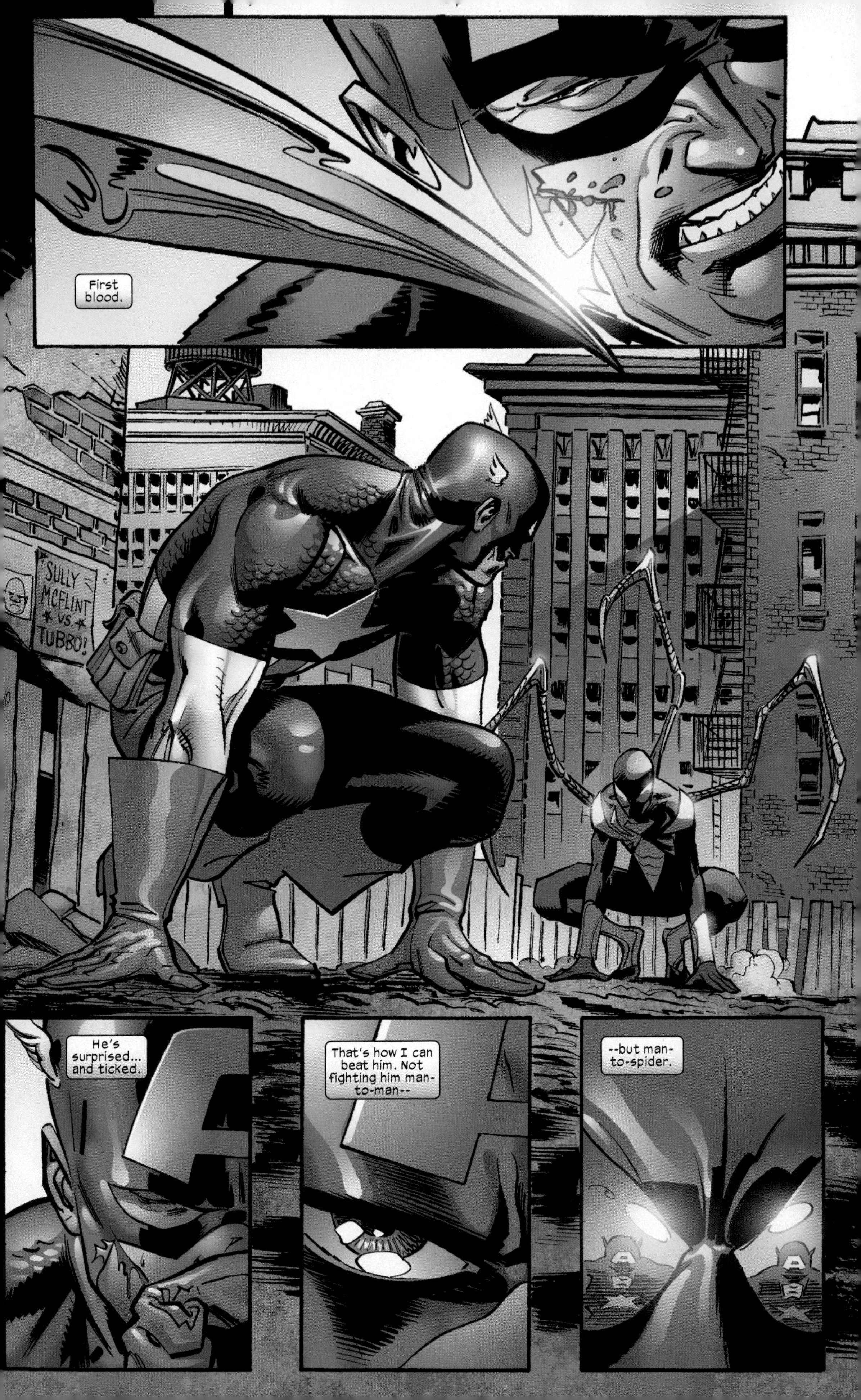
First blood.
SULLY McFLINT VS. TUBBO!
He's surprised... and ticked.
That's how I can beat him. Not fighting him man-to-man--
--but man-to-spider.

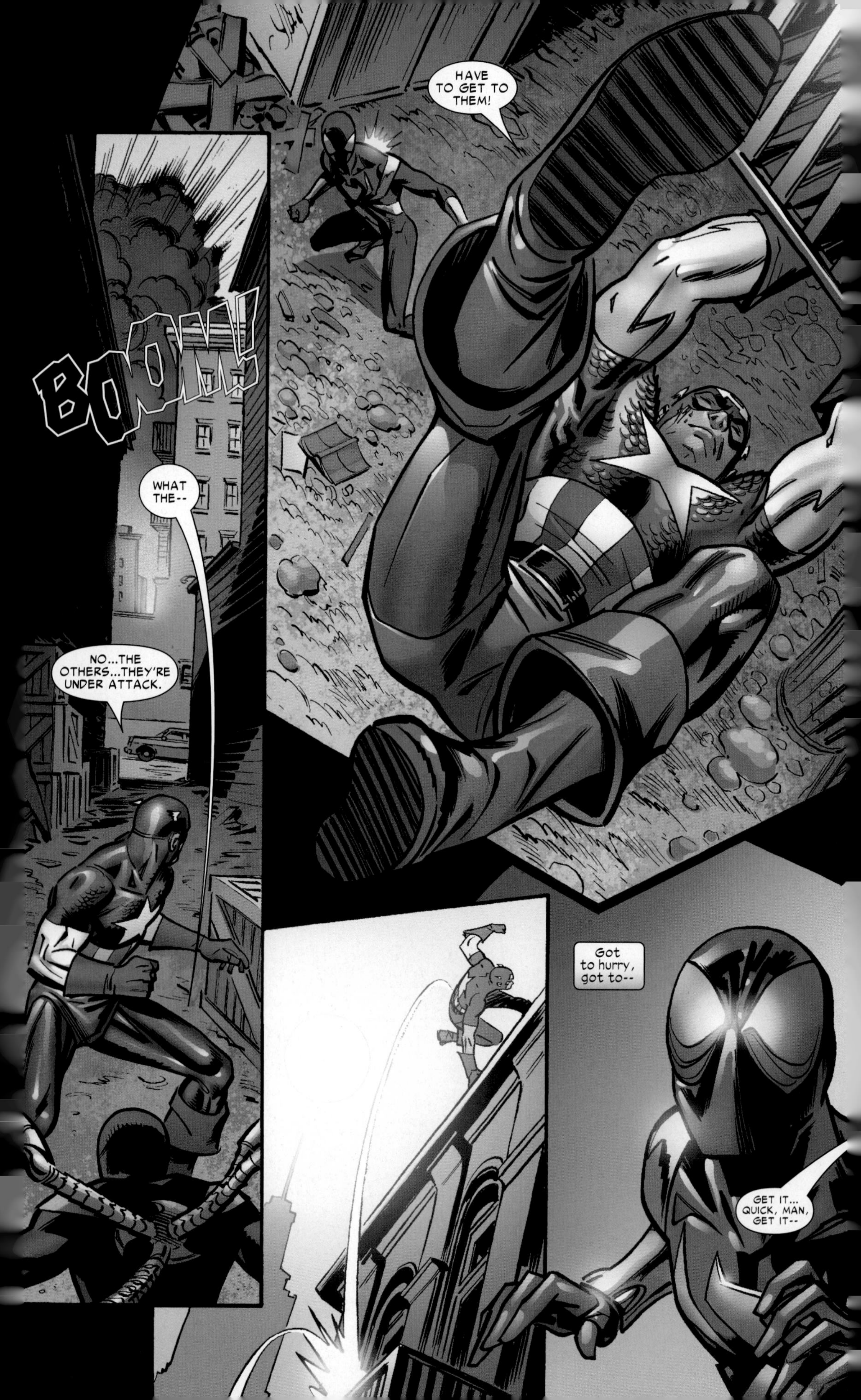
HAVE TO GET TO THEM!
BOOM!
WHAT THE--
NO...THE OTHERS...THEY'RE UNDER ATTACK.
Got to hurry, got to--
GET IT... QUICK, MAN, GET IT--

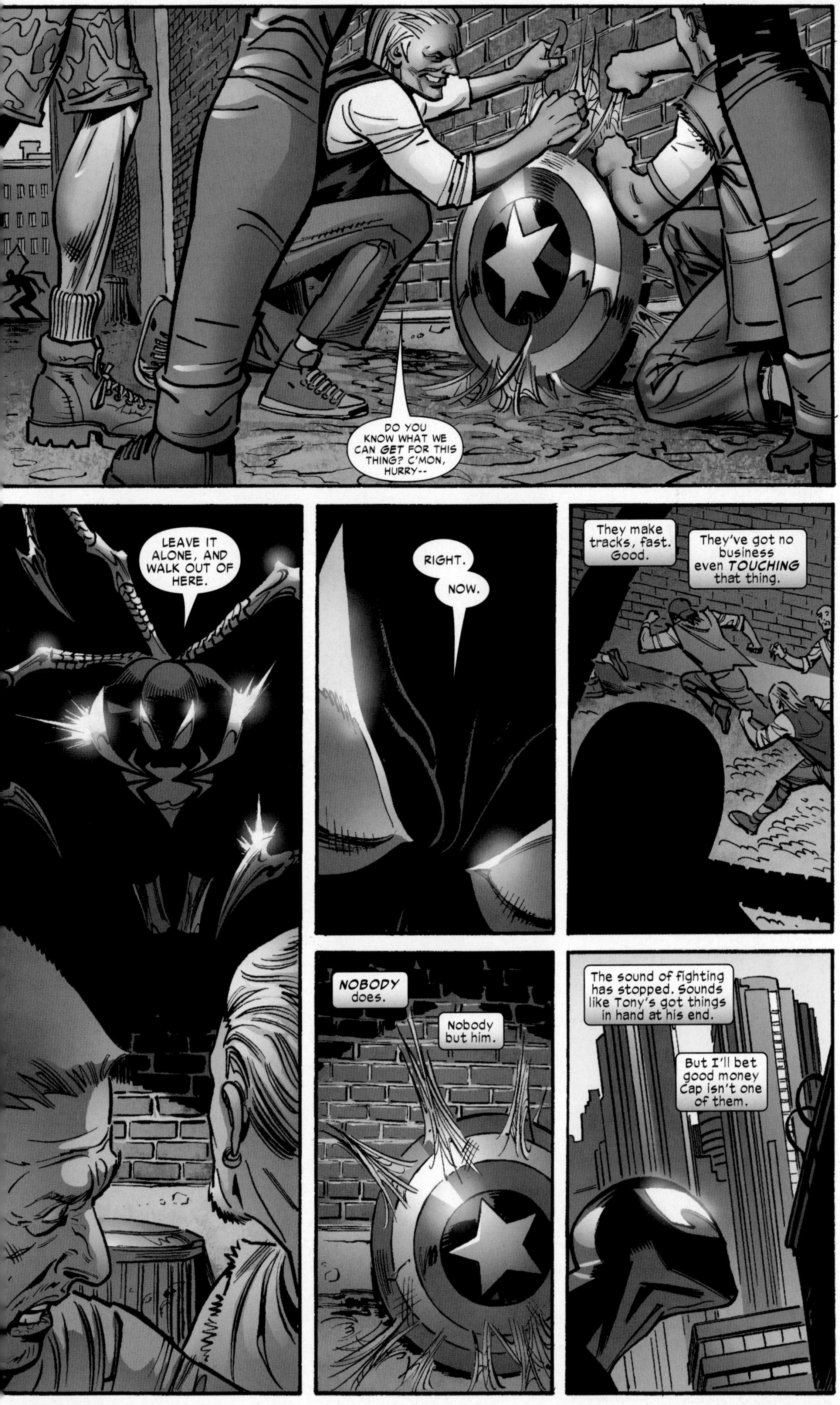
DO YOU KNOW WHAT WE CAN GET FOR THIS THING? C'MON, HURRY--
LEAVE IT ALONE, AND WALK OUT OF HERE.
RIGHT.
NOW.
They make tracks, fast. Good.
They've got no business even TOUCHING that thing.
NOBODY does.
Nobody but him.
The sound of fighting has stopped. Sounds like Tony's got things in hand at his end.
But I'll bet good money Cap isn't one of them.

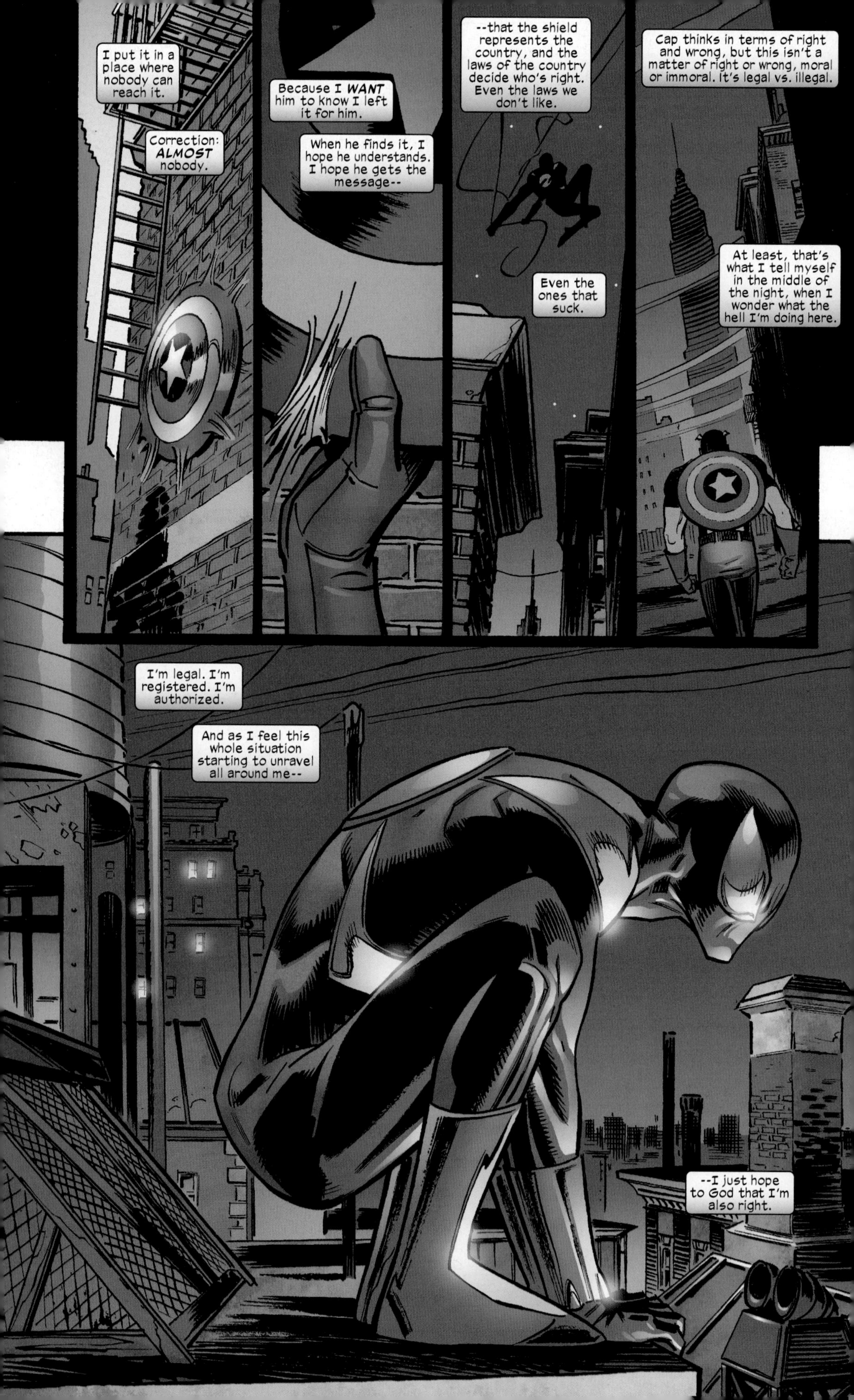

I put it in a place where nobody can reach it.
Correction: ALMOST nobody.
Because I WANT him to know I left it for him.
When he finds it, I hope he understands. I hope he gets the message--
--that the shield represents the country, and the laws of the country decide who's right. Even the laws we don't like.
Even the ones that suck.
Cap thinks in terms of right and wrong, but this isn't a matter of right or wrong, moral or immoral. It's legal vs. illegal.
At least, that's what I tell myself in the middle of the night, when I wonder what the hell I'm doing here.
I'm legal. I'm registered. I'm authorized.
And as I feel this whole situation starting to unravel all around me--
--I just hope to God that I'm also right.

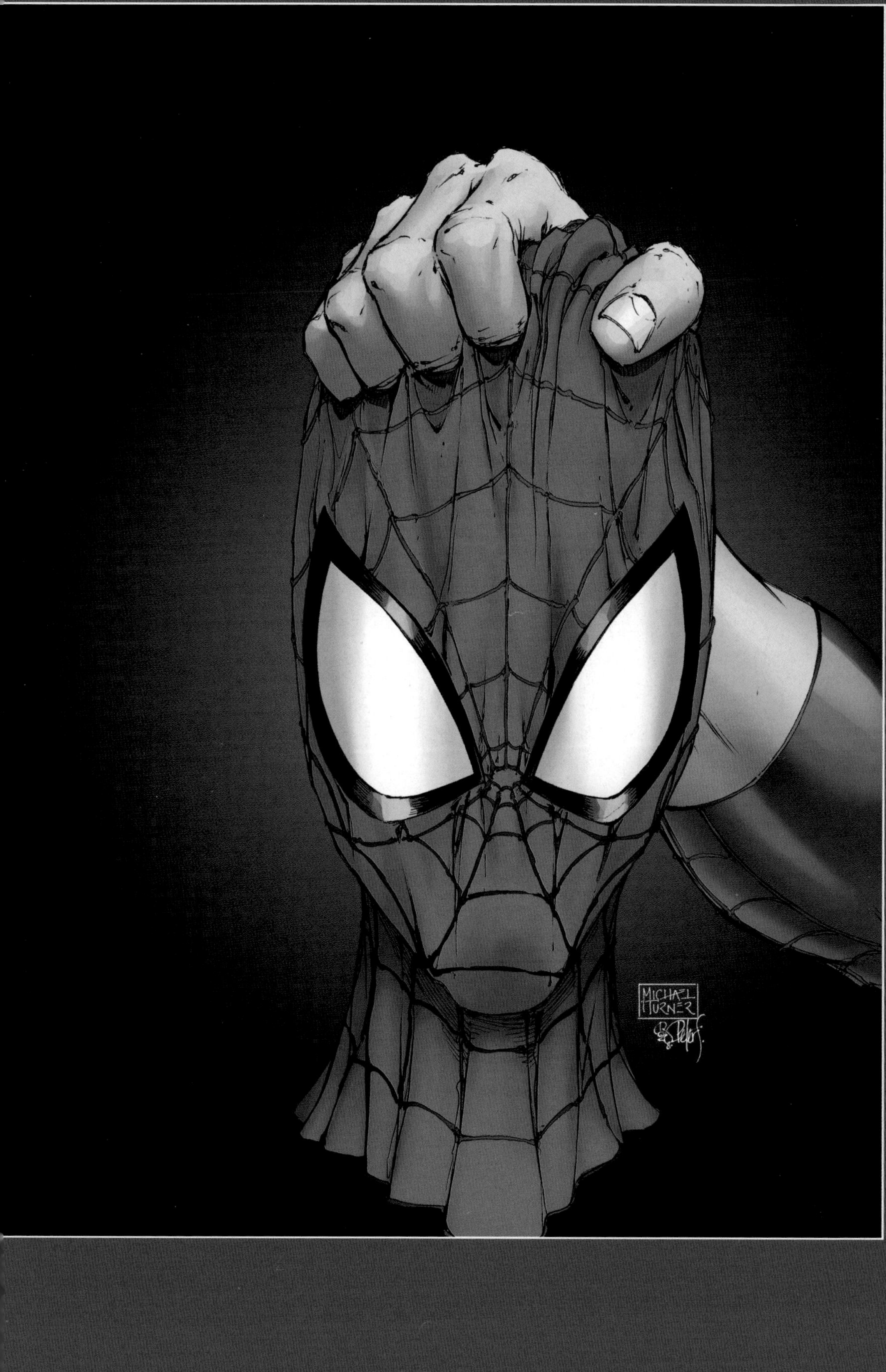
MICHAEL TURNER

WIZARD #179 COVER BY MICHAEL TURNER & PETER STEIGERWALD

THE AMAZING SPIDER-MAN

A MARVEL COMICS EVENT

CIVIL WAR

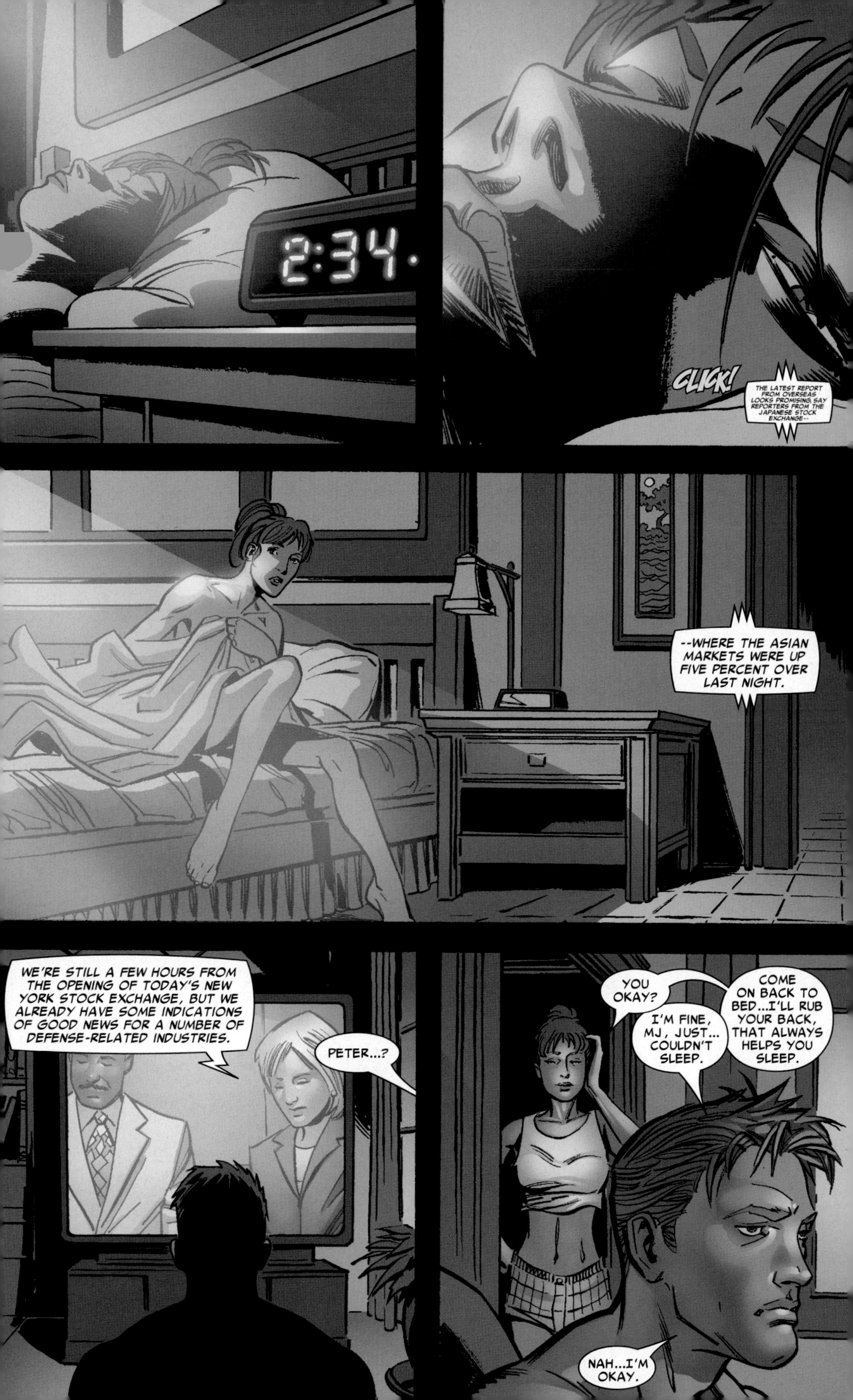
2:34
CLICK!
THE LATEST REPORT FROM OVERSEAS LOOKS PROMISING, SAY REPORTERS FROM THE JAPANESE STOCK EXCHANGE--
--WHERE THE ASIAN MARKETS WERE UP FIVE PERCENT OVER LAST NIGHT.
WE'RE STILL A FEW HOURS FROM THE OPENING OF TODAY'S NEW YORK STOCK EXCHANGE, BUT WE ALREADY HAVE SOME INDICATIONS OF GOOD NEWS FOR A NUMBER OF DEFENSE-RELATED INDUSTRIES.
PETER...?
YOU OKAY?
I'M FINE, MJ, JUST... COULDN'T SLEEP.
COME ON BACK TO BED...I'LL RUB YOUR BACK, THAT ALWAYS HELPS YOU SLEEP.
NAH...I'M OKAY.

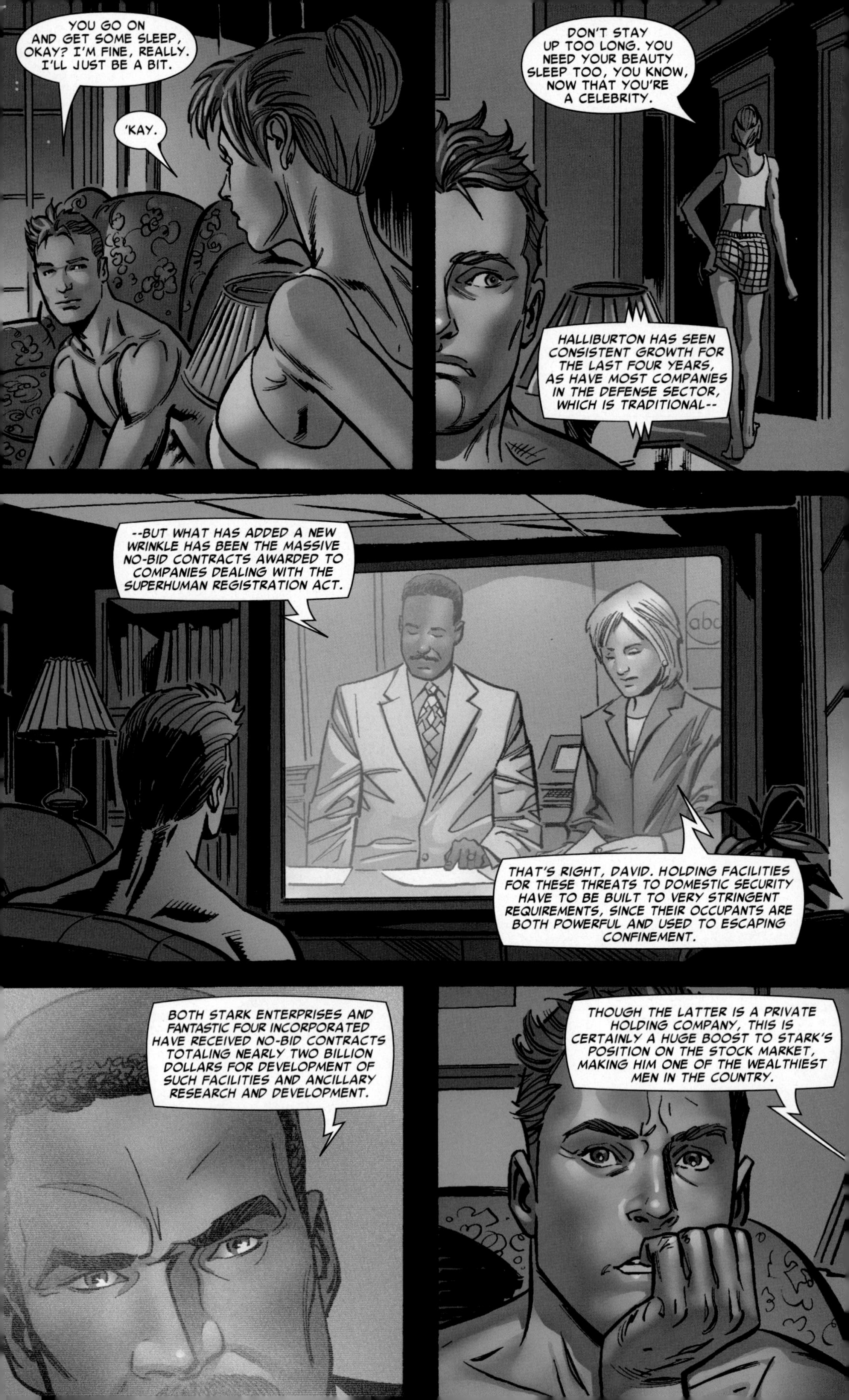
YOU GO ON AND GET SOME SLEEP, OKAY? I'M FINE, REALLY. I'LL JUST BE A BIT.
'KAY.
DON'T STAY UP TOO LONG. YOU NEED YOUR BEAUTY SLEEP TOO, YOU KNOW, NOW THAT YOU'RE A CELEBRITY.
HALLIBURTON HAS SEEN CONSISTENT GROWTH FOR THE LAST FOUR YEARS, AS HAVE MOST COMPANIES IN THE DEFENSE SECTOR, WHICH IS TRADITIONAL--
--BUT WHAT HAS ADDED A NEW WRINKLE HAS BEEN THE MASSIVE NO-BID CONTRACTS AWARDED TO COMPANIES DEALING WITH THE SUPERHUMAN REGISTRATION ACT.
abc
THAT'S RIGHT, DAVID. HOLDING FACILITIES FOR THESE THREATS TO DOMESTIC SECURITY HAVE TO BE BUILT TO VERY STRINGENT REQUIREMENTS, SINCE THEIR OCCUPANTS ARE BOTH POWERFUL AND USED TO ESCAPING CONFINEMENT.
BOTH STARK ENTERPRISES AND FANTASTIC FOUR INCORPORATED HAVE RECEIVED NO-BID CONTRACTS TOTALING NEARLY TWO BILLION DOLLARS FOR DEVELOPMENT OF SUCH FACILITIES AND ANCILLARY RESEARCH AND DEVELOPMENT.
THOUGH THE LATTER IS A PRIVATE HOLDING COMPANY, THIS IS CERTAINLY A HUGE BOOST TO STARK'S POSITION ON THE STOCK MARKET, MAKING HIM ONE OF THE WEALTHIEST MEN IN THE COUNTRY.

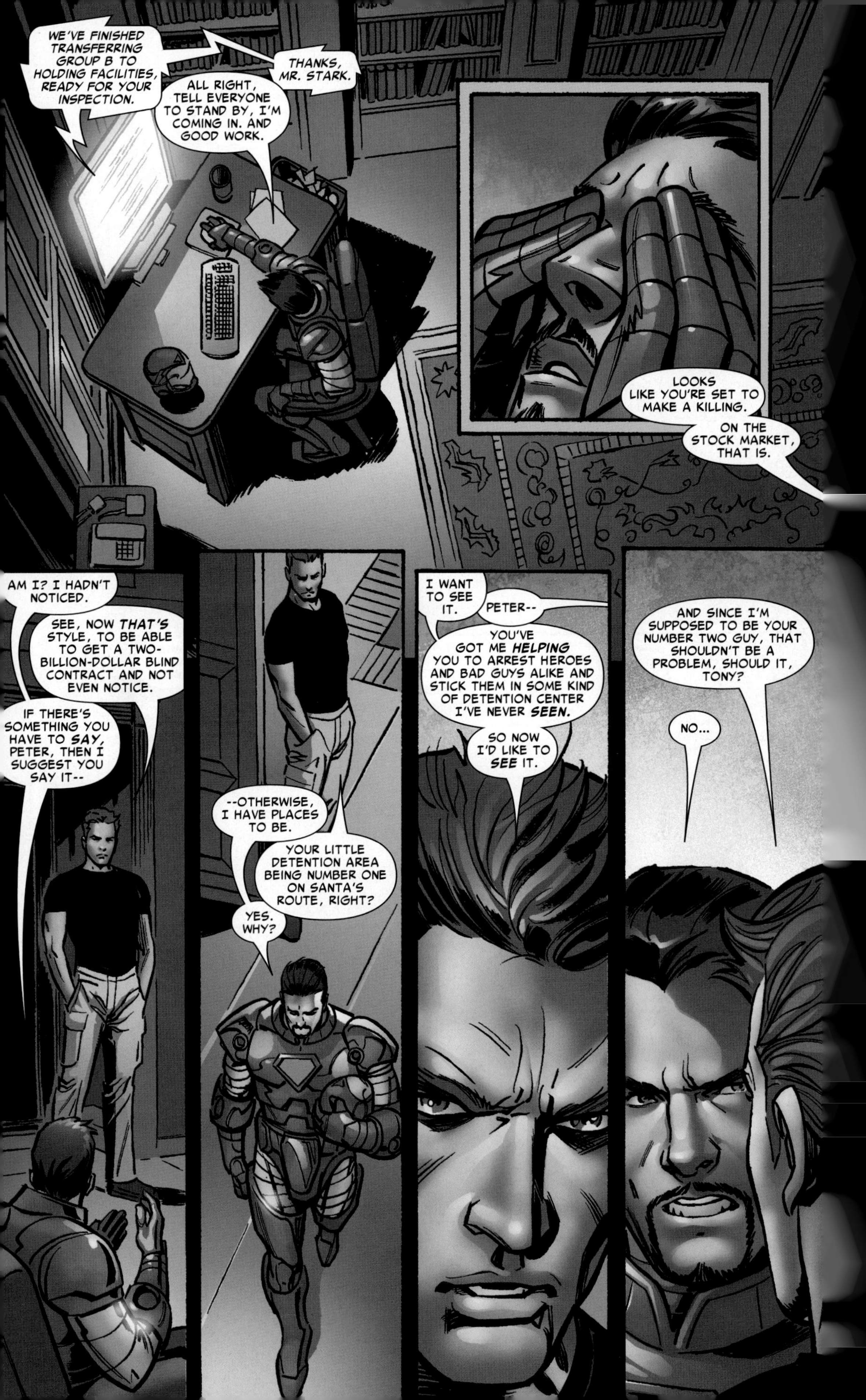
WE'VE FINISHED TRANSFERRING GROUP B TO HOLDING FACILITIES, READY FOR YOUR INSPECTION.
THANKS, MR. STARK.
ALL RIGHT, TELL EVERYONE TO STAND BY, I'M COMING IN. AND GOOD WORK.
LOOKS LIKE YOU'RE SET TO MAKE A KILLING.
ON THE STOCK MARKET, THAT IS.
AM I? I HADN'T NOTICED.
SEE, NOW THAT'S STYLE, TO BE ABLE TO GET A TWO-BILLION-DOLLAR BLIND CONTRACT AND NOT EVEN NOTICE.
IF THERE'S SOMETHING YOU HAVE TO SAY, PETER, THEN I SUGGEST YOU SAY IT--
--OTHERWISE, I HAVE PLACES TO BE.
YOUR LITTLE DETENTION AREA BEING NUMBER ONE ON SANTA'S ROUTE, RIGHT?
YES. WHY?
I WANT TO SEE IT.
PETER--
YOU'VE GOT ME HELPING YOU TO ARREST HEROES AND BAD GUYS ALIKE AND STICK THEM IN SOME KIND OF DETENTION CENTER I'VE NEVER SEEN.
SO NOW I'D LIKE TO SEE IT.
AND SINCE I'M SUPPOSED TO BE YOUR NUMBER TWO GUY, THAT SHOULDN'T BE A PROBLEM, SHOULD IT, TONY?
NO...

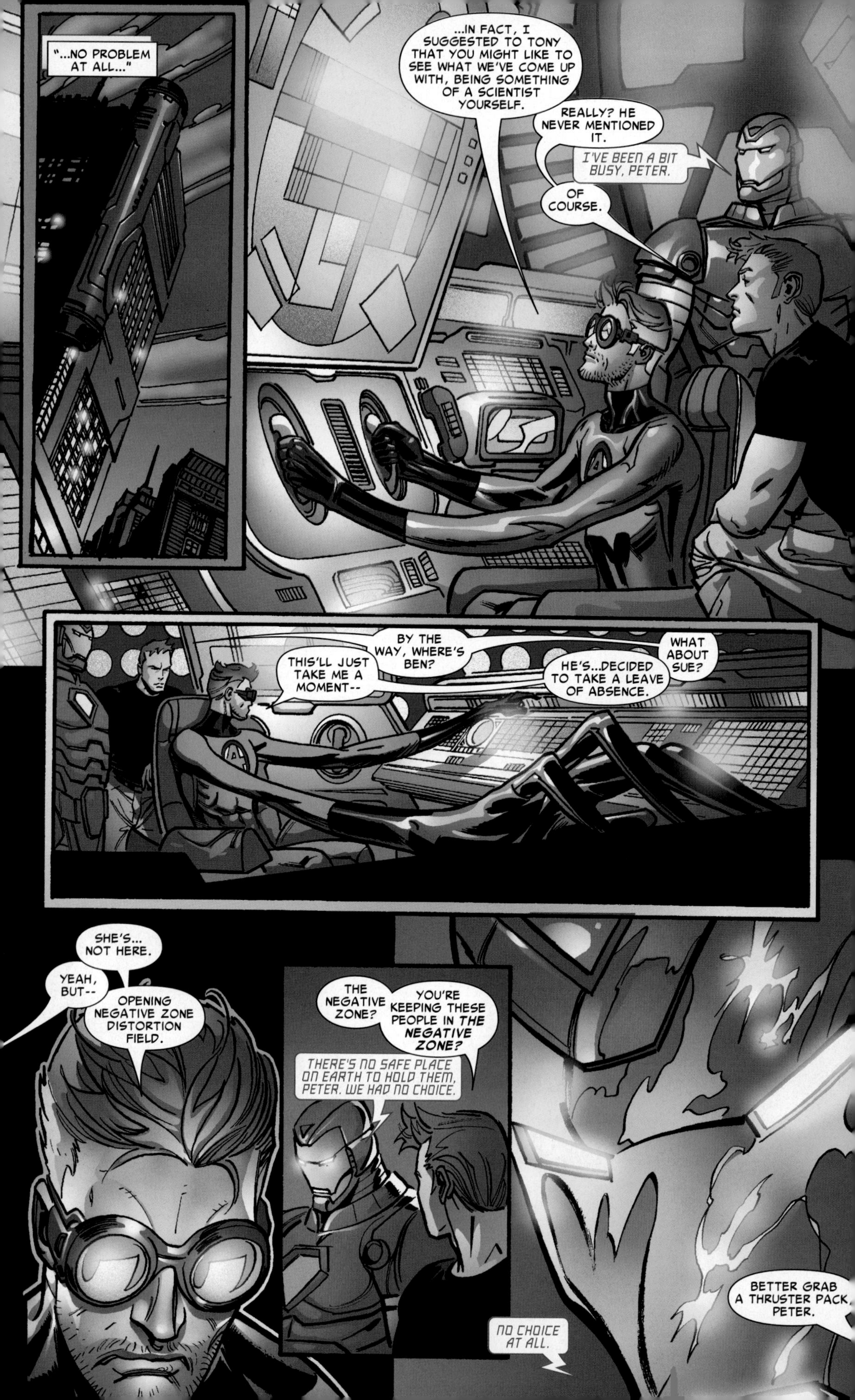
"...NO PROBLEM AT ALL..."
...IN FACT, I SUGGESTED TO TONY THAT YOU MIGHT LIKE TO SEE WHAT WE'VE COME UP WITH, BEING SOMETHING OF A SCIENTIST YOURSELF.
REALLY? HE NEVER MENTIONED IT.
I'VE BEEN A BIT BUSY, PETER.
OF COURSE.
THIS'LL JUST TAKE ME A MOMENT--
BY THE WAY, WHERE'S BEN?
HE'S...DECIDED TO TAKE A LEAVE OF ABSENCE.
WHAT ABOUT SUE?
SHE'S... NOT HERE.
YEAH, BUT--
OPENING NEGATIVE ZONE DISTORTION FIELD.
THE NEGATIVE ZONE?
YOU'RE KEEPING THESE PEOPLE IN THE NEGATIVE ZONE?
THERE'S NO SAFE PLACE ON EARTH TO HOLD THEM, PETER. WE HAD NO CHOICE.
NO CHOICE AT ALL.
BETTER GRAB A THRUSTER PACK, PETER.

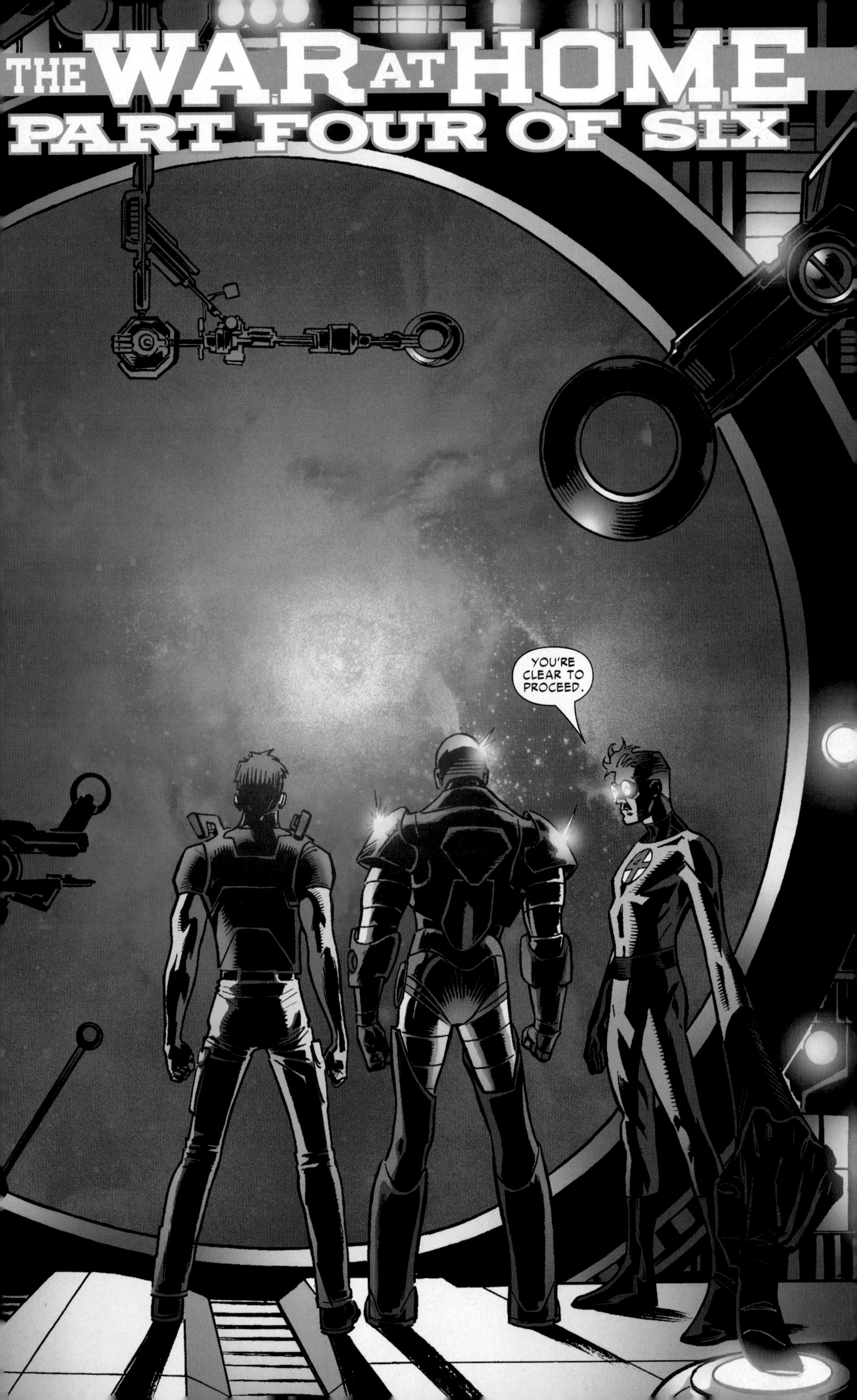
THE WAR AT HOME
PART FOUR OF SIX
YOU'RE CLEAR TO PROCEED.

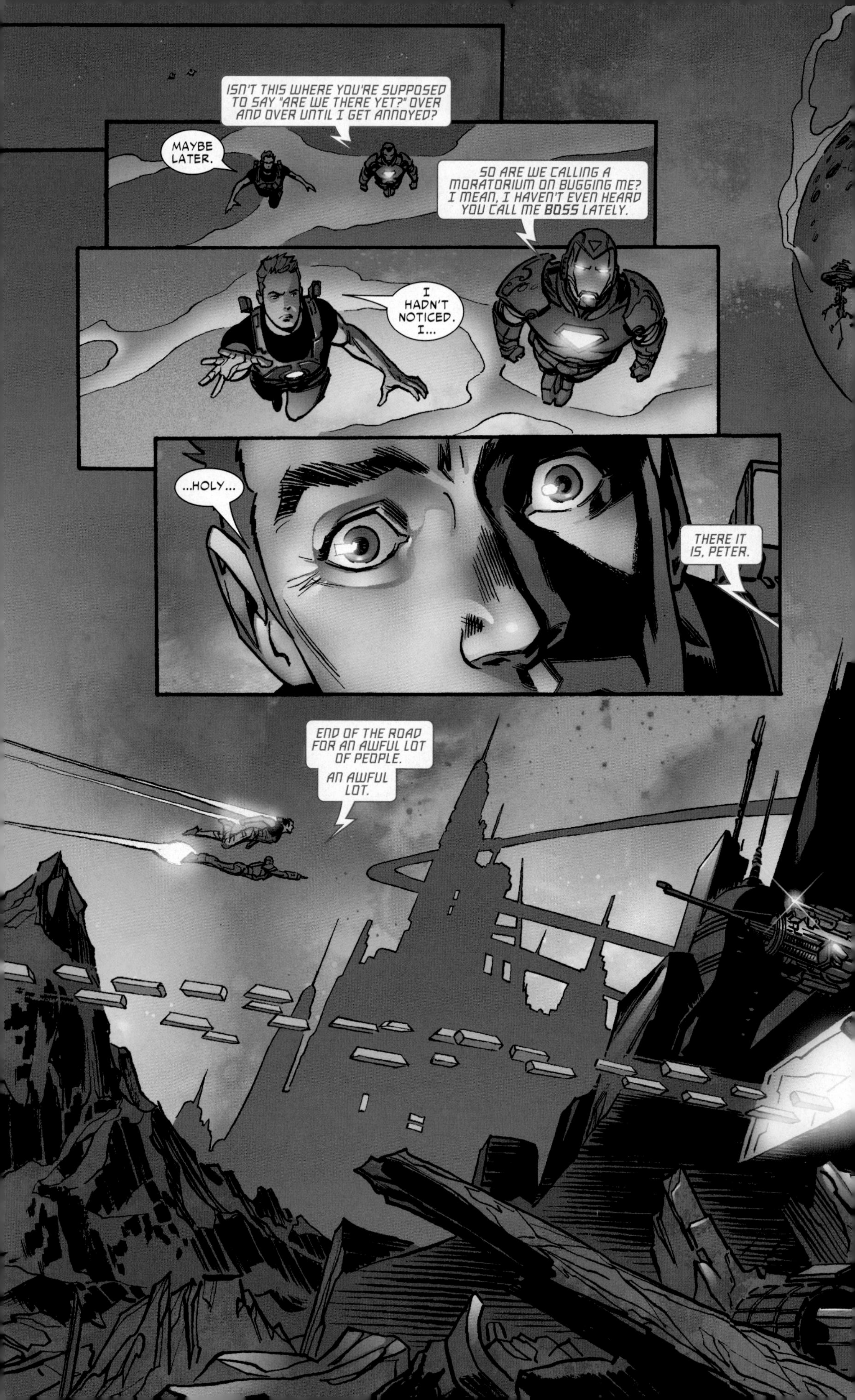
ISN'T THIS WHERE YOU'RE SUPPOSED TO SAY "ARE WE THERE YET?" OVER AND OVER UNTIL I GET ANNOYED?
MAYBE LATER.
SO ARE WE CALLING A MORATORIUM ON BUGGING ME? I MEAN, I HAVEN'T EVEN HEARD YOU CALL ME BOSS LATELY.
I HADN'T NOTICED. I...
...HOLY...
THERE IT IS, PETER.
END OF THE ROAD FOR AN AWFUL LOT OF PEOPLE.
AN AWFUL LOT.

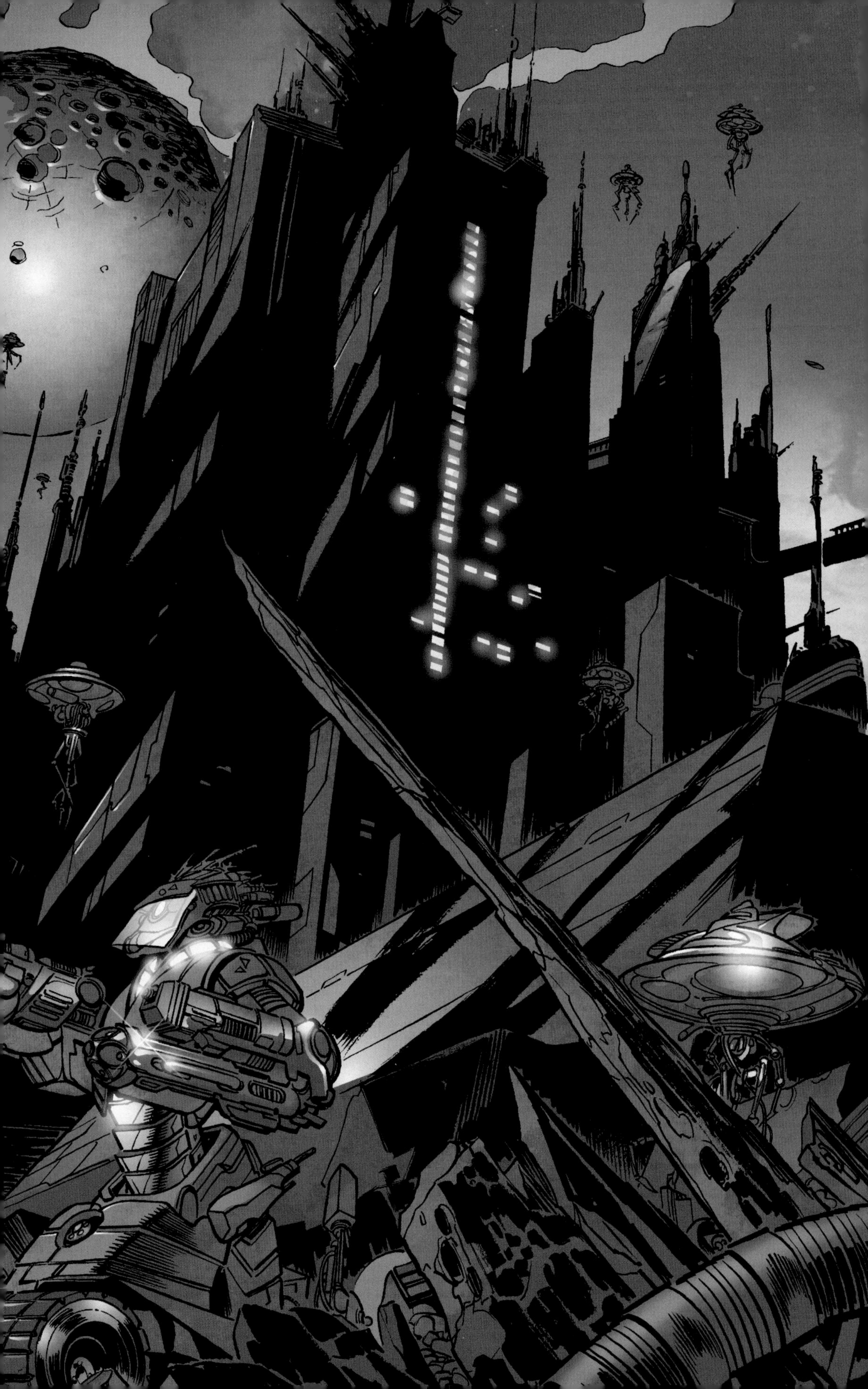

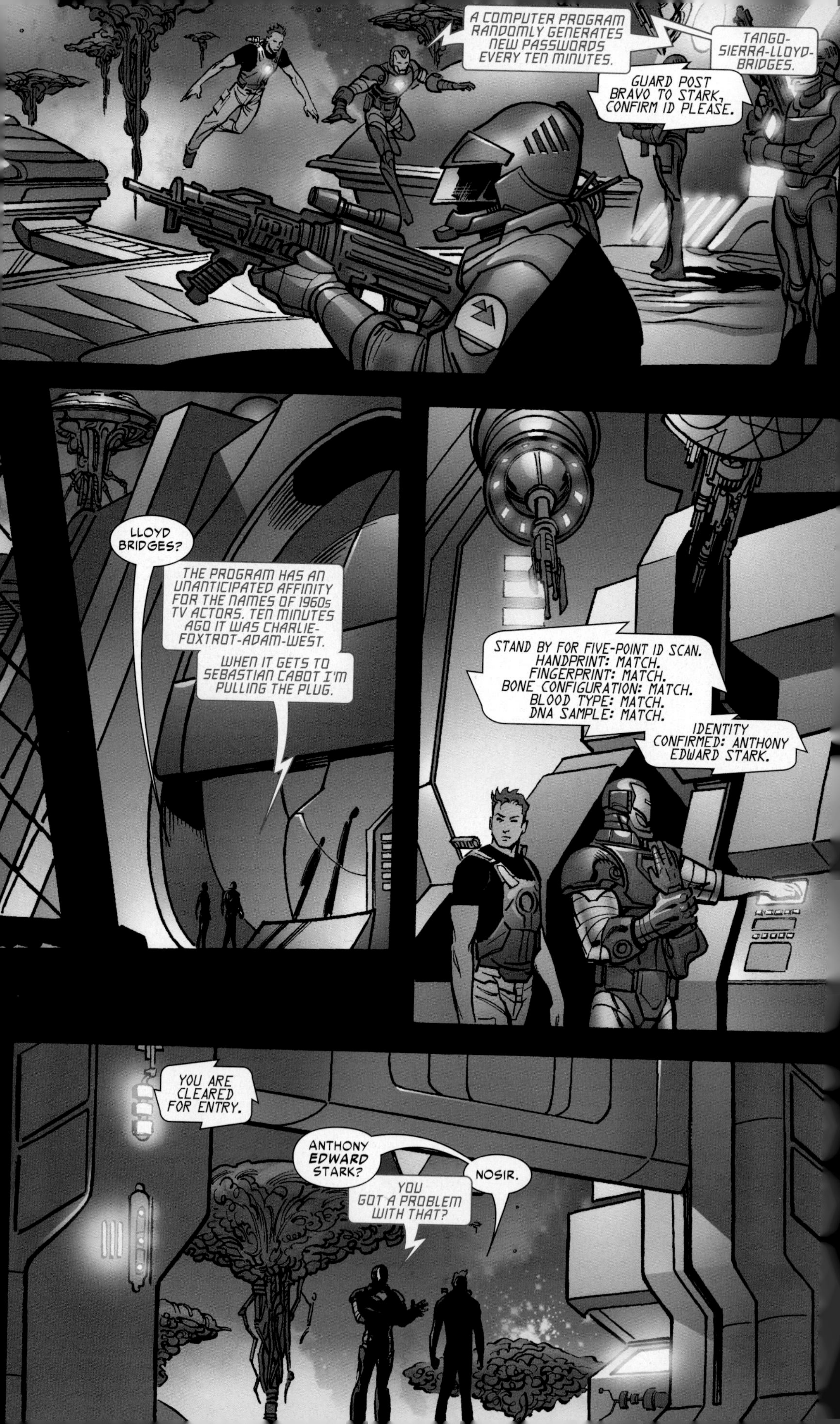
A COMPUTER PROGRAM RANDOMLY GENERATES NEW PASSWORDS EVERY TEN MINUTES.
TANGO-SIERRA-LLOYD-BRIDGES.
GUARD POST BRAVO TO STARK, CONFIRM ID PLEASE.
LLOYD BRIDGES?
THE PROGRAM HAS AN UNANTICIPATED AFFINITY FOR THE NAMES OF 1960s TV ACTORS. TEN MINUTES AGO IT WAS CHARLIE-FOXTROT-ADAM-WEST.
WHEN IT GETS TO SEBASTIAN CABOT I'M PULLING THE PLUG.
STAND BY FOR FIVE-POINT ID SCAN. HANDPRINT: MATCH. FINGERPRINT: MATCH. BONE CONFIGURATION: MATCH. BLOOD TYPE: MATCH. DNA SAMPLE: MATCH.
IDENTITY CONFIRMED: ANTHONY EDWARD STARK.
YOU ARE CLEARED FOR ENTRY.
ANTHONY EDWARD STARK?
NOSIR.
YOU GOT A PROBLEM WITH THAT?

THE DOORS, FLOORS, CEILINGS AND WALLS ARE MADE WITH A NEW KIND OF SYNTHETIC VIBRANIUM. IT'S NOT AS STRONG AS THE REAL THING, BUT WHEN YOU BUILD IT THIS THICK, IT DOESN'T HAVE TO BE.

EVERY CELL IS CUSTOMIZED TO HOLD ITS UNIQUE OCCUPANT. IF HE CONTROLS FIRE, THE ROOM EMITS COLD; IF THE OCCUPANT EMITS A FREQUENCY, THE ROOM EMITS A COUNTER-FREQUENCY.

THEY'RE JUST WORDS, PETER...

"THE OCCUPANT." SOUNDS LIKE A HOTEL. DON'T YOU MEAN "THE PRISONER"?

NAME: RICHARD GILMORE
ALIAS: PRODIGY
PRISONER ID: N

...JUST WORDS.

HEY...HEY! WHOEVER YOU ARE... CAN YOU HELP ME? PLEASE? THERE'S...THERE'S BEEN SOME KIND OF MISUNDERSTANDING... I SHOULDN'T BE HERE...I DIDN'T DO ANYTHING...

THEY ALL SAY PRETTY MUCH THE SAME THING. WE DO ALL WE CAN TO MAKE THEM COMFORTABLE DURING THEIR STAY.

WE EVEN PROVIDE VIRTUAL REALITY SYSTEMS FOR THOSE WHO DON'T REPRESENT A TECH-THREAT.

THIS WAY, EVEN THOUGH THEY'RE INSIDE--

--THEY CAN FEEL AS IF THEY'RE OUTSIDE.

HELP ME... PLEASE... HELP ME...

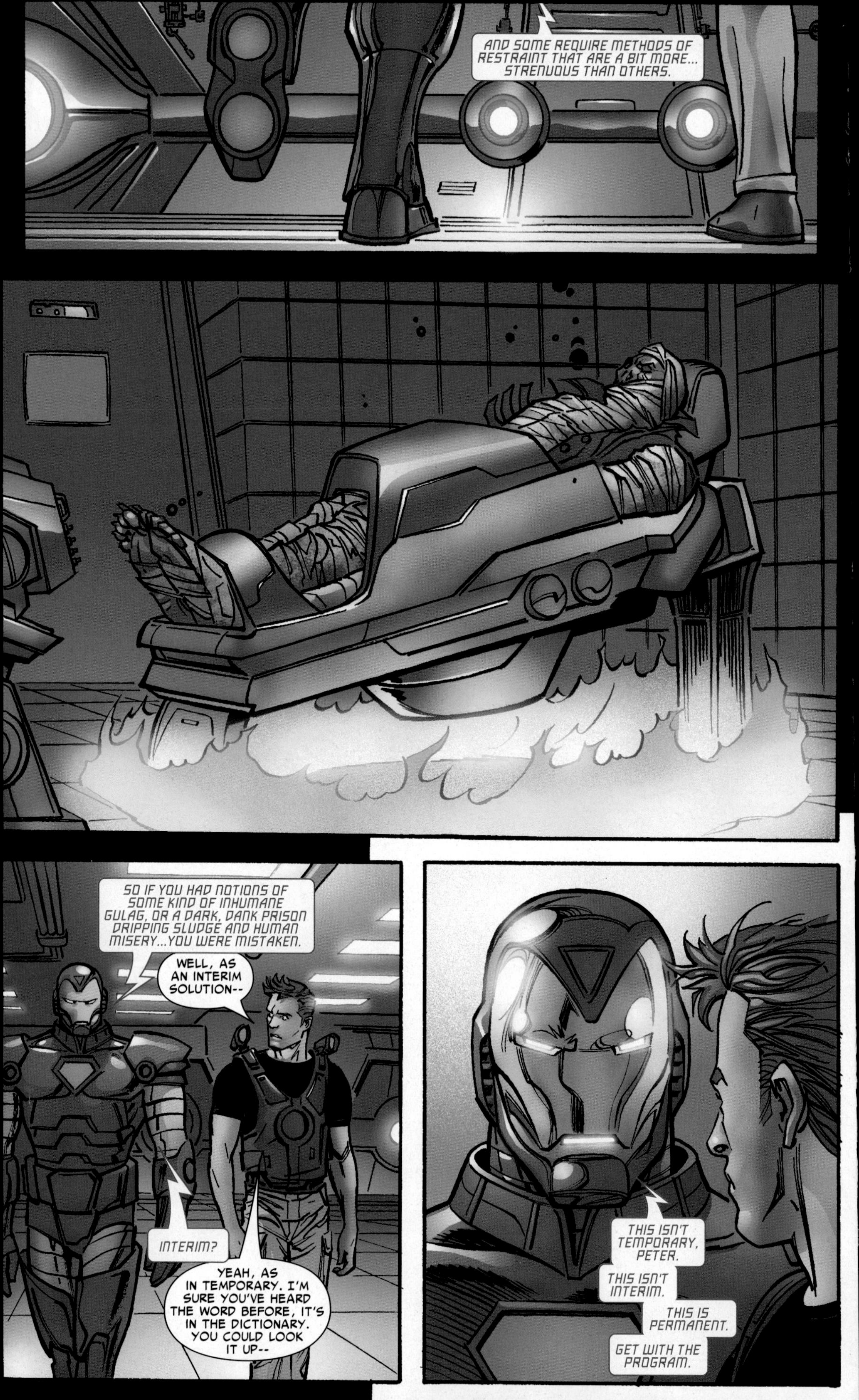
AND SOME REQUIRE METHODS OF RESTRAINT THAT ARE A BIT MORE... STRENUOUS THAN OTHERS.
SO IF YOU HAD NOTIONS OF SOME KIND OF INHUMANE GULAG, OR A DARK, DANK PRISON DRIPPING SLUDGE AND HUMAN MISERY...YOU WERE MISTAKEN.
WELL, AS AN INTERIM SOLUTION--
INTERIM?
YEAH, AS IN TEMPORARY. I'M SURE YOU'VE HEARD THE WORD BEFORE, IT'S IN THE DICTIONARY. YOU COULD LOOK IT UP--
THIS ISN'T TEMPORARY, PETER.
THIS ISN'T INTERIM.
THIS IS PERMANENT.
GET WITH THE PROGRAM.

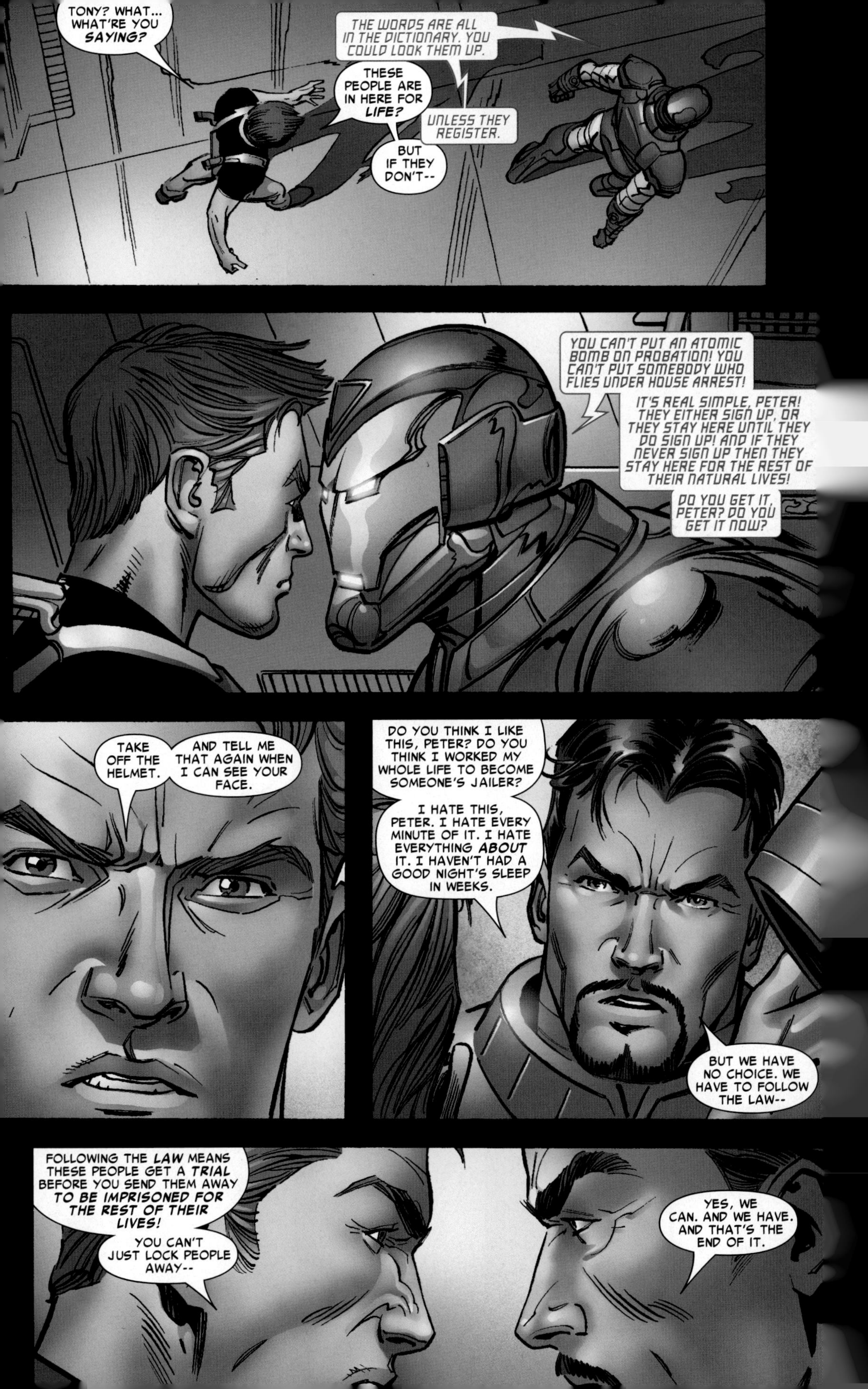

TONY? WHAT... WHAT'RE YOU SAYING?
THE WORDS ARE ALL IN THE DICTIONARY. YOU COULD LOOK THEM UP.
THESE PEOPLE ARE IN HERE FOR LIFE?
UNLESS THEY REGISTER.
BUT IF THEY DON'T--
YOU CAN'T PUT AN ATOMIC BOMB ON PROBATION! YOU CAN'T PUT SOMEBODY WHO FLIES UNDER HOUSE ARREST!
IT'S REAL SIMPLE, PETER! THEY EITHER SIGN UP, OR THEY STAY HERE UNTIL THEY DO SIGN UP! AND IF THEY NEVER SIGN UP THEN THEY STAY HERE FOR THE REST OF THEIR NATURAL LIVES!
DO YOU GET IT, PETER? DO YOU GET IT NOW?
TAKE OFF THE HELMET.
AND TELL ME THAT AGAIN WHEN I CAN SEE YOUR FACE.
DO YOU THINK I LIKE THIS, PETER? DO YOU THINK I WORKED MY WHOLE LIFE TO BECOME SOMEONE'S JAILER?
I HATE THIS, PETER. I HATE EVERY MINUTE OF IT. I HATE EVERYTHING ABOUT IT. I HAVEN'T HAD A GOOD NIGHT'S SLEEP IN WEEKS.
BUT WE HAVE NO CHOICE. WE HAVE TO FOLLOW THE LAW--
FOLLOWING THE LAW MEANS THESE PEOPLE GET A TRIAL BEFORE YOU SEND THEM AWAY TO BE IMPRISONED FOR THE REST OF THEIR LIVES!
YOU CAN'T JUST LOCK PEOPLE AWAY--
YES, WE CAN. AND WE HAVE. AND THAT'S THE END OF IT.

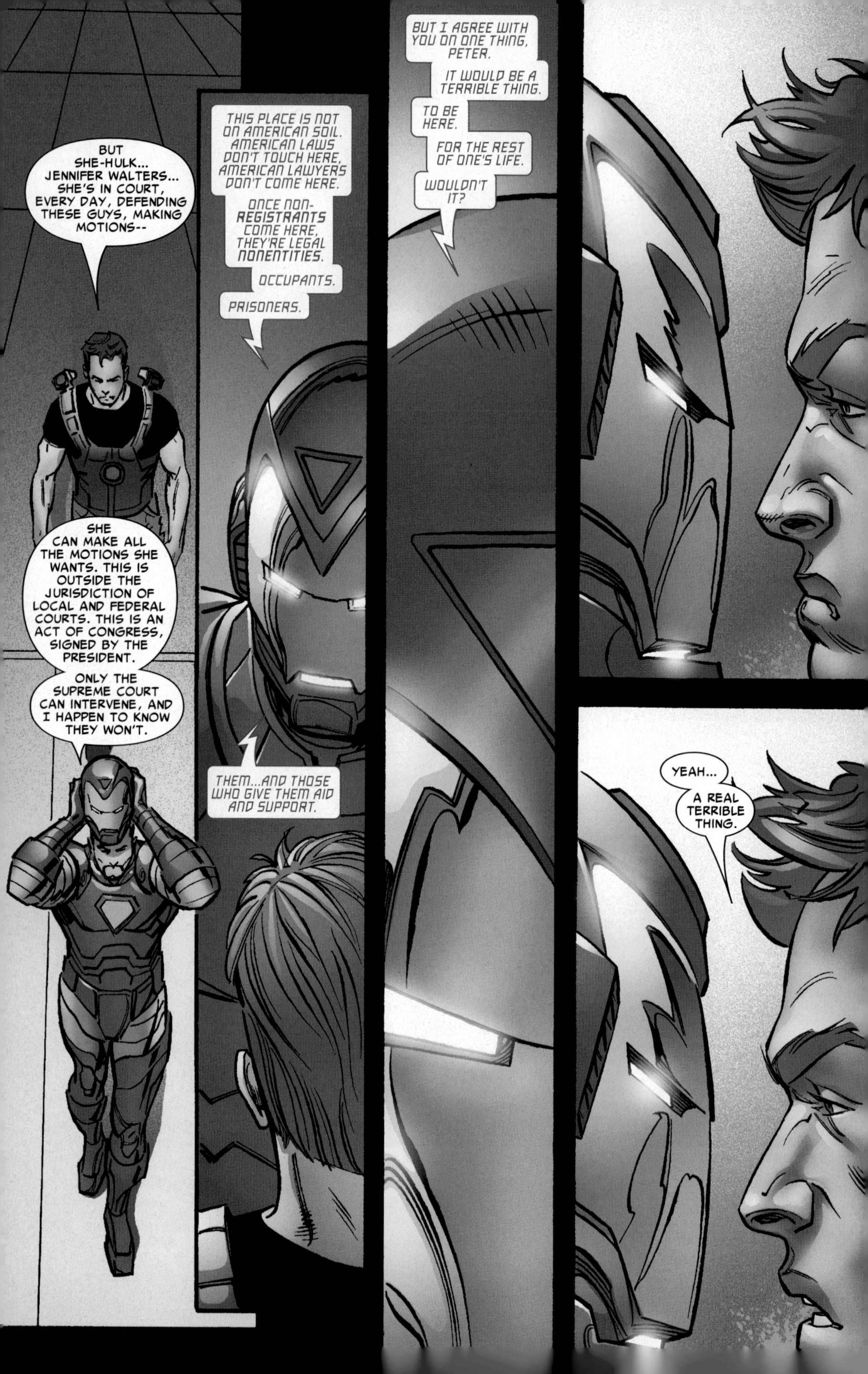
BUT SHE-HULK... JENNIFER WALTERS... SHE'S IN COURT, EVERY DAY, DEFENDING THESE GUYS, MAKING MOTIONS--
SHE CAN MAKE ALL THE MOTIONS SHE WANTS. THIS IS OUTSIDE THE JURISDICTION OF LOCAL AND FEDERAL COURTS. THIS IS AN ACT OF CONGRESS, SIGNED BY THE PRESIDENT.
ONLY THE SUPREME COURT CAN INTERVENE, AND I HAPPEN TO KNOW THEY WON'T.
THIS PLACE IS NOT ON AMERICAN SOIL. AMERICAN LAWS DON'T TOUCH HERE, AMERICAN LAWYERS DON'T COME HERE.
ONCE NON-REGISTRANTS COME HERE, THEY'RE LEGAL NONENTITIES.
OCCUPANTS.
PRISONERS.
THEM...AND THOSE WHO GIVE THEM AID AND SUPPORT.
BUT I AGREE WITH YOU ON ONE THING, PETER.
IT WOULD BE A TERRIBLE THING.
TO BE HERE.
FOR THE REST OF ONE'S LIFE.
WOULDN'T IT?
YEAH...
A REAL TERRIBLE THING.

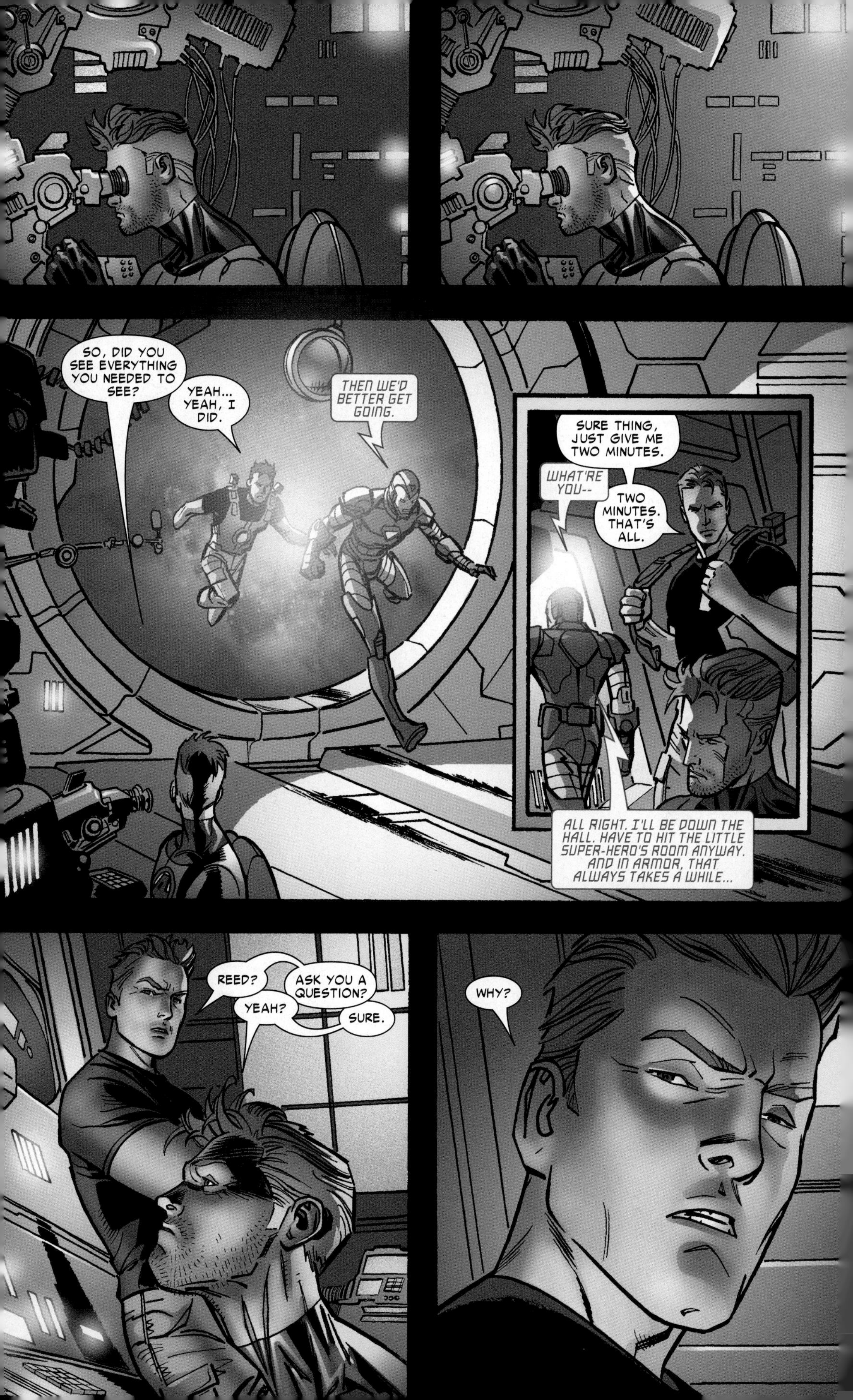
SO, DID YOU SEE EVERYTHING YOU NEEDED TO SEE?
YEAH... YEAH, I DID.
THEN WE'D BETTER GET GOING.
SURE THING, JUST GIVE ME TWO MINUTES.
WHAT'RE YOU--
TWO MINUTES. THAT'S ALL.
ALL RIGHT. I'LL BE DOWN THE HALL. HAVE TO HIT THE LITTLE SUPER-HERO'S ROOM ANYWAY. AND IN ARMOR, THAT ALWAYS TAKES A WHILE...
REED?
YEAH?
ASK YOU A QUESTION?
SURE.
WHY?

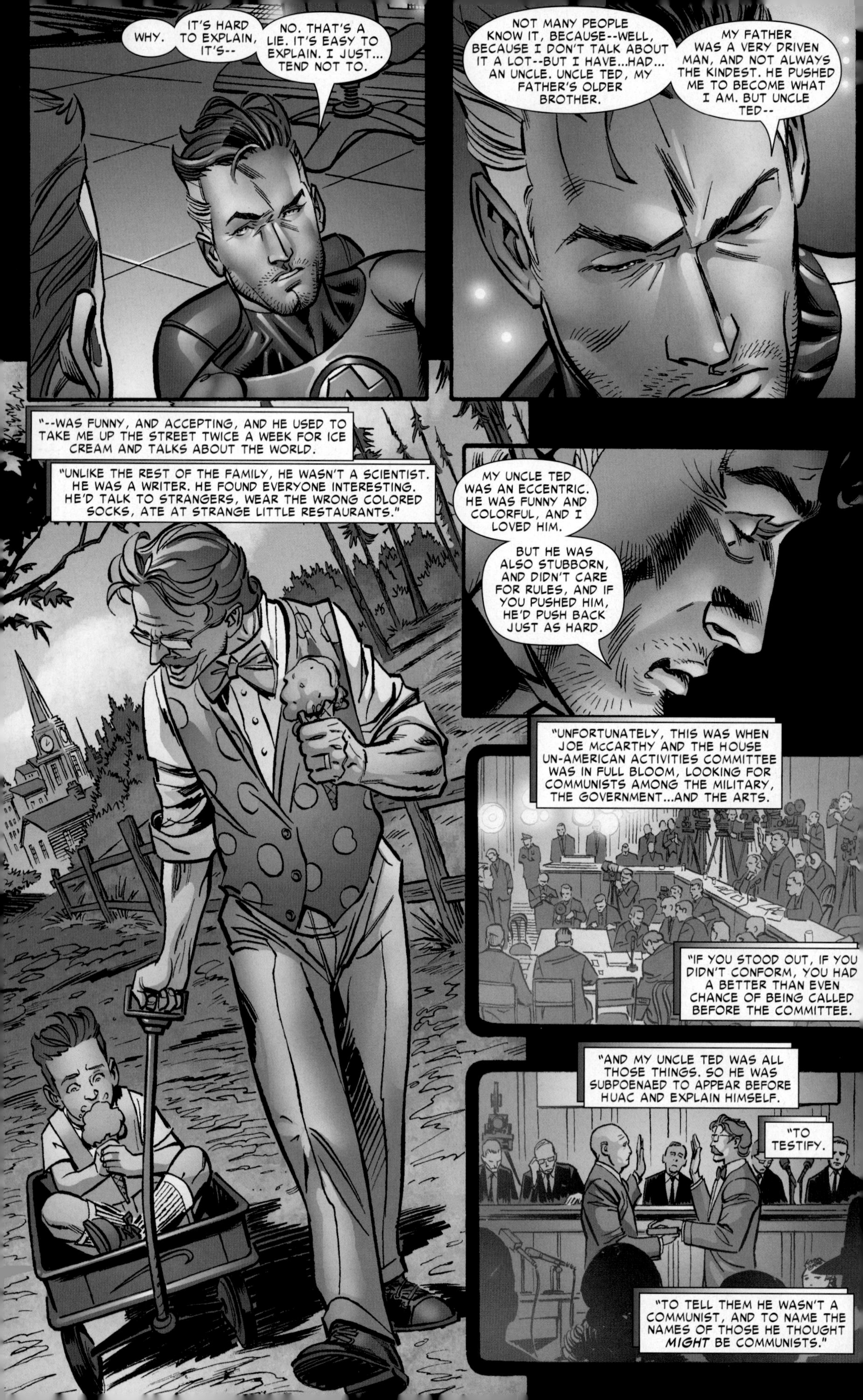
WHY.
IT'S HARD TO EXPLAIN, IT'S--
NO. THAT'S A LIE. IT'S EASY TO EXPLAIN. I JUST... TEND NOT TO.
NOT MANY PEOPLE KNOW IT, BECAUSE--WELL, BECAUSE I DON'T TALK ABOUT IT A LOT--BUT I HAVE...HAD... AN UNCLE. UNCLE TED, MY FATHER'S OLDER BROTHER.
MY FATHER WAS A VERY DRIVEN MAN, AND NOT ALWAYS THE KINDEST. HE PUSHED ME TO BECOME WHAT I AM. BUT UNCLE TED--
"--WAS FUNNY, AND ACCEPTING, AND HE USED TO TAKE ME UP THE STREET TWICE A WEEK FOR ICE CREAM AND TALKS ABOUT THE WORLD.
"UNLIKE THE REST OF THE FAMILY, HE WASN'T A SCIENTIST. HE WAS A WRITER. HE FOUND EVERYONE INTERESTING. HE'D TALK TO STRANGERS, WEAR THE WRONG COLORED SOCKS, ATE AT STRANGE LITTLE RESTAURANTS."
MY UNCLE TED WAS AN ECCENTRIC. HE WAS FUNNY AND COLORFUL, AND I LOVED HIM.
BUT HE WAS ALSO STUBBORN, AND DIDN'T CARE FOR RULES, AND IF YOU PUSHED HIM, HE'D PUSH BACK JUST AS HARD.
"UNFORTUNATELY, THIS WAS WHEN JOE McCARTHY AND THE HOUSE UN-AMERICAN ACTIVITIES COMMITTEE WAS IN FULL BLOOM, LOOKING FOR COMMUNISTS AMONG THE MILITARY, THE GOVERNMENT...AND THE ARTS.
"IF YOU STOOD OUT, IF YOU DIDN'T CONFORM, YOU HAD A BETTER THAN EVEN CHANCE OF BEING CALLED BEFORE THE COMMITTEE.
"AND MY UNCLE TED WAS ALL THOSE THINGS. SO HE WAS SUBPOENAED TO APPEAR BEFORE HUAC AND EXPLAIN HIMSELF.
"TO TESTIFY.
"TO TELL THEM HE WASN'T A COMMUNIST, AND TO NAME THE NAMES OF THOSE HE THOUGHT *MIGHT* BE COMMUNISTS."

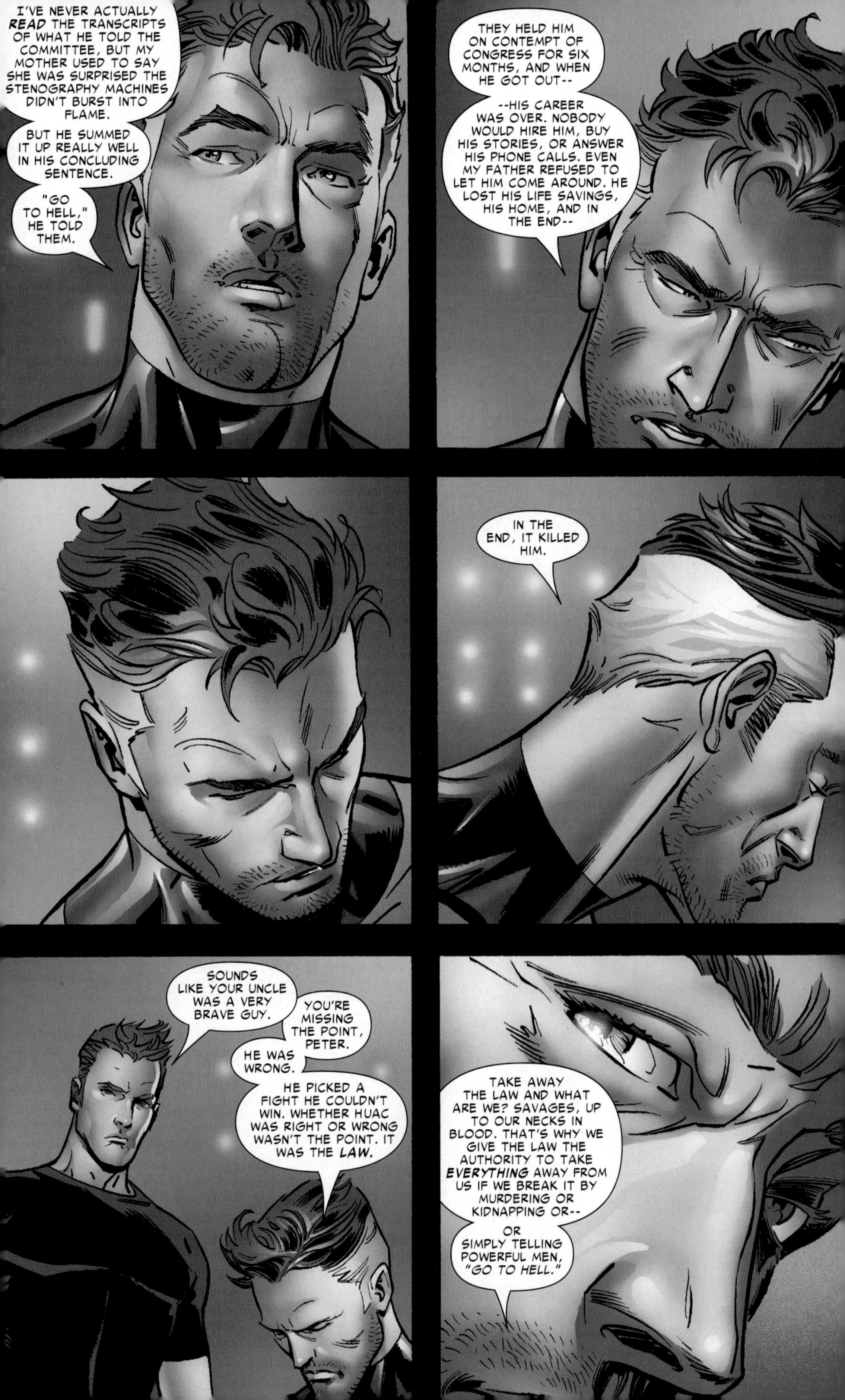
I'VE NEVER ACTUALLY *READ* THE TRANSCRIPTS OF WHAT HE TOLD THE COMMITTEE, BUT MY MOTHER USED TO SAY SHE WAS SURPRISED THE STENOGRAPHY MACHINES DIDN'T BURST INTO FLAME.
BUT HE SUMMED IT UP REALLY WELL IN HIS CONCLUDING SENTENCE.
"GO TO HELL," HE TOLD THEM.
THEY HELD HIM ON CONTEMPT OF CONGRESS FOR SIX MONTHS, AND WHEN HE GOT OUT--
--HIS CAREER WAS OVER. NOBODY WOULD HIRE HIM, BUY HIS STORIES, OR ANSWER HIS PHONE CALLS. EVEN MY FATHER REFUSED TO LET HIM COME AROUND. HE LOST HIS LIFE SAVINGS, HIS HOME, AND IN THE END--
IN THE END, IT KILLED HIM.
SOUNDS LIKE YOUR UNCLE WAS A VERY BRAVE GUY.
YOU'RE MISSING THE POINT, PETER.
HE WAS WRONG.
HE PICKED A FIGHT HE COULDN'T WIN. WHETHER HUAC WAS RIGHT OR WRONG WASN'T THE POINT. IT WAS THE *LAW.*
TAKE AWAY THE LAW AND WHAT ARE WE? SAVAGES, UP TO OUR NECKS IN BLOOD. THAT'S WHY WE GIVE THE LAW THE AUTHORITY TO TAKE *EVERYTHING* AWAY FROM US IF WE BREAK IT BY MURDERING OR KIDNAPPING OR--
OR SIMPLY TELLING POWERFUL MEN, "GO TO HELL."

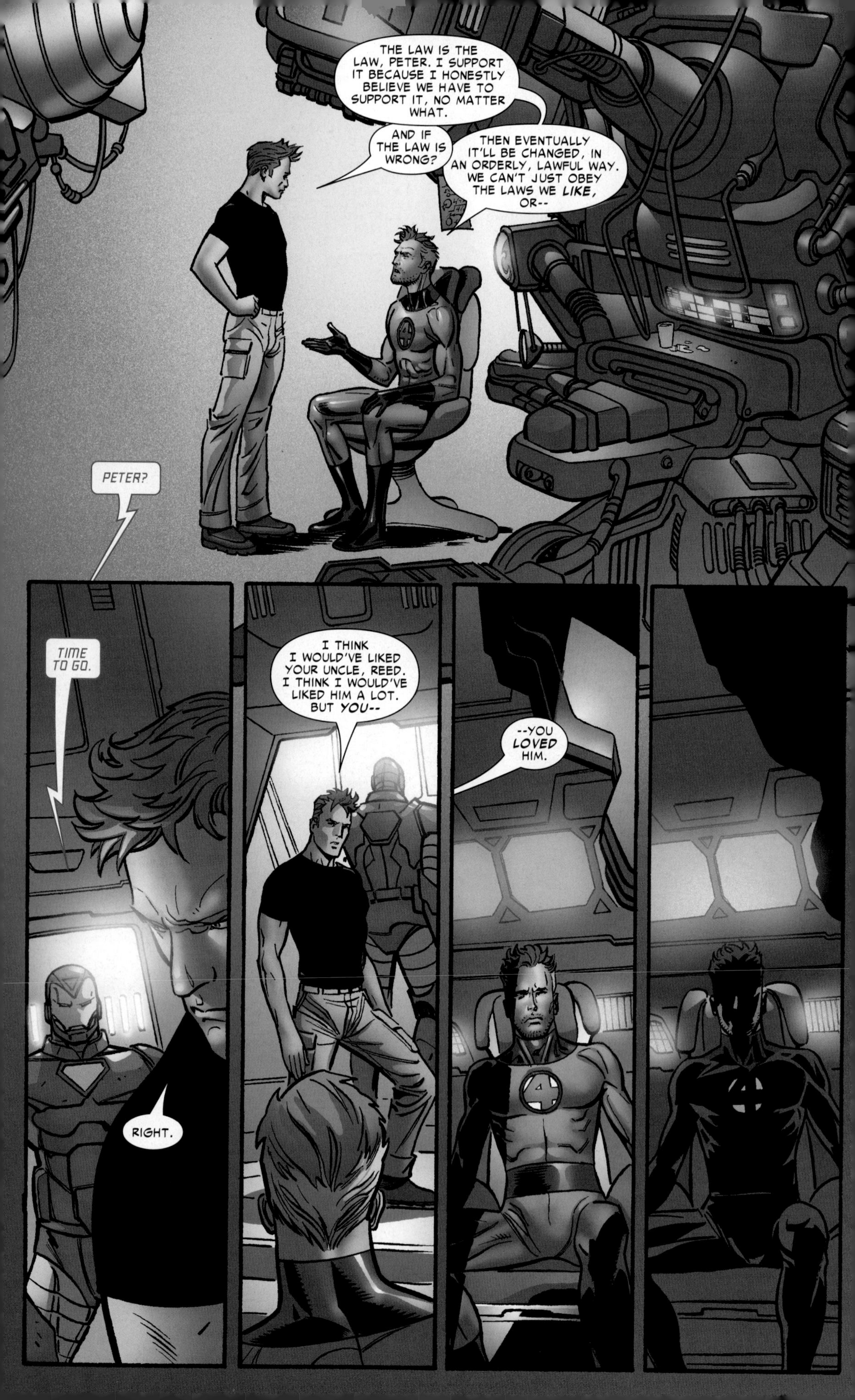
THE LAW IS THE LAW, PETER. I SUPPORT IT BECAUSE I HONESTLY BELIEVE WE HAVE TO SUPPORT IT, NO MATTER WHAT.
AND IF THE LAW IS WRONG?
THEN EVENTUALLY IT'LL BE CHANGED, IN AN ORDERLY, LAWFUL WAY. WE CAN'T JUST OBEY THE LAWS WE LIKE, OR--
PETER?
TIME TO GO.
RIGHT.
I THINK I WOULD'VE LIKED YOUR UNCLE, REED. I THINK I WOULD'VE LIKED HIM A LOT. BUT YOU--
--YOU LOVED HIM.

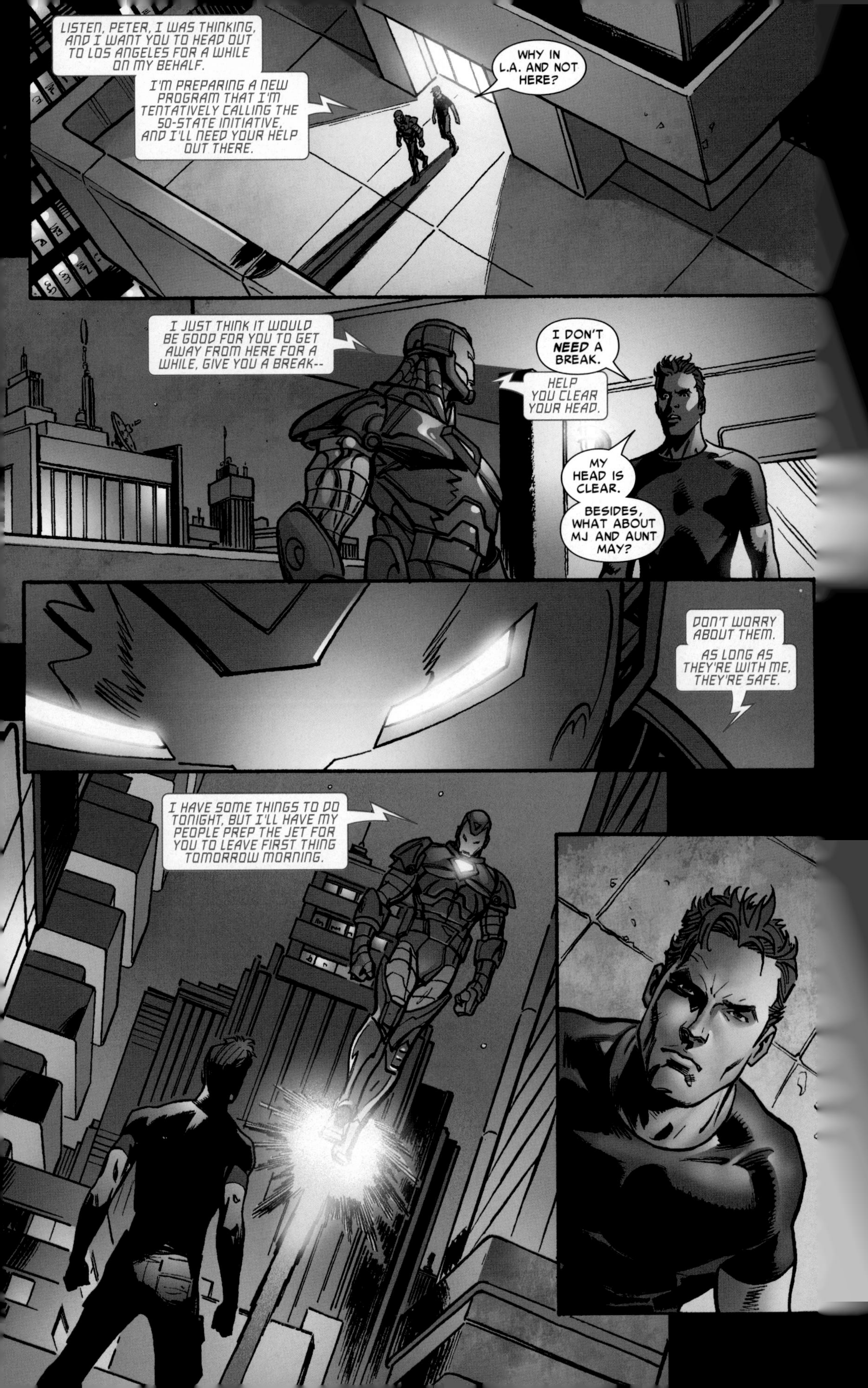
LISTEN, PETER, I WAS THINKING, AND I WANT YOU TO HEAD OUT TO LOS ANGELES FOR A WHILE ON MY BEHALF.
I'M PREPARING A NEW PROGRAM THAT I'M TENTATIVELY CALLING THE 50-STATE INITIATIVE, AND I'LL NEED YOUR HELP OUT THERE.
WHY IN L.A. AND NOT HERE?
I JUST THINK IT WOULD BE GOOD FOR YOU TO GET AWAY FROM HERE FOR A WHILE, GIVE YOU A BREAK--
I DON'T **NEED** A BREAK.
HELP YOU CLEAR YOUR HEAD.
MY HEAD IS CLEAR.
BESIDES, WHAT ABOUT MJ AND AUNT MAY?
DON'T WORRY ABOUT THEM.
AS LONG AS THEY'RE WITH ME, THEY'RE SAFE.
I HAVE SOME THINGS TO DO TONIGHT, BUT I'LL HAVE MY PEOPLE PREP THE JET FOR YOU TO LEAVE FIRST THING TOMORROW MORNING.

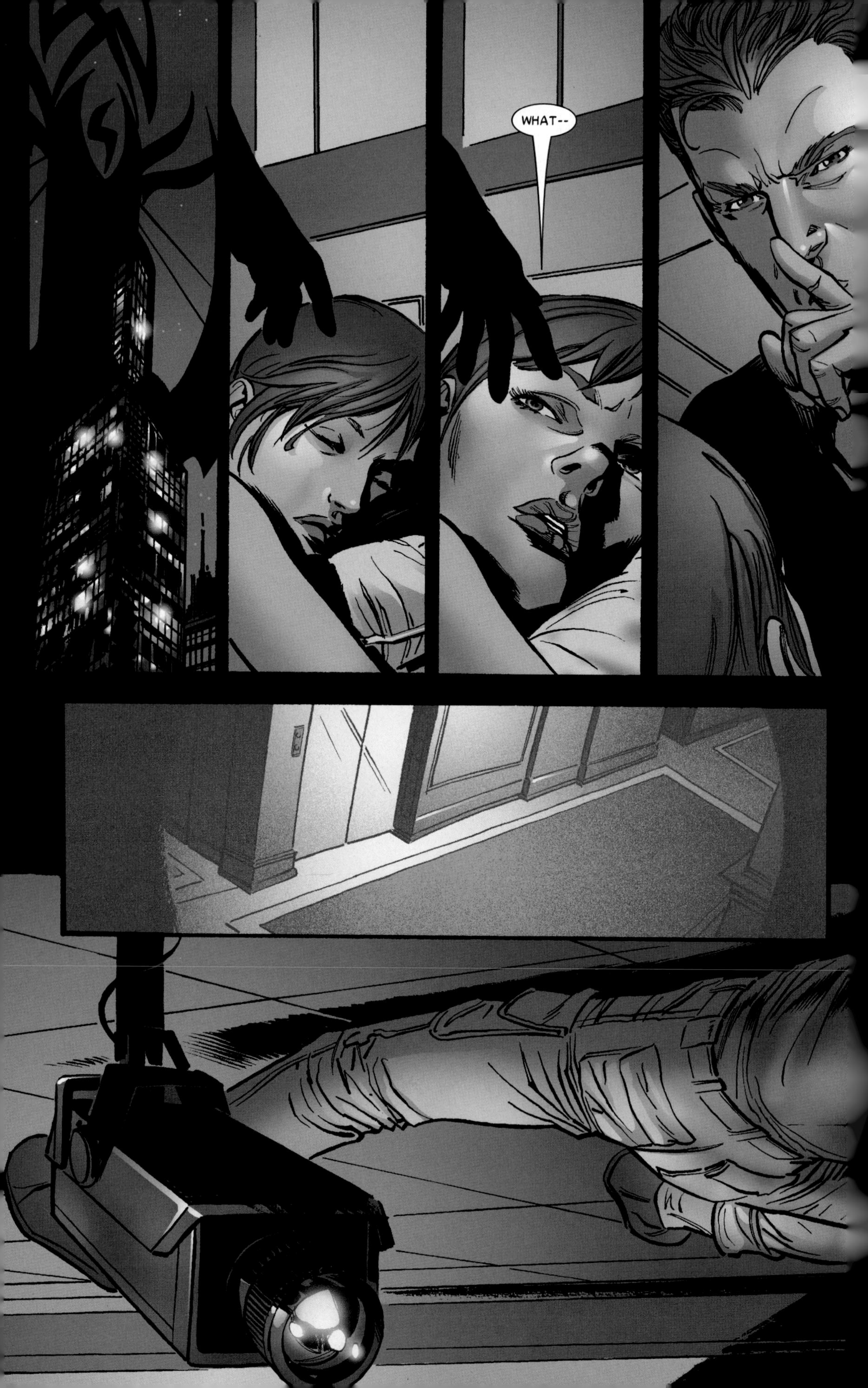
WHAT--

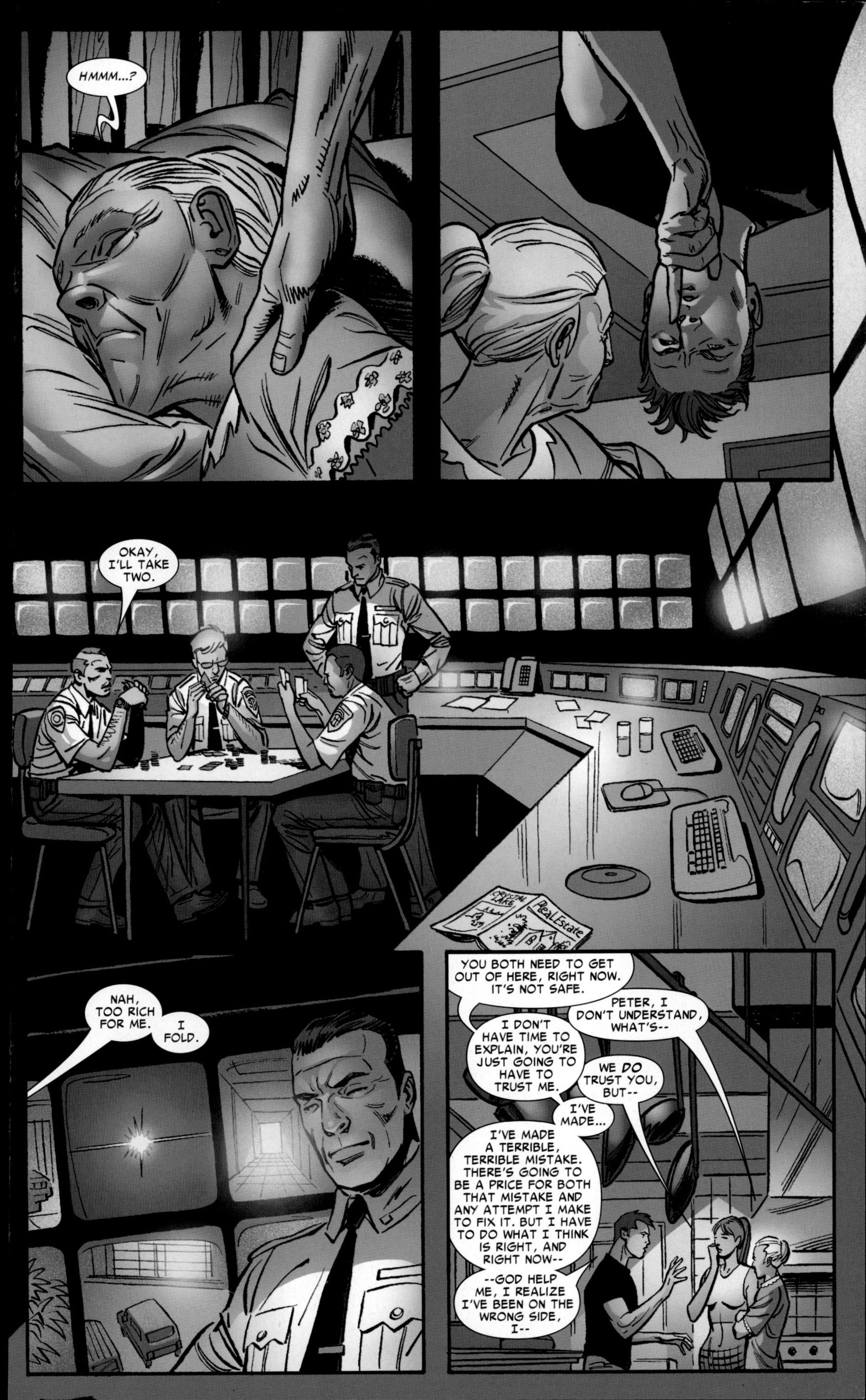
HMMM...?
OKAY, I'LL TAKE TWO.
CRYSTAL LAKE
Real Estate
NAH, TOO RICH FOR ME.
I FOLD.
YOU BOTH NEED TO GET OUT OF HERE, RIGHT NOW. IT'S NOT SAFE.
PETER, I DON'T UNDERSTAND, WHAT'S--
I DON'T HAVE TIME TO EXPLAIN, YOU'RE JUST GOING TO HAVE TO TRUST ME.
WE DO TRUST YOU, BUT--
I'VE MADE...
I'VE MADE A TERRIBLE, TERRIBLE MISTAKE. THERE'S GOING TO BE A PRICE FOR BOTH THAT MISTAKE AND ANY ATTEMPT I MAKE TO FIX IT. BUT I HAVE TO DO WHAT I THINK IS RIGHT, AND RIGHT NOW--
--GOD HELP ME, I REALIZE I'VE BEEN ON THE WRONG SIDE, I--

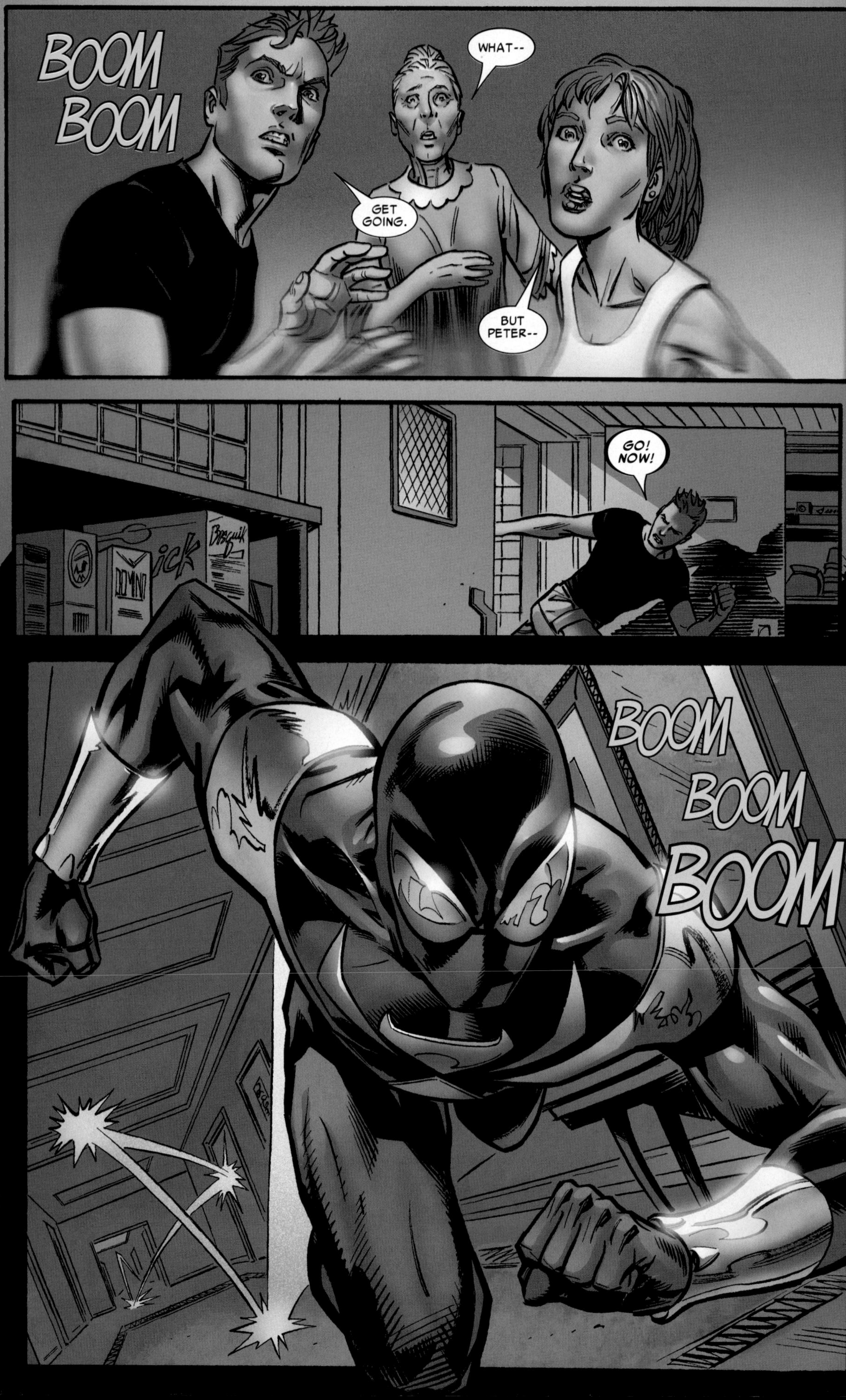
BOOM BOOM
WHAT--
GET GOING.
BUT PETER--
GO! NOW!
BOOM BOOM BOOM

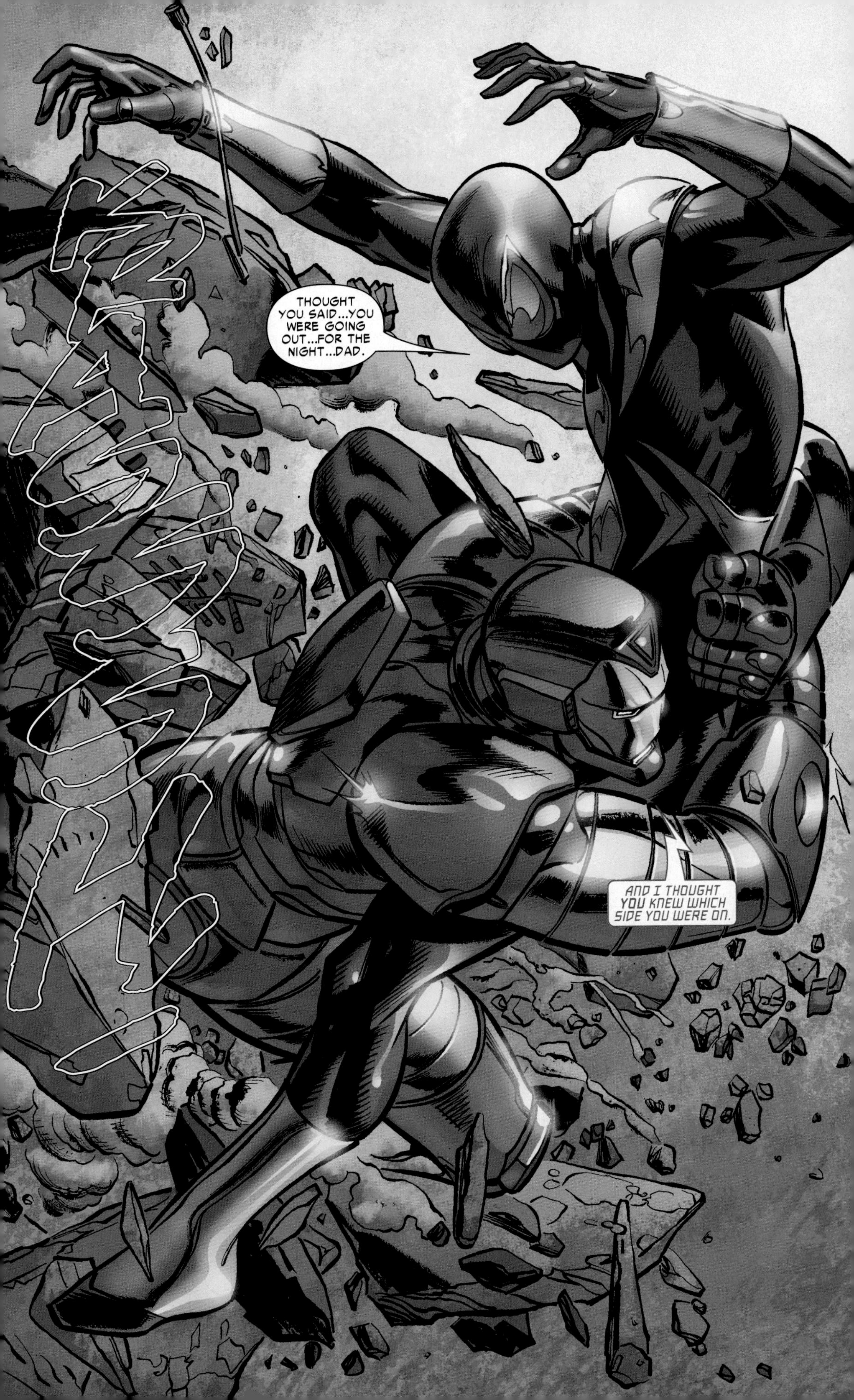
THOUGHT YOU SAID...YOU WERE GOING OUT...FOR THE NIGHT...DAD.
AND I THOUGHT YOU KNEW WHICH SIDE YOU WERE ON.

THE AMAZING
SPIDER-MAN
A MARVEL COMICS EVENT

CIVIL
WAR

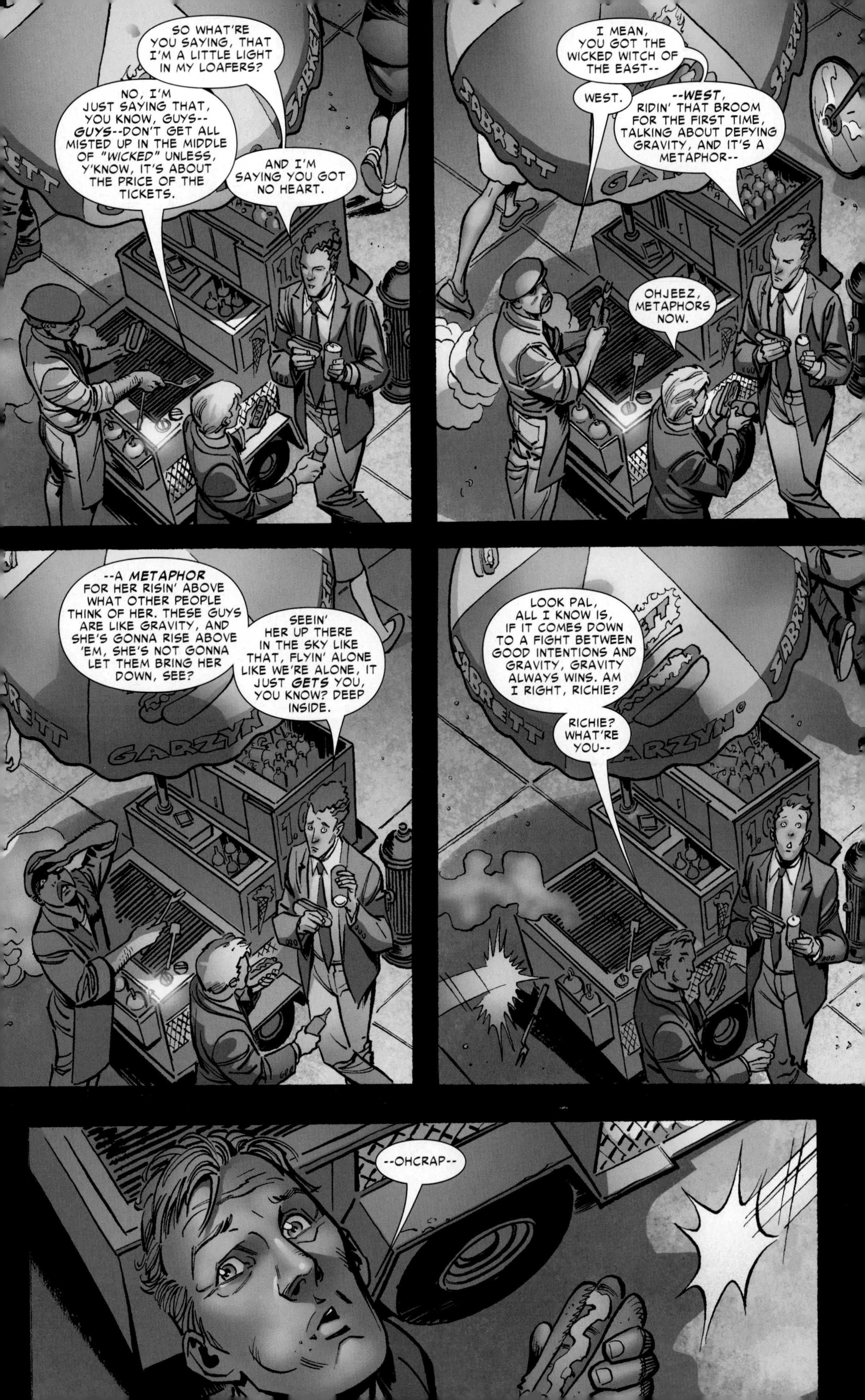
SO WHAT'RE YOU SAYING, THAT I'M A LITTLE LIGHT IN MY LOAFERS?
NO, I'M JUST SAYING THAT, YOU KNOW, GUYS-- *GUYS*--DON'T GET ALL MISTED UP IN THE MIDDLE OF *"WICKED"* UNLESS, Y'KNOW, IT'S ABOUT THE PRICE OF THE TICKETS.
AND I'M SAYING YOU GOT NO HEART.
I MEAN, YOU GOT THE WICKED WITCH OF THE EAST--
WEST.
--WEST, RIDIN' THAT BROOM FOR THE FIRST TIME, TALKING ABOUT DEFYING GRAVITY, AND IT'S A METAPHOR--
OHJEEZ, METAPHORS NOW.
--A *METAPHOR* FOR HER RISIN' ABOVE WHAT OTHER PEOPLE THINK OF HER. THESE GUYS ARE LIKE GRAVITY, AND SHE'S GONNA RISE ABOVE 'EM, SHE'S NOT GONNA LET THEM BRING HER DOWN, SEE?
SEEIN' HER UP THERE IN THE SKY LIKE THAT, FLYIN' ALONE LIKE WE'RE ALONE, IT JUST *GETS* YOU, YOU KNOW? DEEP INSIDE.
LOOK PAL, ALL I KNOW IS, IF IT COMES DOWN TO A FIGHT BETWEEN GOOD INTENTIONS AND GRAVITY, GRAVITY ALWAYS WINS. AM I RIGHT, RICHIE?
RICHIE? WHAT'RE YOU--
--OHCRAP--

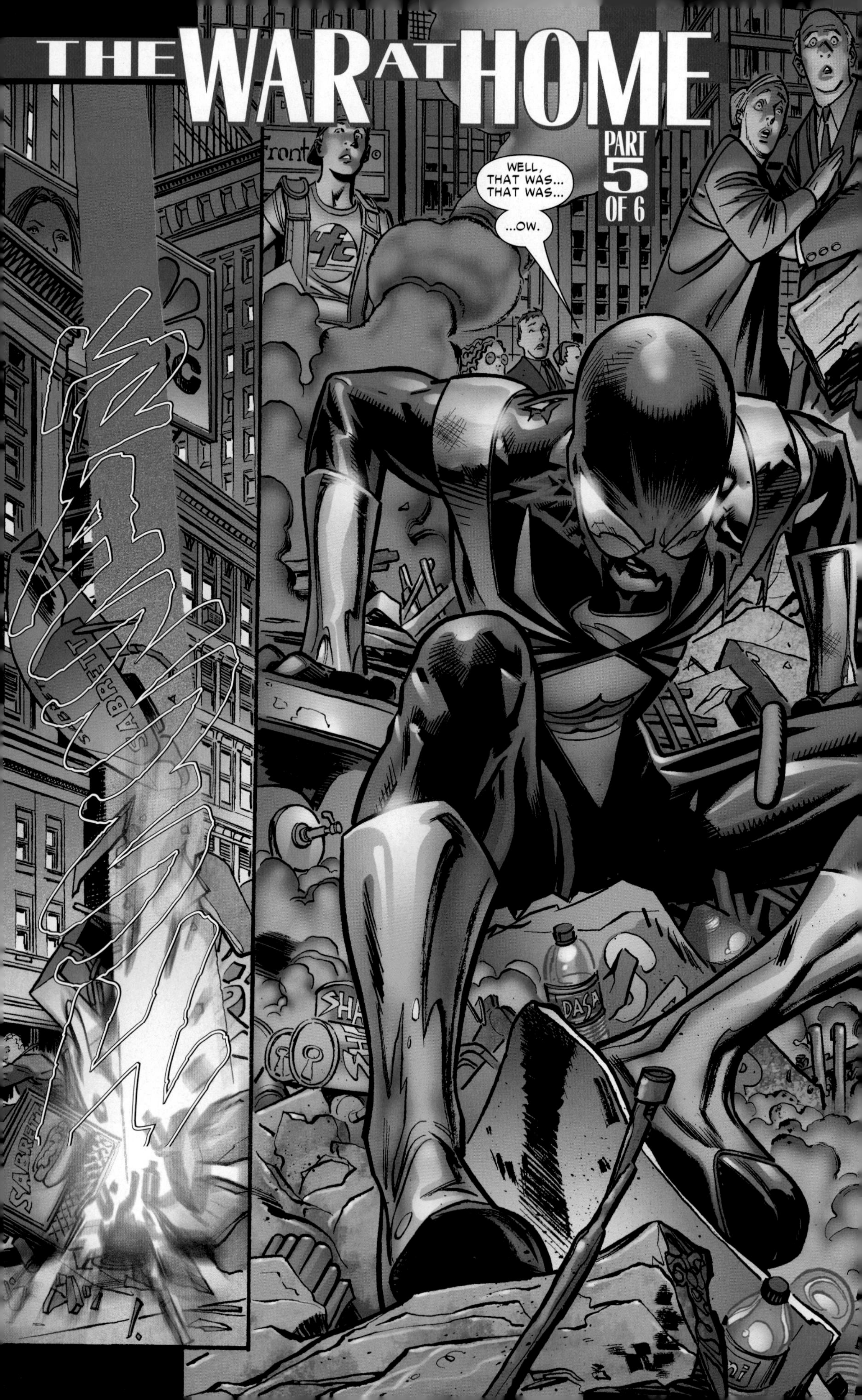
THE WAR AT HOME
PART 5 OF 6
WELL, THAT WAS... THAT WAS...
...OW.

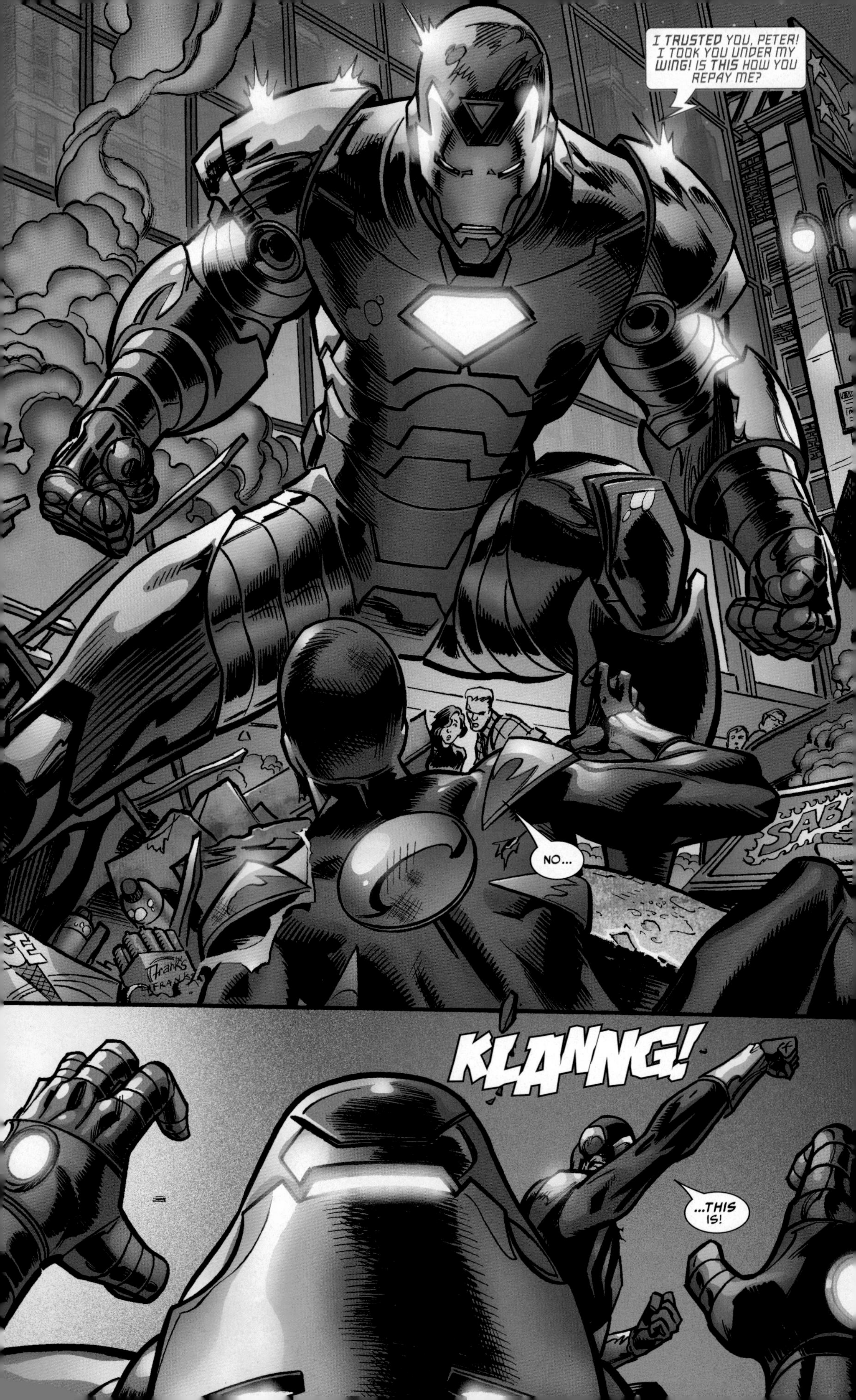
I TRUSTED YOU, PETER! I TOOK YOU UNDER MY WING! IS THIS HOW YOU REPAY ME?
NO...
KLANNG!
...THIS IS!

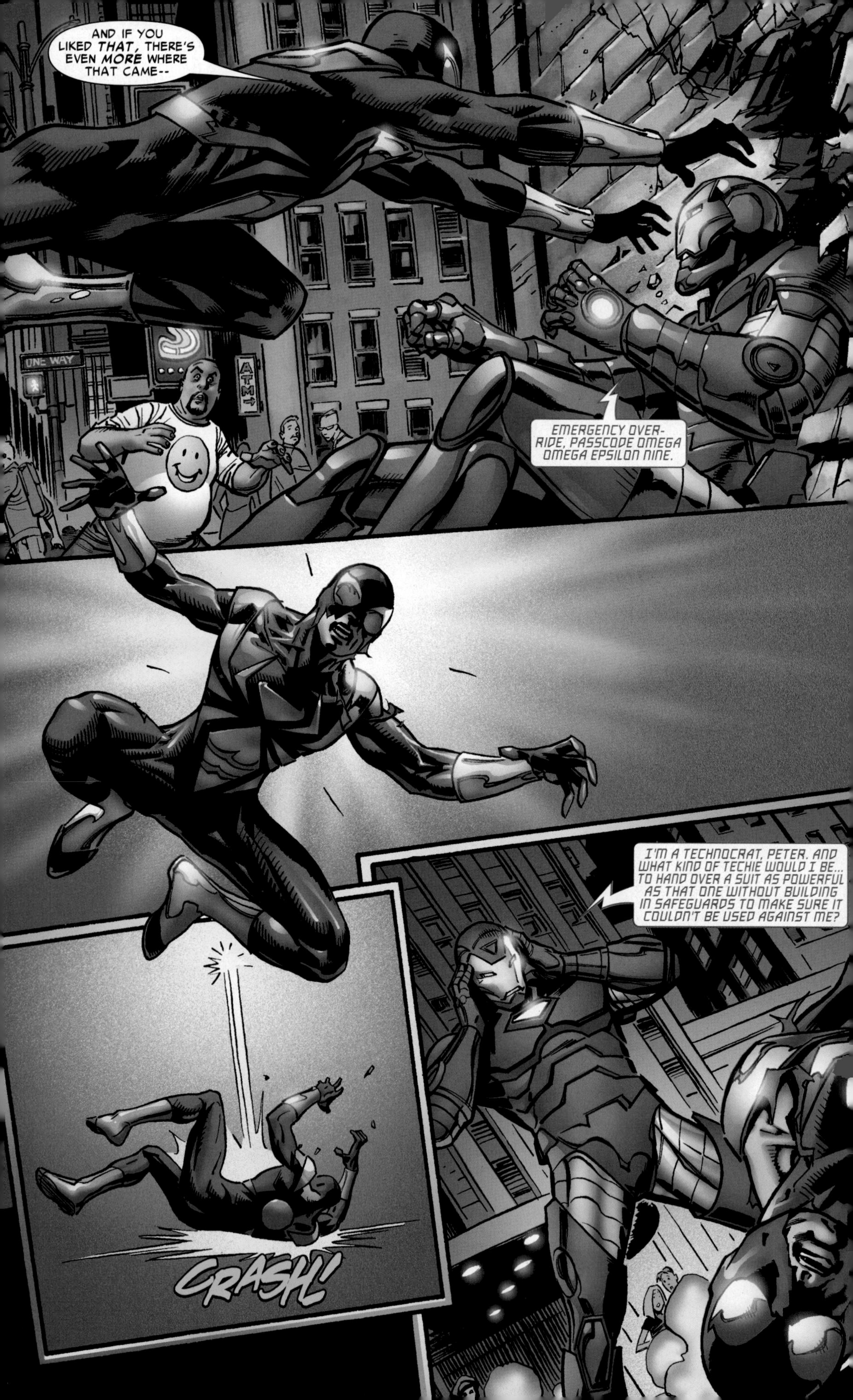
AND IF YOU LIKED THAT, THERE'S EVEN MORE WHERE THAT CAME--
ONE WAY
ATM
EMERGENCY OVER-RIDE, PASSCODE OMEGA OMEGA EPSILON NINE.
I'M A TECHNOCRAT, PETER. AND WHAT KIND OF TECHIE WOULD I BE... TO HAND OVER A SUIT AS POWERFUL AS THAT ONE WITHOUT BUILDING IN SAFEGUARDS TO MAKE SURE IT COULDN'T BE USED AGAINST ME?
CRASH!

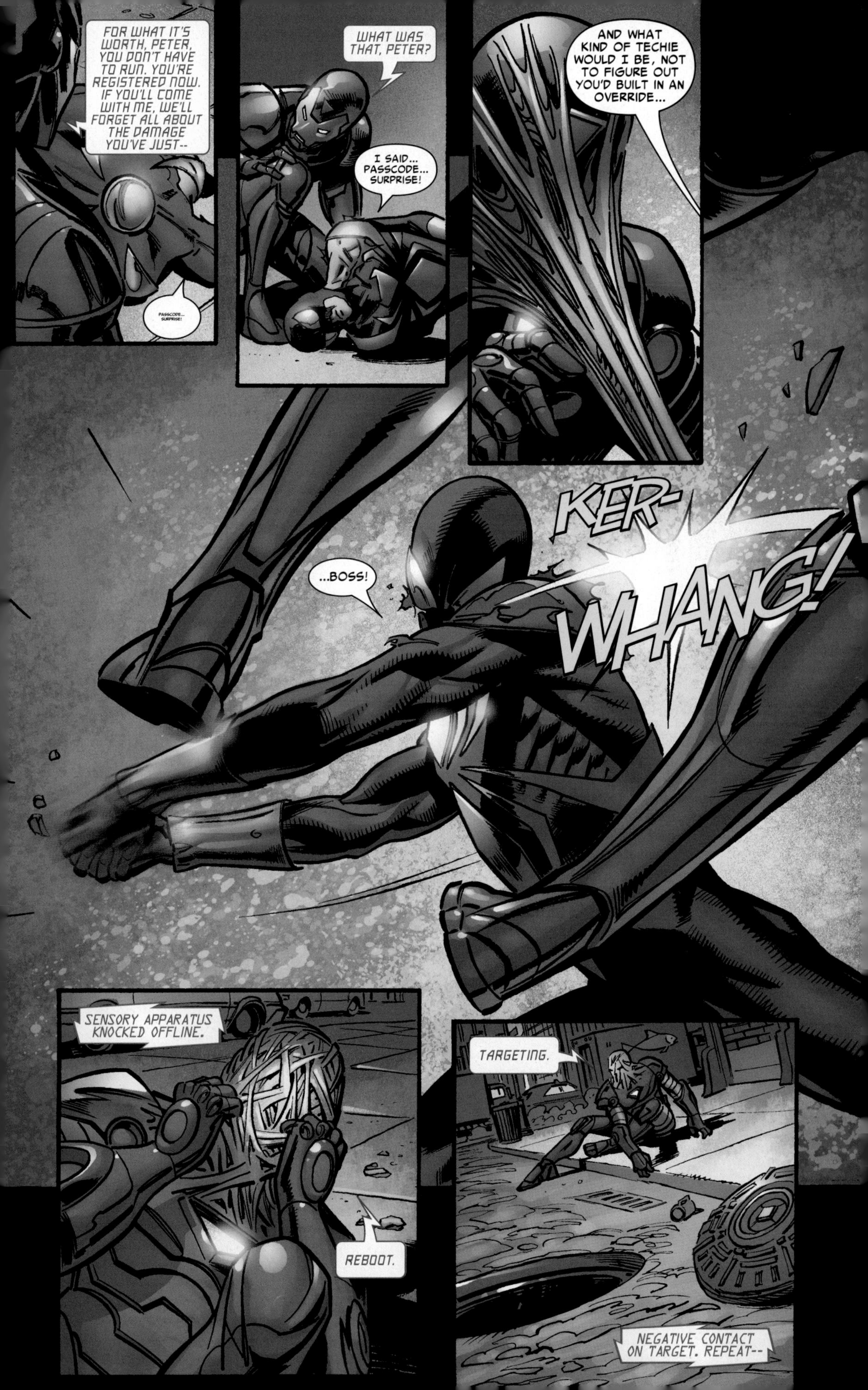
FOR WHAT IT'S WORTH, PETER, YOU DON'T HAVE TO RUN. YOU'RE REGISTERED NOW. IF YOU'LL COME WITH ME, WE'LL FORGET ALL ABOUT THE DAMAGE YOU'VE JUST--
PASSCODE... SURPRISE!
WHAT WAS THAT, PETER?
I SAID... PASSCODE... SURPRISE!
AND WHAT KIND OF TECHIE WOULD I BE, NOT TO FIGURE OUT YOU'D BUILT IN AN OVERRIDE...
...BOSS!
KER-WHANG!
SENSORY APPARATUS KNOCKED OFFLINE.
REBOOT.
TARGETING.
NEGATIVE CONTACT ON TARGET. REPEAT--

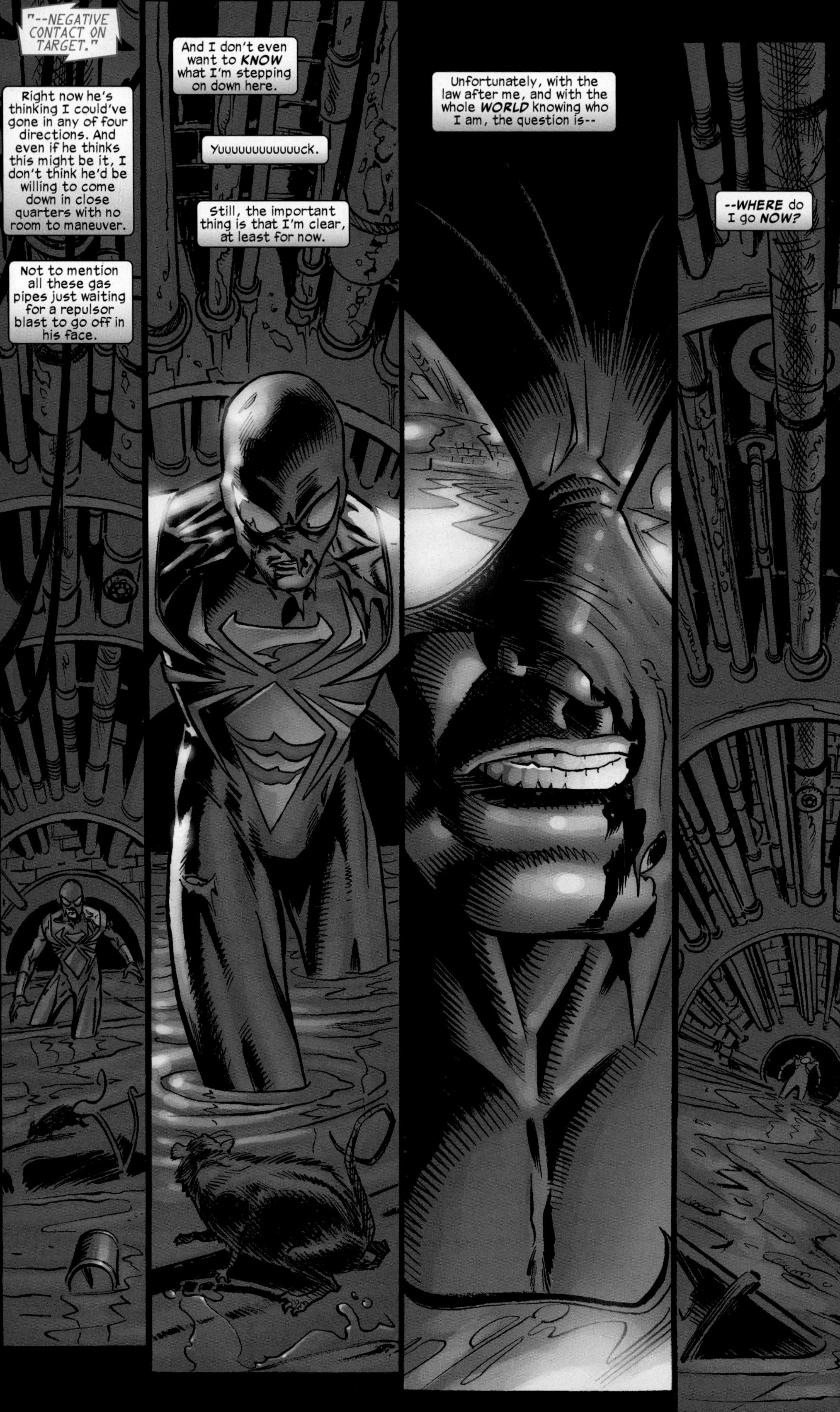
"--NEGATIVE CONTACT ON TARGET."
Right now he's thinking I could've gone in any of four directions. And even if he thinks this might be it, I don't think he'd be willing to come down in close quarters with no room to maneuver.
Not to mention all these gas pipes just waiting for a repulsor blast to go off in his face.
And I don't even want to KNOW what I'm stepping on down here.
Yuuuuuuuuuuuuck.
Still, the important thing is that I'm clear, at least for now.
Unfortunately, with the law after me, and with the whole WORLD knowing who I am, the question is--
--WHERE do I go NOW?

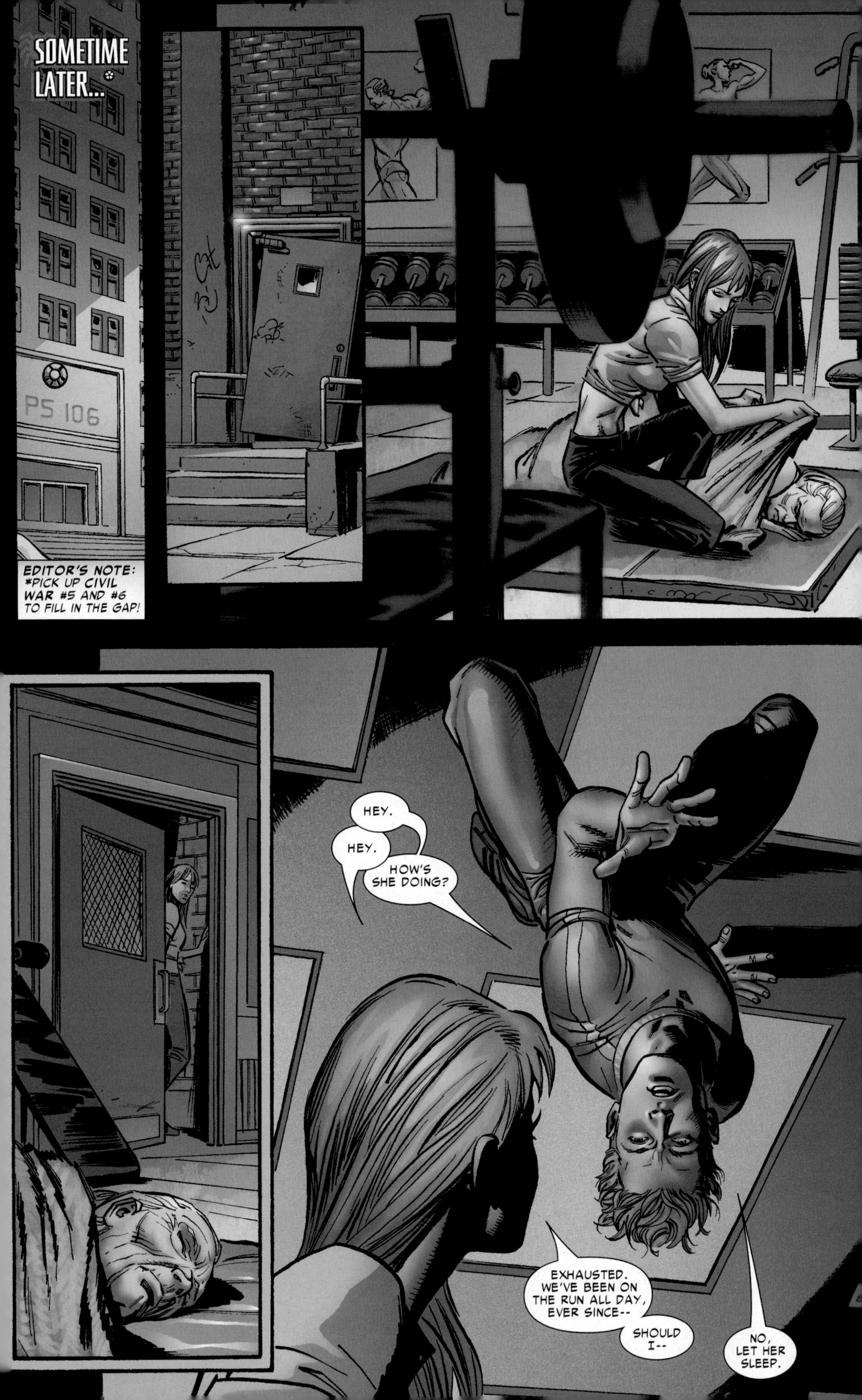
SOMETIME LATER...*
PS 106
EDITOR'S NOTE: *PICK UP CIVIL WAR #5 AND #6 TO FILL IN THE GAP!
HEY.
HEY.
HOW'S SHE DOING?
EXHAUSTED. WE'VE BEEN ON THE RUN ALL DAY, EVER SINCE--
SHOULD I--
NO, LET HER SLEEP.

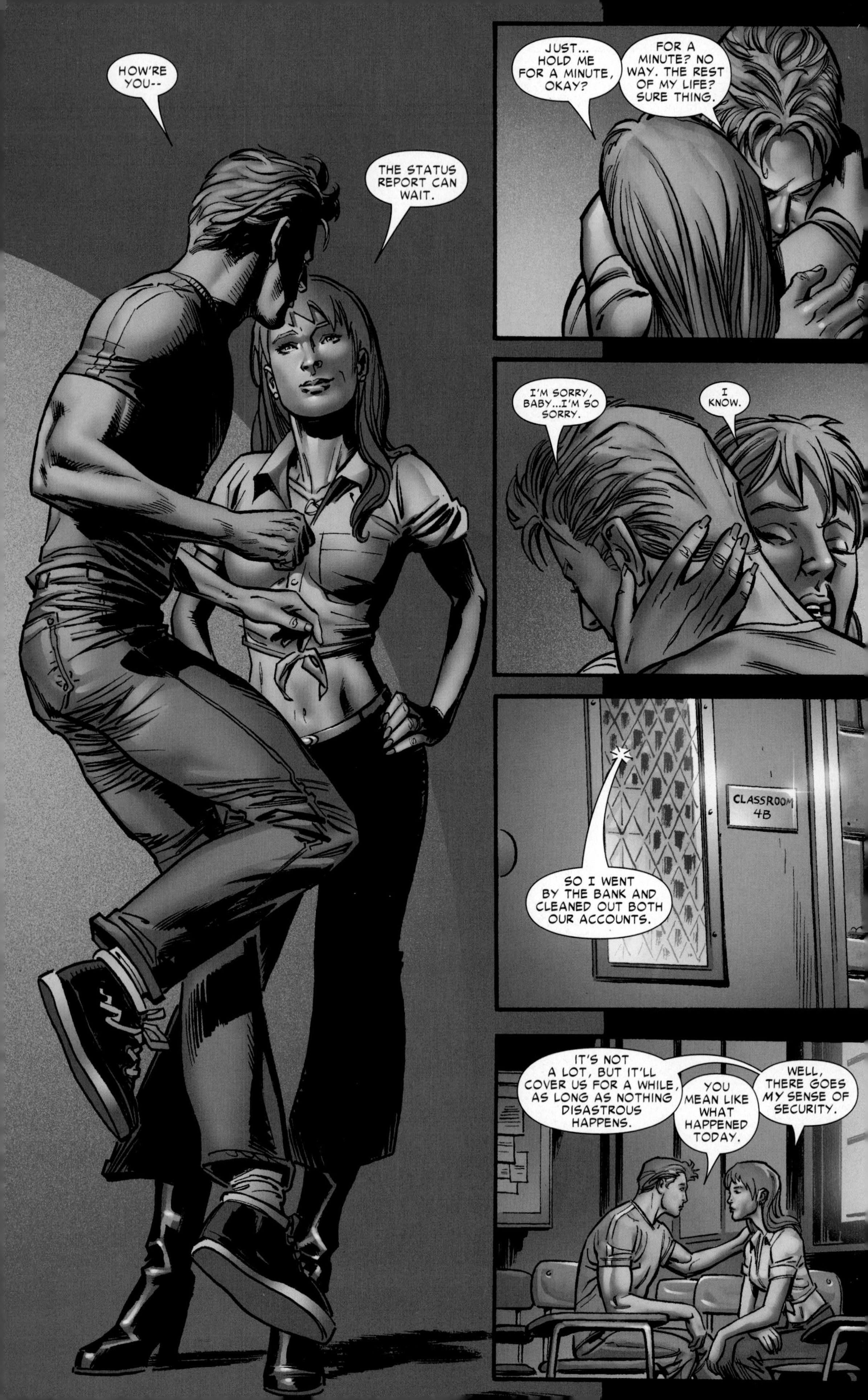
HOW'RE YOU--
THE STATUS REPORT CAN WAIT.
JUST... HOLD ME FOR A MINUTE, OKAY?
FOR A MINUTE? NO WAY. THE REST OF MY LIFE? SURE THING.
I'M SORRY, BABY...I'M SO SORRY.
I KNOW.
CLASSROOM 4B
SO I WENT BY THE BANK AND CLEANED OUT BOTH OUR ACCOUNTS.
IT'S NOT A LOT, BUT IT'LL COVER US FOR A WHILE, AS LONG AS NOTHING DISASTROUS HAPPENS.
YOU MEAN LIKE WHAT HAPPENED TODAY.
WELL, THERE GOES MY SENSE OF SECURITY.

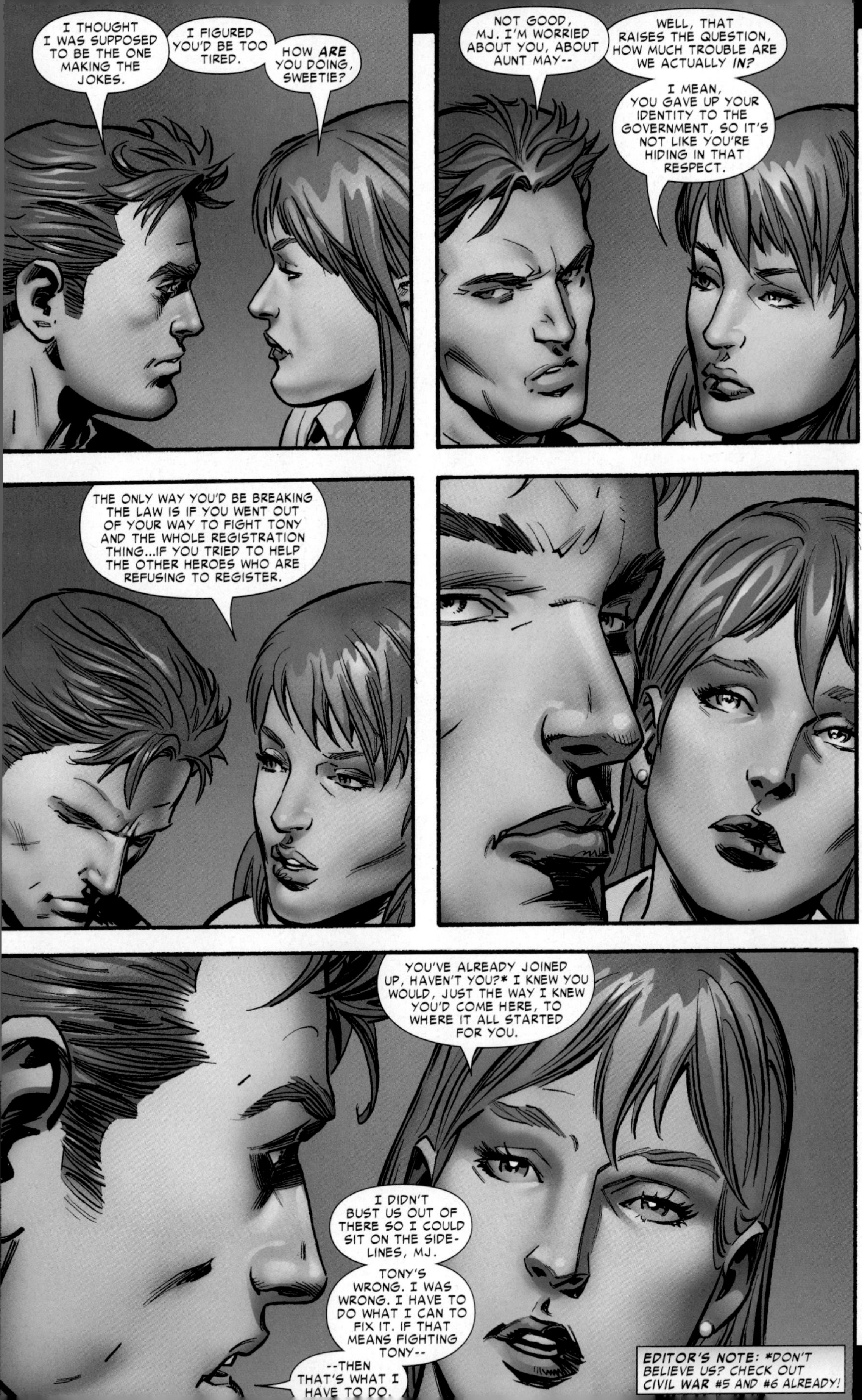
I THOUGHT I WAS SUPPOSED TO BE THE ONE MAKING THE JOKES.
I FIGURED YOU'D BE TOO TIRED.
HOW ARE YOU DOING, SWEETIE?
NOT GOOD, MJ. I'M WORRIED ABOUT YOU, ABOUT AUNT MAY--
WELL, THAT RAISES THE QUESTION, HOW MUCH TROUBLE ARE WE ACTUALLY IN?
I MEAN, YOU GAVE UP YOUR IDENTITY TO THE GOVERNMENT, SO IT'S NOT LIKE YOU'RE HIDING IN THAT RESPECT.
THE ONLY WAY YOU'D BE BREAKING THE LAW IS IF YOU WENT OUT OF YOUR WAY TO FIGHT TONY AND THE WHOLE REGISTRATION THING...IF YOU TRIED TO HELP THE OTHER HEROES WHO ARE REFUSING TO REGISTER.
YOU'VE ALREADY JOINED UP, HAVEN'T YOU?* I KNEW YOU WOULD, JUST THE WAY I KNEW YOU'D COME HERE, TO WHERE IT ALL STARTED FOR YOU.
I DIDN'T BUST US OUT OF THERE SO I COULD SIT ON THE SIDE-LINES, MJ.
TONY'S WRONG. I WAS WRONG. I HAVE TO DO WHAT I CAN TO FIX IT. IF THAT MEANS FIGHTING TONY--
--THEN THAT'S WHAT I HAVE TO DO.
EDITOR'S NOTE: *DON'T BELIEVE US? CHECK OUT CIVIL WAR #5 AND #6 ALREADY!

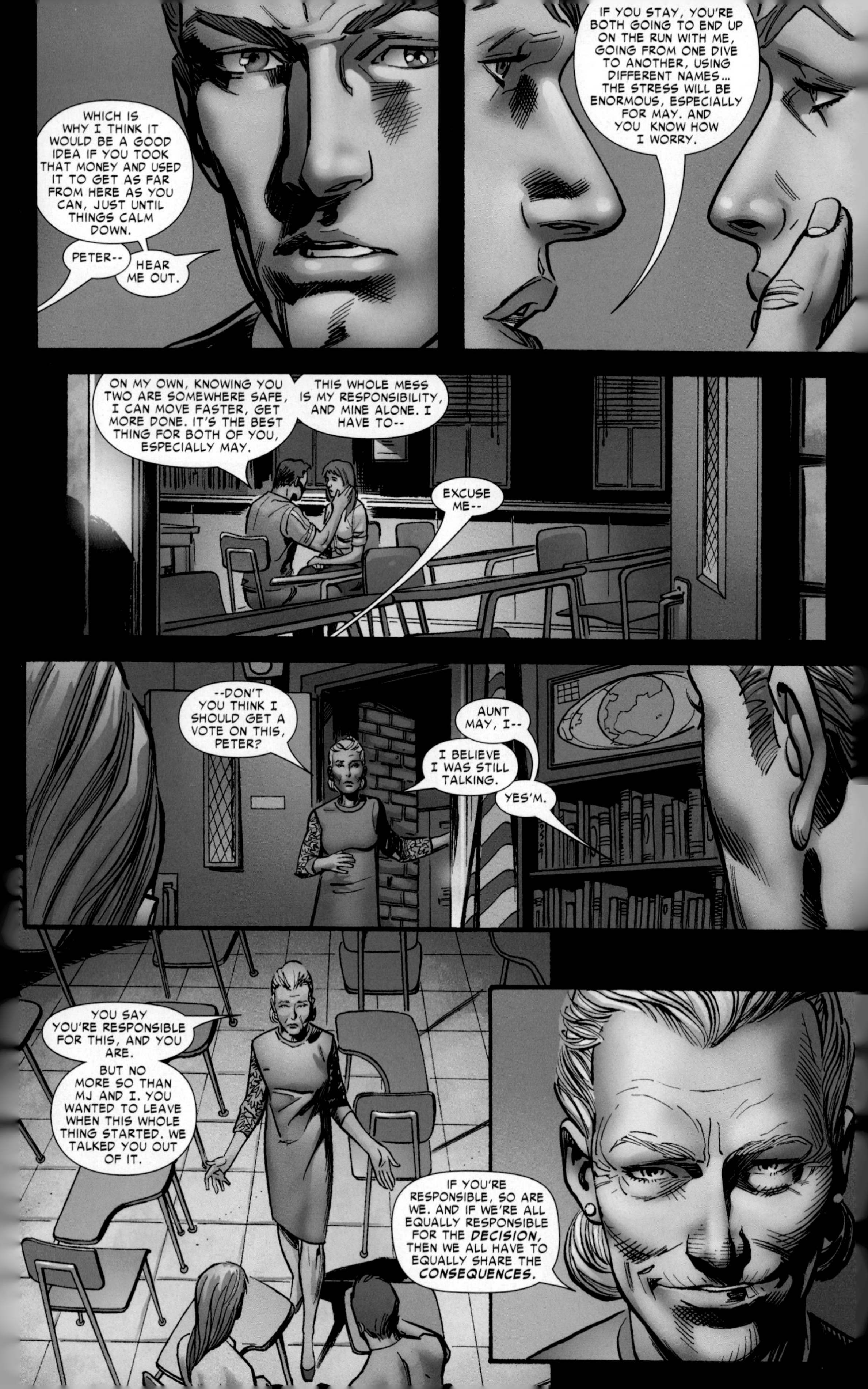
WHICH IS WHY I THINK IT WOULD BE A GOOD IDEA IF YOU TOOK THAT MONEY AND USED IT TO GET AS FAR FROM HERE AS YOU CAN, JUST UNTIL THINGS CALM DOWN.
PETER--
HEAR ME OUT.
IF YOU STAY, YOU'RE BOTH GOING TO END UP ON THE RUN WITH ME, GOING FROM ONE DIVE TO ANOTHER, USING DIFFERENT NAMES... THE STRESS WILL BE ENORMOUS, ESPECIALLY FOR MAY. AND YOU KNOW HOW I WORRY.
ON MY OWN, KNOWING YOU TWO ARE SOMEWHERE SAFE, I CAN MOVE FASTER, GET MORE DONE. IT'S THE BEST THING FOR BOTH OF YOU, ESPECIALLY MAY.
THIS WHOLE MESS IS MY RESPONSIBILITY, AND MINE ALONE. I HAVE TO--
EXCUSE ME--
--DON'T YOU THINK I SHOULD GET A VOTE ON THIS, PETER?
AUNT MAY, I--
I BELIEVE I WAS STILL TALKING.
YES'M.
YOU SAY YOU'RE RESPONSIBLE FOR THIS, AND YOU ARE.
BUT NO MORE SO THAN MJ AND I. YOU WANTED TO LEAVE WHEN THIS WHOLE THING STARTED. WE TALKED YOU OUT OF IT.
IF YOU'RE RESPONSIBLE, SO ARE WE. AND IF WE'RE ALL EQUALLY RESPONSIBLE FOR THE DECISION, THEN WE ALL HAVE TO EQUALLY SHARE THE CONSEQUENCES.

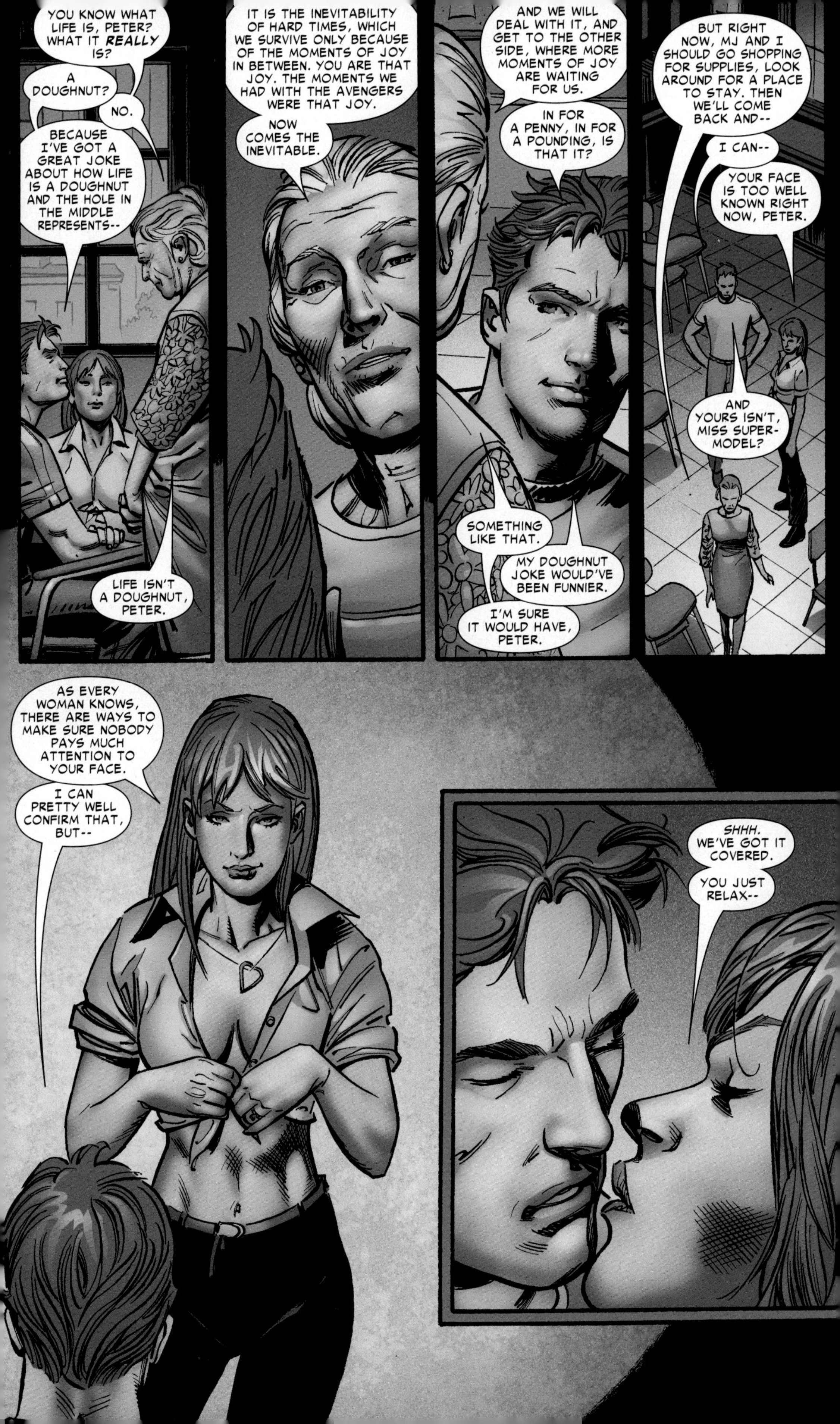
YOU KNOW WHAT LIFE IS, PETER? WHAT IT REALLY IS?
A DOUGHNUT?
NO.
BECAUSE I'VE GOT A GREAT JOKE ABOUT HOW LIFE IS A DOUGHNUT AND THE HOLE IN THE MIDDLE REPRESENTS--
LIFE ISN'T A DOUGHNUT, PETER.
IT IS THE INEVITABILITY OF HARD TIMES, WHICH WE SURVIVE ONLY BECAUSE OF THE MOMENTS OF JOY IN BETWEEN. YOU ARE THAT JOY. THE MOMENTS WE HAD WITH THE AVENGERS WERE THAT JOY.
NOW COMES THE INEVITABLE.
AND WE WILL DEAL WITH IT, AND GET TO THE OTHER SIDE, WHERE MORE MOMENTS OF JOY ARE WAITING FOR US.
IN FOR A PENNY, IN FOR A POUNDING, IS THAT IT?
SOMETHING LIKE THAT.
MY DOUGHNUT JOKE WOULD'VE BEEN FUNNIER.
I'M SURE IT WOULD HAVE, PETER.
BUT RIGHT NOW, MJ AND I SHOULD GO SHOPPING FOR SUPPLIES, LOOK AROUND FOR A PLACE TO STAY. THEN WE'LL COME BACK AND--
I CAN--
YOUR FACE IS TOO WELL KNOWN RIGHT NOW, PETER.
AND YOURS ISN'T, MISS SUPER-MODEL?
AS EVERY WOMAN KNOWS, THERE ARE WAYS TO MAKE SURE NOBODY PAYS MUCH ATTENTION TO YOUR FACE.
I CAN PRETTY WELL CONFIRM THAT, BUT--
SHHH. WE'VE GOT IT COVERED.
YOU JUST RELAX--

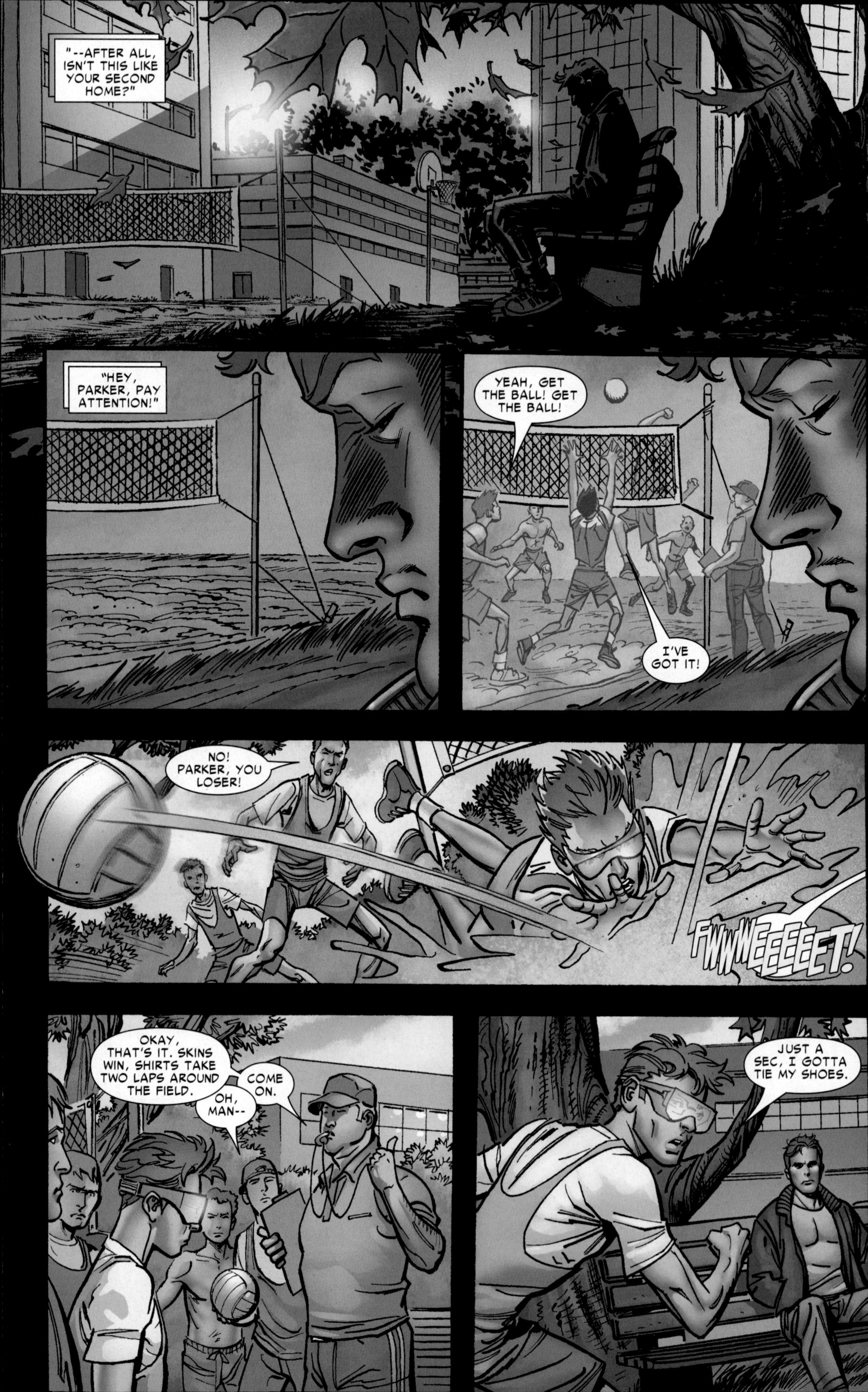
"--AFTER ALL, ISN'T THIS LIKE YOUR SECOND HOME?"
"HEY, PARKER, PAY ATTENTION!"
YEAH, GET THE BALL! GET THE BALL!
I'VE GOT IT!
NO! PARKER, YOU LOSER!
FWWWEEEEET!
OKAY, THAT'S IT. SKINS WIN, SHIRTS TAKE TWO LAPS AROUND THE FIELD.
OH, MAN--
COME ON.
JUST A SEC, I GOTTA TIE MY SHOES.

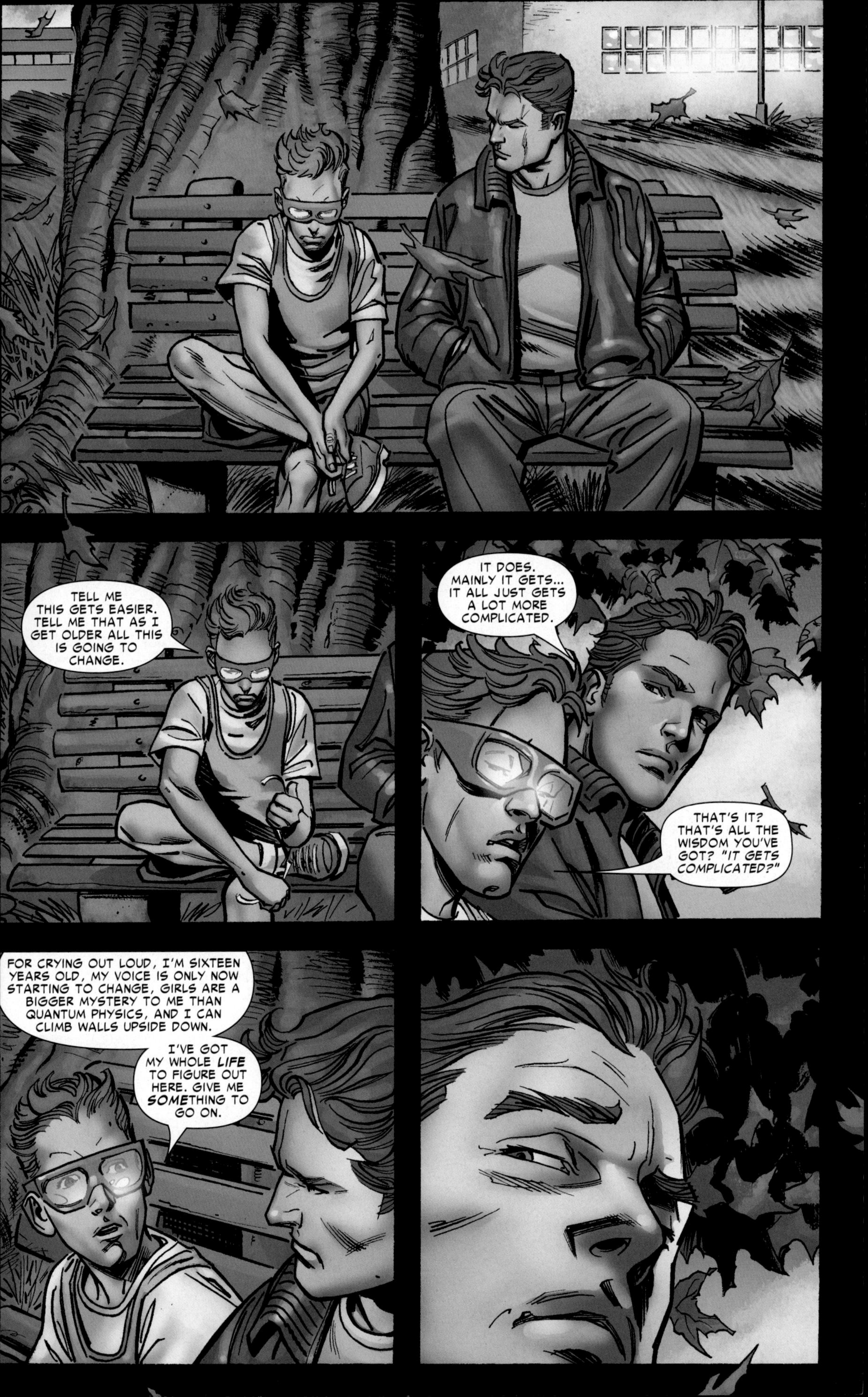
TELL ME THIS GETS EASIER. TELL ME THAT AS I GET OLDER ALL THIS IS GOING TO CHANGE.
IT DOES. MAINLY IT GETS... IT ALL JUST GETS A LOT MORE COMPLICATED.
THAT'S IT? THAT'S ALL THE WISDOM YOU'VE GOT? "IT GETS COMPLICATED?"
FOR CRYING OUT LOUD, I'M SIXTEEN YEARS OLD, MY VOICE IS ONLY NOW STARTING TO CHANGE, GIRLS ARE A BIGGER MYSTERY TO ME THAN QUANTUM PHYSICS, AND I CAN CLIMB WALLS UPSIDE DOWN.
I'VE GOT MY WHOLE *LIFE* TO FIGURE OUT HERE. GIVE ME ***SOME***THING TO GO ON.

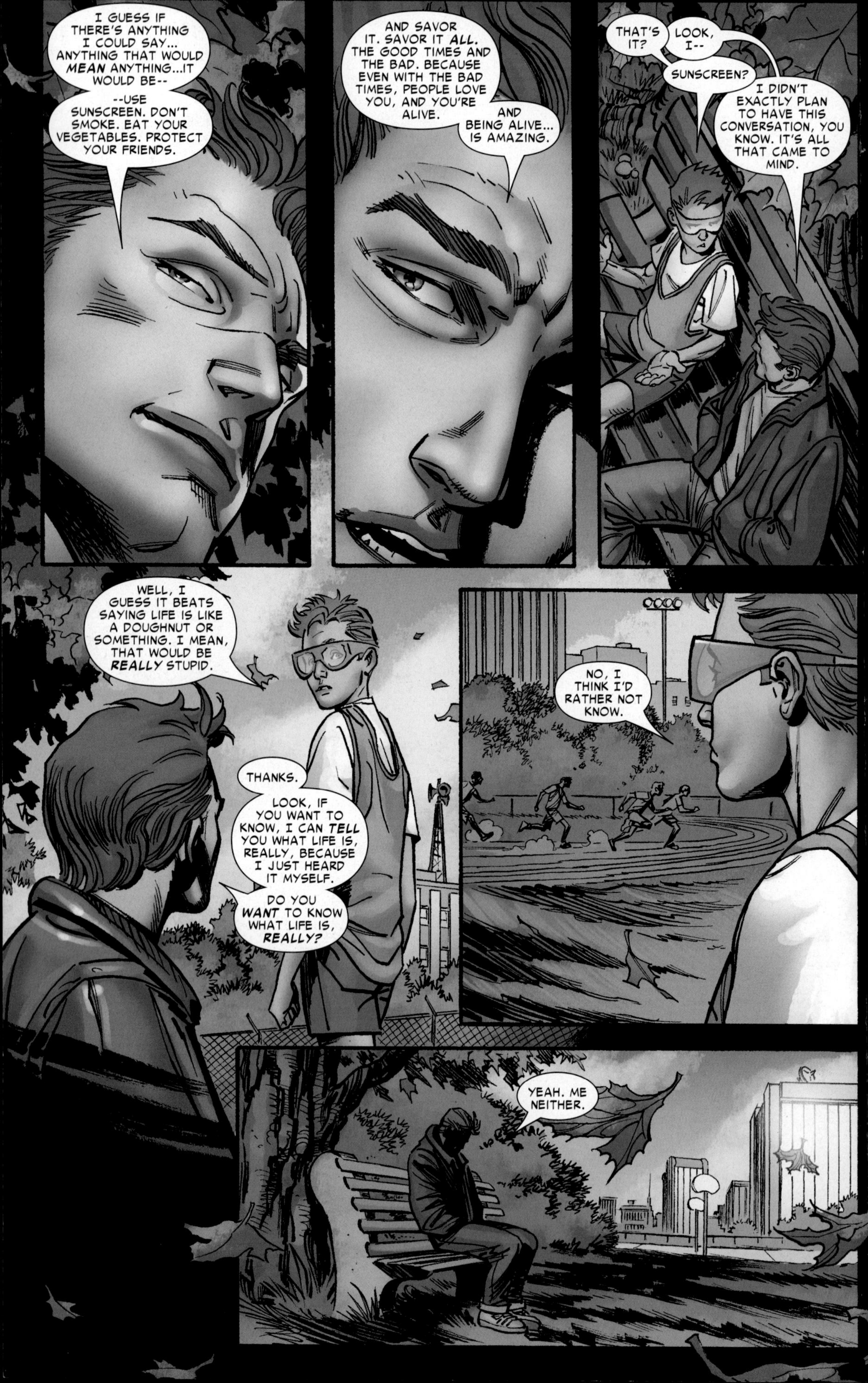
I GUESS IF THERE'S ANYTHING I COULD SAY... ANYTHING THAT WOULD MEAN ANYTHING...IT WOULD BE--
--USE SUNSCREEN. DON'T SMOKE. EAT YOUR VEGETABLES. PROTECT YOUR FRIENDS.
AND SAVOR IT. SAVOR IT ALL. THE GOOD TIMES AND THE BAD. BECAUSE EVEN WITH THE BAD TIMES, PEOPLE LOVE YOU, AND YOU'RE ALIVE.
AND BEING ALIVE... IS AMAZING.
THAT'S IT?
SUNSCREEN?
LOOK, I--
I DIDN'T EXACTLY PLAN TO HAVE THIS CONVERSATION, YOU KNOW. IT'S ALL THAT CAME TO MIND.
WELL, I GUESS IT BEATS SAYING LIFE IS LIKE A DOUGHNUT OR SOMETHING. I MEAN, THAT WOULD BE REALLY STUPID.
THANKS.
LOOK, IF YOU WANT TO KNOW, I CAN TELL YOU WHAT LIFE IS, REALLY, BECAUSE I JUST HEARD IT MYSELF.
DO YOU WANT TO KNOW WHAT LIFE IS, REALLY?
NO, I THINK I'D RATHER NOT KNOW.
YEAH. ME NEITHER.

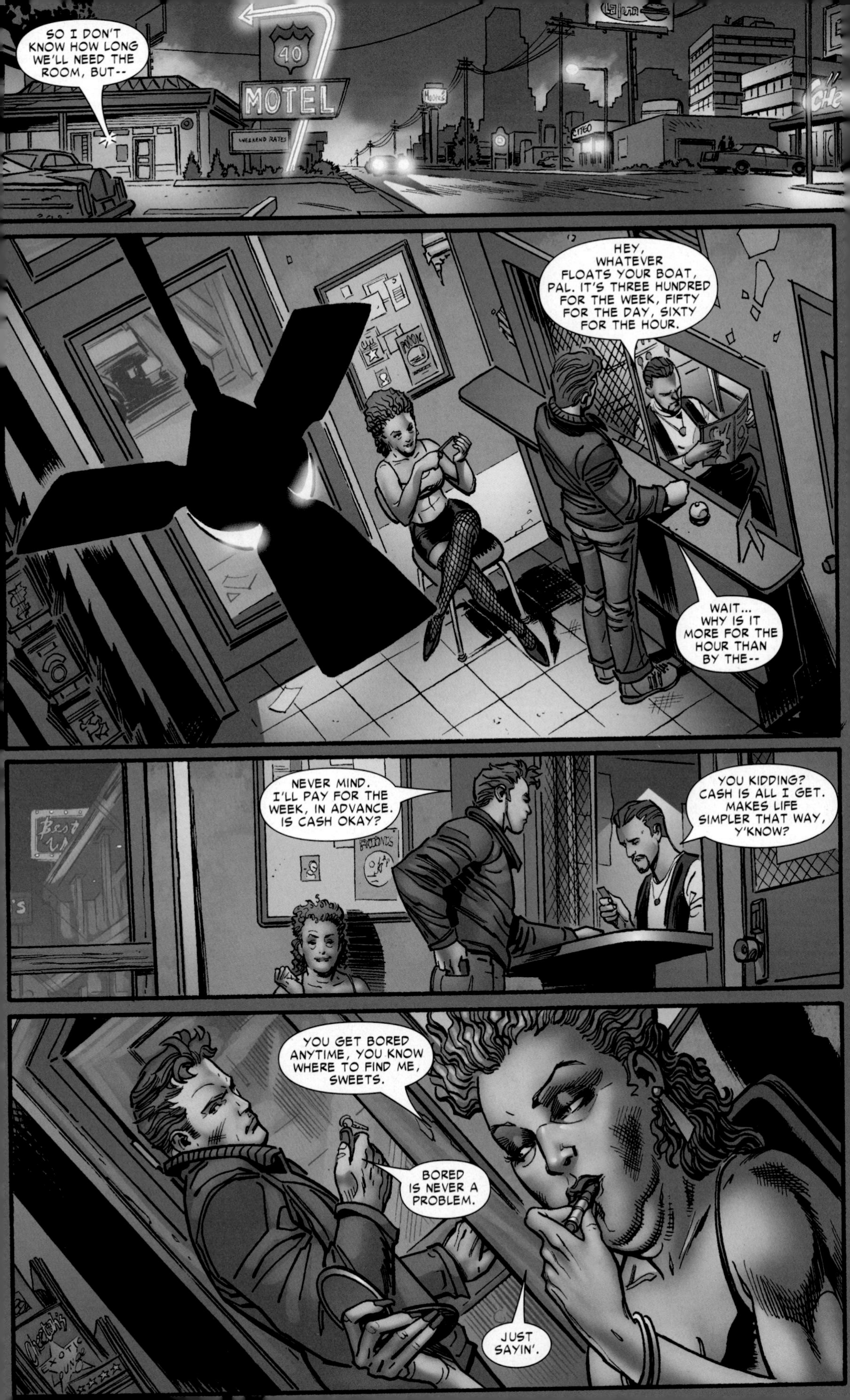
SO I DON'T KNOW HOW LONG WE'LL NEED THE ROOM, BUT--
40
MOTEL
WEEKEND RATES
HEY, WHATEVER FLOATS YOUR BOAT, PAL. IT'S THREE HUNDRED FOR THE WEEK, FIFTY FOR THE DAY, SIXTY FOR THE HOUR.
WAIT... WHY IS IT MORE FOR THE HOUR THAN BY THE--
NEVER MIND. I'LL PAY FOR THE WEEK, IN ADVANCE. IS CASH OKAY?
YOU KIDDING? CASH IS ALL I GET. MAKES LIFE SIMPLER THAT WAY, Y'KNOW?
YOU GET BORED ANYTIME, YOU KNOW WHERE TO FIND ME, SWEETS.
BORED IS NEVER A PROBLEM.
JUST SAYIN'.
EXOTIC LOUNGE

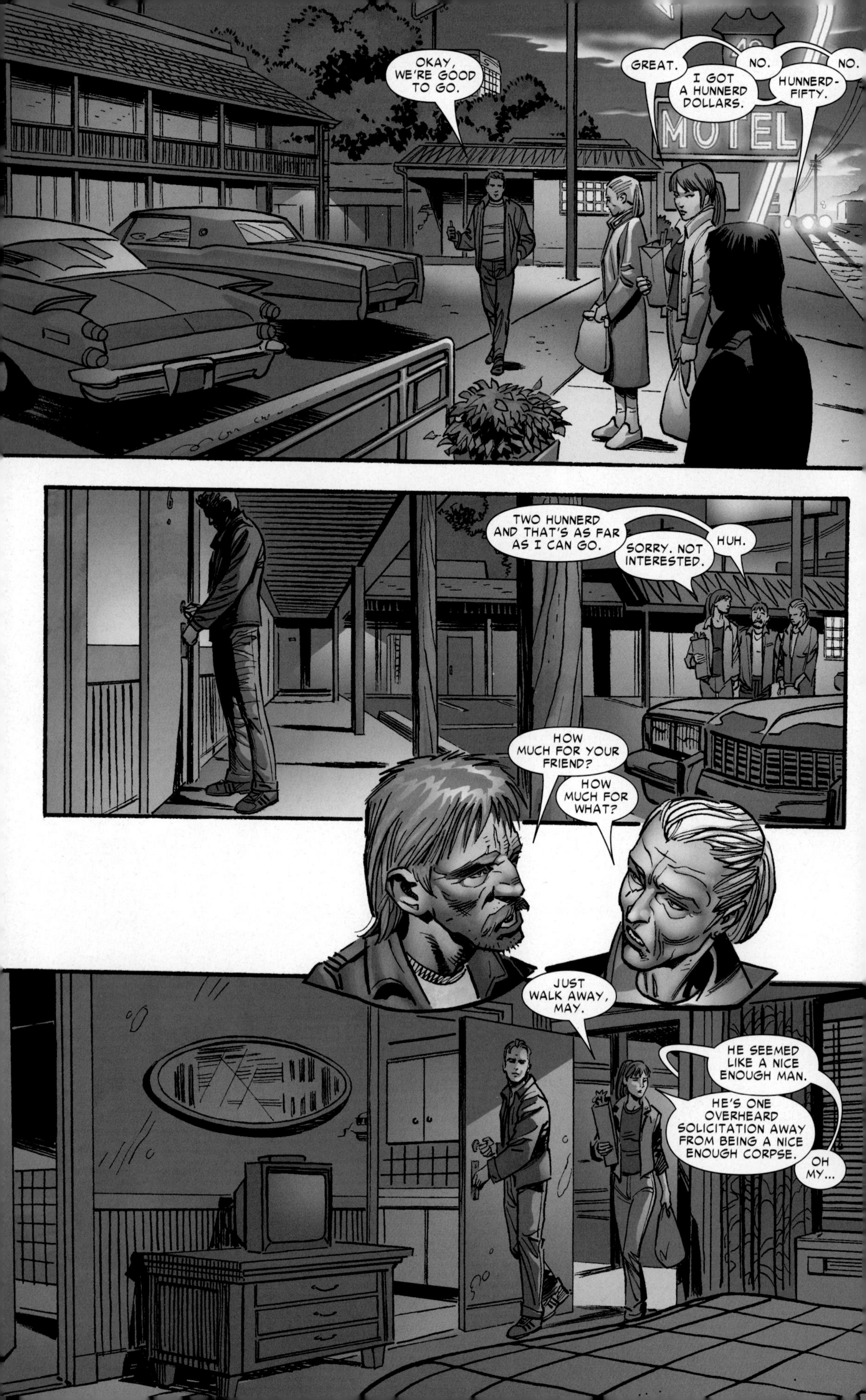
OKAY, WE'RE GOOD TO GO.
MOTEL
GREAT.
I GOT A HUNNERD DOLLARS.
NO.
HUNNERD-FIFTY.
NO.
TWO HUNNERD AND THAT'S AS FAR AS I CAN GO.
SORRY. NOT INTERESTED.
HUH.
HOW MUCH FOR YOUR FRIEND?
HOW MUCH FOR WHAT?
JUST WALK AWAY, MAY.
HE SEEMED LIKE A NICE ENOUGH MAN.
HE'S ONE OVERHEARD SOLICITATION AWAY FROM BEING A NICE ENOUGH CORPSE.
OH MY...

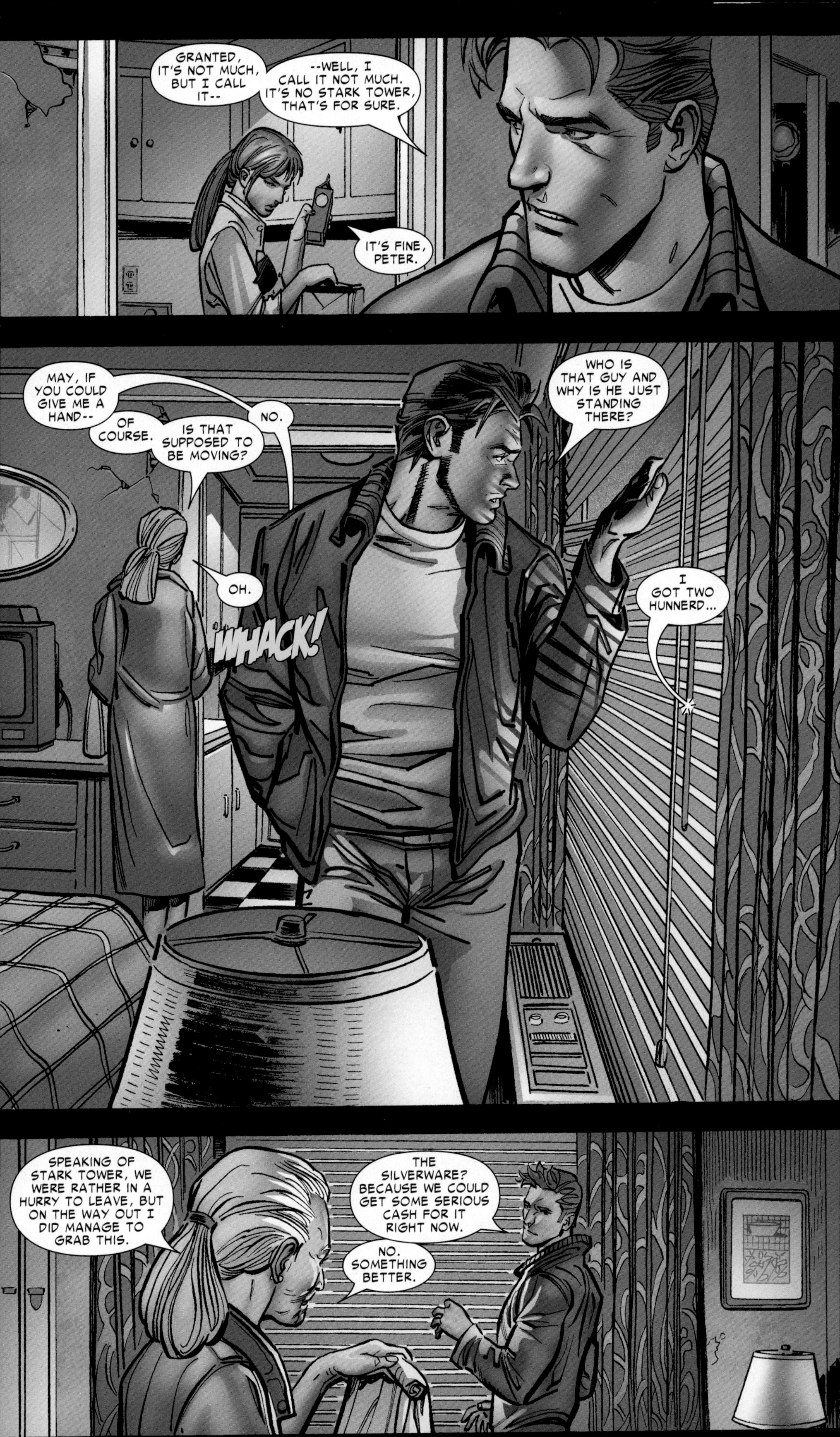
GRANTED, IT'S NOT MUCH, BUT I CALL IT--
--WELL, I CALL IT NOT MUCH. IT'S NO STARK TOWER, THAT'S FOR SURE.
IT'S FINE, PETER.
MAY, IF YOU COULD GIVE ME A HAND--
OF COURSE.
IS THAT SUPPOSED TO BE MOVING?
NO.
WHO IS THAT GUY AND WHY IS HE JUST STANDING THERE?
OH.
WHACK!
I GOT TWO HUNNERD...
SPEAKING OF STARK TOWER, WE WERE RATHER IN A HURRY TO LEAVE, BUT ON THE WAY OUT I DID MANAGE TO GRAB THIS.
THE SILVERWARE? BECAUSE WE COULD GET SOME SERIOUS CASH FOR IT RIGHT NOW.
NO. SOMETHING BETTER.

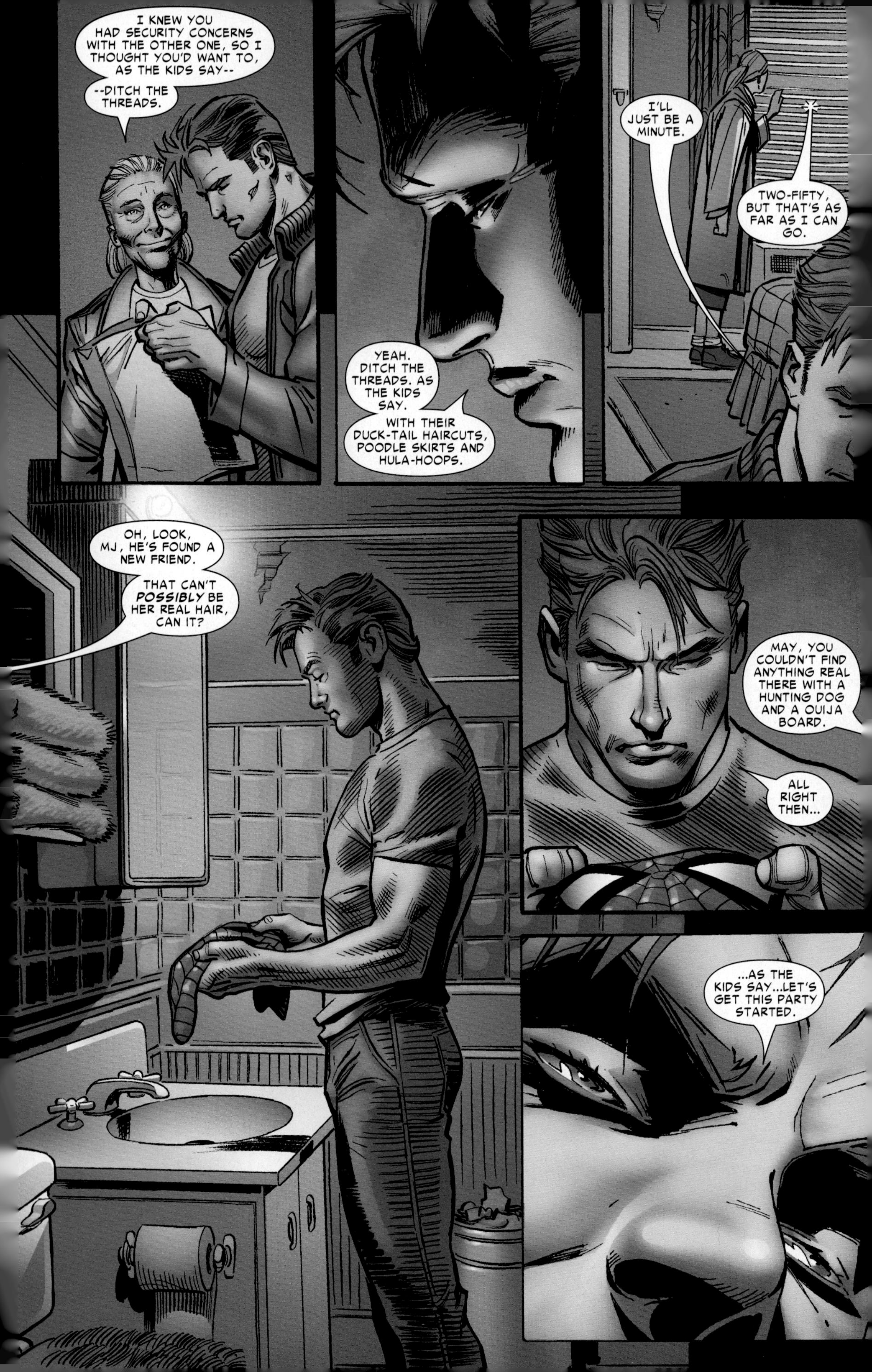
I KNEW YOU HAD SECURITY CONCERNS WITH THE OTHER ONE, SO I THOUGHT YOU'D WANT TO, AS THE KIDS SAY--
--DITCH THE THREADS.
YEAH. DITCH THE THREADS. AS THE KIDS SAY.
WITH THEIR DUCK-TAIL HAIRCUTS, POODLE SKIRTS AND HULA-HOOPS.
I'LL JUST BE A MINUTE.
TWO-FIFTY, BUT THAT'S AS FAR AS I CAN GO.
OH, LOOK, MJ, HE'S FOUND A NEW FRIEND.
THAT CAN'T *POSSIBLY* BE HER REAL HAIR, CAN IT?
MAY, YOU COULDN'T FIND ANYTHING REAL THERE WITH A HUNTING DOG AND A OUIJA BOARD.
ALL RIGHT THEN...
...AS THE KIDS SAY...LET'S GET THIS PARTY STARTED.

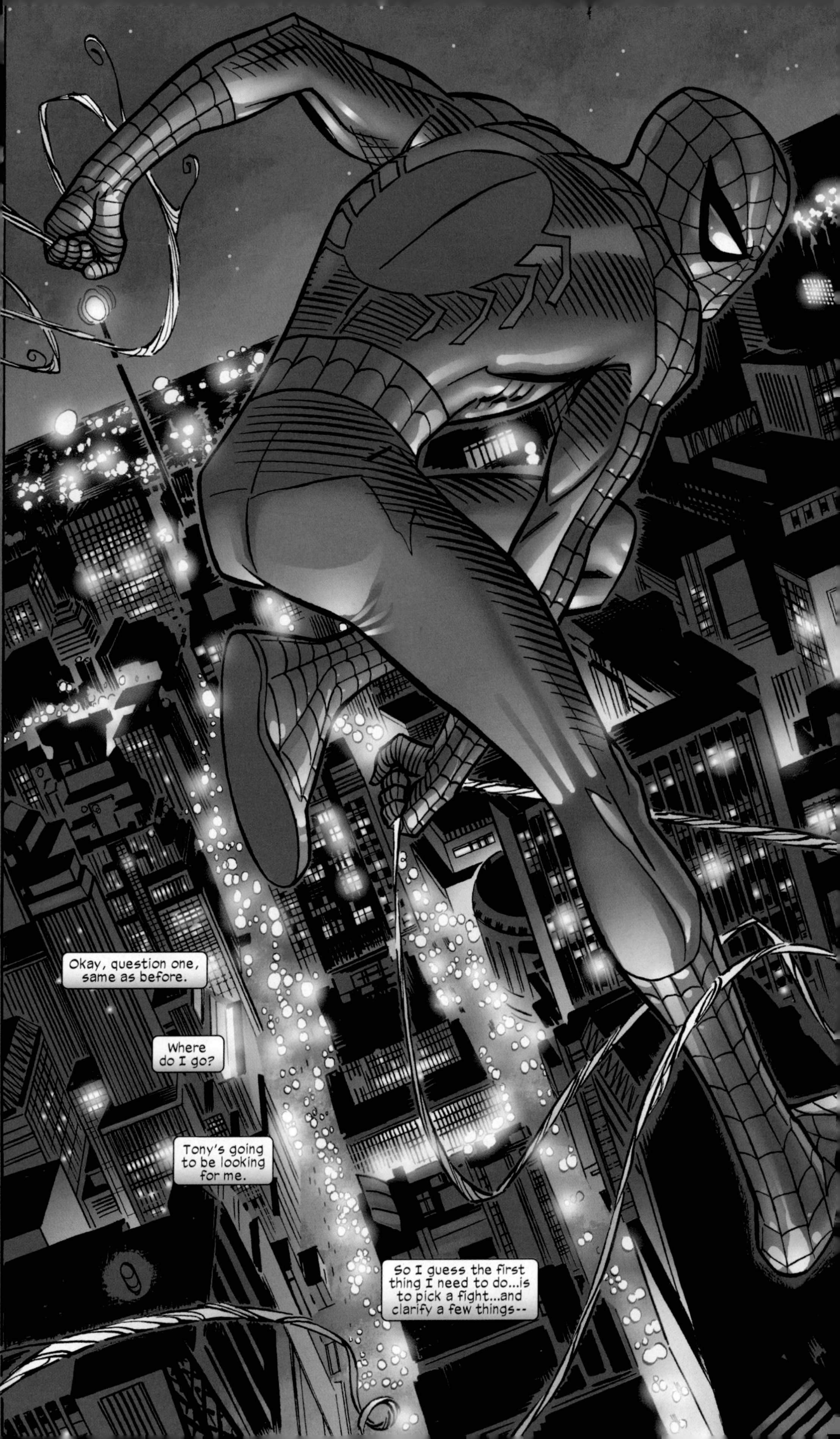
Okay, question one, same as before.
Where do I go?
Tony's going to be looking for me.
So I guess the first thing I need to do...is to pick a fight...and clarify a few things--

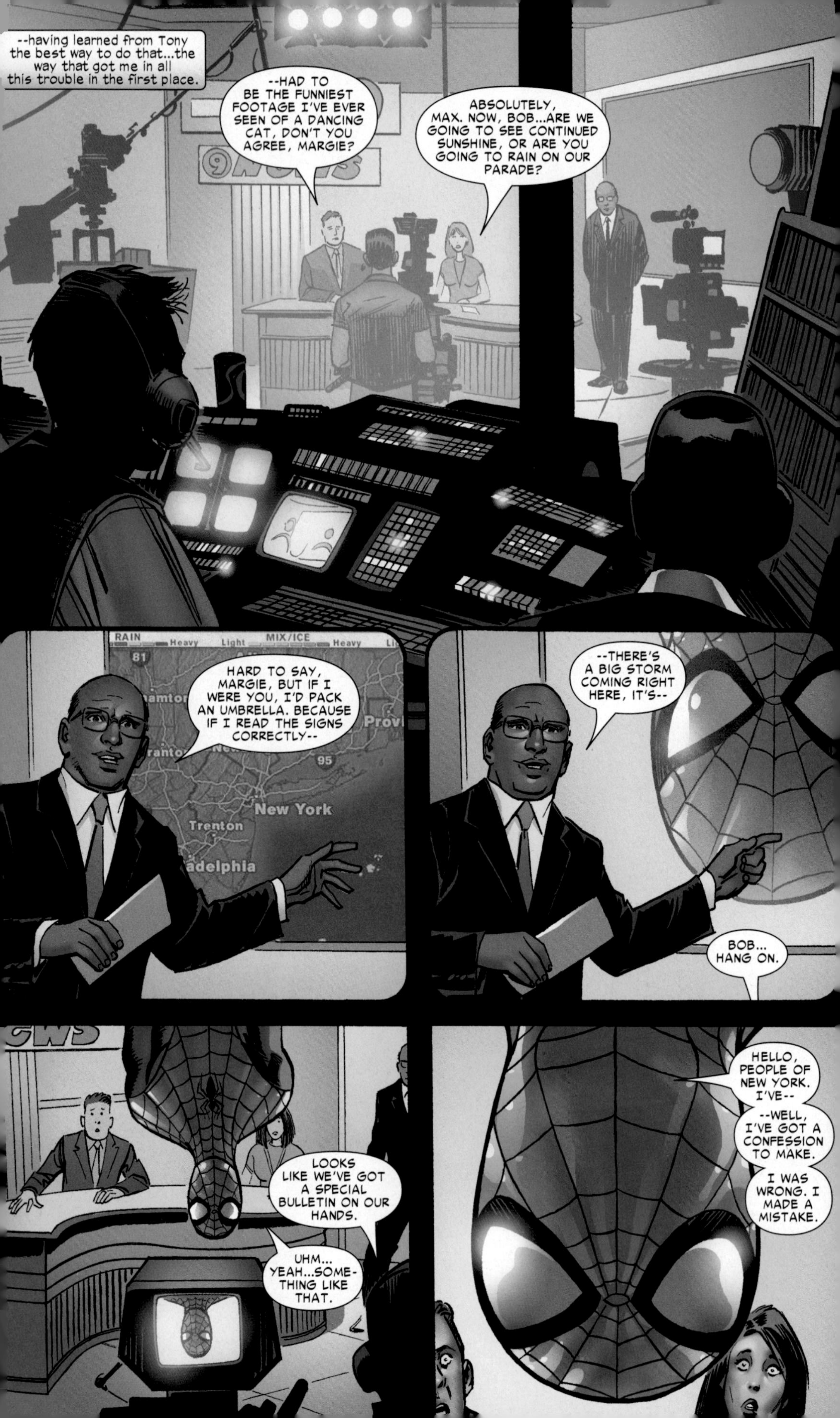
--having learned from Tony the best way to do that...the way that got me in all this trouble in the first place.
--HAD TO BE THE FUNNIEST FOOTAGE I'VE EVER SEEN OF A DANCING CAT, DON'T YOU AGREE, MARGIE?
ABSOLUTELY, MAX. NOW, BOB...ARE WE GOING TO SEE CONTINUED SUNSHINE, OR ARE YOU GOING TO RAIN ON OUR PARADE?
RAIN Heavy Light MIX/ICE Heavy
New York
Trenton
HARD TO SAY, MARGIE, BUT IF I WERE YOU, I'D PACK AN UMBRELLA. BECAUSE IF I READ THE SIGNS CORRECTLY--
--THERE'S A BIG STORM COMING RIGHT HERE, IT'S--
BOB... HANG ON.
LOOKS LIKE WE'VE GOT A SPECIAL BULLETIN ON OUR HANDS.
UHM... YEAH...SOME-THING LIKE THAT.
HELLO, PEOPLE OF NEW YORK. I'VE--
--WELL, I'VE GOT A CONFESSION TO MAKE.
I WAS WRONG. I MADE A MISTAKE.

FOR THE LAST MONTH OR SO, I'VE BEEN THE CLOSEST PERSON TO TONY STARK--IRON MAN--AND I'VE HAD A CHANCE TO SEE HIS OPERATION FIRSTHAND.

I'VE SEEN THE VERY CONCEPT OF JUSTICE DESTROYED. I'VE SEEN HEROES AND BAD GUYS ALIKE--

--DANGEROUS GUYS, NO MISTAKE, BUT STILL BORN IN THIS COUNTRY FOR THE MOST PART, DENIED DUE PROCESS--

GO GET 'EM, TIGER.

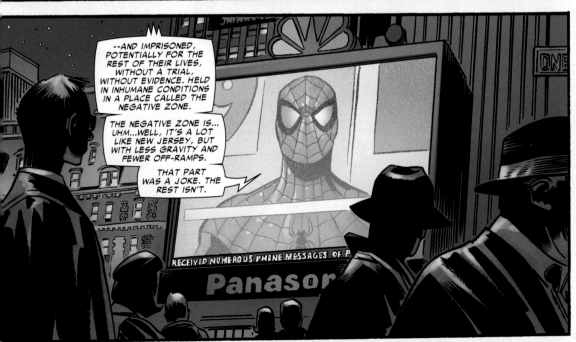

--AND IMPRISONED, POTENTIALLY FOR THE REST OF THEIR LIVES, WITHOUT A TRIAL, WITHOUT EVIDENCE. HELD IN INHUMANE CONDITIONS IN A PLACE CALLED THE NEGATIVE ZONE.

THE NEGATIVE ZONE IS... UHM...WELL, IT'S A LOT LIKE NEW JERSEY, BUT WITH LESS GRAVITY AND FEWER OFF-RAMPS.

THAT PART WAS A JOKE. THE REST ISN'T.

RECEIVED NUMEROUS PHONE MESSAGES OF P

Panasor

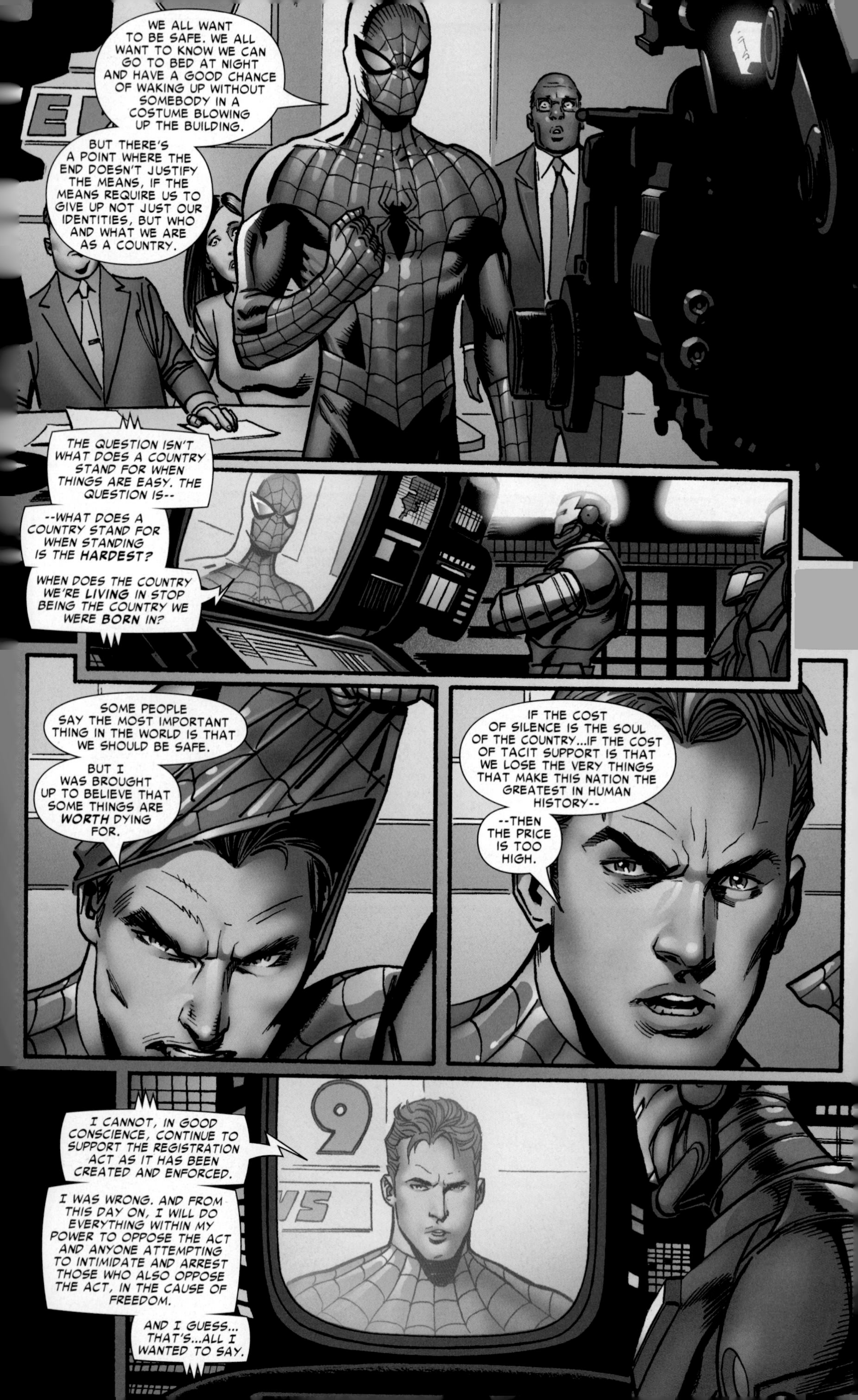
WE ALL WANT TO BE SAFE. WE ALL WANT TO KNOW WE CAN GO TO BED AT NIGHT AND HAVE A GOOD CHANCE OF WAKING UP WITHOUT SOMEBODY IN A COSTUME BLOWING UP THE BUILDING.
BUT THERE'S A POINT WHERE THE END DOESN'T JUSTIFY THE MEANS, IF THE MEANS REQUIRE US TO GIVE UP NOT JUST OUR IDENTITIES, BUT WHO AND WHAT WE ARE AS A COUNTRY.
THE QUESTION ISN'T WHAT DOES A COUNTRY STAND FOR WHEN THINGS ARE EASY. THE QUESTION IS--
--WHAT DOES A COUNTRY STAND FOR WHEN STANDING IS THE HARDEST?
WHEN DOES THE COUNTRY WE'RE LIVING IN STOP BEING THE COUNTRY WE WERE BORN IN?
SOME PEOPLE SAY THE MOST IMPORTANT THING IN THE WORLD IS THAT WE SHOULD BE SAFE.
BUT I WAS BROUGHT UP TO BELIEVE THAT SOME THINGS ARE WORTH DYING FOR.
IF THE COST OF SILENCE IS THE SOUL OF THE COUNTRY...IF THE COST OF TACIT SUPPORT IS THAT WE LOSE THE VERY THINGS THAT MAKE THIS NATION THE GREATEST IN HUMAN HISTORY--
--THEN THE PRICE IS TOO HIGH.
I CANNOT, IN GOOD CONSCIENCE, CONTINUE TO SUPPORT THE REGISTRATION ACT AS IT HAS BEEN CREATED AND ENFORCED.
I WAS WRONG. AND FROM THIS DAY ON, I WILL DO EVERYTHING WITHIN MY POWER TO OPPOSE THE ACT AND ANYONE ATTEMPTING TO INTIMIDATE AND ARREST THOSE WHO ALSO OPPOSE THE ACT, IN THE CAUSE OF FREEDOM.
AND I GUESS... THAT'S...ALL I WANTED TO SAY.

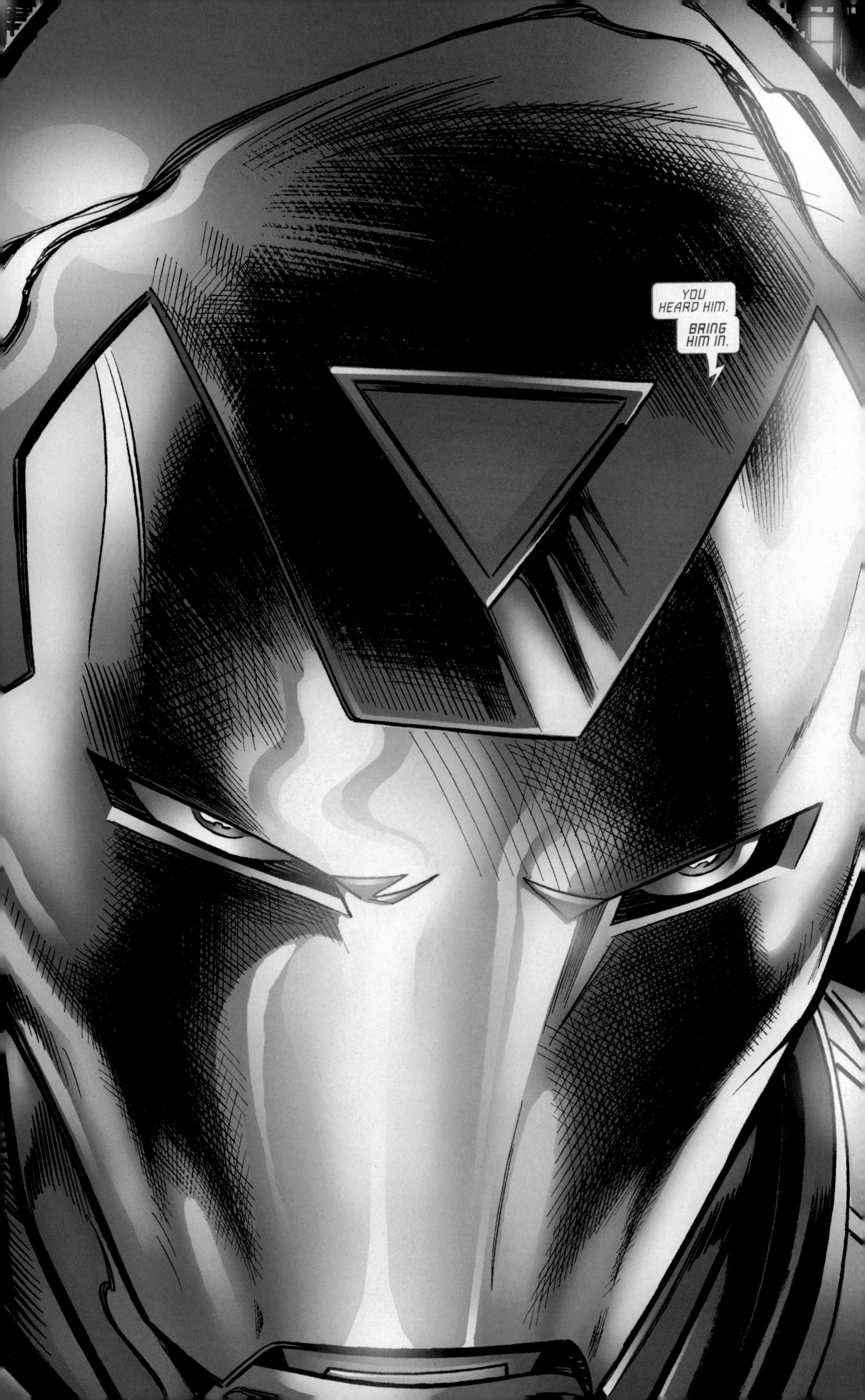
YOU HEARD HIM.
BRING HIM IN.

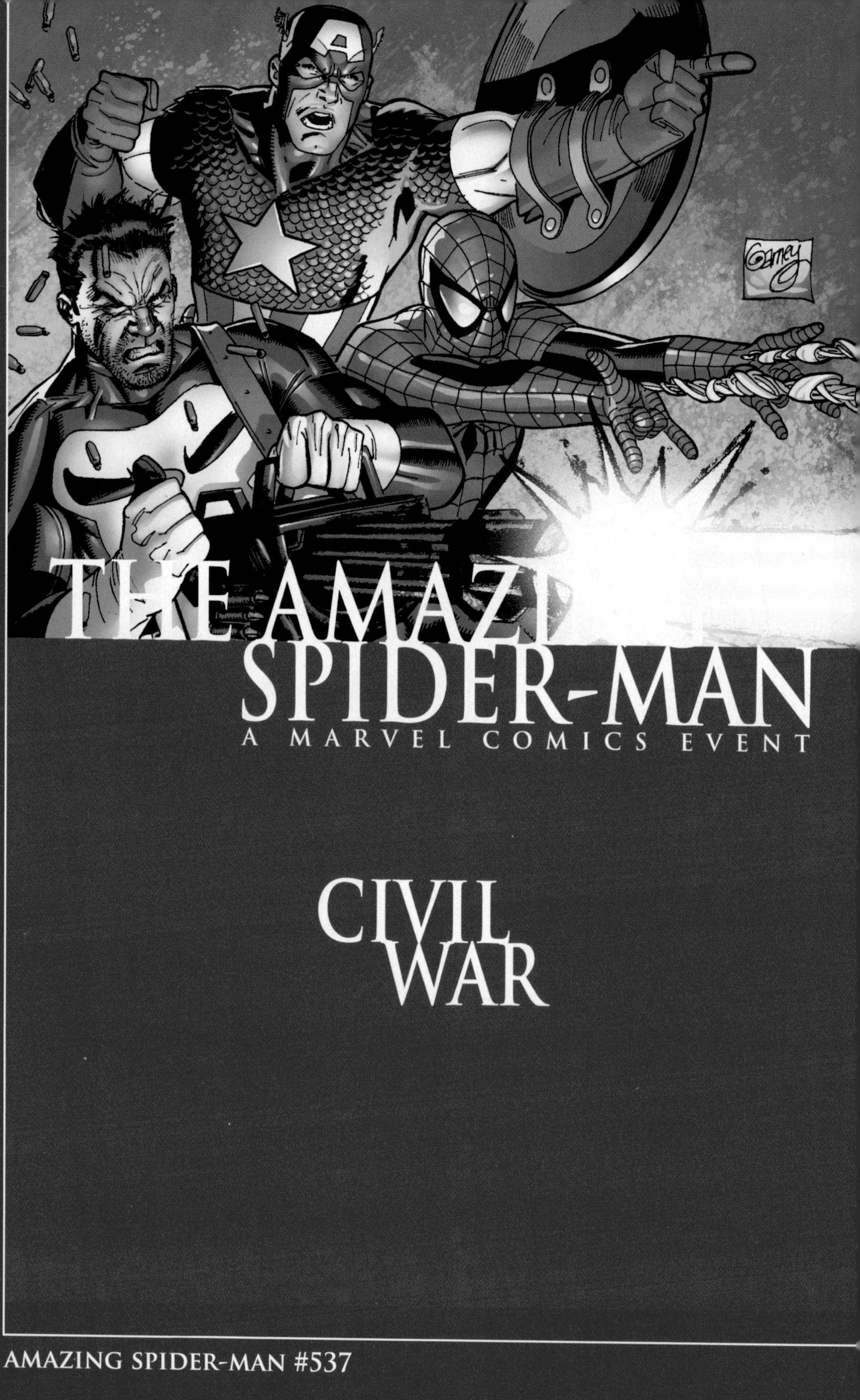
THE AMAZI
SPIDER-MAN
A MARVEL COMICS EVENT
CIVIL
WAR

AMAZING SPIDER-MAN #537

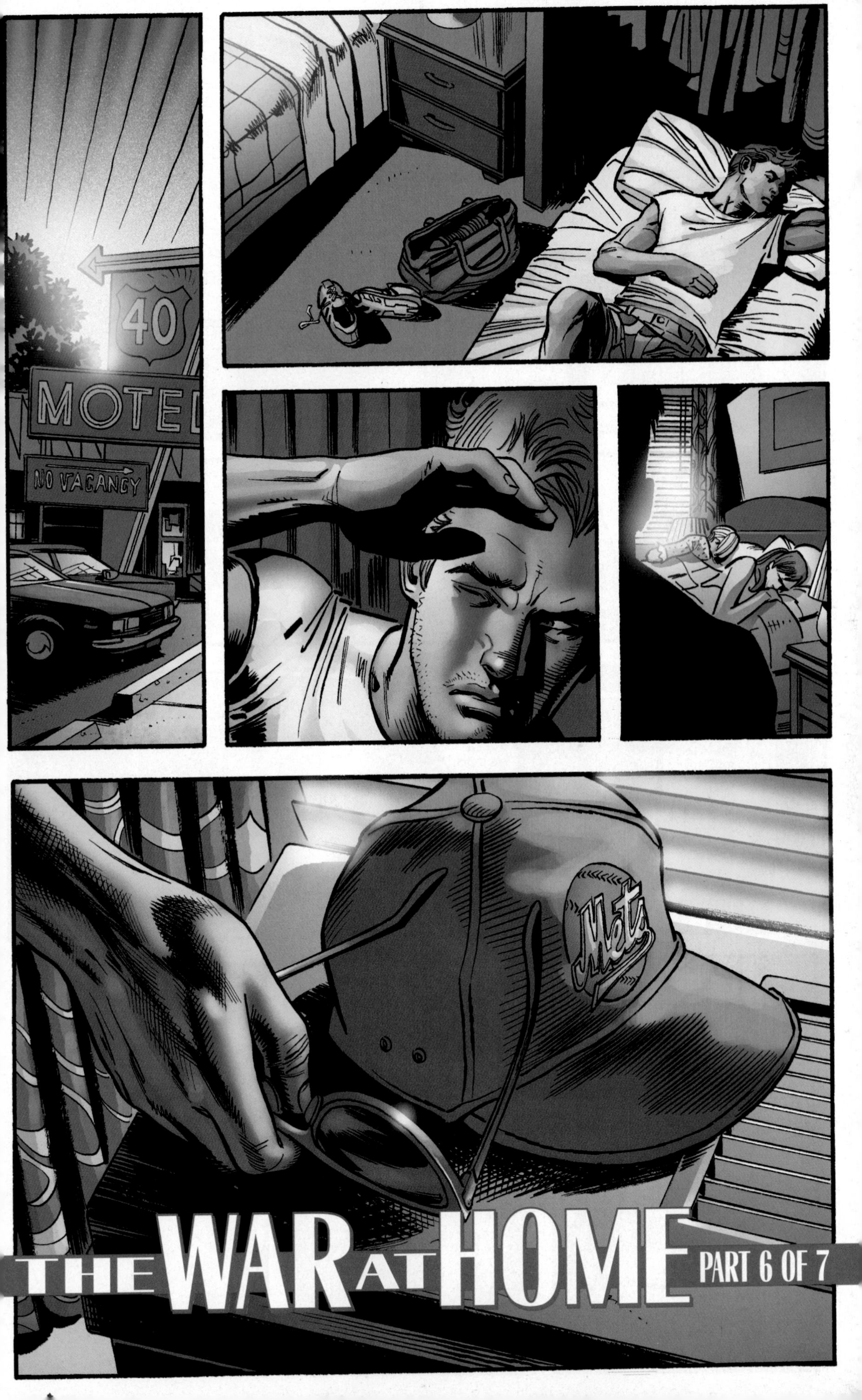
40
MOTEL
NO VACANCY
Mets
THE WAR AT HOME
PART 6 OF 7

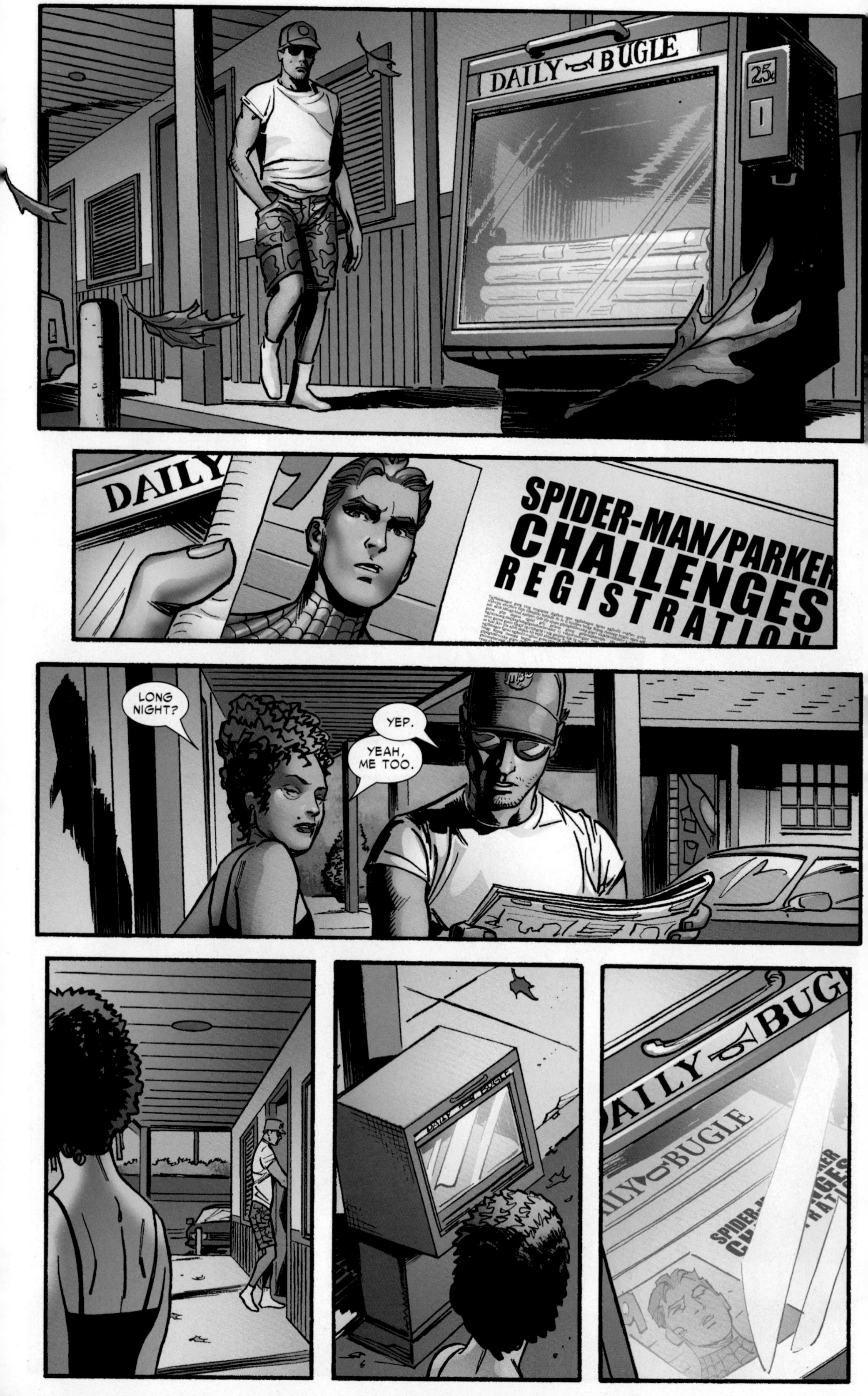
DAILY BUGLE
25¢
DAILY
SPIDER-MAN/PARKER
CHALLENGES
REGISTRATION
LONG NIGHT?
YEP.
YEAH, ME TOO.
DAILY BUGLE
DAILY BUGLE

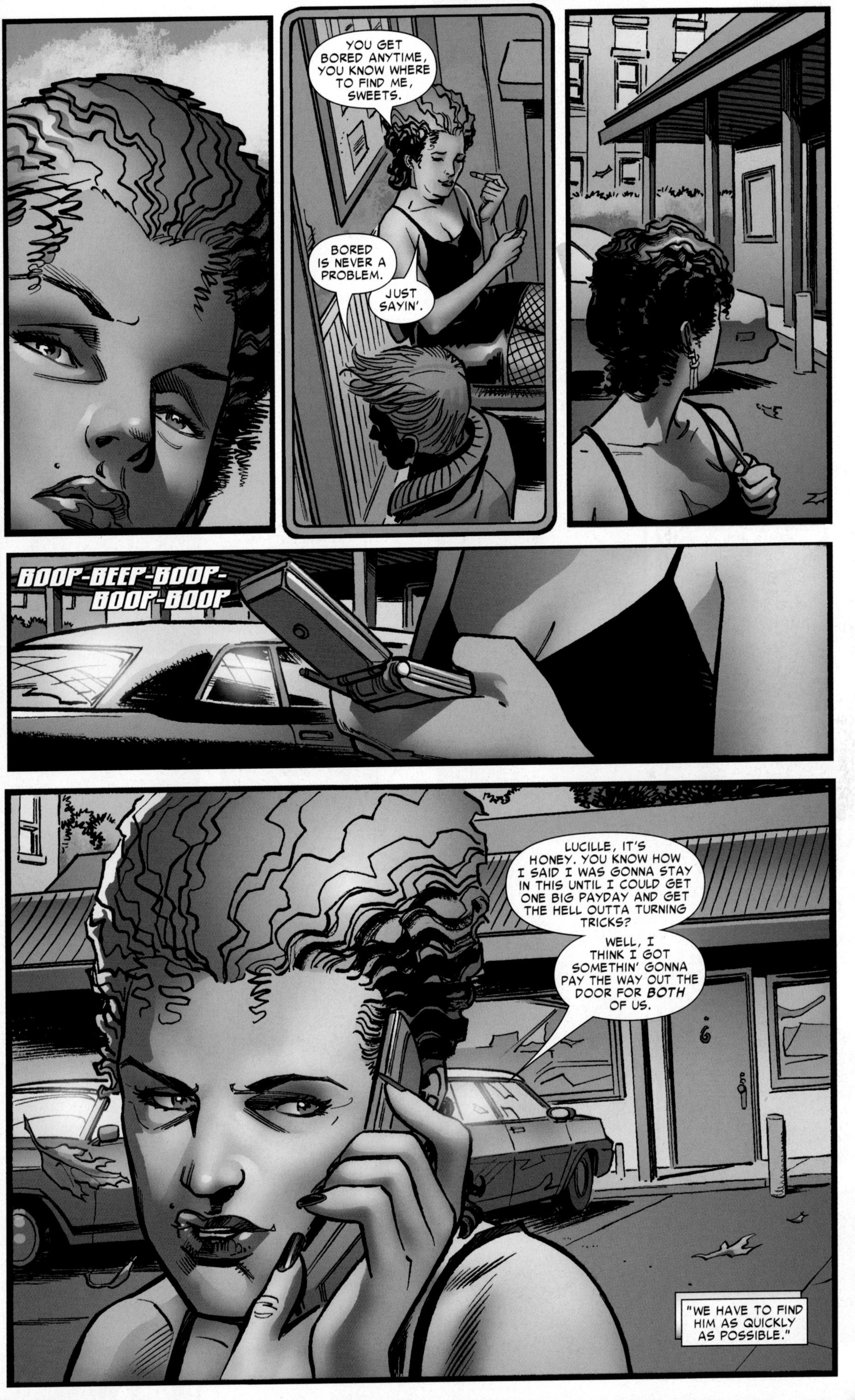
YOU GET BORED ANYTIME, YOU KNOW WHERE TO FIND ME, SWEETS.
BORED IS NEVER A PROBLEM.
JUST SAYIN'.
BOOP-BEEP-BOOP-BOOP-BOOP
LUCILLE, IT'S HONEY. YOU KNOW HOW I SAID I WAS GONNA STAY IN THIS UNTIL I COULD GET ONE BIG PAYDAY AND GET THE HELL OUTTA TURNING TRICKS?
WELL, I THINK I GOT SOMETHIN' GONNA PAY THE WAY OUT THE DOOR FOR *BOTH* OF US.
"WE HAVE TO FIND HIM AS QUICKLY AS POSSIBLE."

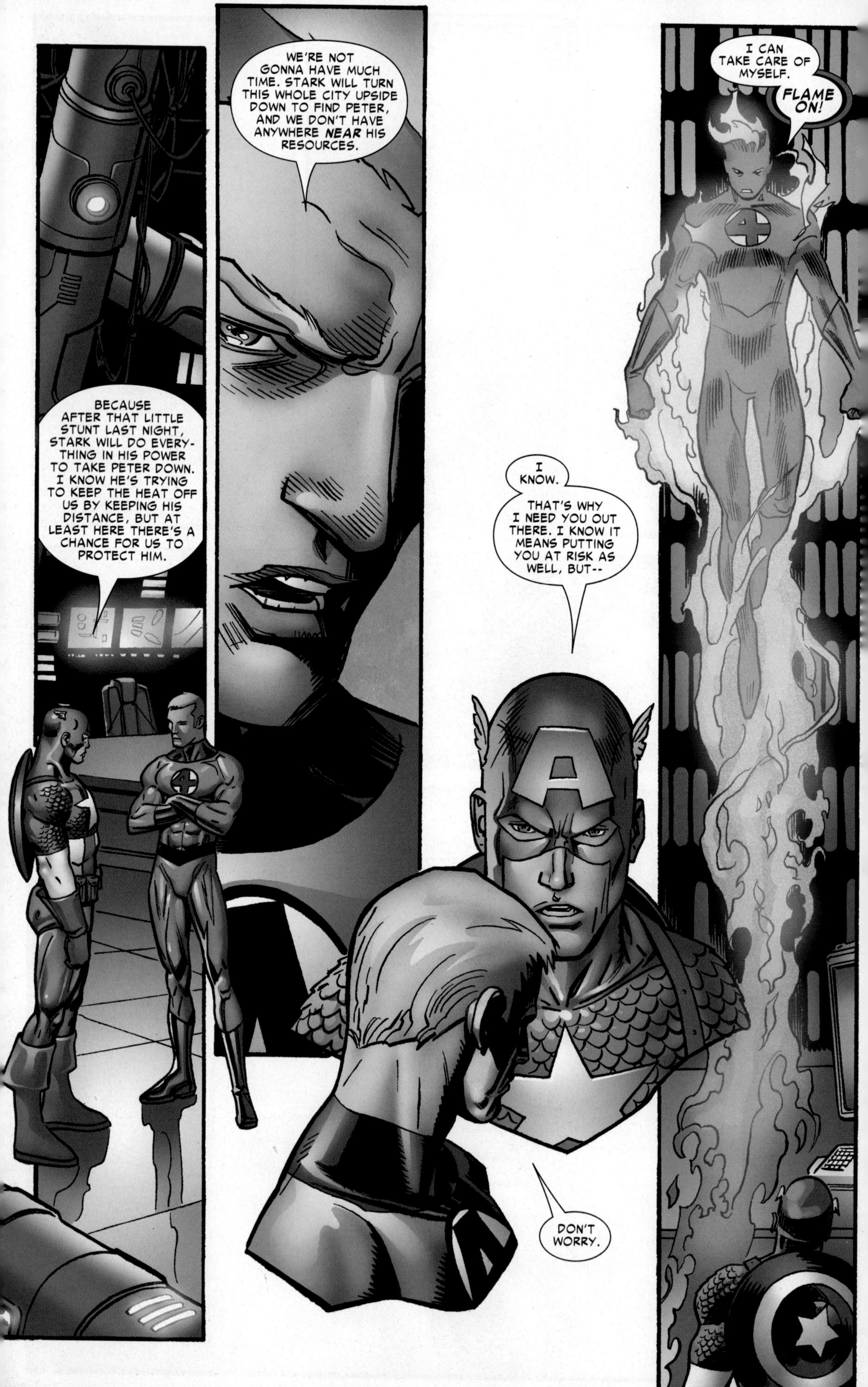
WE'RE NOT GONNA HAVE MUCH TIME. STARK WILL TURN THIS WHOLE CITY UPSIDE DOWN TO FIND PETER, AND WE DON'T HAVE ANYWHERE NEAR HIS RESOURCES.
BECAUSE AFTER THAT LITTLE STUNT LAST NIGHT, STARK WILL DO EVERY-THING IN HIS POWER TO TAKE PETER DOWN. I KNOW HE'S TRYING TO KEEP THE HEAT OFF US BY KEEPING HIS DISTANCE, BUT AT LEAST HERE THERE'S A CHANCE FOR US TO PROTECT HIM.
I KNOW.
THAT'S WHY I NEED YOU OUT THERE. I KNOW IT MEANS PUTTING YOU AT RISK AS WELL, BUT--
DON'T WORRY.
I CAN TAKE CARE OF MYSELF.
FLAME ON!

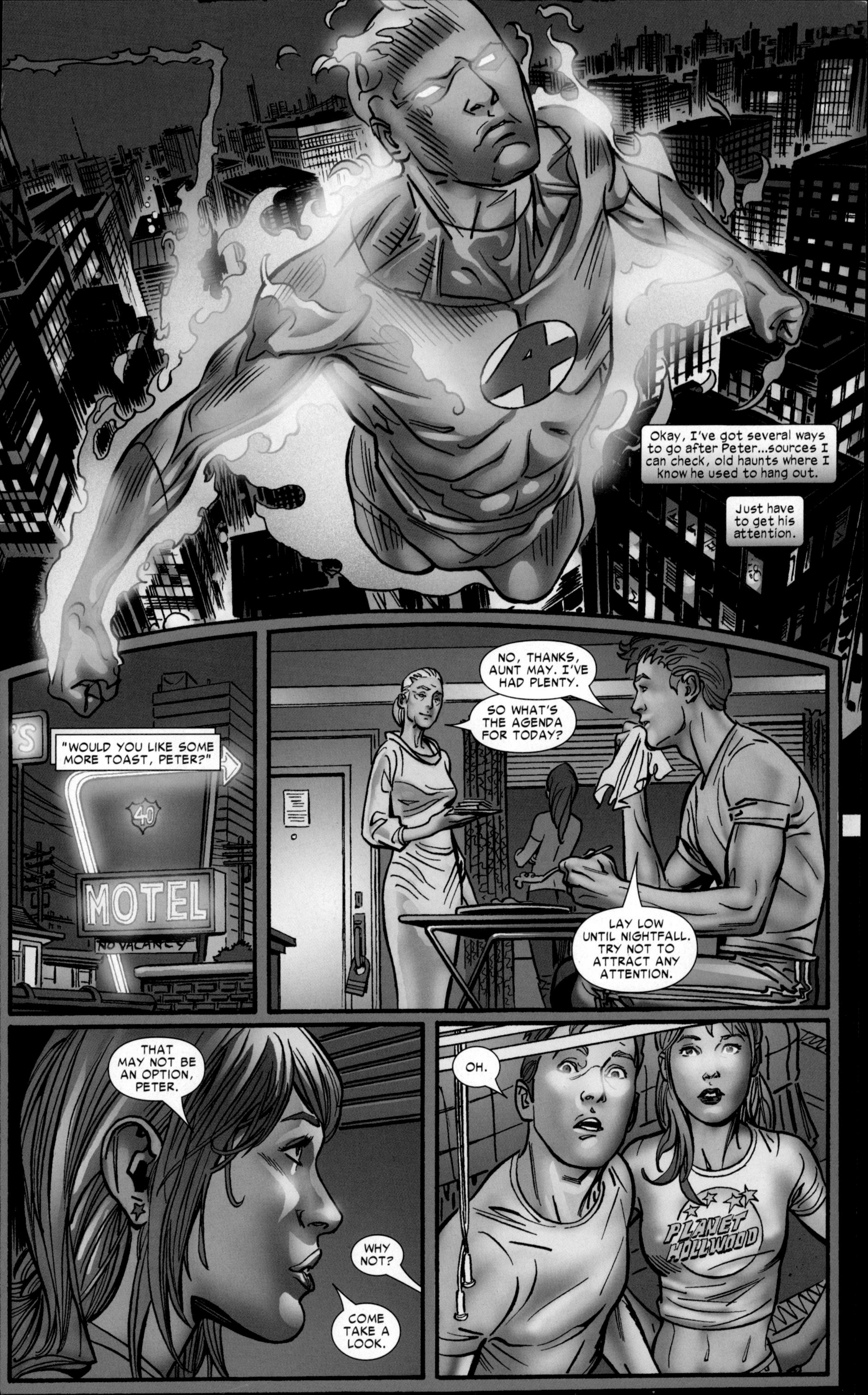
Okay, I've got several ways to go after Peter...sources I can check, old haunts where I know he used to hang out.
Just have to get his attention.
"WOULD YOU LIKE SOME MORE TOAST, PETER?"
MOTEL
NO, THANKS, AUNT MAY. I'VE HAD PLENTY.
SO WHAT'S THE AGENDA FOR TODAY?
LAY LOW UNTIL NIGHTFALL. TRY NOT TO ATTRACT ANY ATTENTION.
THAT MAY NOT BE AN OPTION, PETER.
WHY NOT?
COME TAKE A LOOK.
OH.
PLANET HOLLWOOD

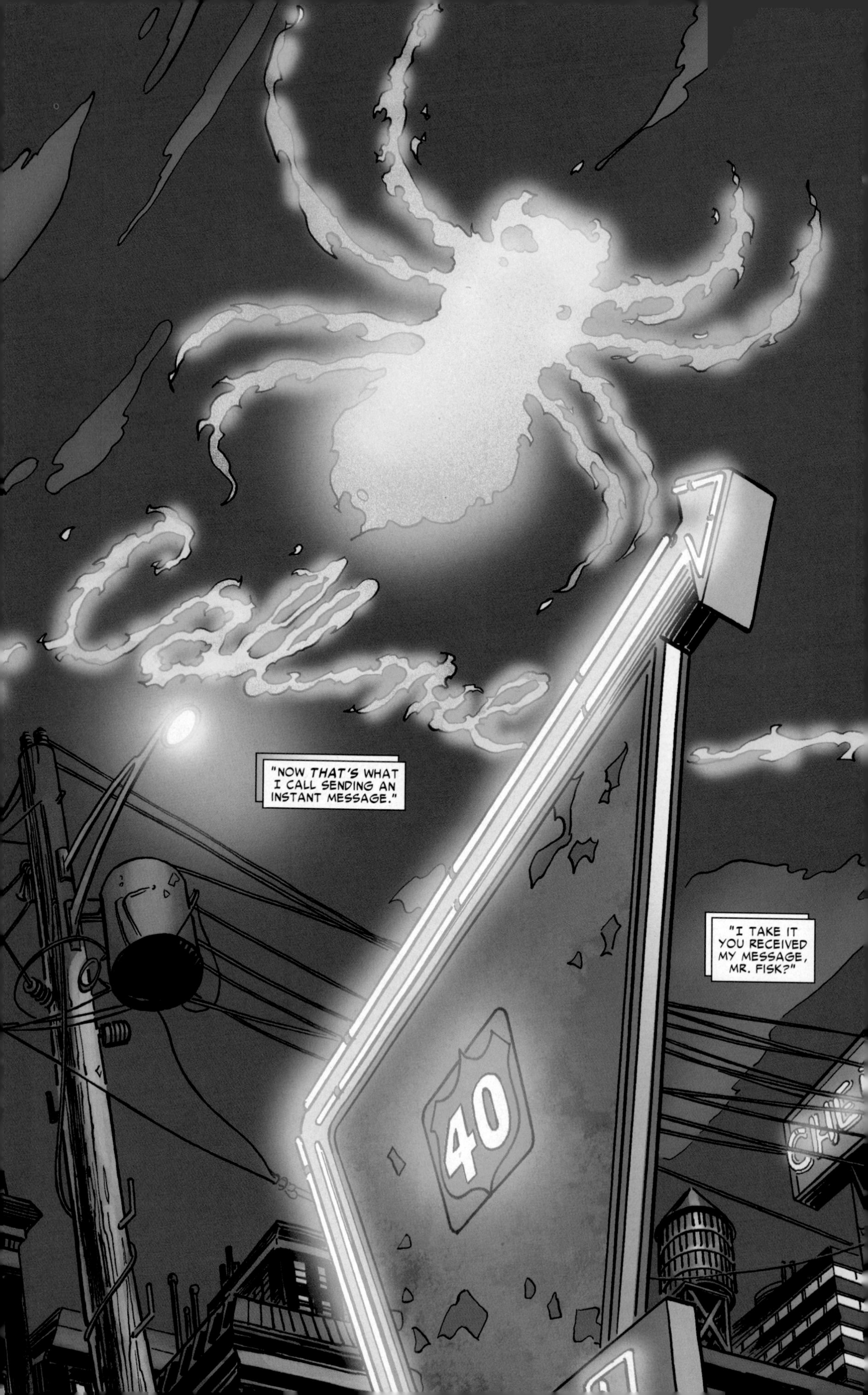
"NOW THAT'S WHAT I CALL SENDING AN INSTANT MESSAGE."
"I TAKE IT YOU RECEIVED MY MESSAGE, MR. FISK?"
40

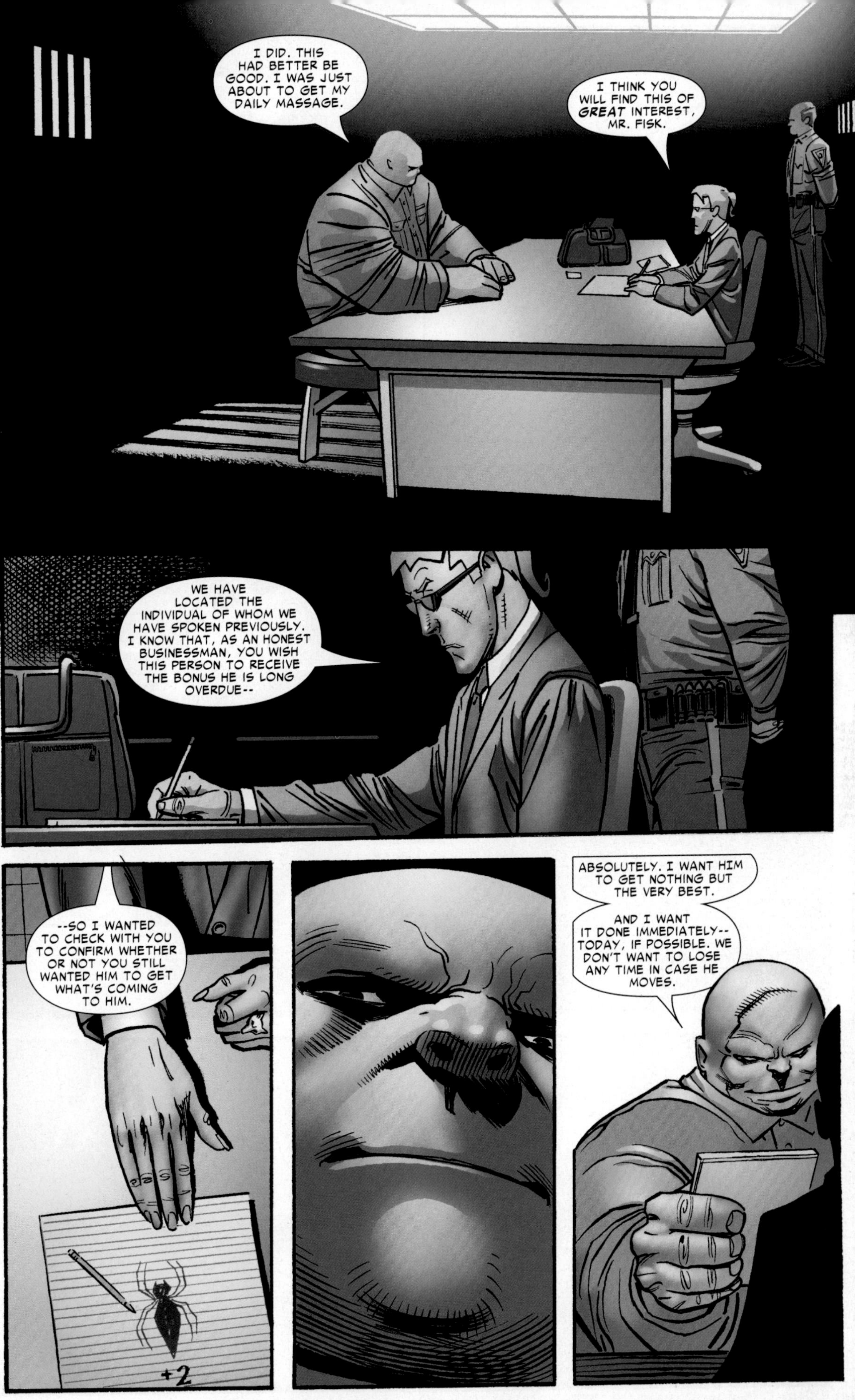
I DID. THIS HAD BETTER BE GOOD. I WAS JUST ABOUT TO GET MY DAILY MASSAGE.
I THINK YOU WILL FIND THIS OF GREAT INTEREST, MR. FISK.
WE HAVE LOCATED THE INDIVIDUAL OF WHOM WE HAVE SPOKEN PREVIOUSLY. I KNOW THAT, AS AN HONEST BUSINESSMAN, YOU WISH THIS PERSON TO RECEIVE THE BONUS HE IS LONG OVERDUE--
--SO I WANTED TO CHECK WITH YOU TO CONFIRM WHETHER OR NOT YOU STILL WANTED HIM TO GET WHAT'S COMING TO HIM.
+2
ABSOLUTELY. I WANT HIM TO GET NOTHING BUT THE VERY BEST.
AND I WANT IT DONE IMMEDIATELY-- TODAY, IF POSSIBLE. WE DON'T WANT TO LOSE ANY TIME IN CASE HE MOVES.

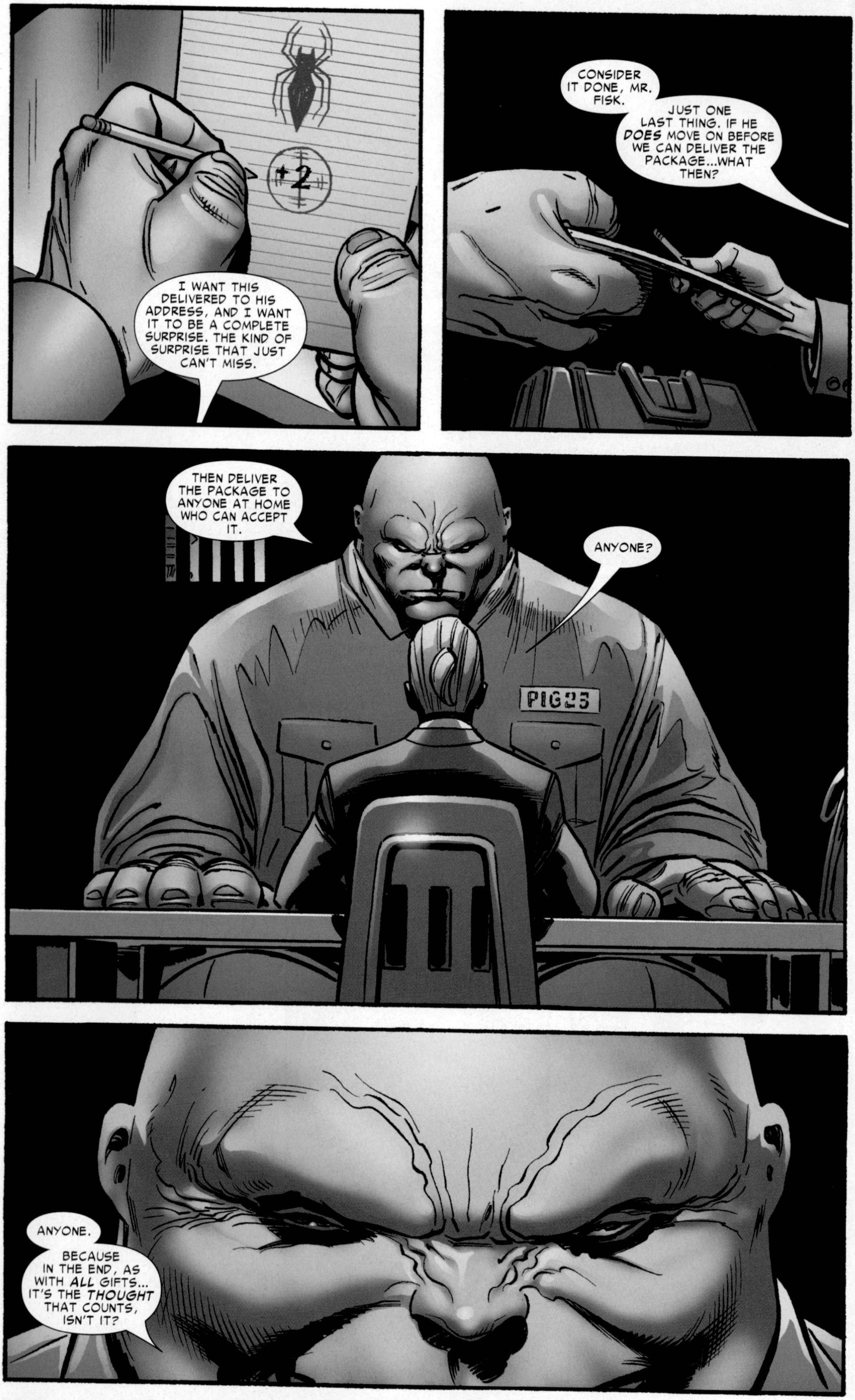

I WANT THIS DELIVERED TO HIS ADDRESS, AND I WANT IT TO BE A COMPLETE SURPRISE. THE KIND OF SURPRISE THAT JUST CAN'T MISS.
CONSIDER IT DONE, MR. FISK.
JUST ONE LAST THING. IF HE DOES MOVE ON BEFORE WE CAN DELIVER THE PACKAGE...WHAT THEN?
THEN DELIVER THE PACKAGE TO ANYONE AT HOME WHO CAN ACCEPT IT.
ANYONE?
PIG25
ANYONE.
BECAUSE IN THE END, AS WITH ALL GIFTS... IT'S THE THOUGHT THAT COUNTS, ISN'T IT?

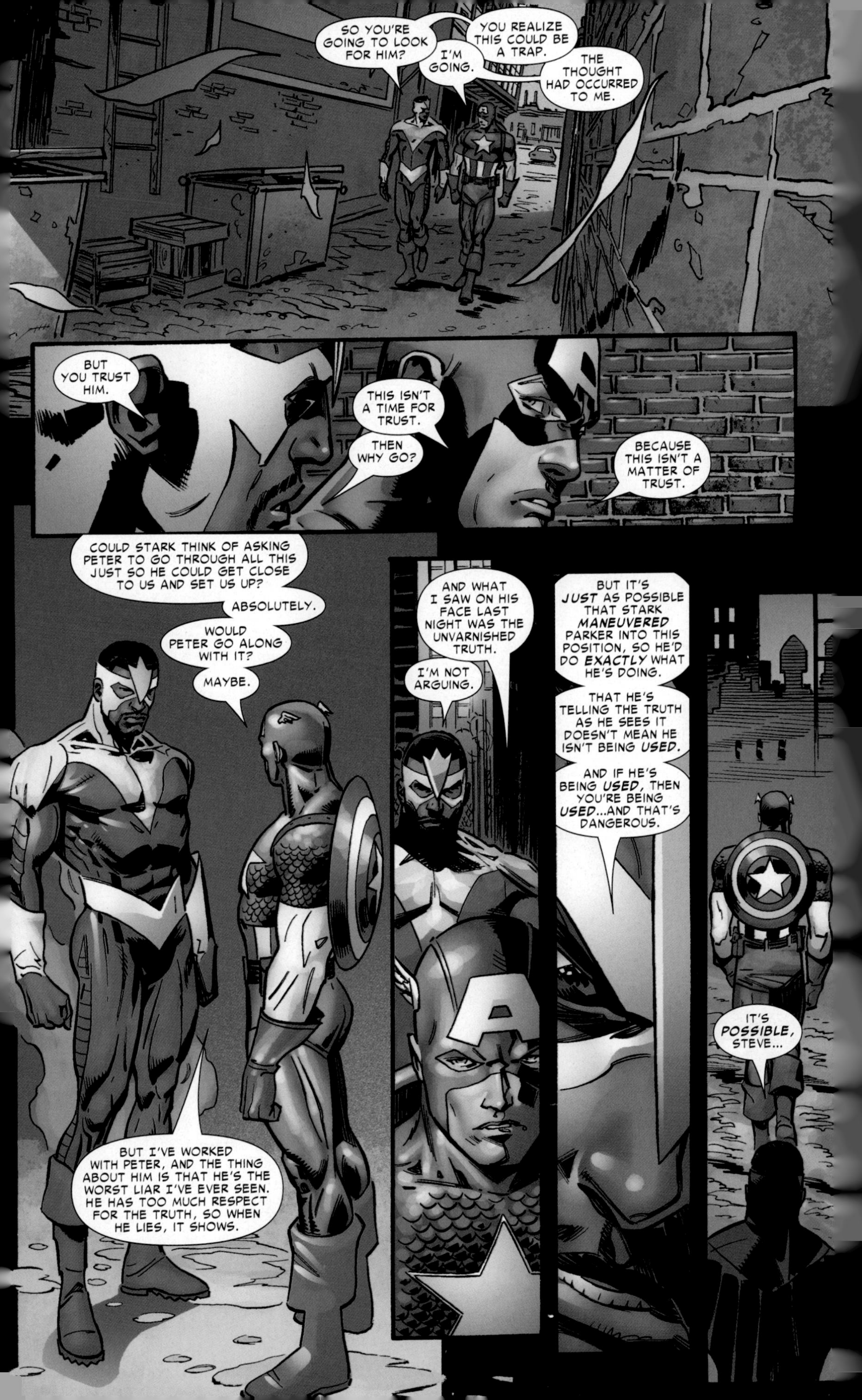
SO YOU'RE GOING TO LOOK FOR HIM?
I'M GOING.
YOU REALIZE THIS COULD BE A TRAP.
THE THOUGHT HAD OCCURRED TO ME.
BUT YOU TRUST HIM.
THIS ISN'T A TIME FOR TRUST.
THEN WHY GO?
BECAUSE THIS ISN'T A MATTER OF TRUST.
COULD STARK THINK OF ASKING PETER TO GO THROUGH ALL THIS JUST SO HE COULD GET CLOSE TO US AND SET US UP?
ABSOLUTELY.
WOULD PETER GO ALONG WITH IT?
MAYBE.
BUT I'VE WORKED WITH PETER, AND THE THING ABOUT HIM IS THAT HE'S THE WORST LIAR I'VE EVER SEEN. HE HAS TOO MUCH RESPECT FOR THE TRUTH, SO WHEN HE LIES, IT SHOWS.
AND WHAT I SAW ON HIS FACE LAST NIGHT WAS THE UNVARNISHED TRUTH.
I'M NOT ARGUING.
BUT IT'S *JUST* AS POSSIBLE THAT STARK *MANEUVERED* PARKER INTO THIS POSITION, SO HE'D DO *EXACTLY* WHAT HE'S DOING.
THAT HE'S TELLING THE TRUTH AS HE SEES IT DOESN'T MEAN HE ISN'T BEING *USED*.
AND IF HE'S BEING *USED*, THEN YOU'RE BEING *USED*...AND THAT'S DANGEROUS.
IT'S *POSSIBLE*, STEVE...

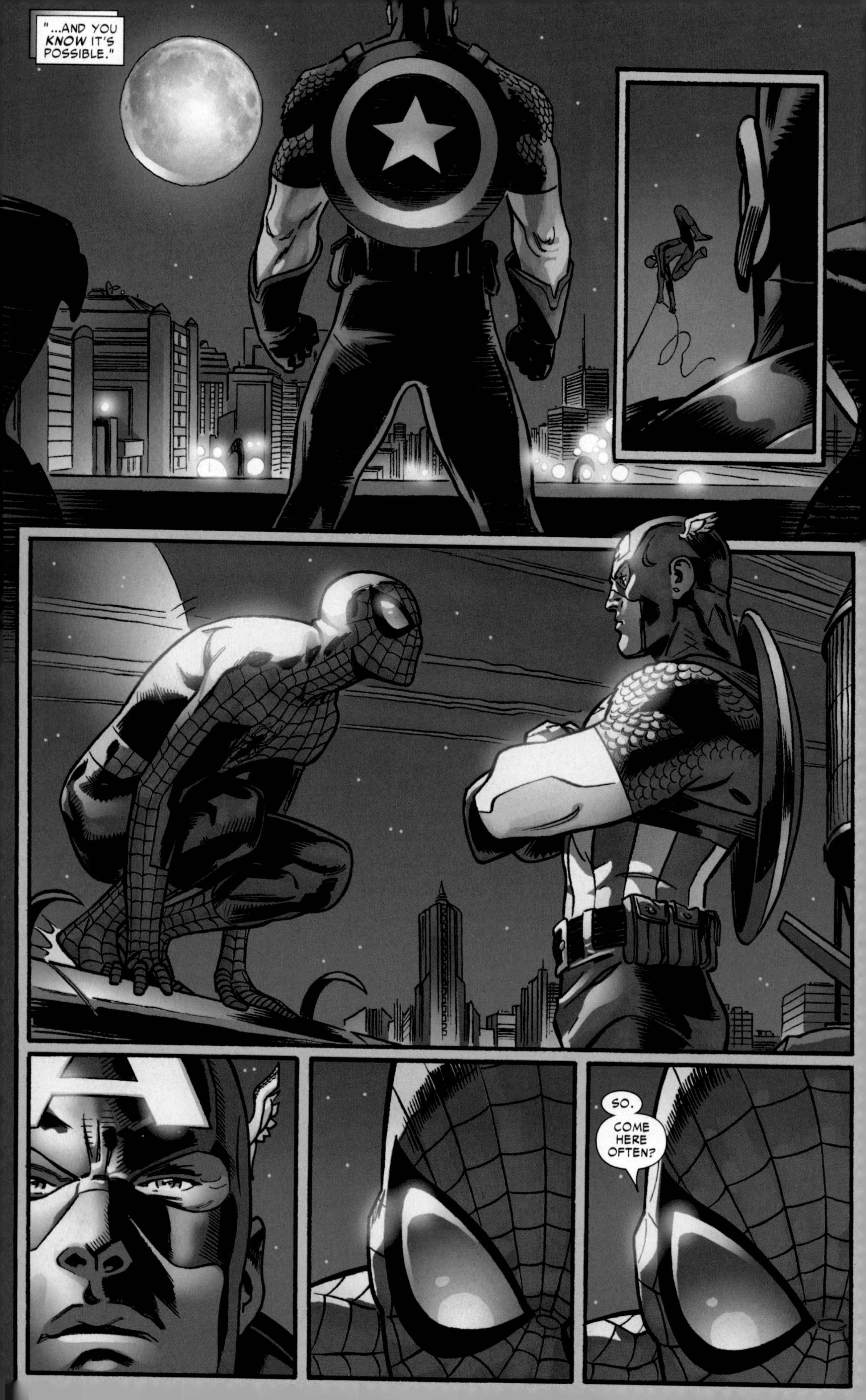
"...AND YOU KNOW IT'S POSSIBLE."
SO.
COME HERE OFTEN?

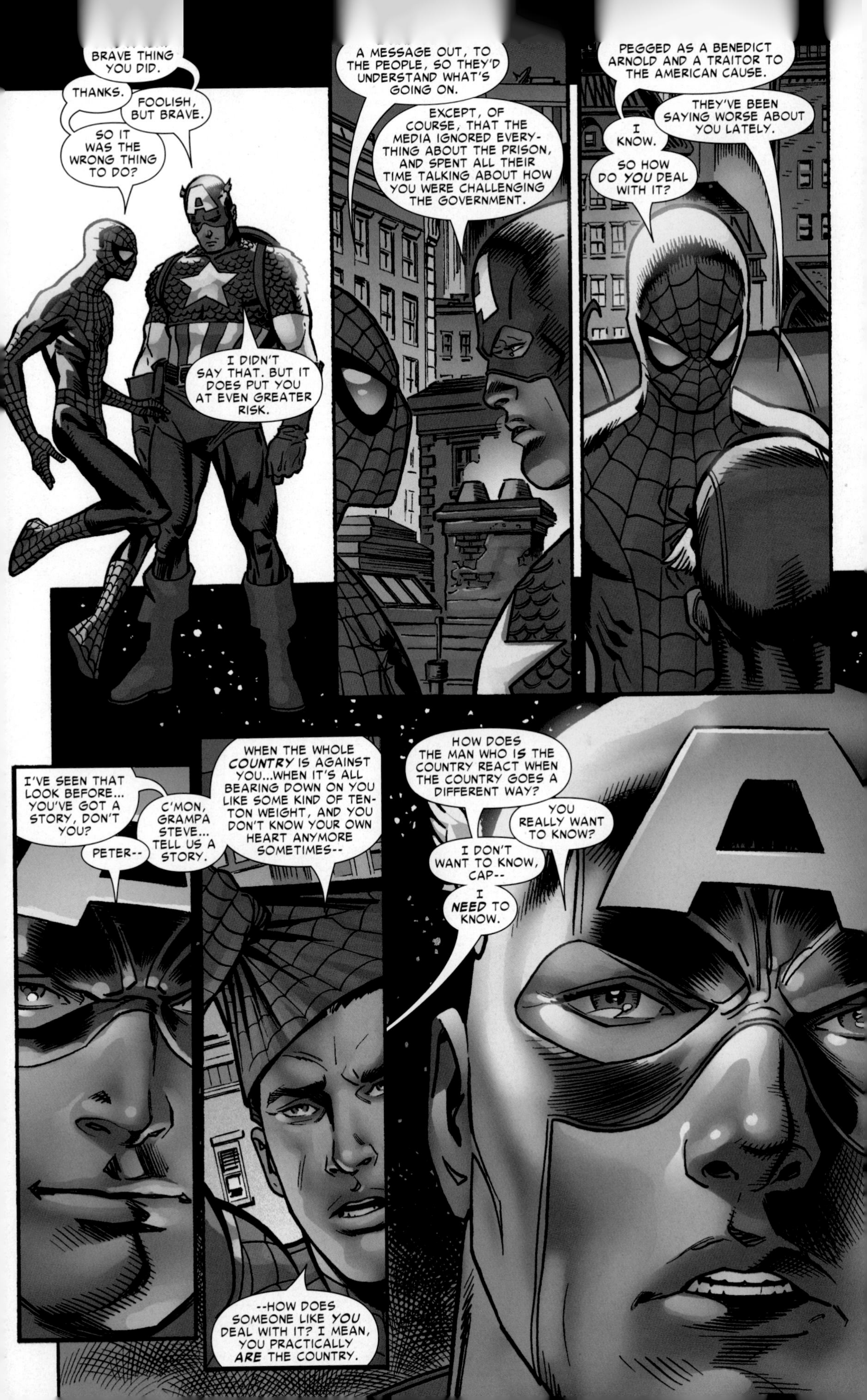
BRAVE THING YOU DID.
THANKS.
FOOLISH, BUT BRAVE.
SO IT WAS THE WRONG THING TO DO?
I DIDN'T SAY THAT. BUT IT DOES PUT YOU AT EVEN GREATER RISK.
A MESSAGE OUT, TO THE PEOPLE, SO THEY'D UNDERSTAND WHAT'S GOING ON.
EXCEPT, OF COURSE, THAT THE MEDIA IGNORED EVERY-THING ABOUT THE PRISON, AND SPENT ALL THEIR TIME TALKING ABOUT HOW YOU WERE CHALLENGING THE GOVERNMENT.
PEGGED AS A BENEDICT ARNOLD AND A TRAITOR TO THE AMERICAN CAUSE.
I KNOW.
THEY'VE BEEN SAYING WORSE ABOUT YOU LATELY.
SO HOW DO YOU DEAL WITH IT?
I'VE SEEN THAT LOOK BEFORE... YOU'VE GOT A STORY, DON'T YOU?
C'MON, GRAMPA STEVE... TELL US A STORY.
PETER--
WHEN THE WHOLE COUNTRY IS AGAINST YOU...WHEN IT'S ALL BEARING DOWN ON YOU LIKE SOME KIND OF TEN-TON WEIGHT, AND YOU DON'T KNOW YOUR OWN HEART ANYMORE SOMETIMES--
--HOW DOES SOMEONE LIKE YOU DEAL WITH IT? I MEAN, YOU PRACTICALLY ARE THE COUNTRY.
HOW DOES THE MAN WHO IS THE COUNTRY REACT WHEN THE COUNTRY GOES A DIFFERENT WAY?
YOU REALLY WANT TO KNOW?
I DON'T WANT TO KNOW, CAP--
I NEED TO KNOW.

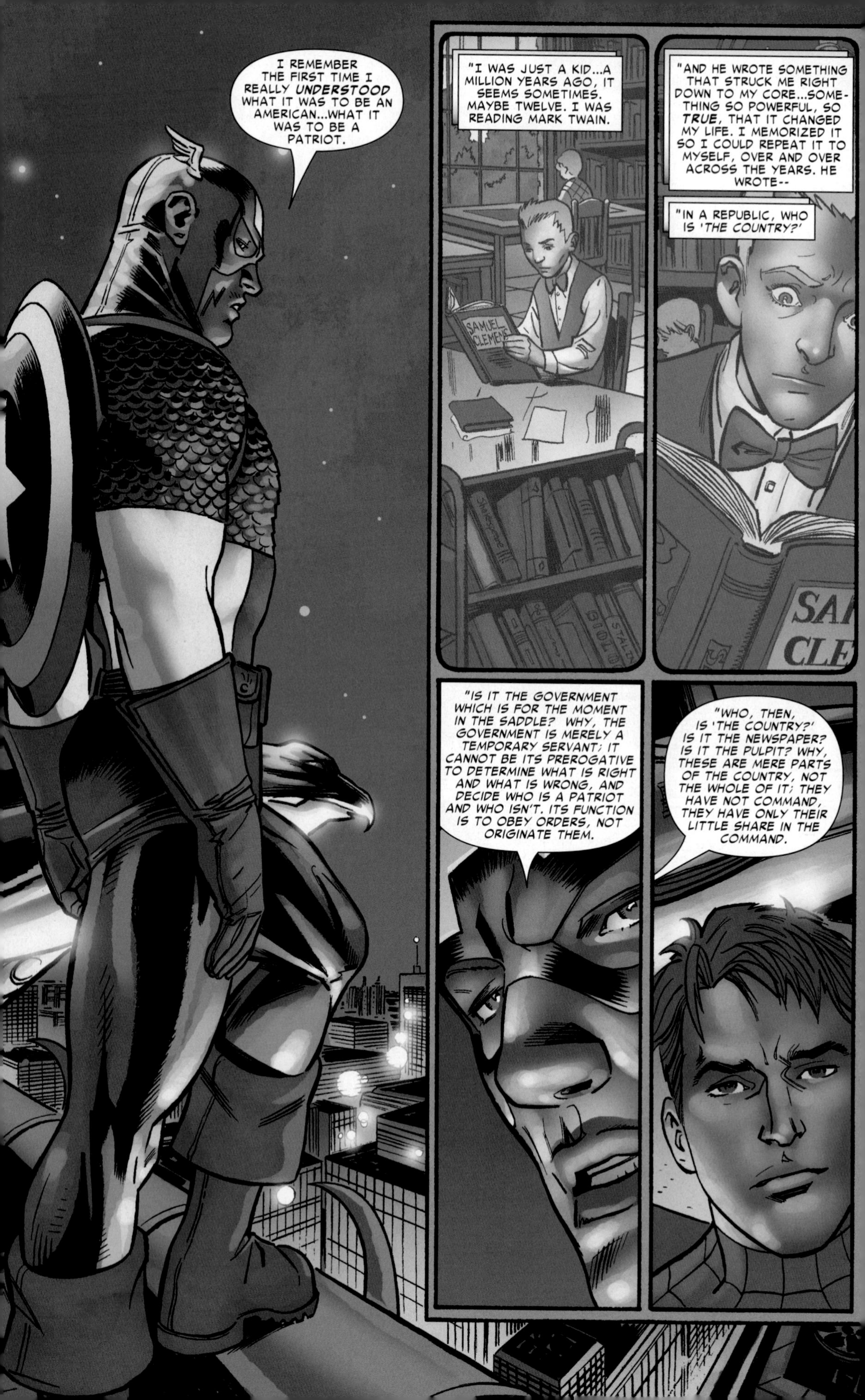

I REMEMBER THE FIRST TIME I REALLY *UNDERSTOOD* WHAT IT WAS TO BE AN AMERICAN...WHAT IT WAS TO BE A PATRIOT.
"I WAS JUST A KID...A MILLION YEARS AGO, IT SEEMS SOMETIMES. MAYBE TWELVE. I WAS READING MARK TWAIN.
SAMUEL CLEMENS
"AND HE WROTE SOMETHING THAT STRUCK ME RIGHT DOWN TO MY CORE...SOMETHING SO POWERFUL, SO *TRUE*, THAT IT CHANGED MY LIFE. I MEMORIZED IT SO I COULD REPEAT IT TO MYSELF, OVER AND OVER ACROSS THE YEARS. HE WROTE--
"IN A REPUBLIC, WHO IS *'THE COUNTRY?'*
"IS IT THE GOVERNMENT WHICH IS FOR THE MOMENT IN THE SADDLE? WHY, THE GOVERNMENT IS MERELY A TEMPORARY SERVANT; IT CANNOT BE ITS PREROGATIVE TO DETERMINE WHAT IS RIGHT AND WHAT IS WRONG, AND DECIDE WHO IS A PATRIOT AND WHO ISN'T. ITS FUNCTION IS TO OBEY ORDERS, NOT ORIGINATE THEM.
"WHO, THEN, IS 'THE COUNTRY?' IS IT THE NEWSPAPER? IS IT THE PULPIT? WHY, THESE ARE MERE PARTS OF THE COUNTRY, NOT THE WHOLE OF IT; THEY HAVE NOT COMMAND, THEY HAVE ONLY THEIR LITTLE SHARE IN THE COMMAND.

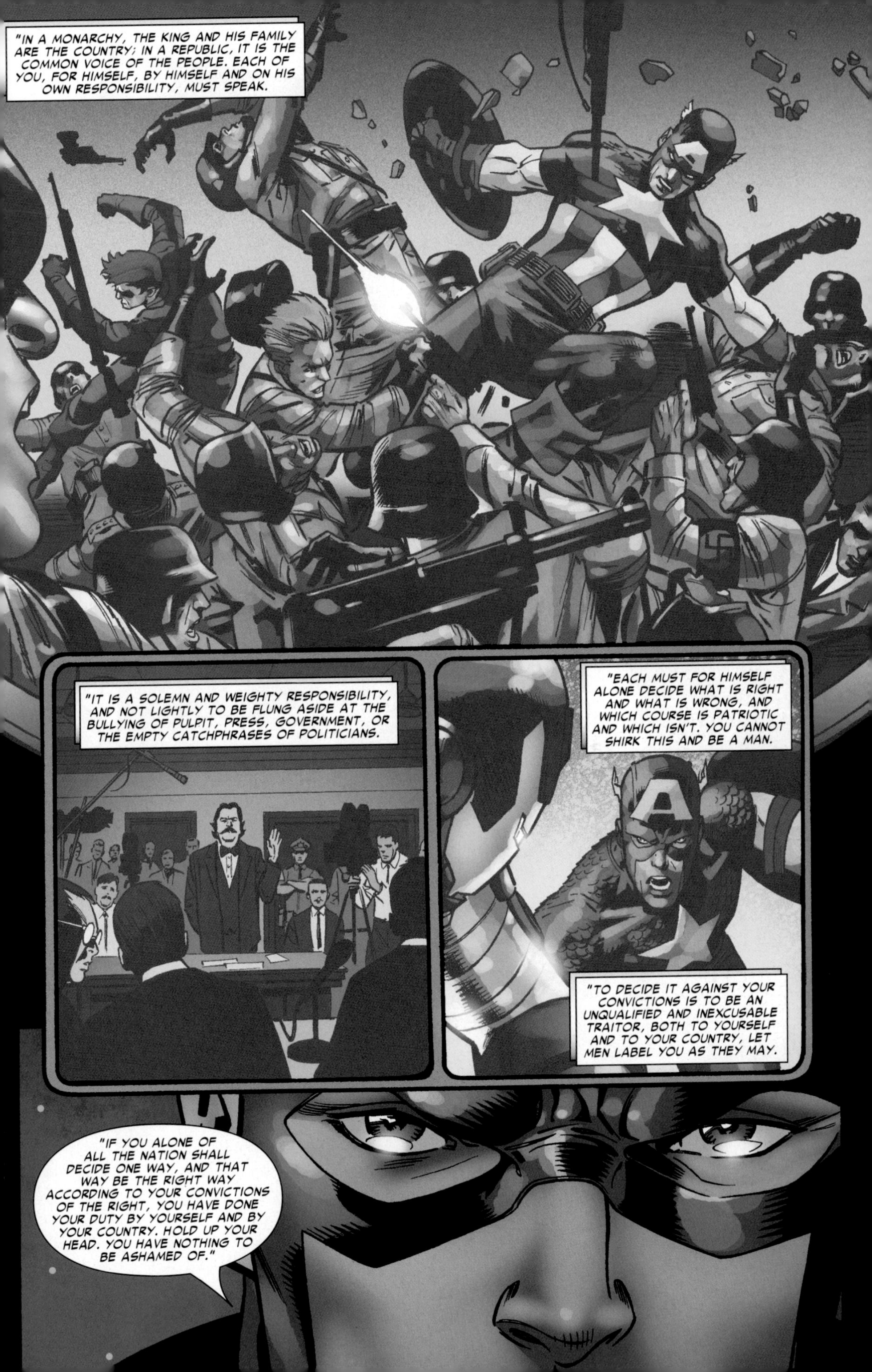
"IN A MONARCHY, THE KING AND HIS FAMILY ARE THE COUNTRY; IN A REPUBLIC, IT IS THE COMMON VOICE OF THE PEOPLE. EACH OF YOU, FOR HIMSELF, BY HIMSELF AND ON HIS OWN RESPONSIBILITY, MUST SPEAK.
"IT IS A SOLEMN AND WEIGHTY RESPONSIBILITY, AND NOT LIGHTLY TO BE FLUNG ASIDE AT THE BULLYING OF PULPIT, PRESS, GOVERNMENT, OR THE EMPTY CATCHPHRASES OF POLITICIANS.
"EACH MUST FOR HIMSELF ALONE DECIDE WHAT IS RIGHT AND WHAT IS WRONG, AND WHICH COURSE IS PATRIOTIC AND WHICH ISN'T. YOU CANNOT SHIRK THIS AND BE A MAN.
"TO DECIDE IT AGAINST YOUR CONVICTIONS IS TO BE AN UNQUALIFIED AND INEXCUSABLE TRAITOR, BOTH TO YOURSELF AND TO YOUR COUNTRY, LET MEN LABEL YOU AS THEY MAY.
"IF YOU ALONE OF ALL THE NATION SHALL DECIDE ONE WAY, AND THAT WAY BE THE RIGHT WAY ACCORDING TO YOUR CONVICTIONS OF THE RIGHT, YOU HAVE DONE YOUR DUTY BY YOURSELF AND BY YOUR COUNTRY. HOLD UP YOUR HEAD. YOU HAVE NOTHING TO BE ASHAMED OF."

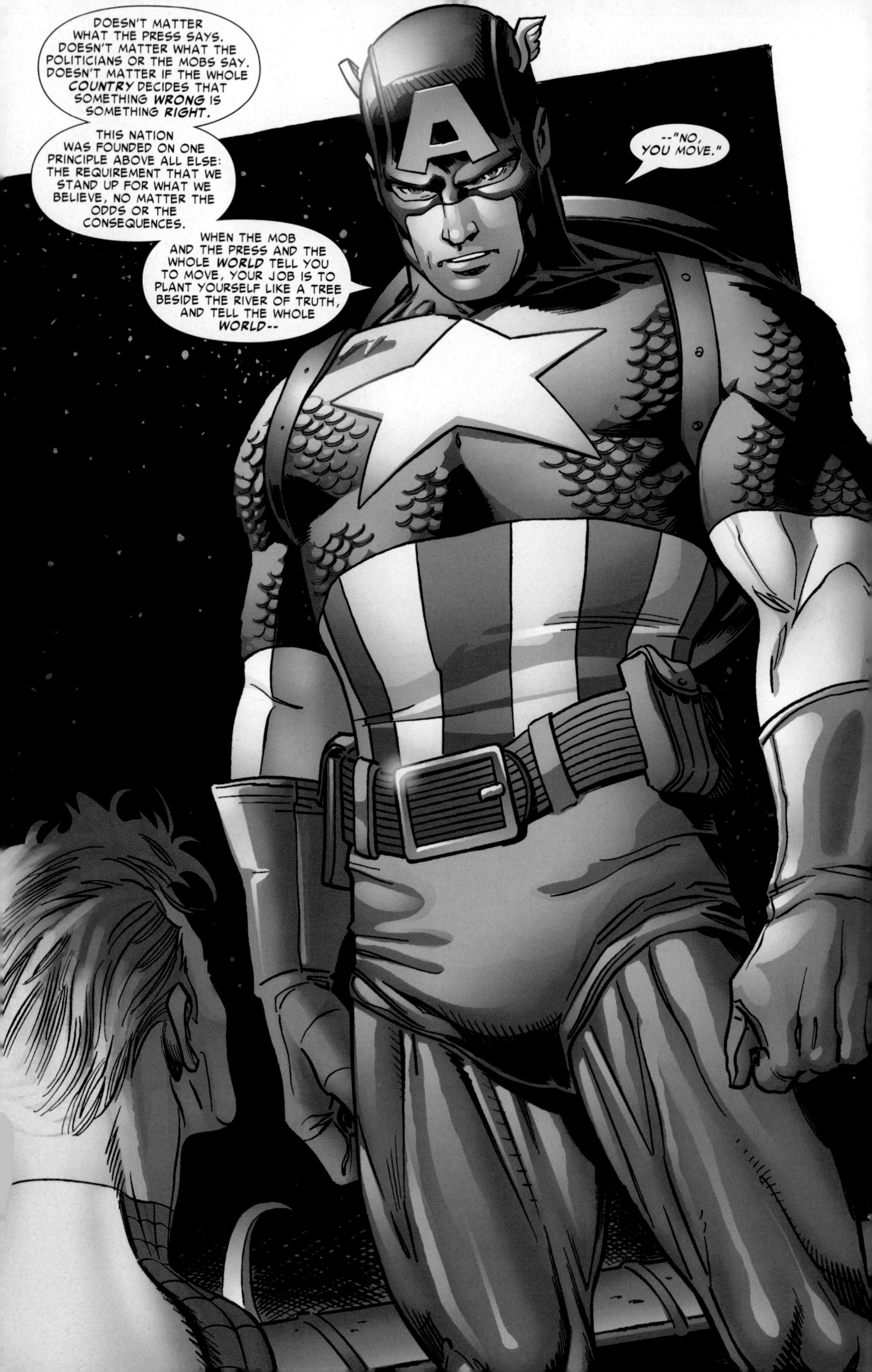
DOESN'T MATTER WHAT THE PRESS SAYS. DOESN'T MATTER WHAT THE POLITICIANS OR THE MOBS SAY. DOESN'T MATTER IF THE WHOLE COUNTRY DECIDES THAT SOMETHING WRONG IS SOMETHING RIGHT.
THIS NATION WAS FOUNDED ON ONE PRINCIPLE ABOVE ALL ELSE: THE REQUIREMENT THAT WE STAND UP FOR WHAT WE BELIEVE, NO MATTER THE ODDS OR THE CONSEQUENCES.
WHEN THE MOB AND THE PRESS AND THE WHOLE WORLD TELL YOU TO MOVE, YOUR JOB IS TO PLANT YOURSELF LIKE A TREE BESIDE THE RIVER OF TRUTH, AND TELL THE WHOLE WORLD--
--"NO, YOU MOVE."

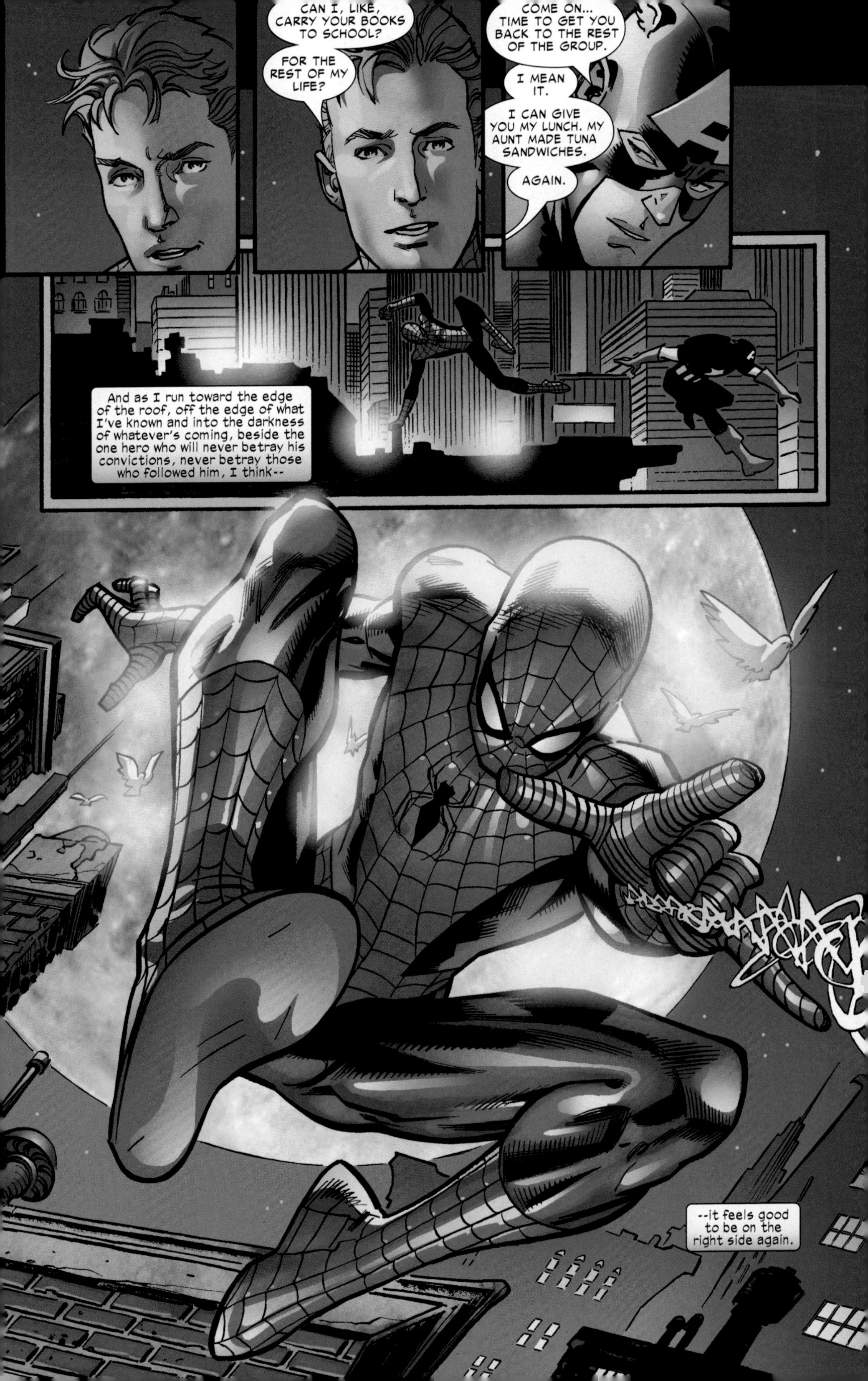

CAN I, LIKE, CARRY YOUR BOOKS TO SCHOOL?
FOR THE REST OF MY LIFE?
COME ON... TIME TO GET YOU BACK TO THE REST OF THE GROUP.
I MEAN IT.
I CAN GIVE YOU MY LUNCH. MY AUNT MADE TUNA SANDWICHES.
AGAIN.
And as I run toward the edge of the roof, off the edge of what I've known and into the darkness of whatever's coming, beside the one hero who will never betray his convictions, never betray those who followed him, I think--
--it feels good to be on the right side again.

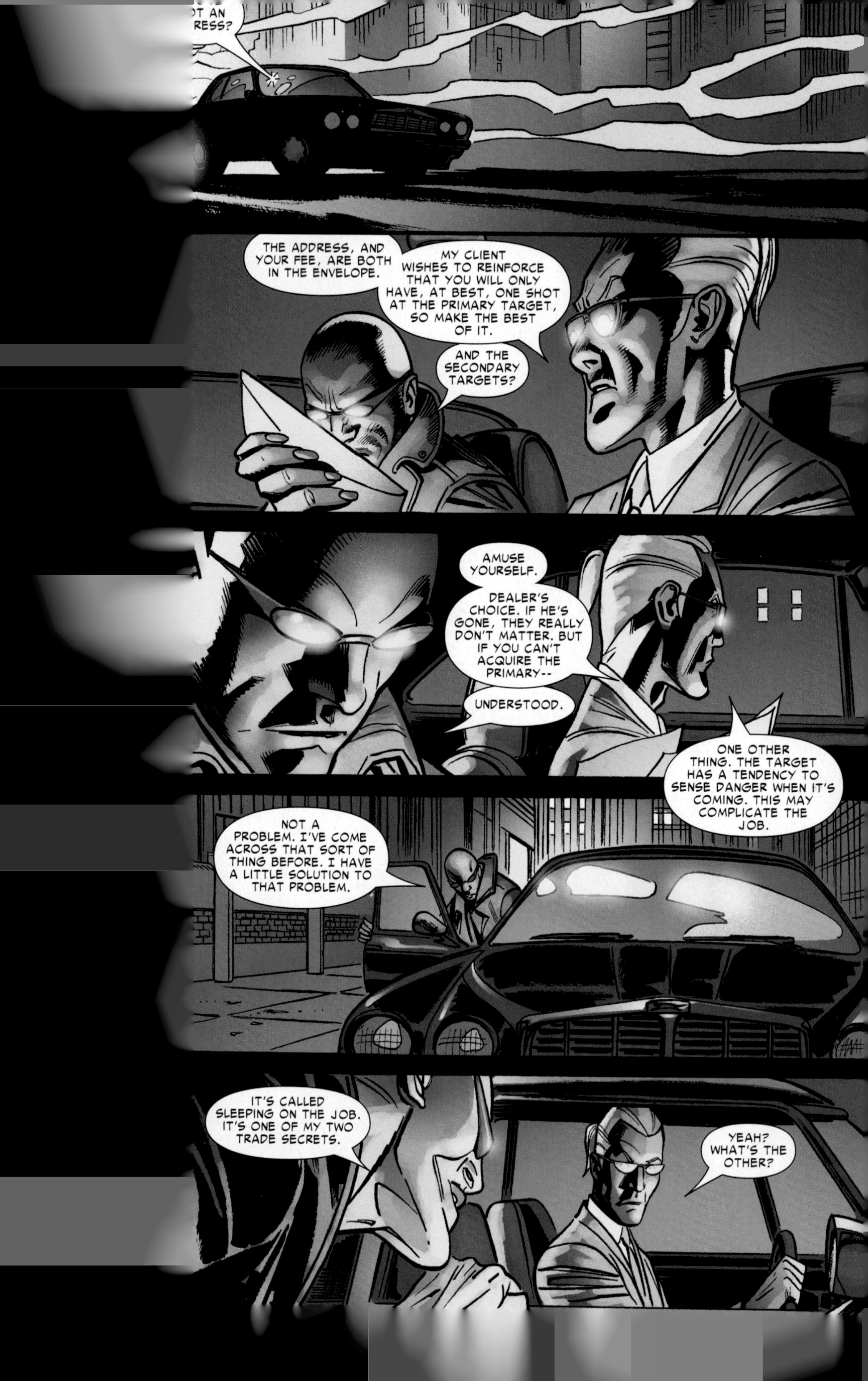
THE ADDRESS, AND YOUR FEE, ARE BOTH IN THE ENVELOPE.
MY CLIENT WISHES TO REINFORCE THAT YOU WILL ONLY HAVE, AT BEST, ONE SHOT AT THE PRIMARY TARGET, SO MAKE THE BEST OF IT.
AND THE SECONDARY TARGETS?
AMUSE YOURSELF.
DEALER'S CHOICE. IF HE'S GONE, THEY REALLY DON'T MATTER. BUT IF YOU CAN'T ACQUIRE THE PRIMARY--
UNDERSTOOD.
ONE OTHER THING. THE TARGET HAS A TENDENCY TO SENSE DANGER WHEN IT'S COMING. THIS MAY COMPLICATE THE JOB.
NOT A PROBLEM. I'VE COME ACROSS THAT SORT OF THING BEFORE. I HAVE A LITTLE SOLUTION TO THAT PROBLEM.
IT'S CALLED SLEEPING ON THE JOB. IT'S ONE OF MY TWO TRADE SECRETS.
YEAH? WHAT'S THE OTHER?

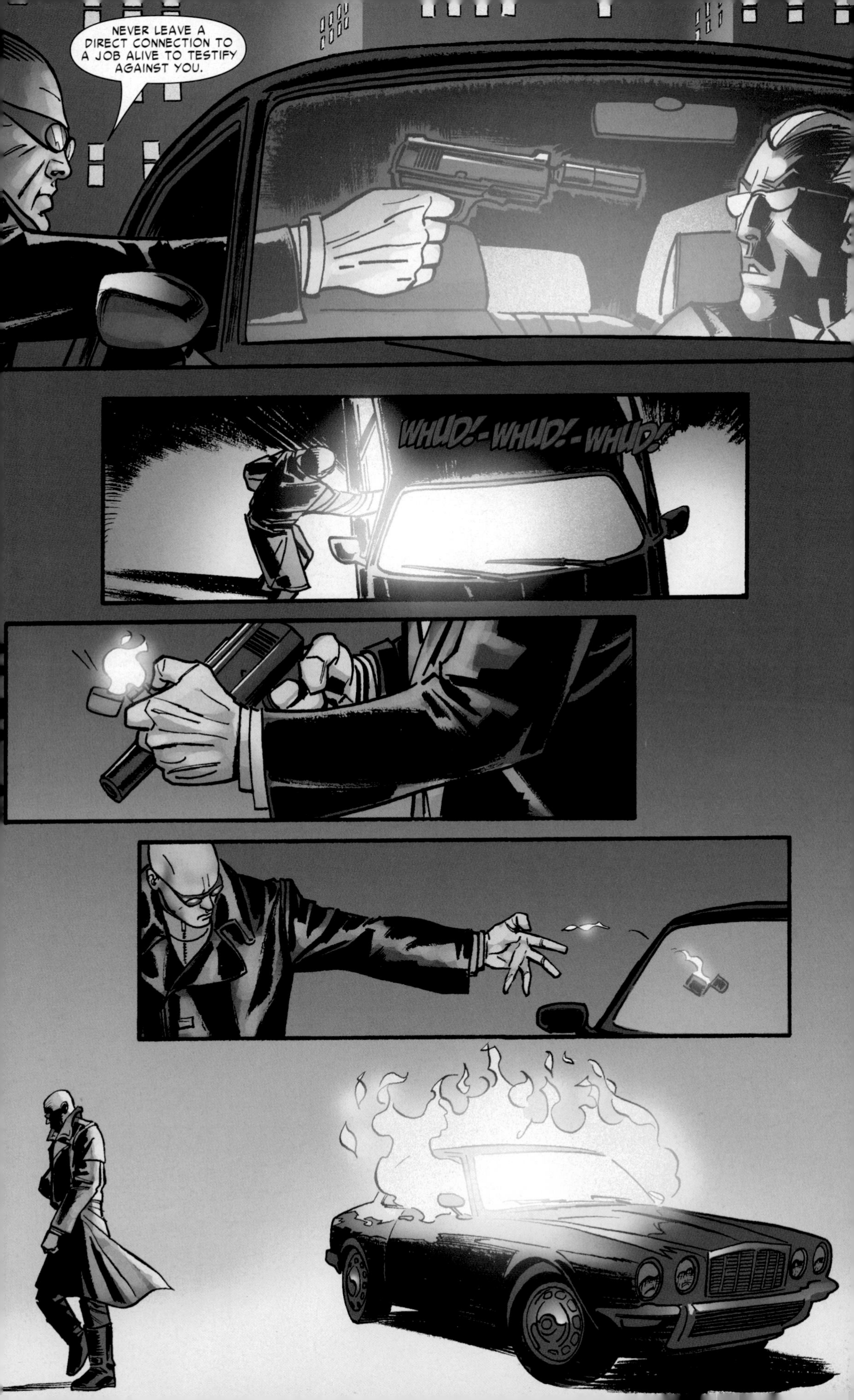
NEVER LEAVE A DIRECT CONNECTION TO A JOB ALIVE TO TESTIFY AGAINST YOU.
WHUD!-WHUD!-WHUD!

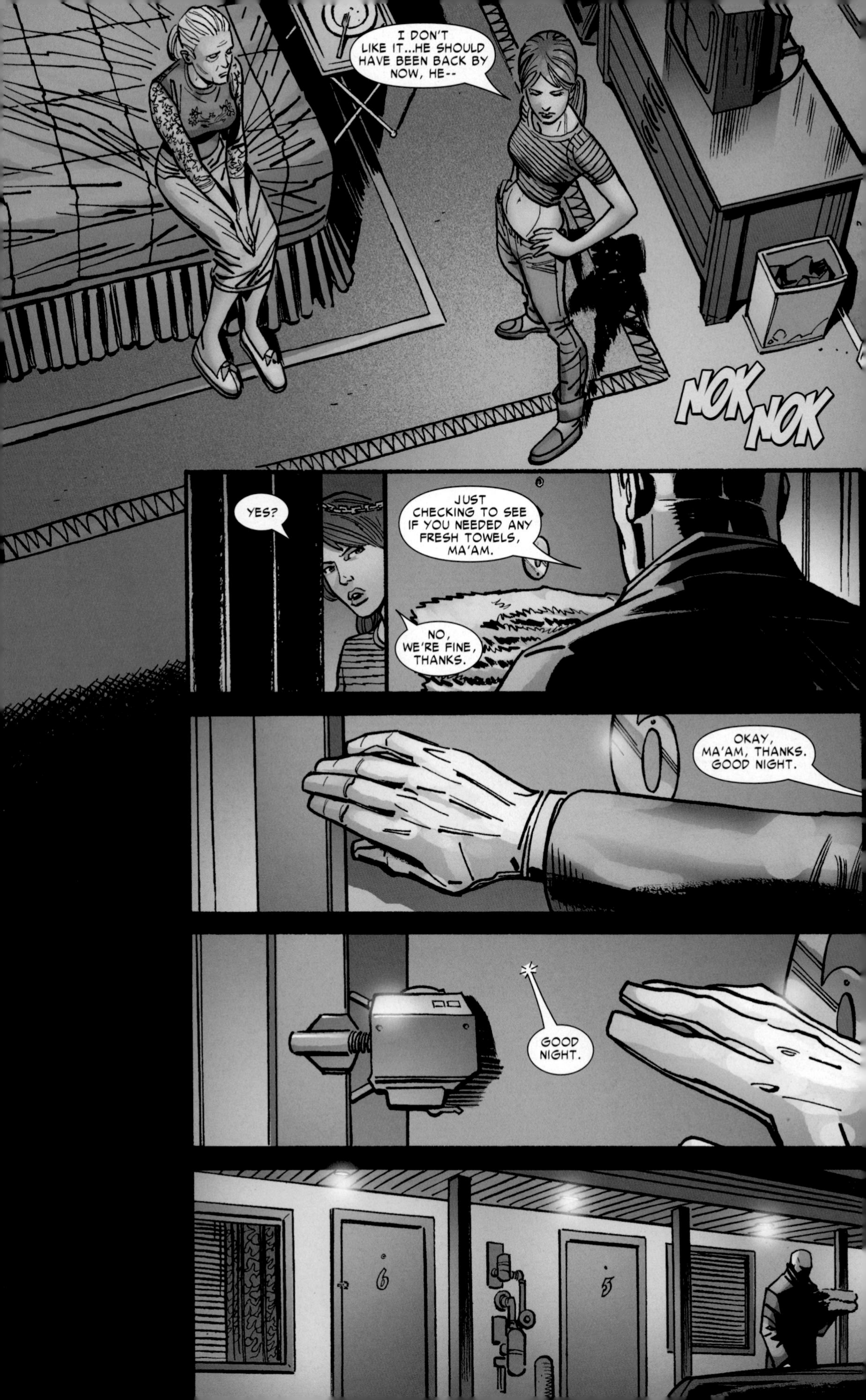
I DON'T LIKE IT...HE SHOULD HAVE BEEN BACK BY NOW, HE--
NOK NOK
YES?
JUST CHECKING TO SEE IF YOU NEEDED ANY FRESH TOWELS, MA'AM.
NO, WE'RE FINE, THANKS.
OKAY, MA'AM, THANKS. GOOD NIGHT.
GOOD NIGHT.
6
5

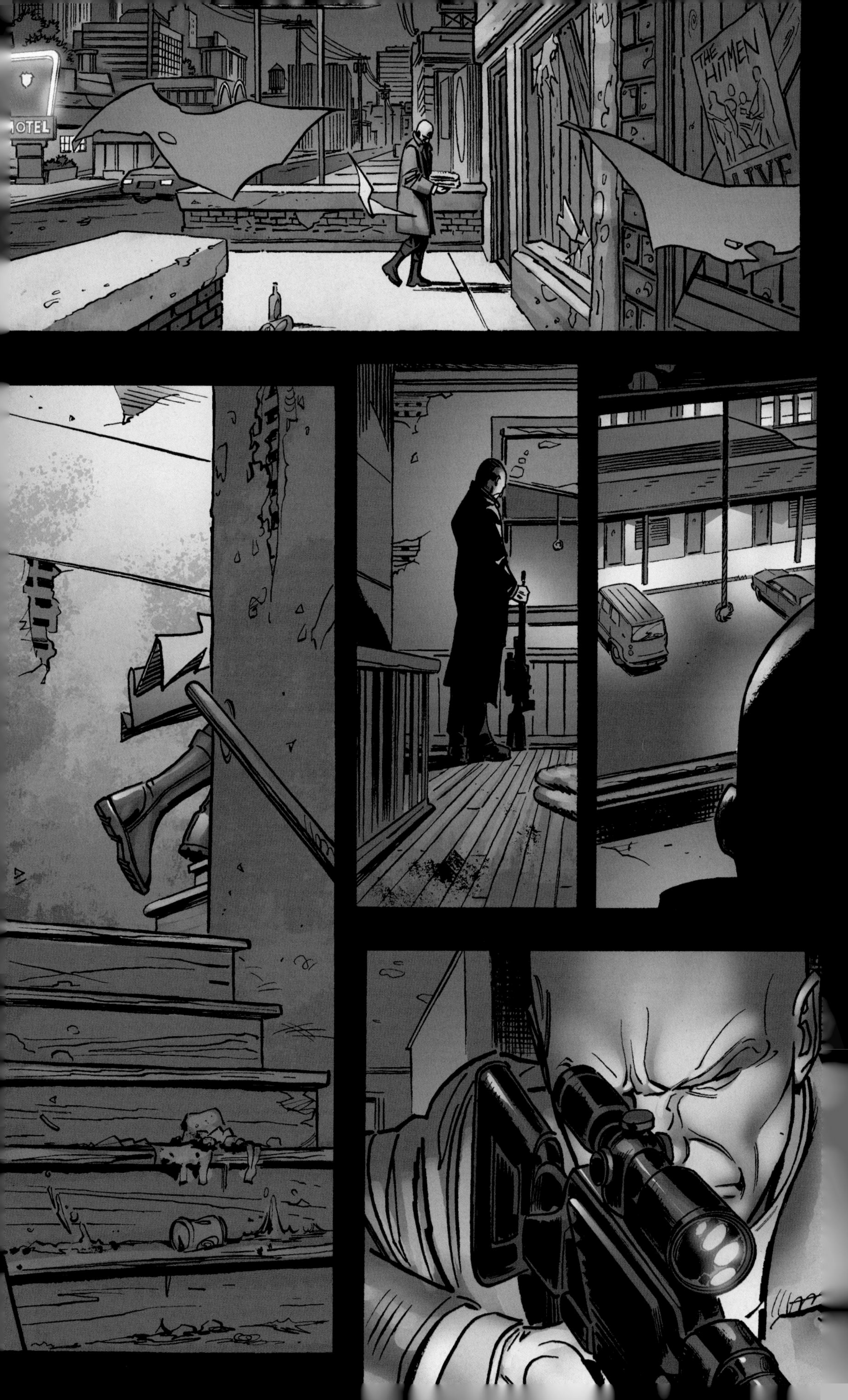
MOTEL
THE HITMEN
LIVE

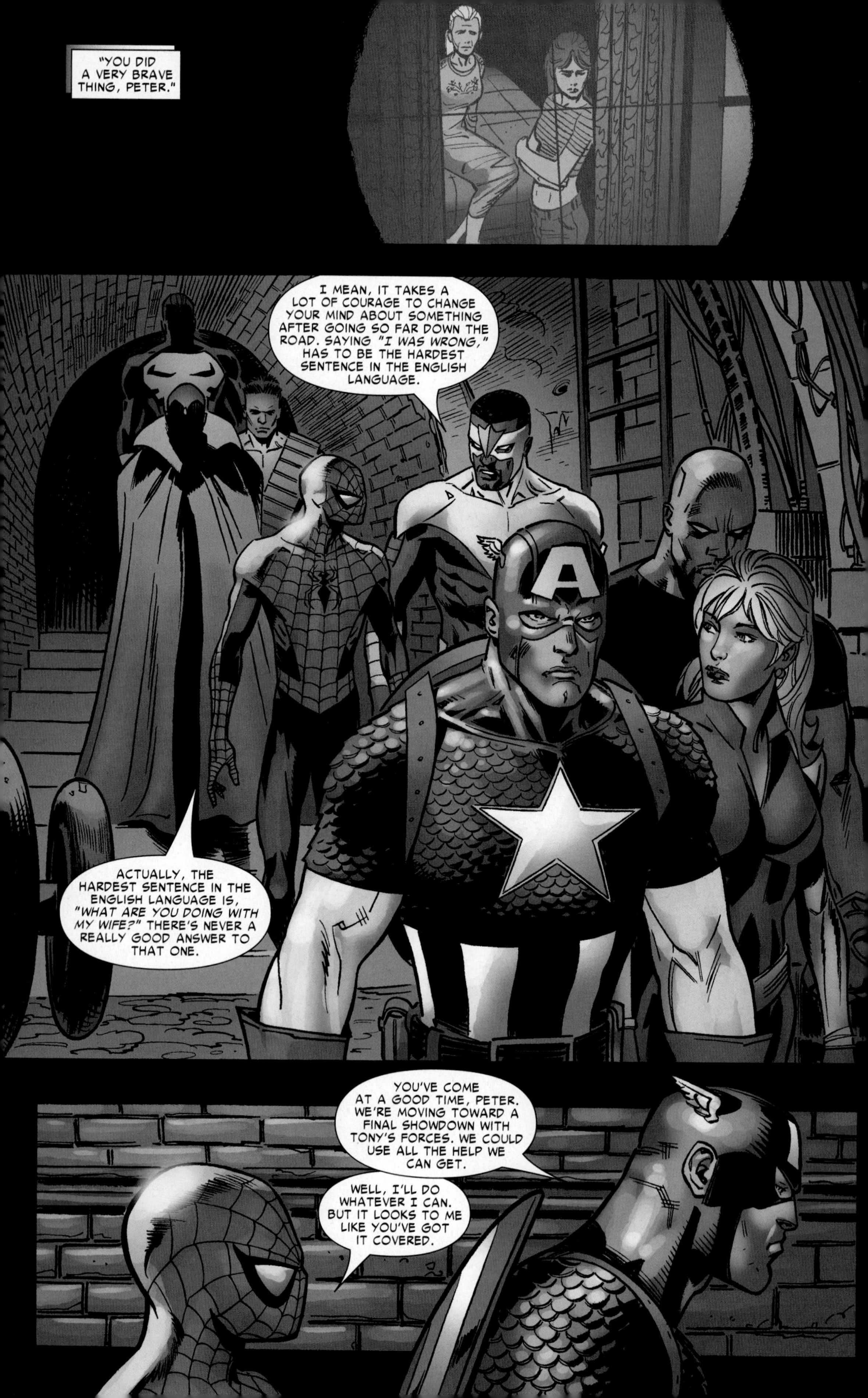
"YOU DID A VERY BRAVE THING, PETER."
I MEAN, IT TAKES A LOT OF COURAGE TO CHANGE YOUR MIND ABOUT SOMETHING AFTER GOING SO FAR DOWN THE ROAD. SAYING "I WAS WRONG," HAS TO BE THE HARDEST SENTENCE IN THE ENGLISH LANGUAGE.
ACTUALLY, THE HARDEST SENTENCE IN THE ENGLISH LANGUAGE IS, "WHAT ARE YOU DOING WITH MY WIFE?" THERE'S NEVER A REALLY GOOD ANSWER TO THAT ONE.
YOU'VE COME AT A GOOD TIME, PETER. WE'RE MOVING TOWARD A FINAL SHOWDOWN WITH TONY'S FORCES. WE COULD USE ALL THE HELP WE CAN GET.
WELL, I'LL DO WHATEVER I CAN. BUT IT LOOKS TO ME LIKE YOU'VE GOT IT COVERED.

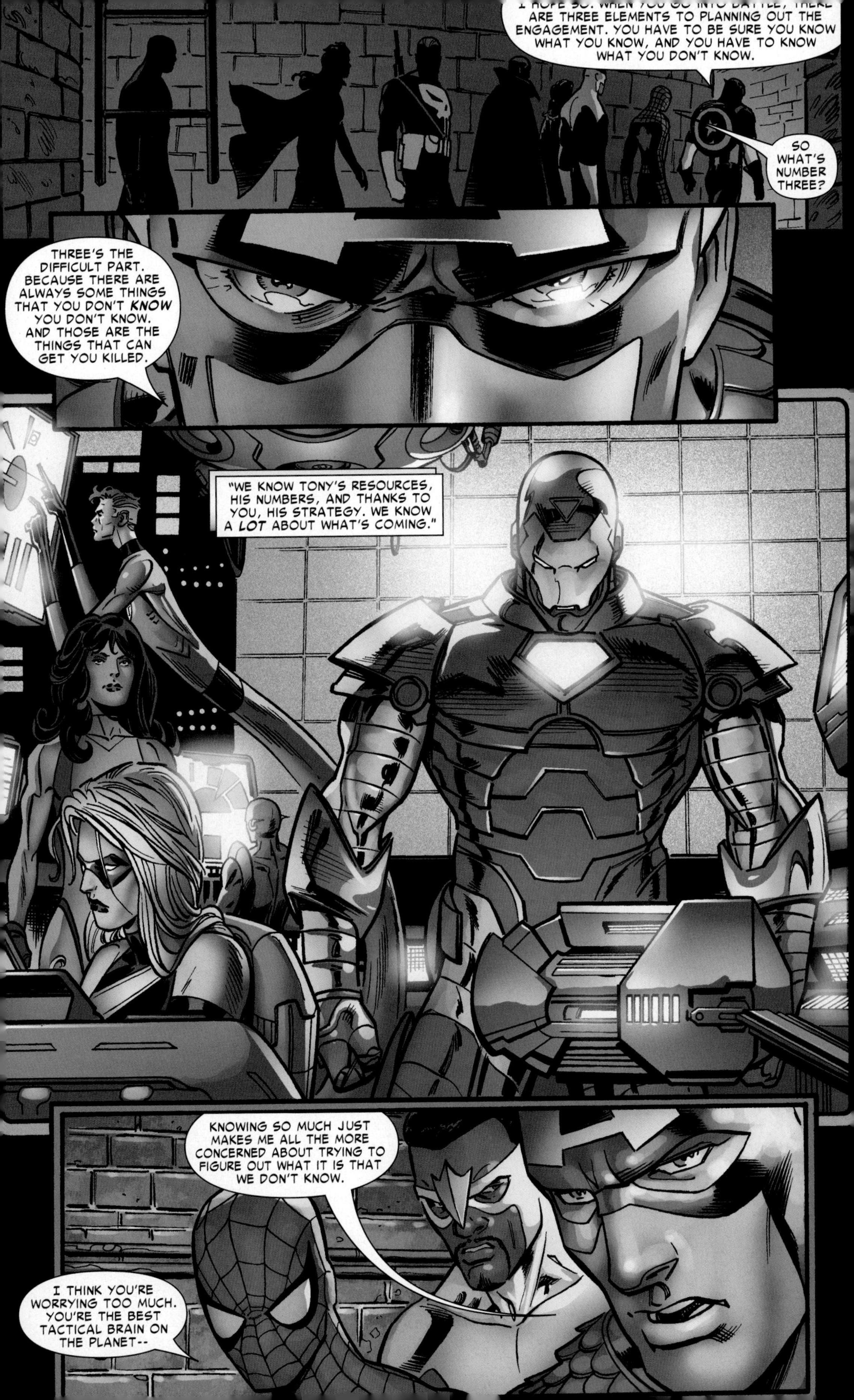

ARE THREE ELEMENTS TO PLANNING OUT THE ENGAGEMENT. YOU HAVE TO BE SURE YOU KNOW WHAT YOU KNOW, AND YOU HAVE TO KNOW WHAT YOU DON'T KNOW.
SO WHAT'S NUMBER THREE?
THREE'S THE DIFFICULT PART. BECAUSE THERE ARE ALWAYS SOME THINGS THAT YOU DON'T KNOW YOU DON'T KNOW. AND THOSE ARE THE THINGS THAT CAN GET YOU KILLED.
"WE KNOW TONY'S RESOURCES, HIS NUMBERS, AND THANKS TO YOU, HIS STRATEGY. WE KNOW A LOT ABOUT WHAT'S COMING."
KNOWING SO MUCH JUST MAKES ME ALL THE MORE CONCERNED ABOUT TRYING TO FIGURE OUT WHAT IT IS THAT WE DON'T KNOW.
I THINK YOU'RE WORRYING TOO MUCH. YOU'RE THE BEST TACTICAL BRAIN ON THE PLANET--

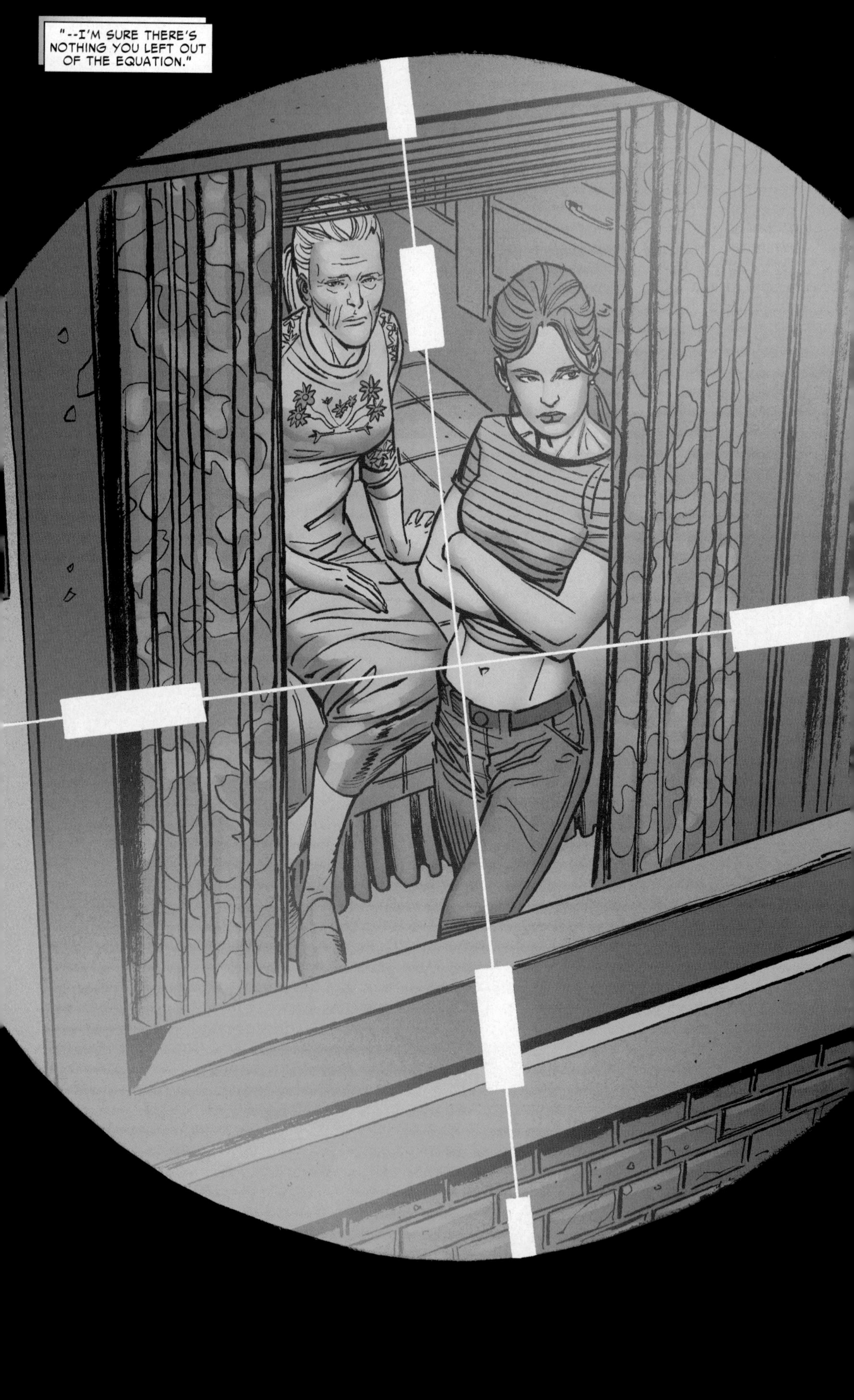
"--I'M SURE THERE'S NOTHING YOU LEFT OUT OF THE EQUATION."

THE AMAZING
SPIDER-MAN
A MARVEL COMICS EVENT

CIVIL
WAR

AMAZING SPIDER-MAN #538

THE WAR AT HOME PART 7 OF 7

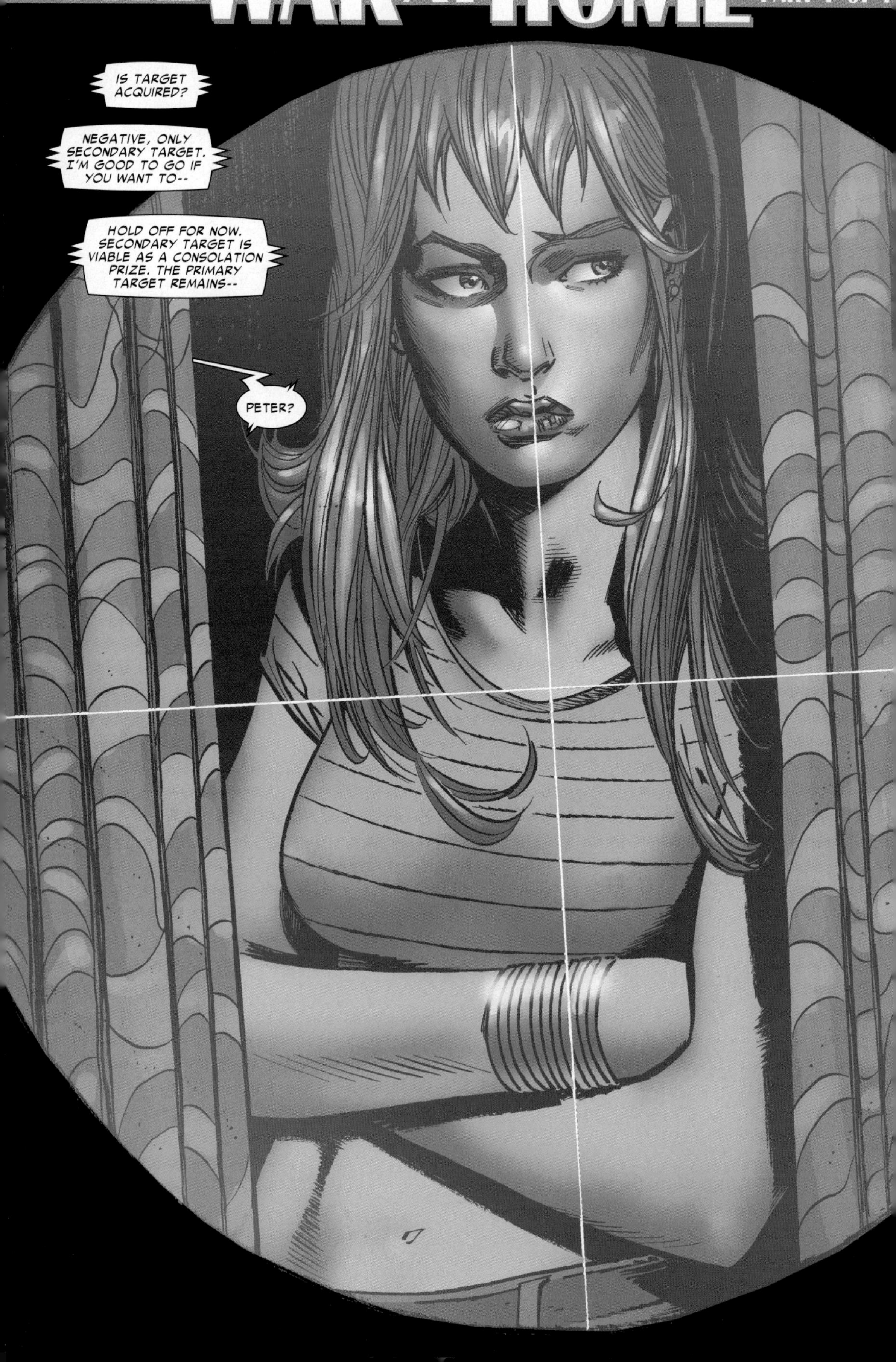

IS TARGET ACQUIRED?
NEGATIVE, ONLY SECONDARY TARGET. I'M GOOD TO GO IF YOU WANT TO--
HOLD OFF FOR NOW. SECONDARY TARGET IS VIABLE AS A CONSOLATION PRIZE. THE PRIMARY TARGET REMAINS--
PETER?

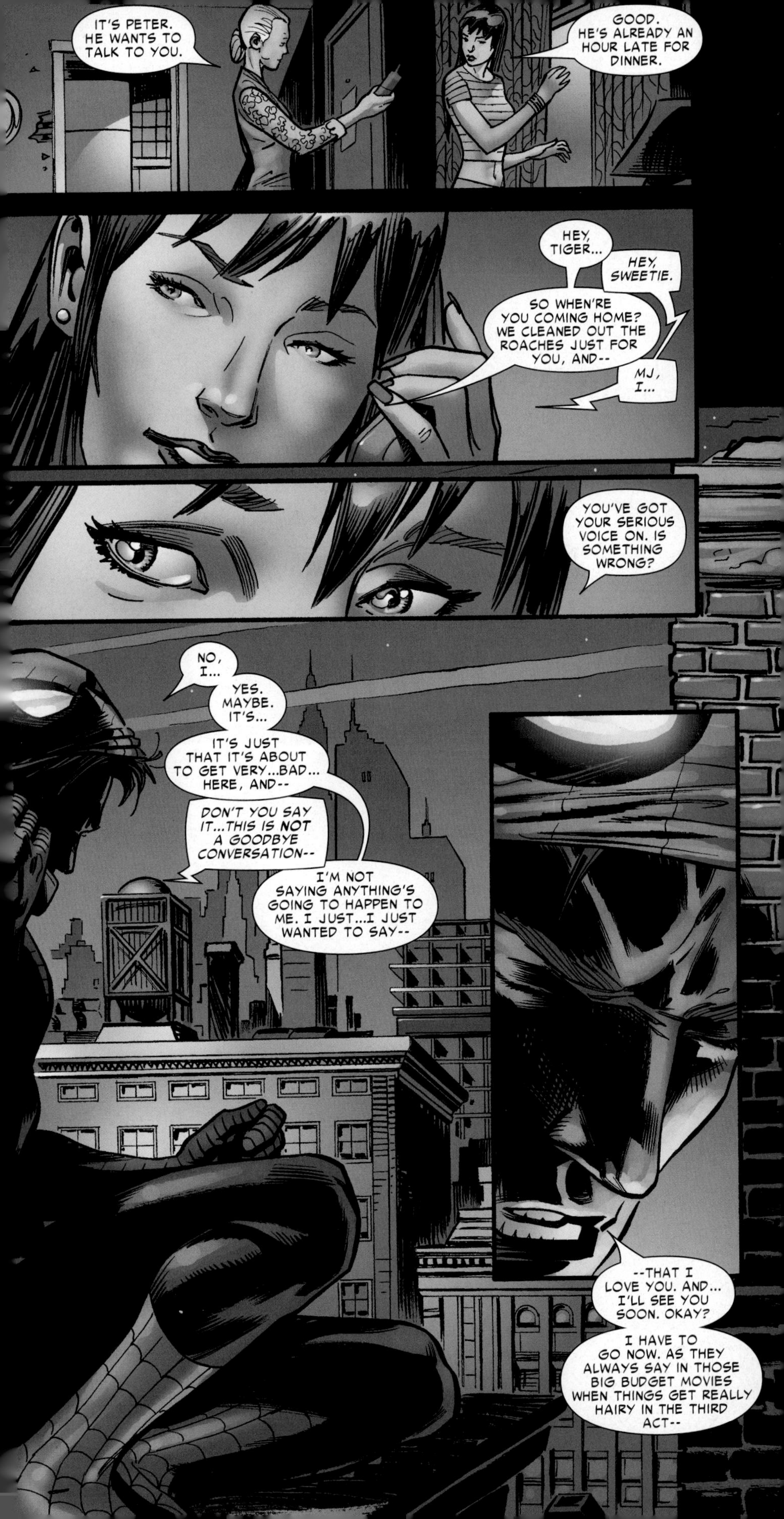
IT'S PETER. HE WANTS TO TALK TO YOU.
GOOD. HE'S ALREADY AN HOUR LATE FOR DINNER.
HEY, TIGER...
HEY, SWEETIE.
SO WHEN'RE YOU COMING HOME? WE CLEANED OUT THE ROACHES JUST FOR YOU, AND--
MJ, I...
YOU'VE GOT YOUR SERIOUS VOICE ON. IS SOMETHING WRONG?
NO, I...
YES. MAYBE. IT'S...
IT'S JUST THAT IT'S ABOUT TO GET VERY...BAD... HERE, AND--
DON'T YOU SAY IT...THIS IS NOT A GOODBYE CONVERSATION--
I'M NOT SAYING ANYTHING'S GOING TO HAPPEN TO ME. I JUST...I JUST WANTED TO SAY--
--THAT I LOVE YOU. AND... I'LL SEE YOU SOON. OKAY?
I HAVE TO GO NOW. AS THEY ALWAYS SAY IN THOSE BIG BUDGET MOVIES WHEN THINGS GET REALLY HAIRY IN THE THIRD ACT--

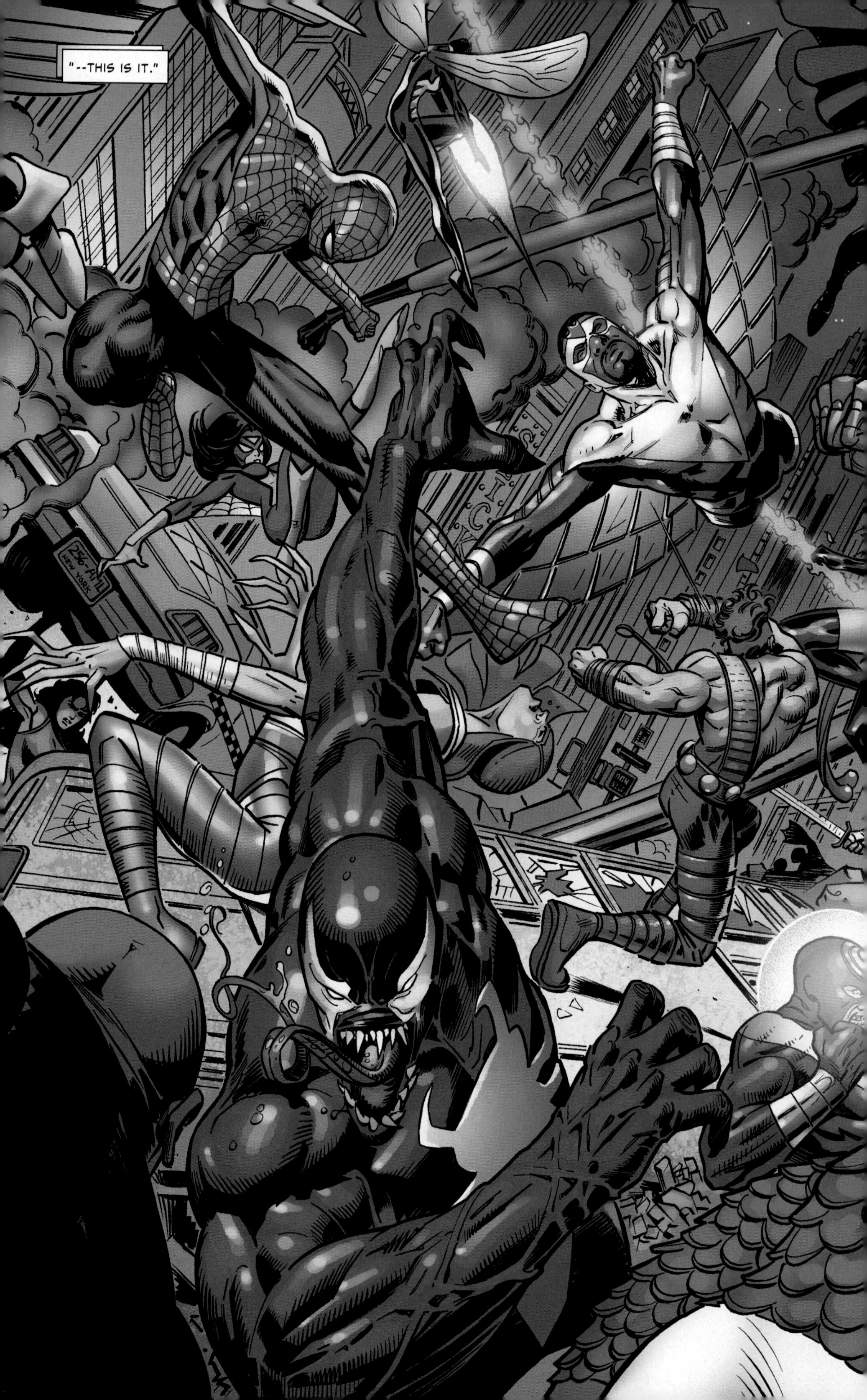
"--THIS IS IT."

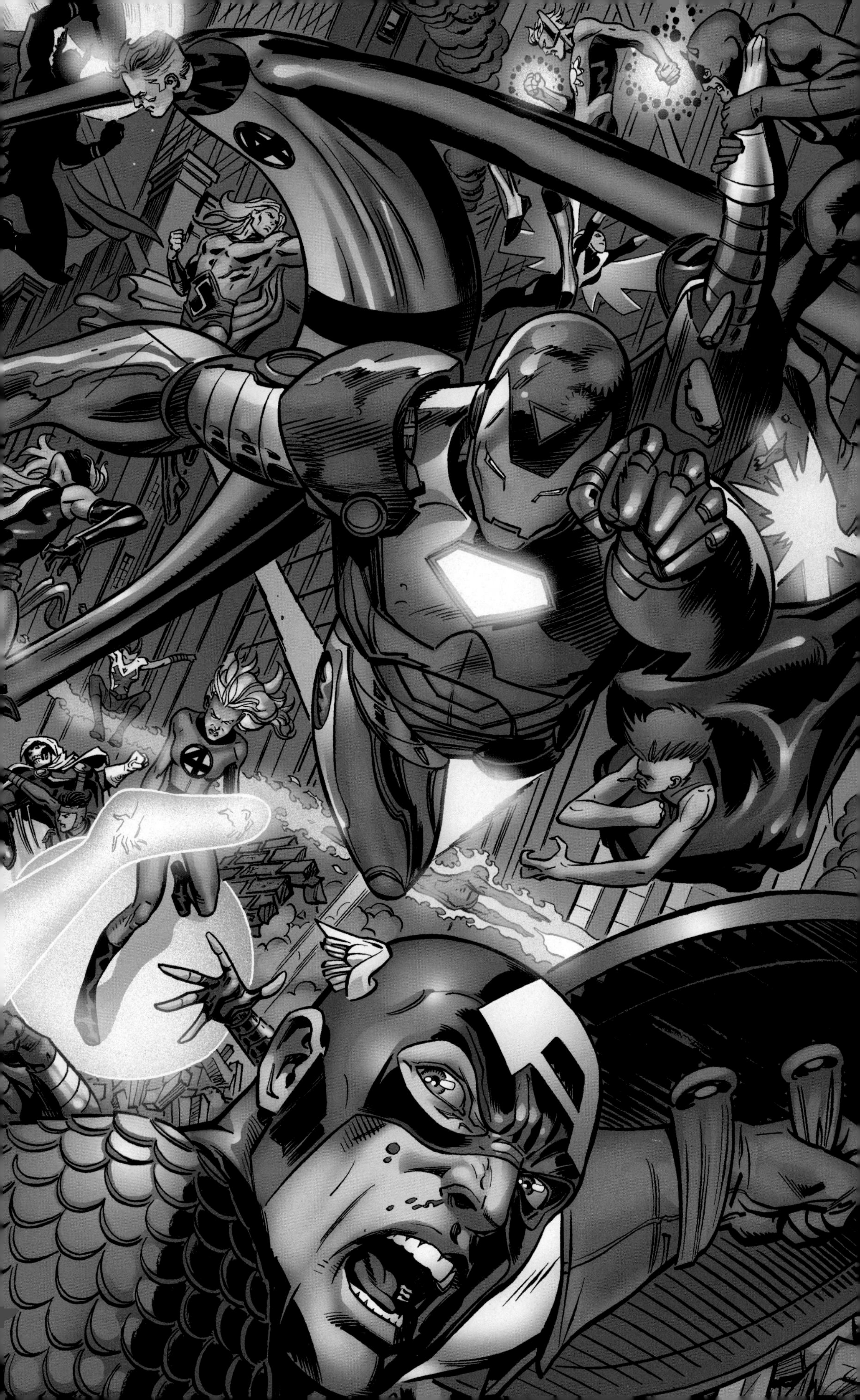

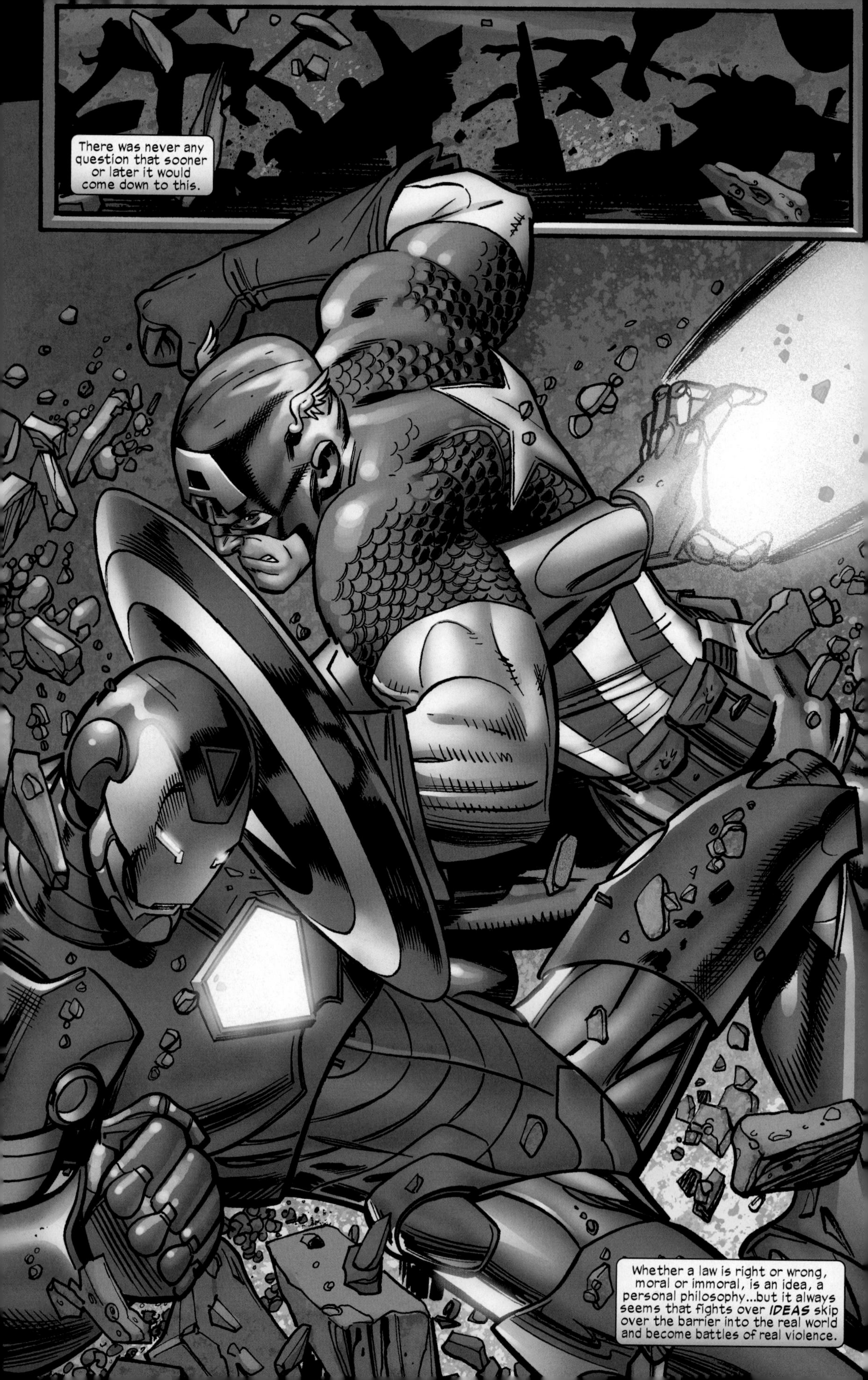
There was never any question that sooner or later it would come down to this.
Whether a law is right or wrong, moral or immoral, is an idea, a personal philosophy...but it always seems that fights over IDEAS skip over the barrier into the real world and become battles of real violence.

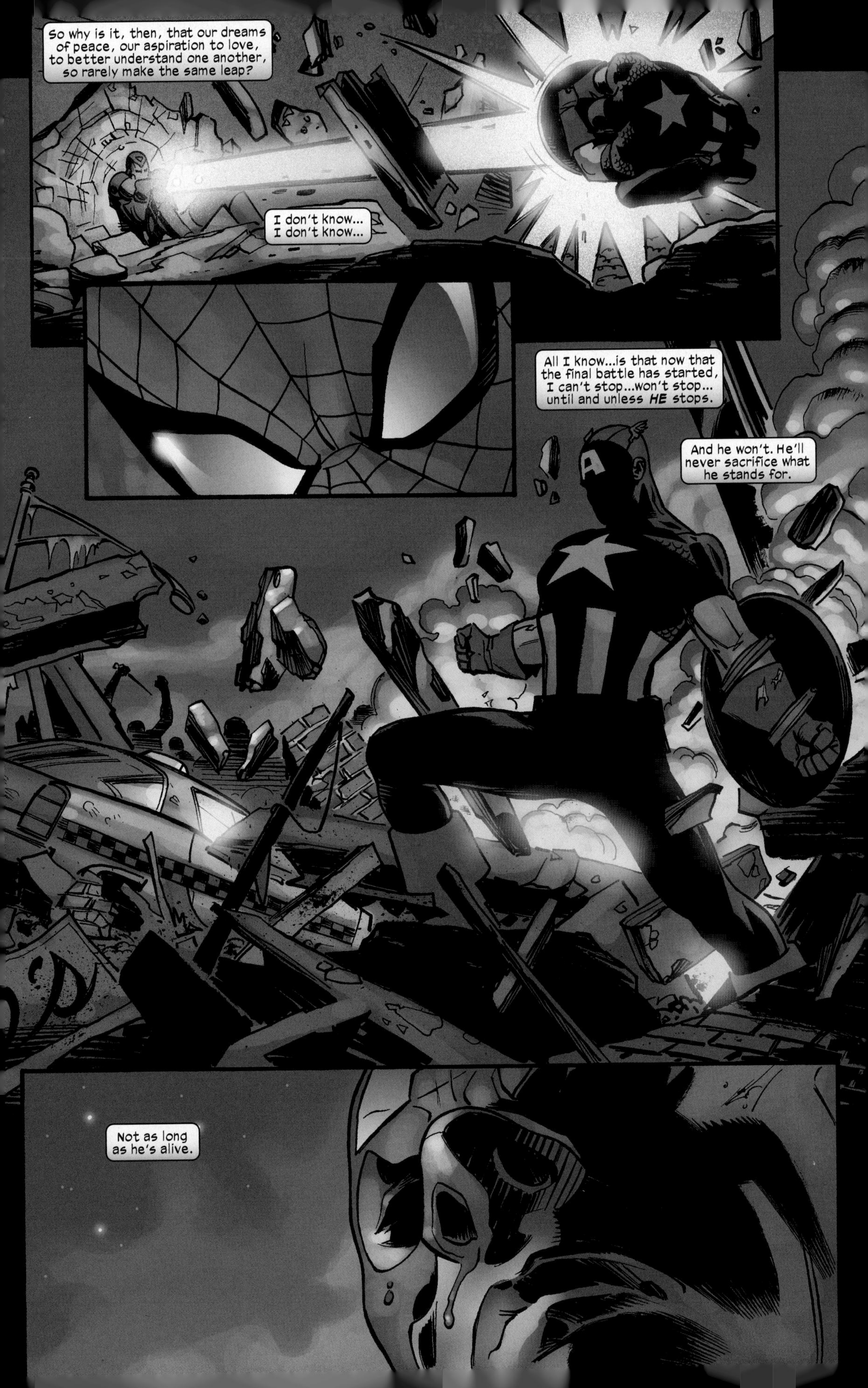

So why is it, then, that our dreams of peace, our aspiration to love, to better understand one another, so rarely make the same leap?
I don't know... I don't know...
All I know...is that now that the final battle has started, I can't stop...won't stop... until and unless HE stops.
And he won't. He'll never sacrifice what he stands for.
Not as long as he's alive.

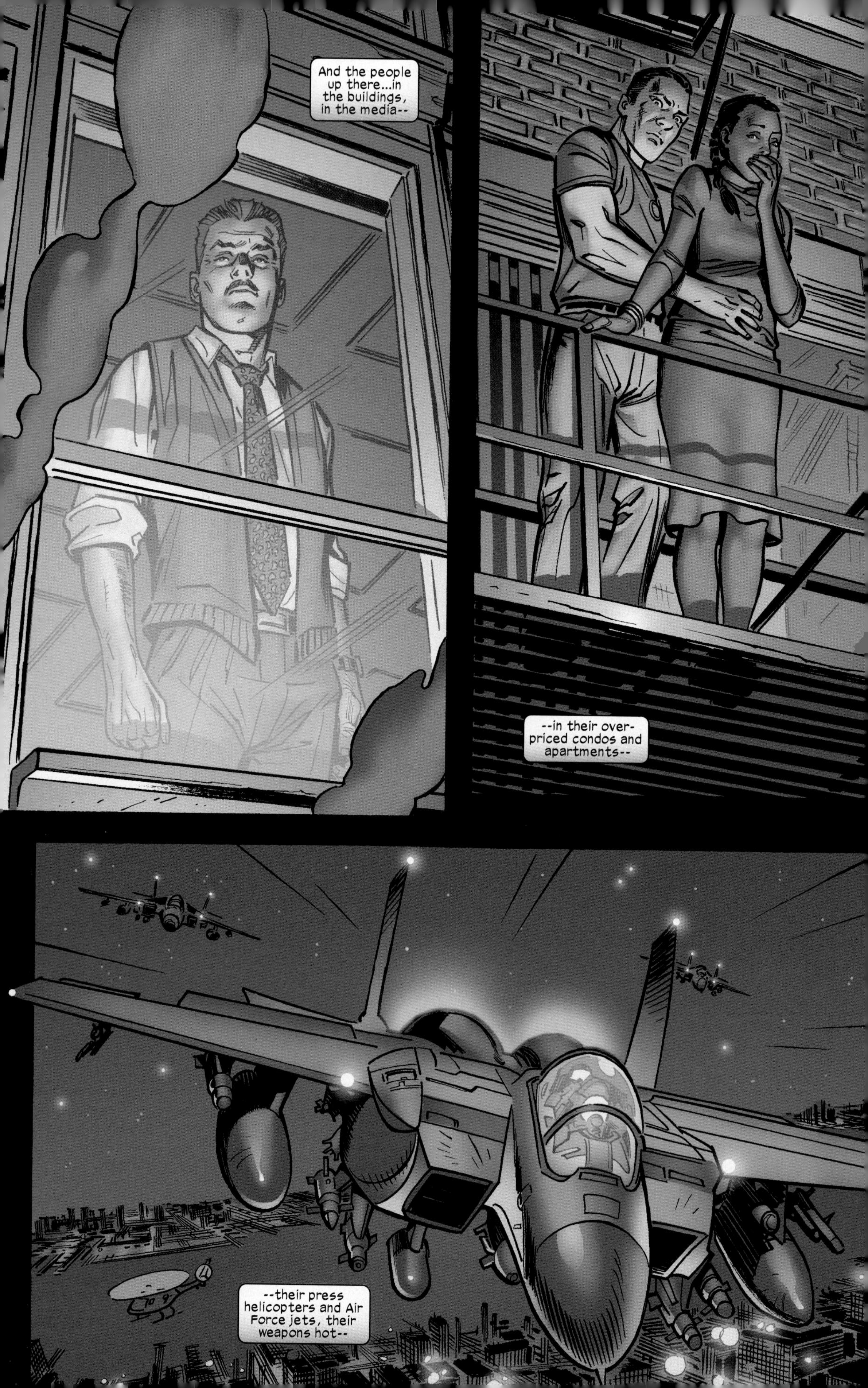
And the people up there...in the buildings, in the media--
--in their over-priced condos and apartments--
--their press helicopters and Air Force jets, their weapons hot--

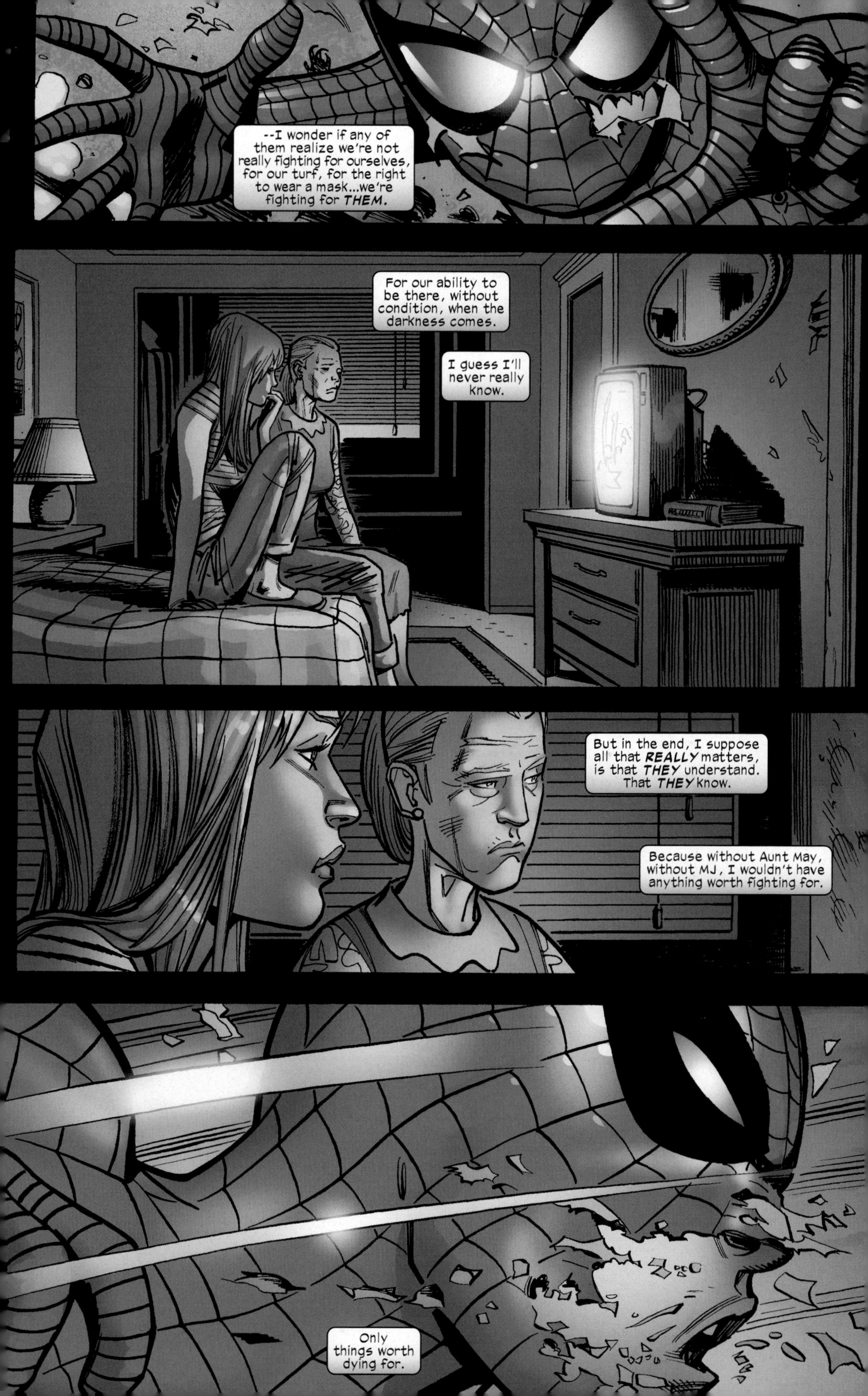
--I wonder if any of them realize we're not really fighting for ourselves, for our turf, for the right to wear a mask...we're fighting for THEM.
For our ability to be there, without condition, when the darkness comes.
I guess I'll never really know.
But in the end, I suppose all that REALLY matters, is that THEY understand. That THEY know.
Because without Aunt May, without MJ, I wouldn't have anything worth fighting for.
Only things worth dying for.

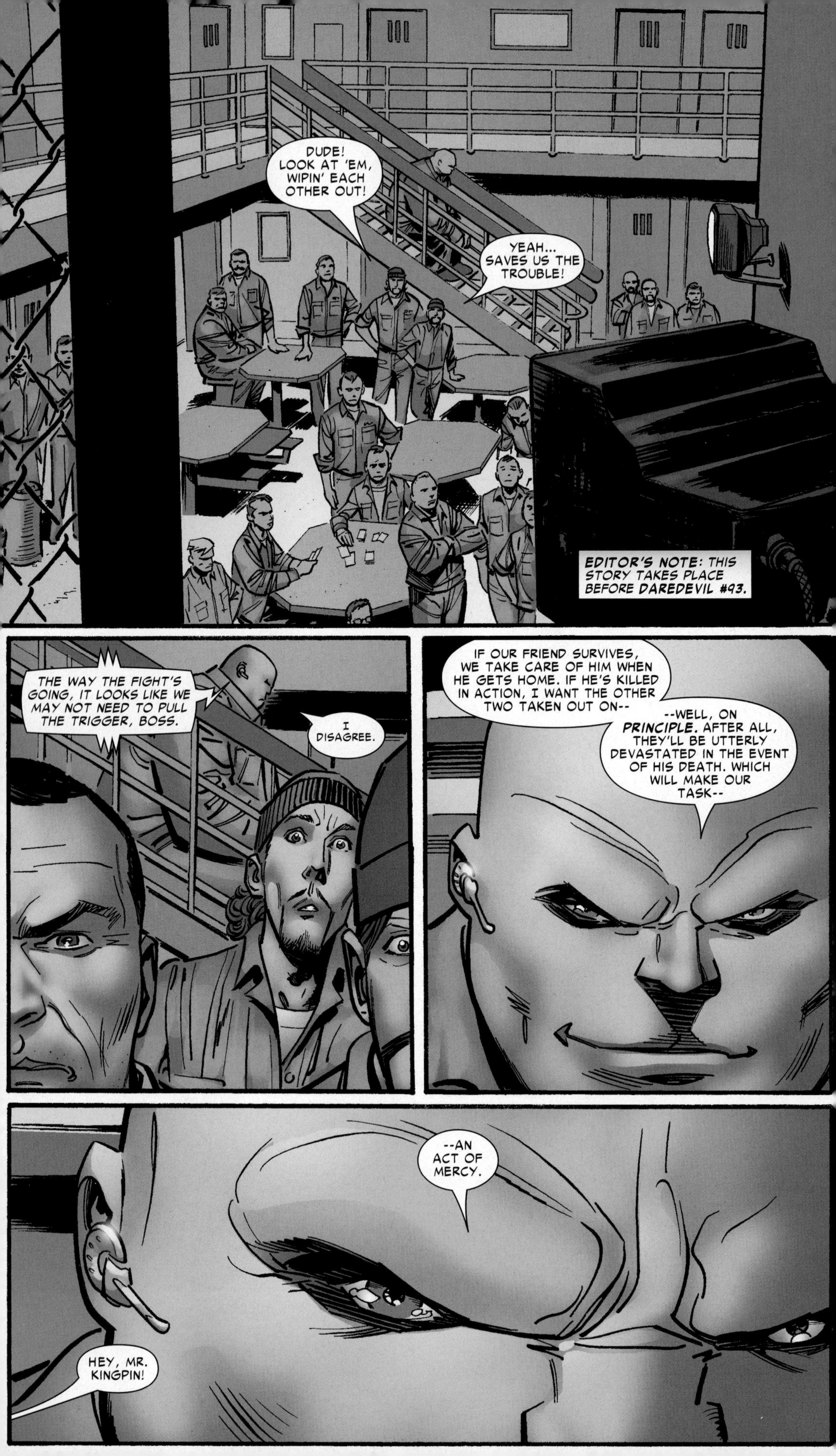
DUDE! LOOK AT 'EM, WIPIN' EACH OTHER OUT!
YEAH... SAVES US THE TROUBLE!
EDITOR'S NOTE: THIS STORY TAKES PLACE BEFORE DAREDEVIL #93.
THE WAY THE FIGHT'S GOING, IT LOOKS LIKE WE MAY NOT NEED TO PULL THE TRIGGER, BOSS.
I DISAGREE.
IF OUR FRIEND SURVIVES, WE TAKE CARE OF HIM WHEN HE GETS HOME. IF HE'S KILLED IN ACTION, I WANT THE OTHER TWO TAKEN OUT ON--
--WELL, ON PRINCIPLE. AFTER ALL, THEY'LL BE UTTERLY DEVASTATED IN THE EVENT OF HIS DEATH. WHICH WILL MAKE OUR TASK--
--AN ACT OF MERCY.
HEY, MR. KINGPIN!

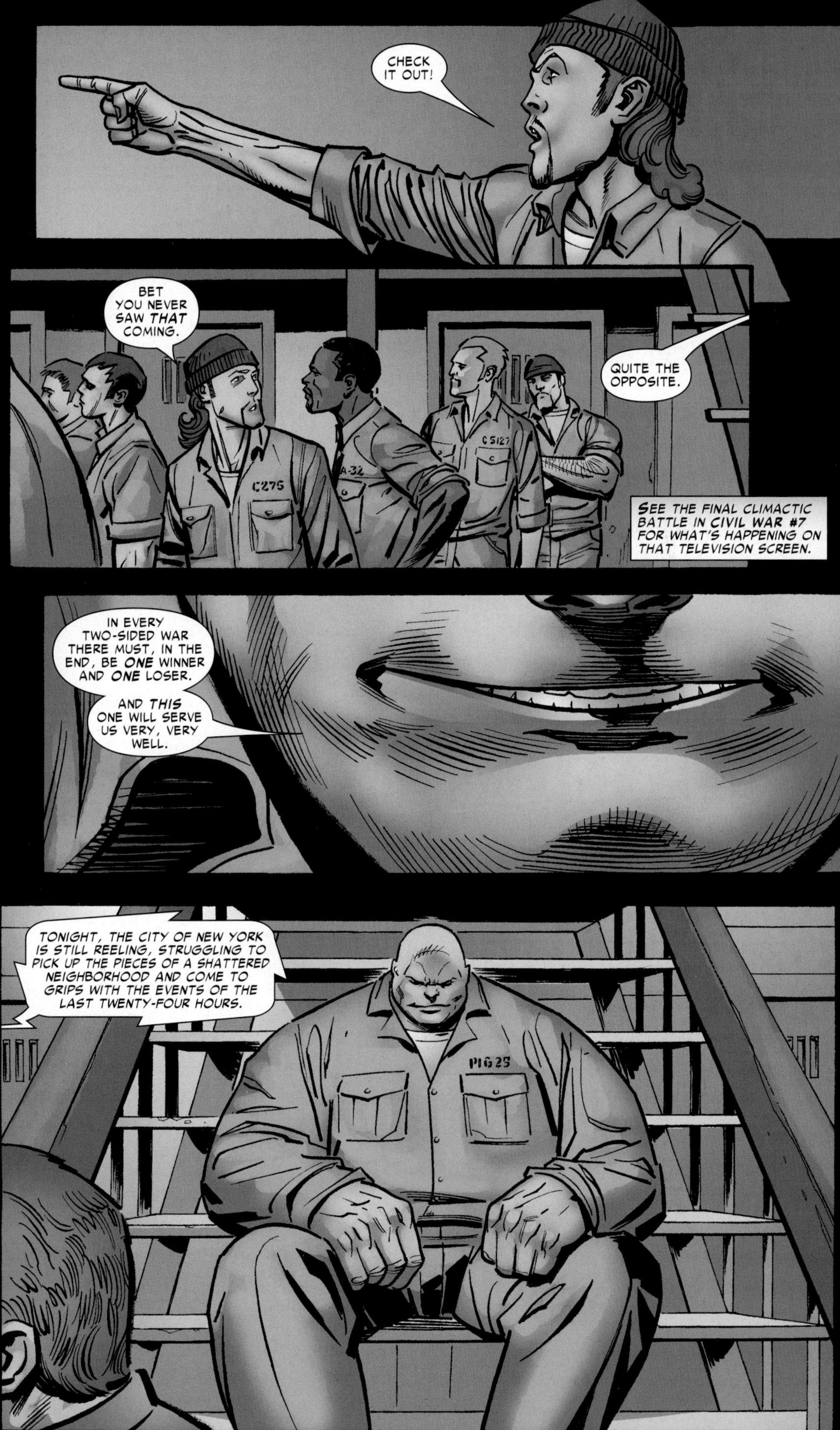
CHECK IT OUT!
BET YOU NEVER SAW THAT COMING.
QUITE THE OPPOSITE.
C275
A-32
C5127
SEE THE FINAL CLIMACTIC BATTLE IN CIVIL WAR #7 FOR WHAT'S HAPPENING ON THAT TELEVISION SCREEN.
IN EVERY TWO-SIDED WAR THERE MUST, IN THE END, BE ONE WINNER AND ONE LOSER.
AND THIS ONE WILL SERVE US VERY, VERY WELL.
TONIGHT, THE CITY OF NEW YORK IS STILL REELING, STRUGGLING TO PICK UP THE PIECES OF A SHATTERED NEIGHBORHOOD AND COME TO GRIPS WITH THE EVENTS OF THE LAST TWENTY-FOUR HOURS.
P1623

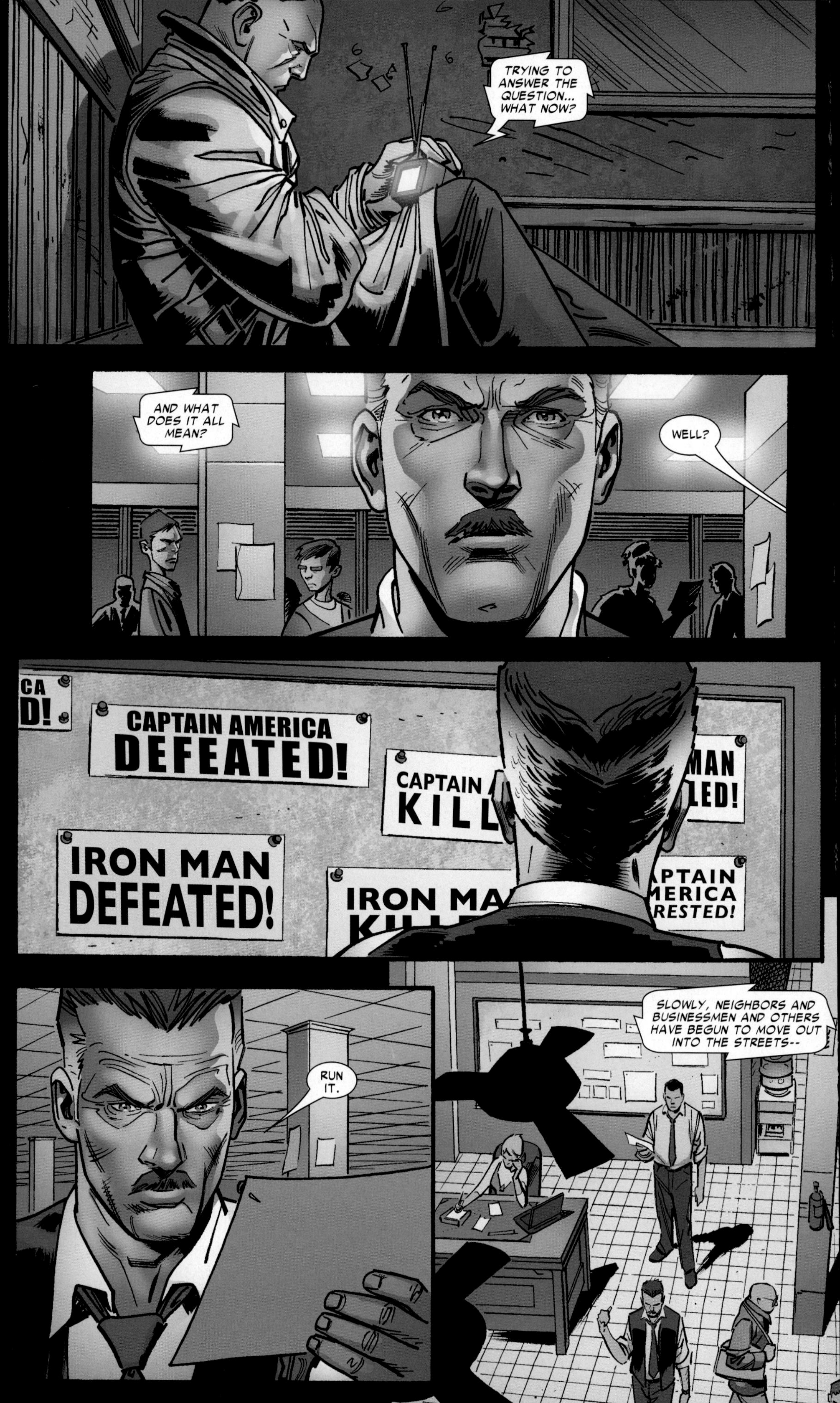
TRYING TO ANSWER THE QUESTION... WHAT NOW?
AND WHAT DOES IT ALL MEAN?
WELL?
CAPTAIN AMERICA DEFEATED!
CAPTAIN A... KILL...
...MAN ...LED!
IRON MAN DEFEATED!
IRON MA...
...PTAIN ...MERICA ...RESTED!
RUN IT.
SLOWLY, NEIGHBORS AND BUSINESSMEN AND OTHERS HAVE BEGUN TO MOVE OUT INTO THE STREETS--

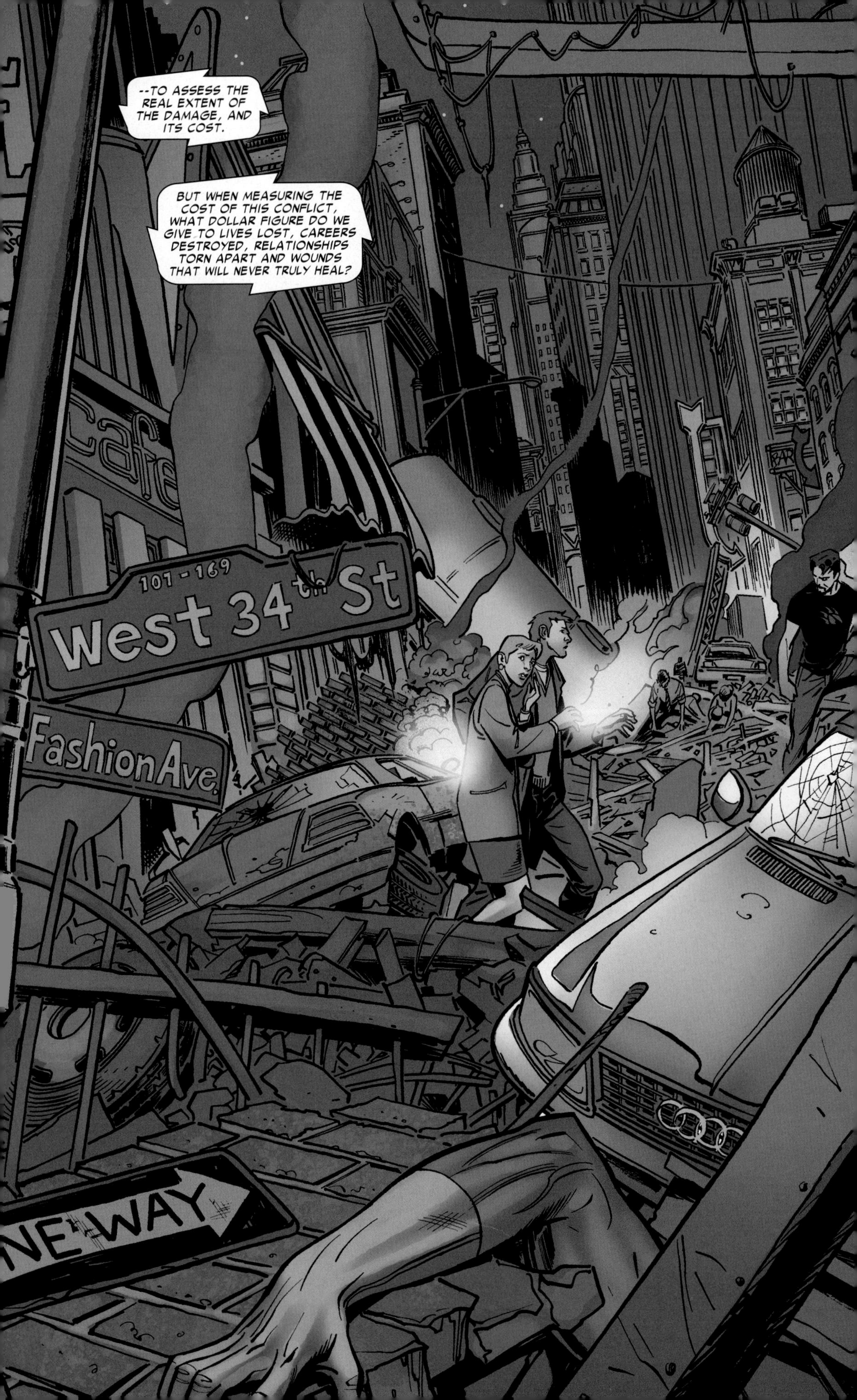
--TO ASSESS THE REAL EXTENT OF THE DAMAGE, AND ITS COST.
BUT WHEN MEASURING THE COST OF THIS CONFLICT, WHAT DOLLAR FIGURE DO WE GIVE TO LIVES LOST, CAREERS DESTROYED, RELATIONSHIPS TORN APART AND WOUNDS THAT WILL NEVER TRULY HEAL?
Cafe
101-169
West 34th St
Fashion Ave.
ONE WAY

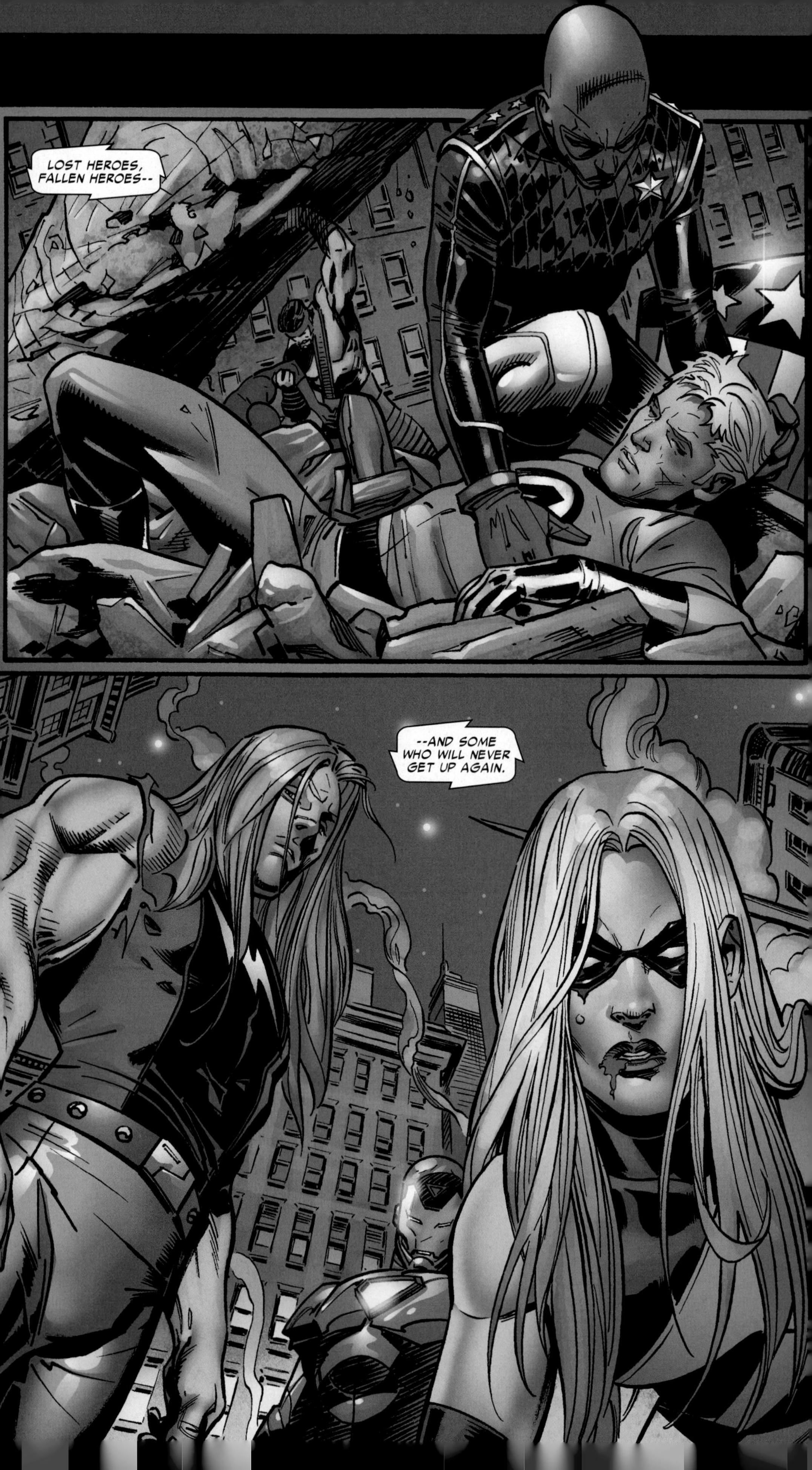
LOST HEROES,
FALLEN HEROES--
--AND SOME
WHO WILL NEVER
GET UP AGAIN.

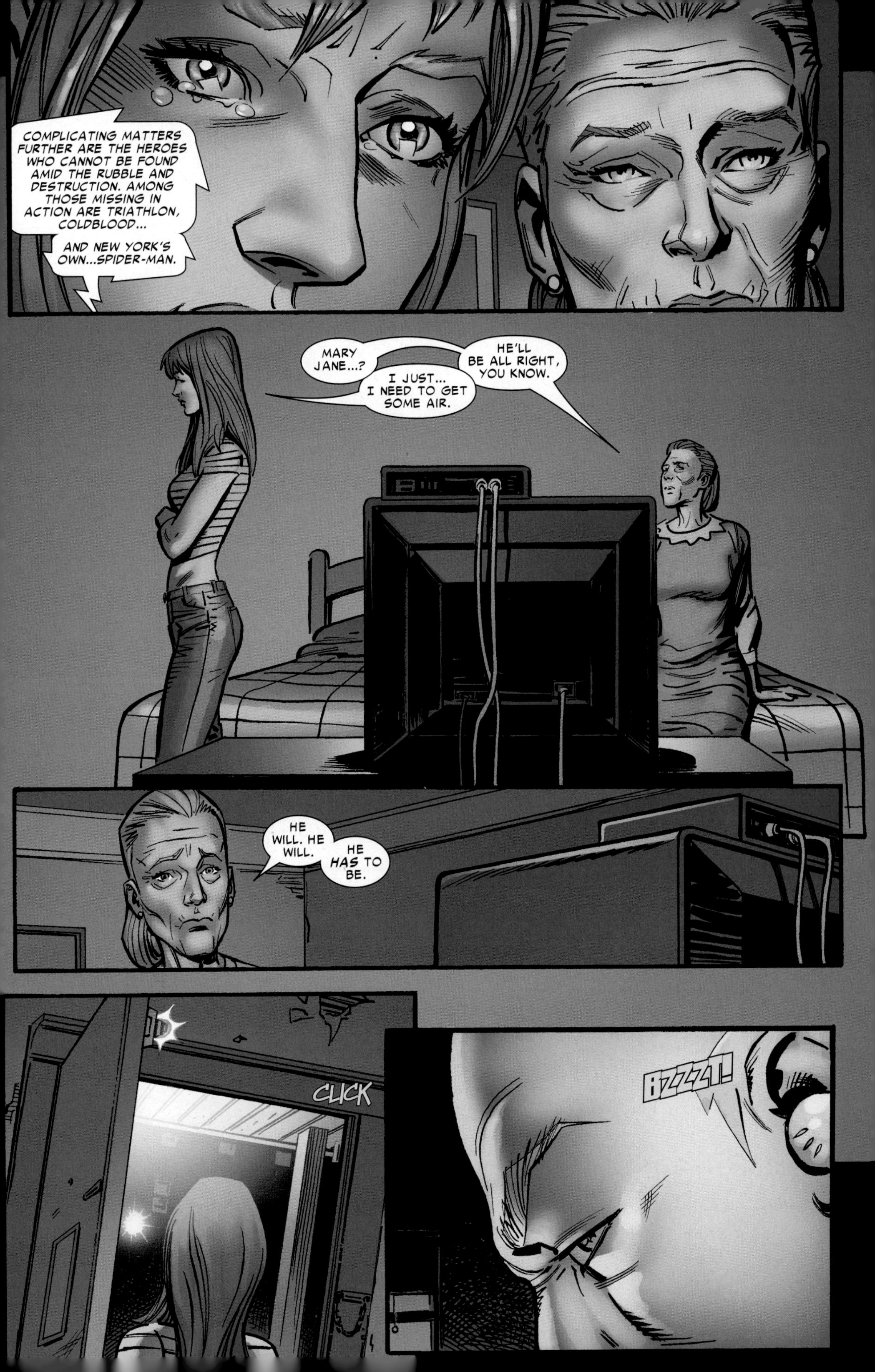
COMPLICATING MATTERS FURTHER ARE THE HEROES WHO CANNOT BE FOUND AMID THE RUBBLE AND DESTRUCTION. AMONG THOSE MISSING IN ACTION ARE TRIATHLON, COLDBLOOD...
AND NEW YORK'S OWN...SPIDER-MAN.
MARY JANE...?
HE'LL BE ALL RIGHT, YOU KNOW.
I JUST... I NEED TO GET SOME AIR.
HE WILL. HE WILL.
HE *HAS* TO BE.
CLICK
BZZZZT!

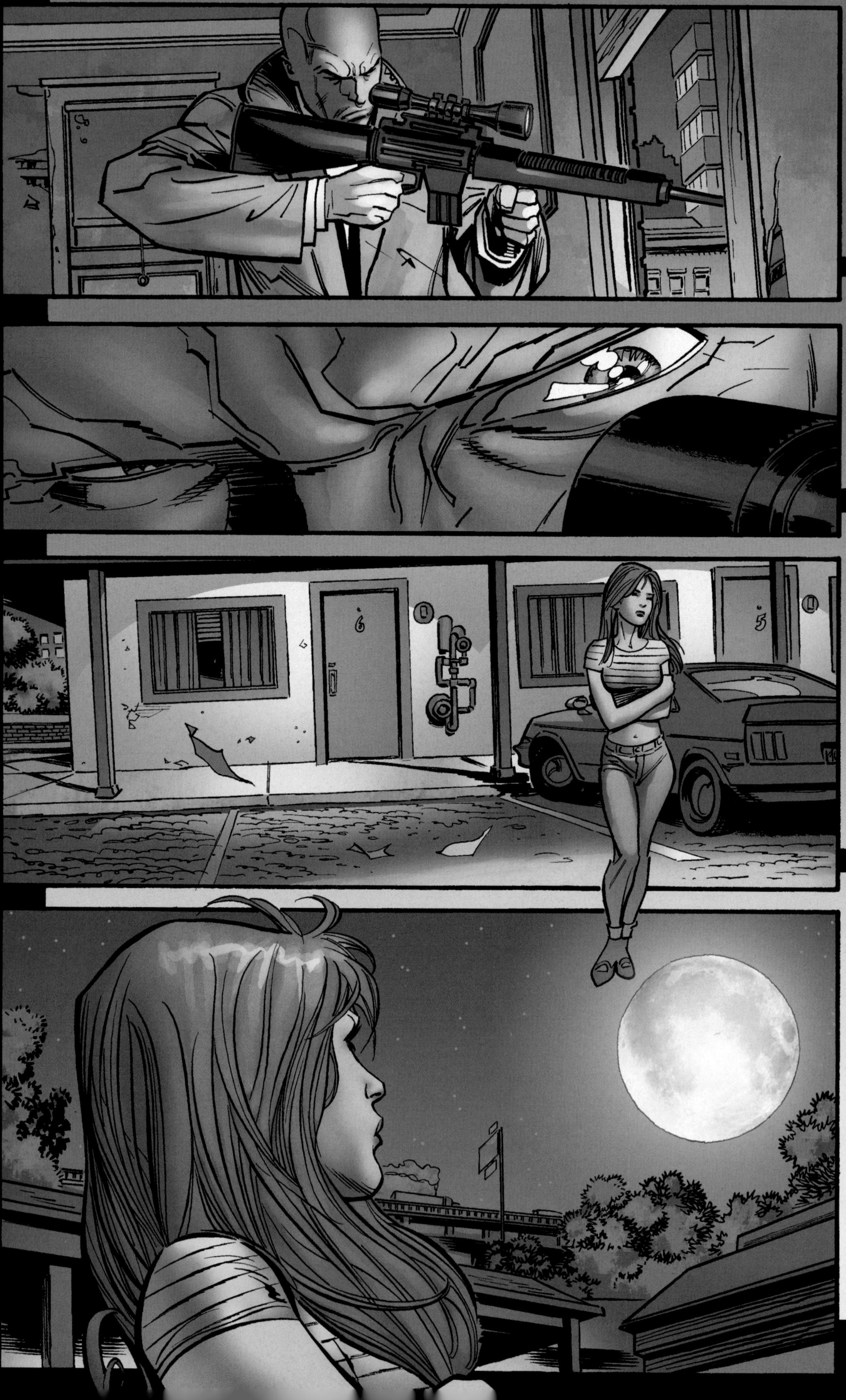
6
5

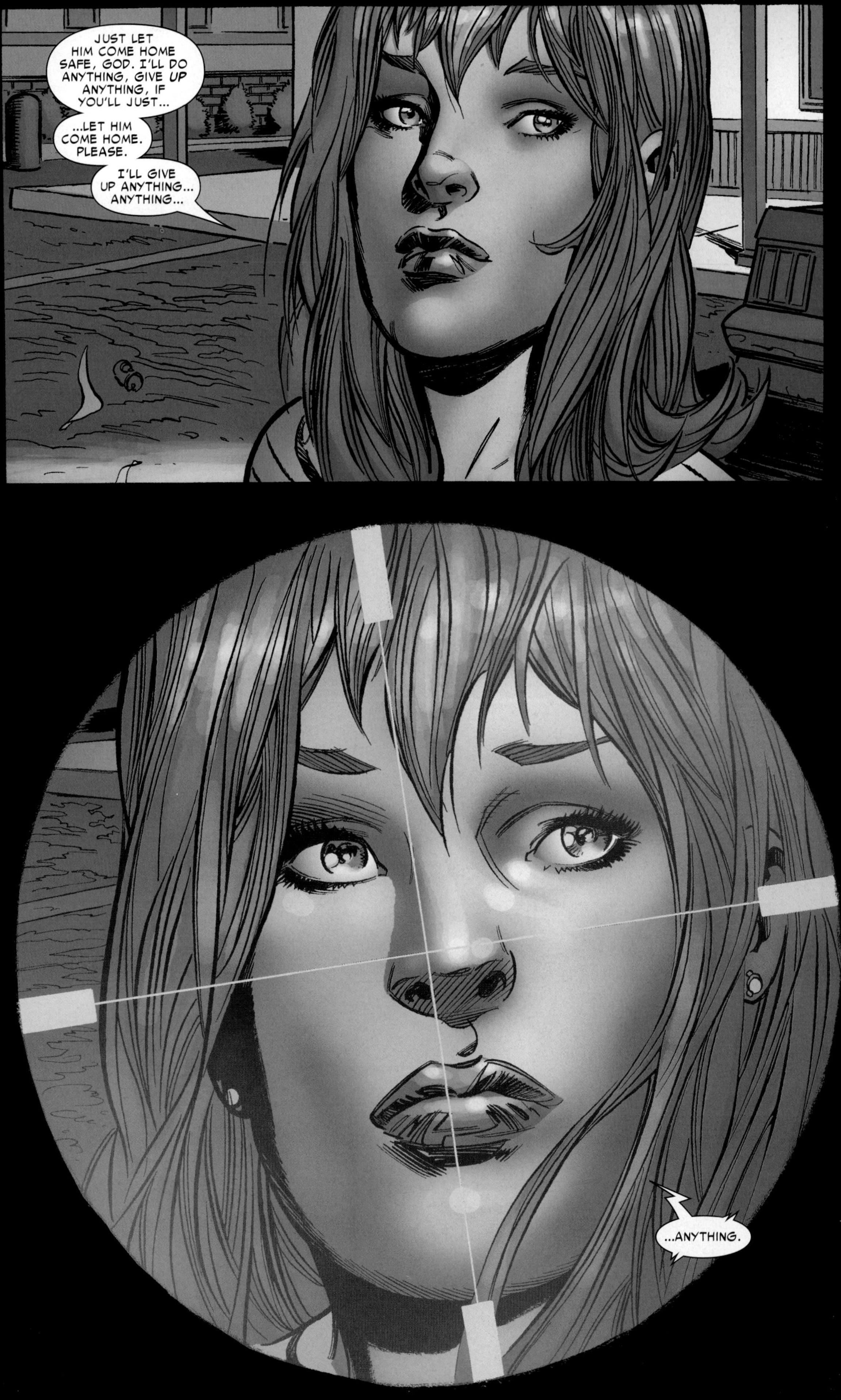
JUST LET HIM COME HOME SAFE, GOD. I'LL DO ANYTHING, GIVE UP ANYTHING, IF YOU'LL JUST...
...LET HIM COME HOME. PLEASE.
I'LL GIVE UP ANYTHING... ANYTHING...
...ANYTHING.

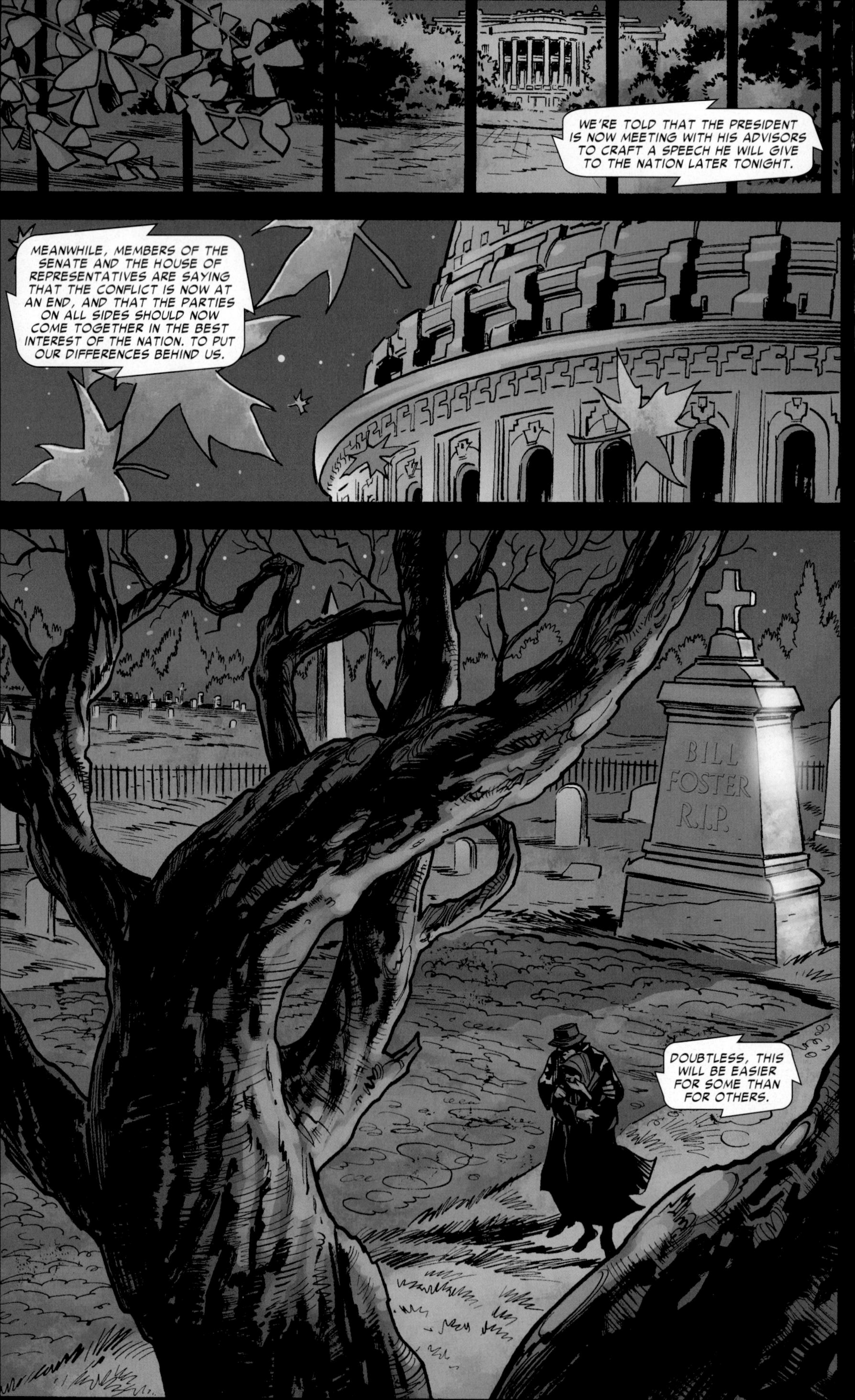
WE'RE TOLD THAT THE PRESIDENT IS NOW MEETING WITH HIS ADVISORS TO CRAFT A SPEECH HE WILL GIVE TO THE NATION LATER TONIGHT.
MEANWHILE, MEMBERS OF THE SENATE AND THE HOUSE OF REPRESENTATIVES ARE SAYING THAT THE CONFLICT IS NOW AT AN END, AND THAT THE PARTIES ON ALL SIDES SHOULD NOW COME TOGETHER IN THE BEST INTEREST OF THE NATION. TO PUT OUR DIFFERENCES BEHIND US.
BILL FOSTER R.I.P.
DOUBTLESS, THIS WILL BE EASIER FOR SOME THAN FOR OTHERS.

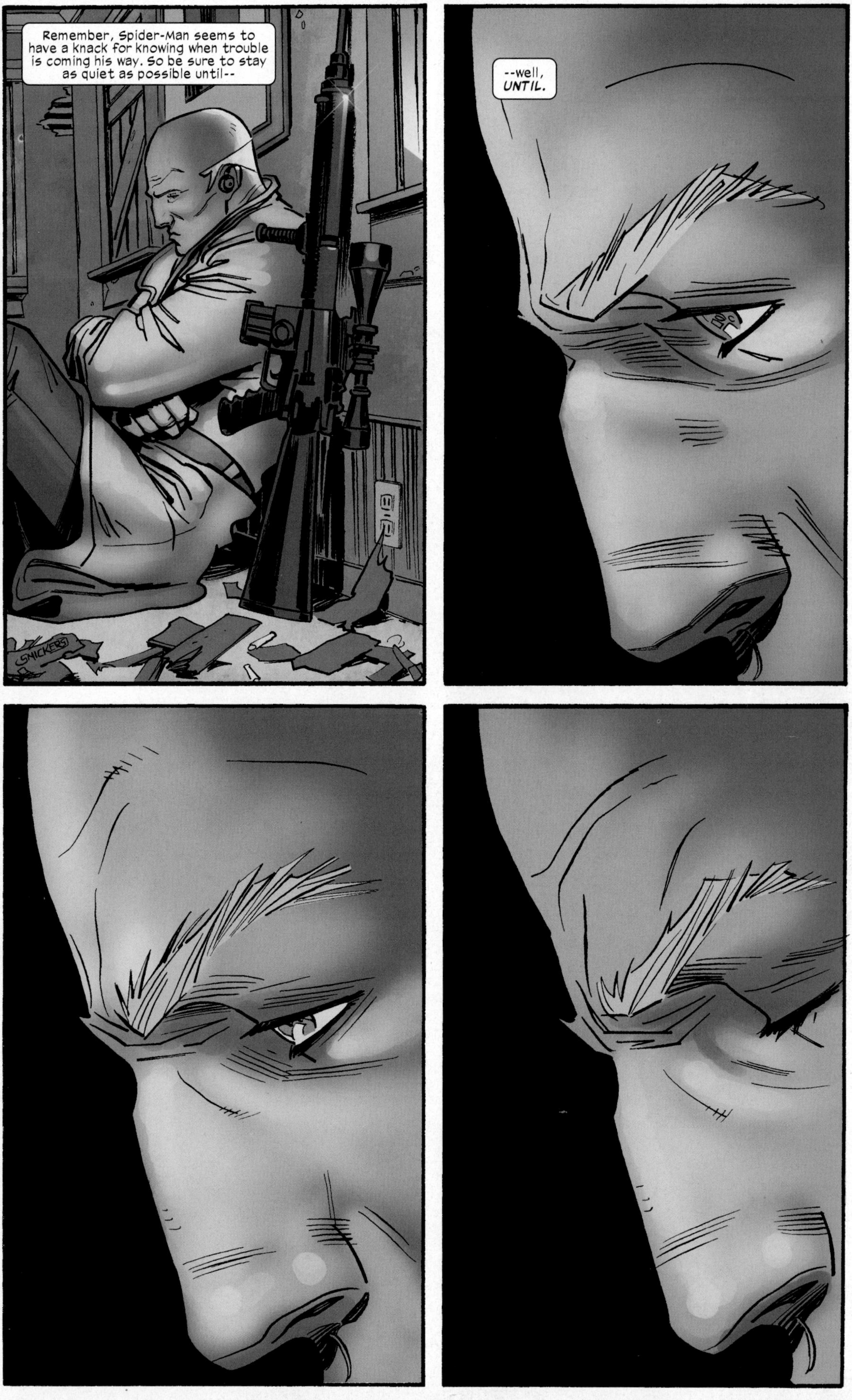
Remember, Spider-Man seems to have a knack for knowing when trouble is coming his way. So be sure to stay as quiet as possible until--
SNICKERS
--well, UNTIL.

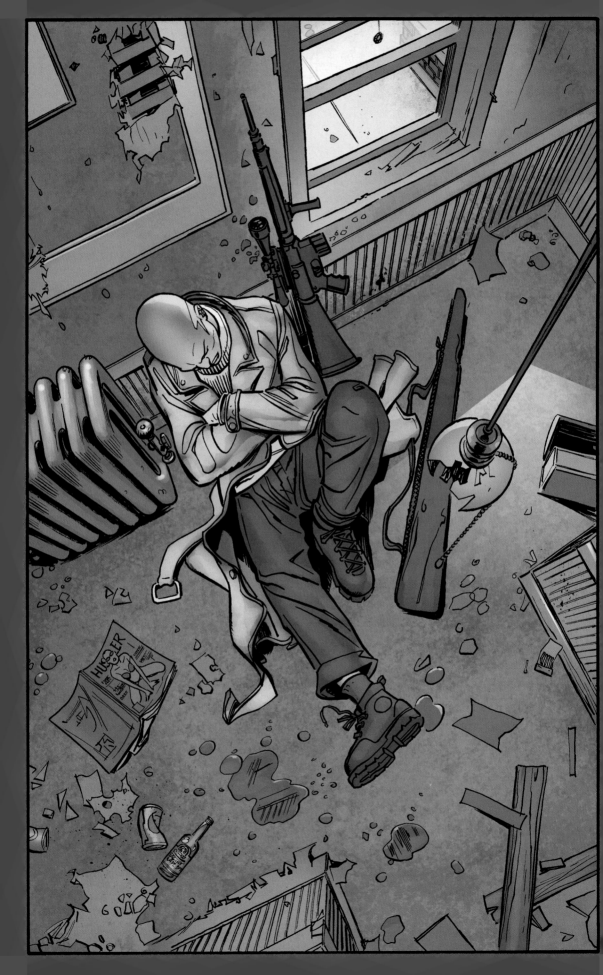

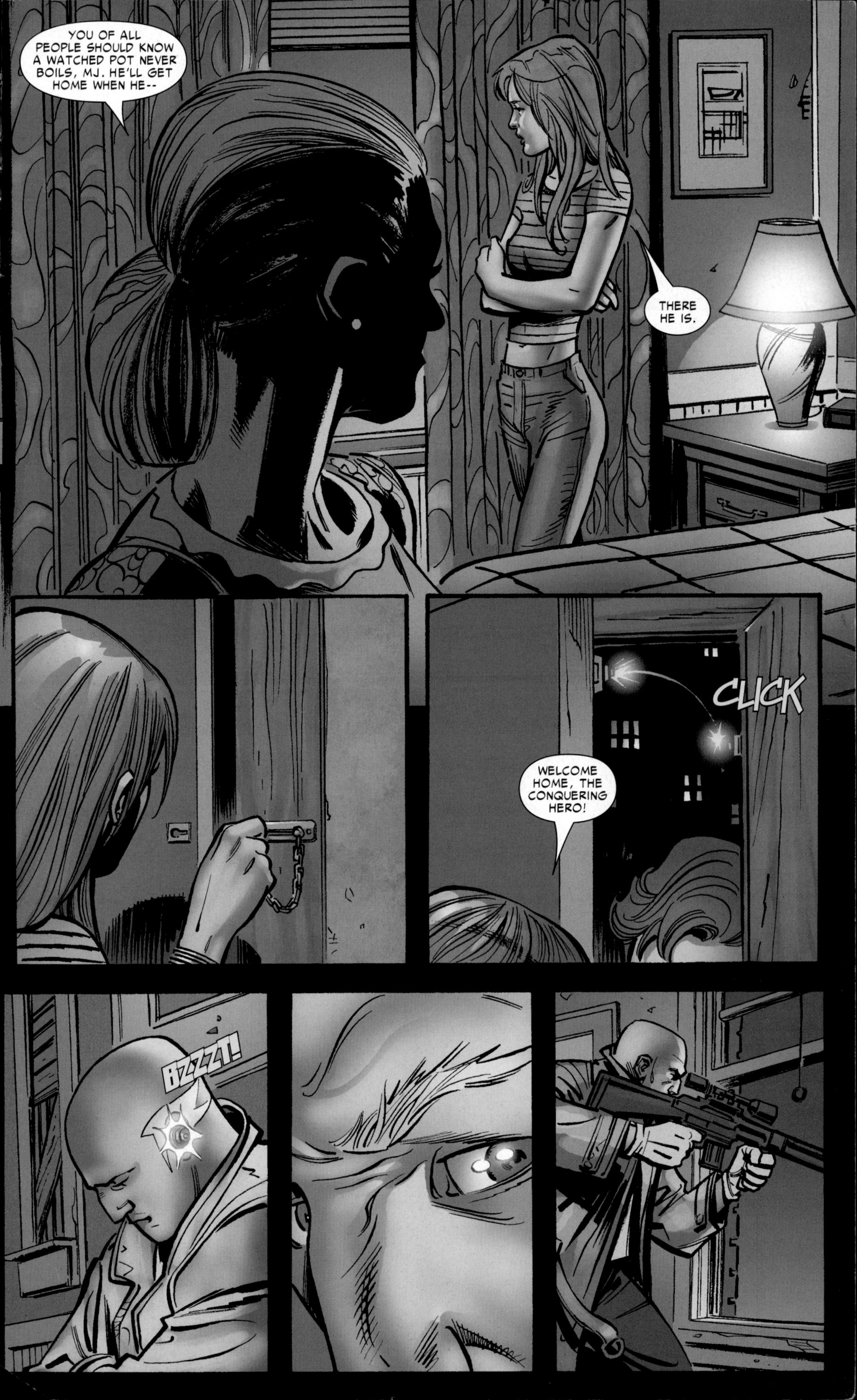
YOU OF ALL PEOPLE SHOULD KNOW A WATCHED POT NEVER BOILS, MJ. HE'LL GET HOME WHEN HE--
THERE HE IS.
CLICK
WELCOME HOME, THE CONQUERING HERO!
BZZZT!

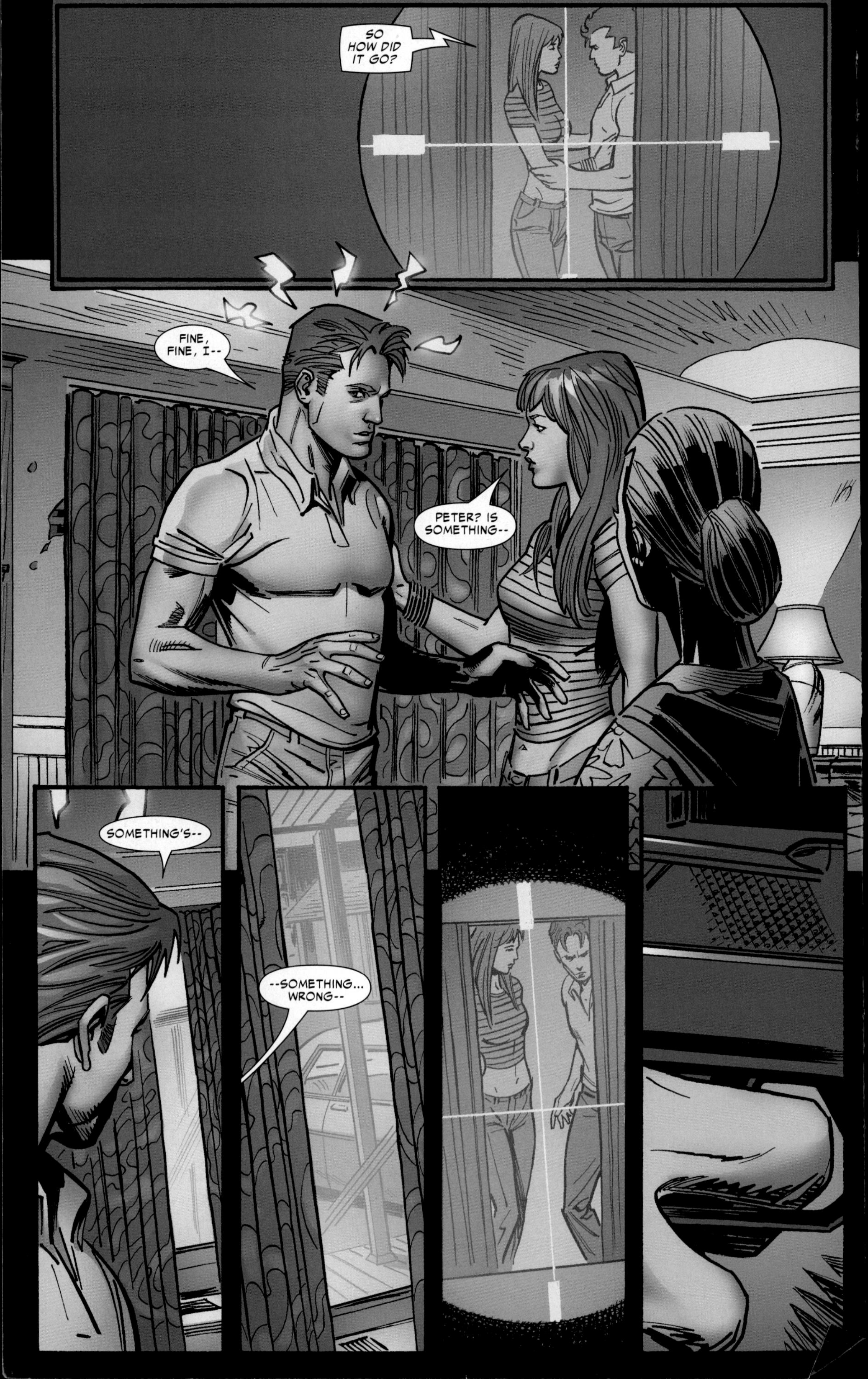
SO HOW DID IT GO?
FINE, FINE, I--
PETER? IS SOMETHING--
SOMETHING'S--
--SOMETHING... WRONG--

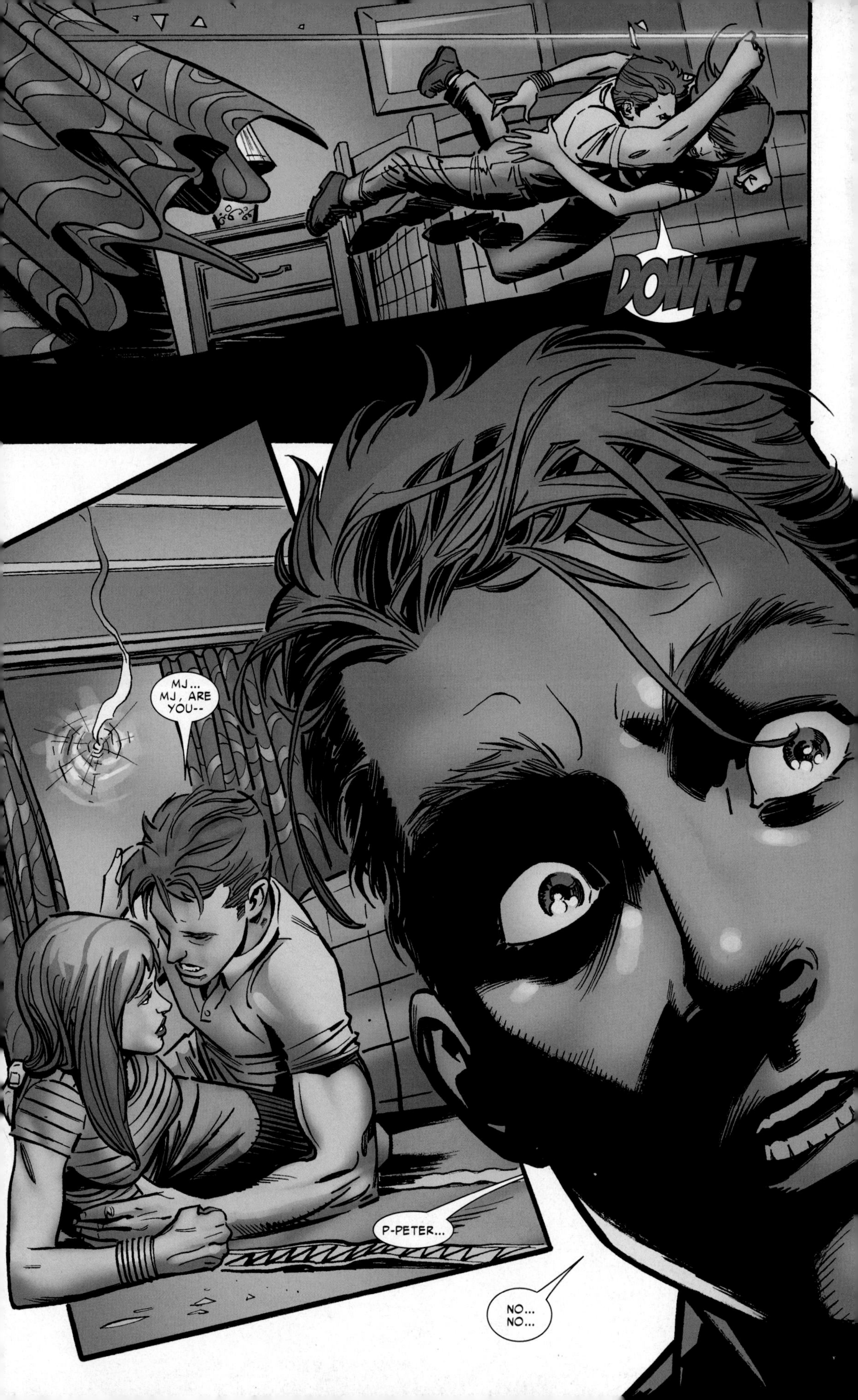
DOWN!
MJ... MJ, ARE YOU--
P-PETER...
NO... NO...

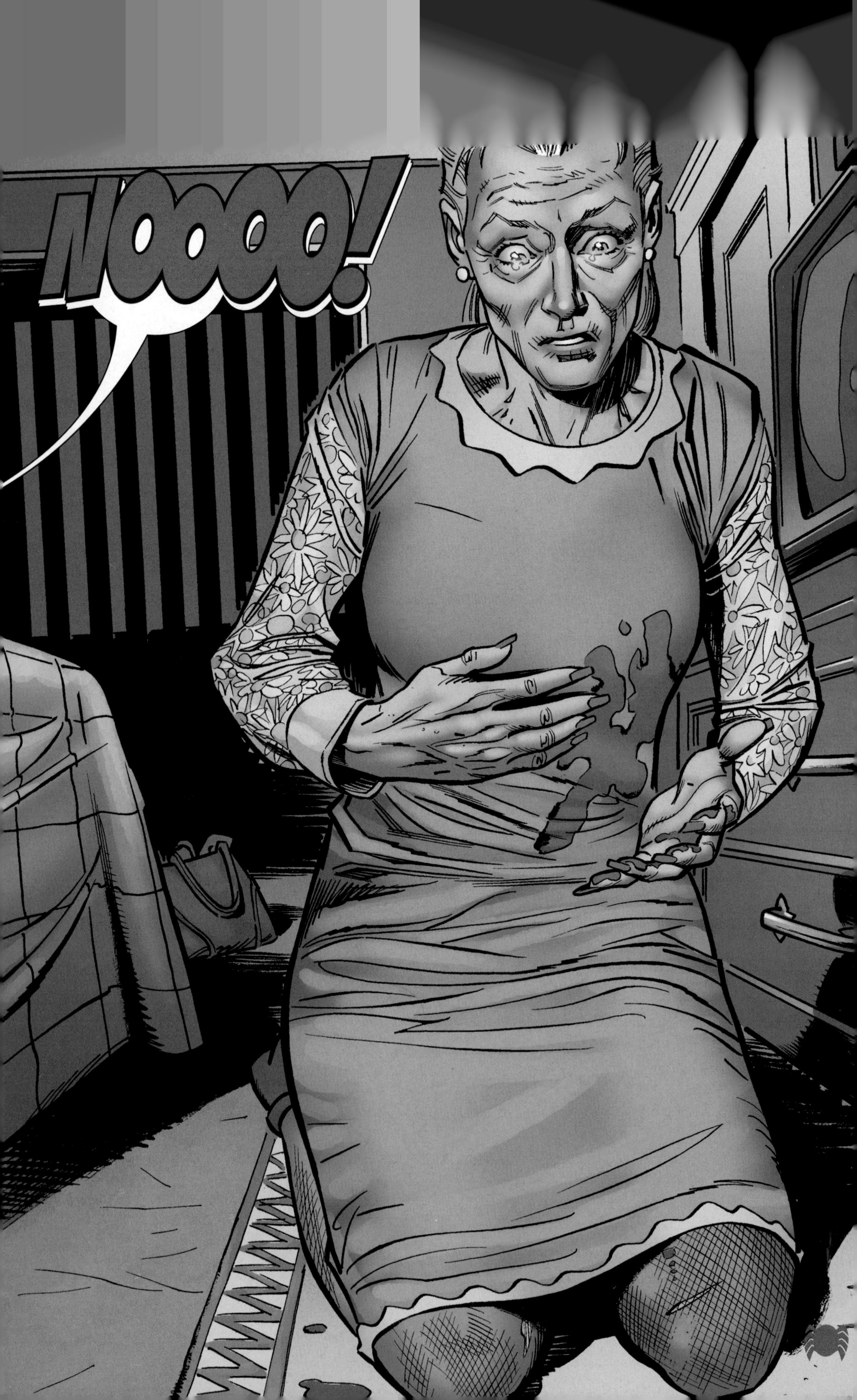
NOOOO!

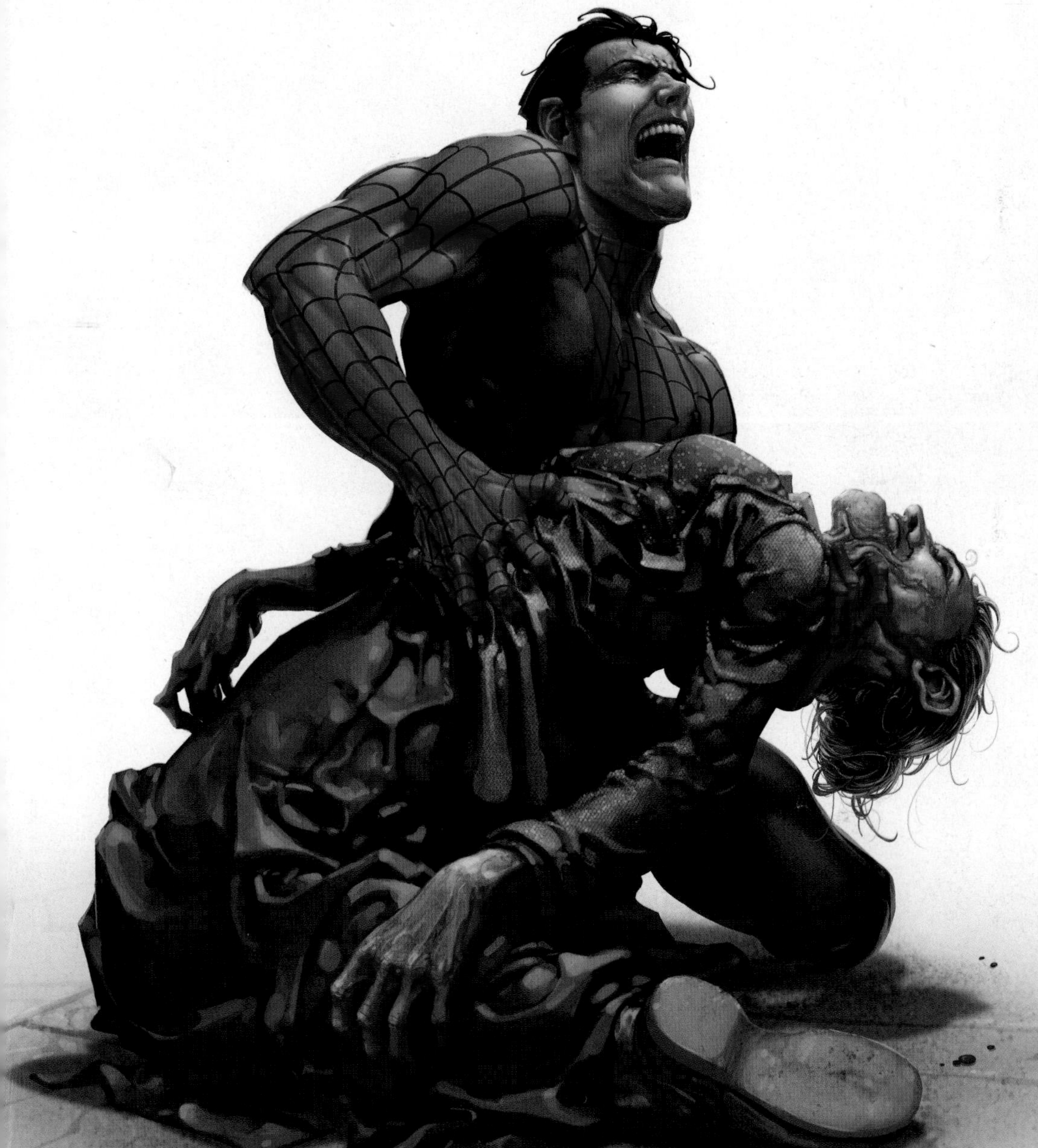
-Crain-

AMAZING SPIDER-MAN #538 VARIANT BY CLAYTON CRAIN

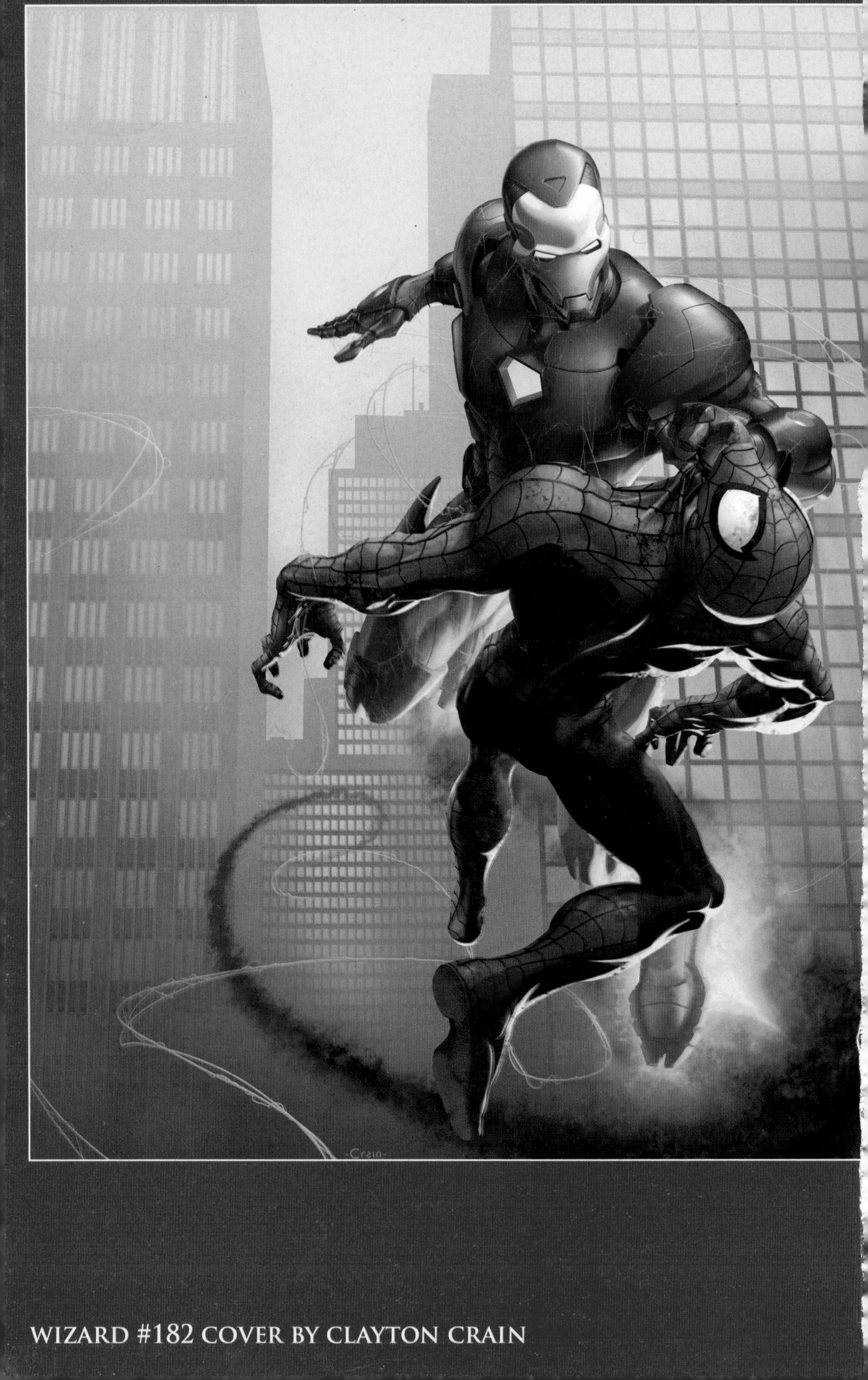
-Crain-

WIZARD #182 COVER BY CLAYTON CRAIN